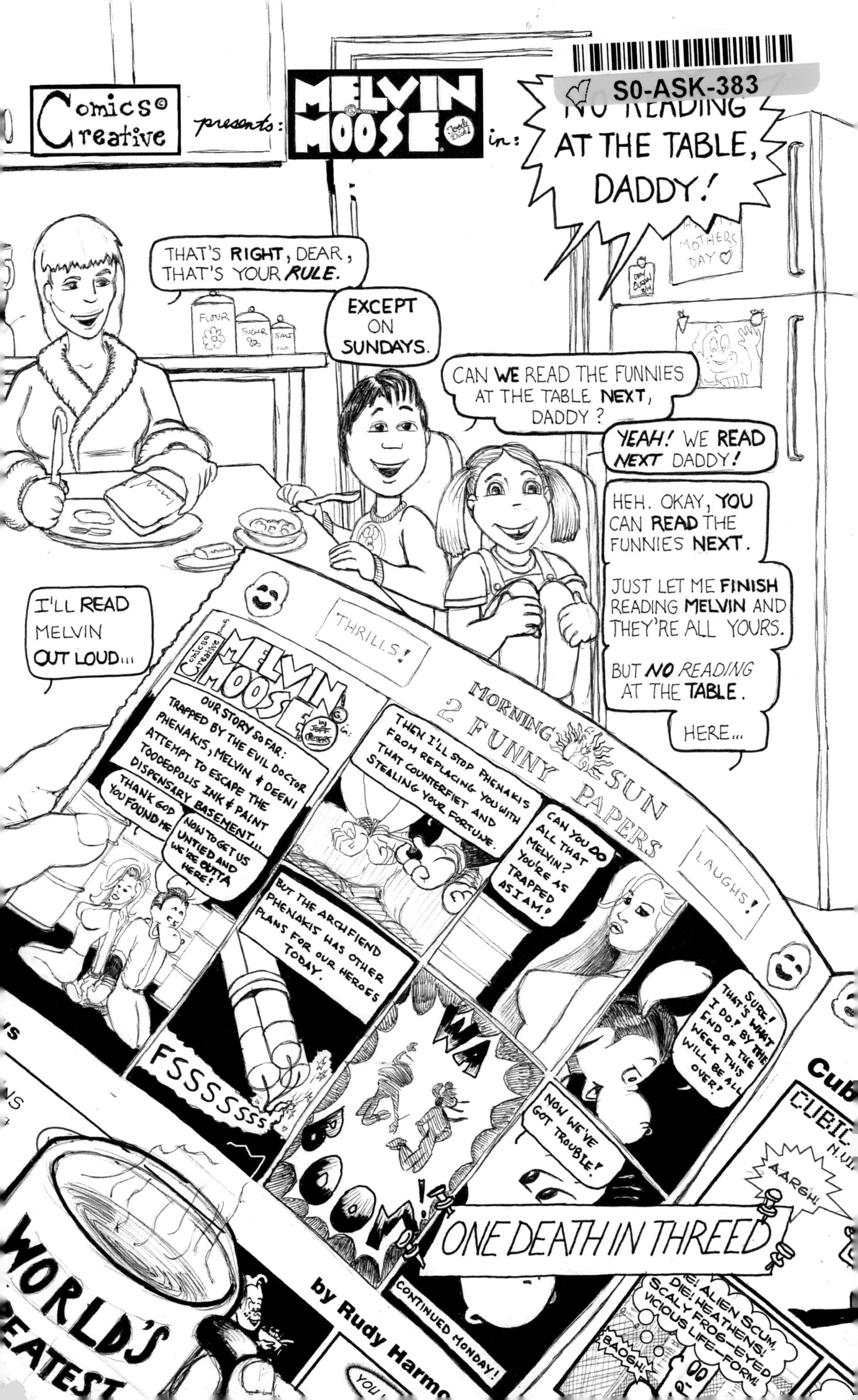
S0-ASK-383
Comics Creative
presents:
MELVIN MOOSE
Toodle Dicks
in:
NO READING AT THE TABLE, DADDY!
HAPPY MOTHERS DAY
THAT'S RIGHT, DEAR, THAT'S YOUR RULE.
FLOUR
SUGAR
SALT
EXCEPT ON SUNDAYS.
CAN WE READ THE FUNNIES AT THE TABLE NEXT, DADDY?
YEAH! WE READ NEXT DADDY!
HEH. OKAY, YOU CAN READ THE FUNNIES NEXT.
JUST LET ME FINISH READING MELVIN AND THEY'RE ALL YOURS.
BUT NO READING AT THE TABLE.
HERE...
I'LL READ MELVIN OUT LOUD...
THRILLS!
MORNING SUN FUNNY PAPERS
LAUGHS!
Comics Creative presents MELVIN MOOSE by JEFF PETERS in:
OUR STORY SO FAR: TRAPPED BY THE EVIL DOCTOR PHENAKIS, MELVIN & DEENI ATTEMPT TO ESCAPE THE TOODEOPOLIS INK & PAINT DISPENSARY BASEMENT...
THANK GOD YOU FOUND ME
NOW TO GET US UNTIED AND WE'RE OUTTA HERE!
THEN I'LL STOP PHENAKIS FROM REPLACING YOU WITH THAT COUNTERFIET AND STEALING YOUR FORTUNE.
CAN YOU DO ALL THAT MELVIN? YOU'RE AS TRAPPED AS I AM!
SURE! THAT'S WHAT I DO! BY THE END OF THE WEEK THIS WILL BE ALL OVER!
BUT THE ARCHFIEND PHENAKIS HAS OTHER PLANS FOR OUR HEROES TODAY.
FSSSSSSS
KA BOOOM!
NOW WE'VE GOT TROUBLE!
ONE DEATH IN THREED
CONTINUED MONDAY!
WORLD'S GREATEST
by Rudy Harmo
CUBICLE
AARGH!
DIE! ALIEN SCUM, DIE! HEATHENS! SCALY FROG-EYED VICIOUS LIFE-FORM!
BAOSH!

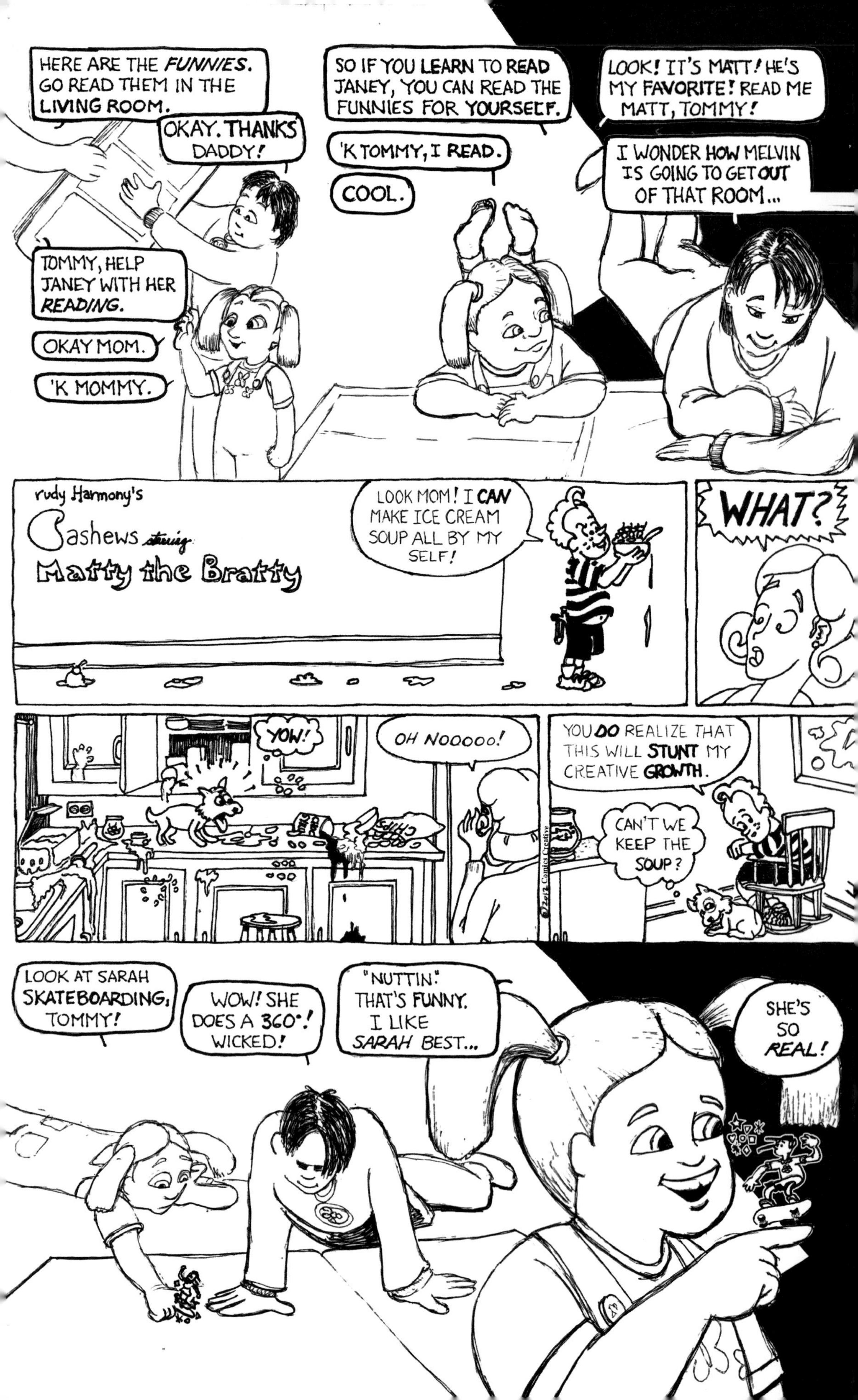
HERE ARE THE *FUNNIES*. GO READ THEM IN THE LIVING ROOM.
OKAY. THANKS DADDY!
TOMMY, HELP JANEY WITH HER *READING*.
OKAY MOM.
'K MOMMY.
SO IF YOU LEARN TO READ JANEY, YOU CAN READ THE FUNNIES FOR YOURSELF.
'K TOMMY, I READ.
COOL.
LOOK! IT'S MATT! HE'S MY FAVORITE! READ ME MATT, TOMMY!
I WONDER HOW MELVIN IS GOING TO GET OUT OF THAT ROOM...
rudy Harmony's
Cashews starring
Matty the Bratty
LOOK MOM! I CAN MAKE ICE CREAM SOUP ALL BY MY SELF!
WHAT?
YOW!
OH NOOOOO!
©2012 Comics Creative
YOU DO REALIZE THAT THIS WILL STUNT MY CREATIVE GROWTH.
CAN'T WE KEEP THE SOUP?
LOOK AT SARAH SKATEBOARDING, TOMMY!
WOW! SHE DOES A 360°! WICKED!
"NUTTIN." THAT'S FUNNY. I LIKE *SARAH* BEST...
SHE'S SO *REAL*!

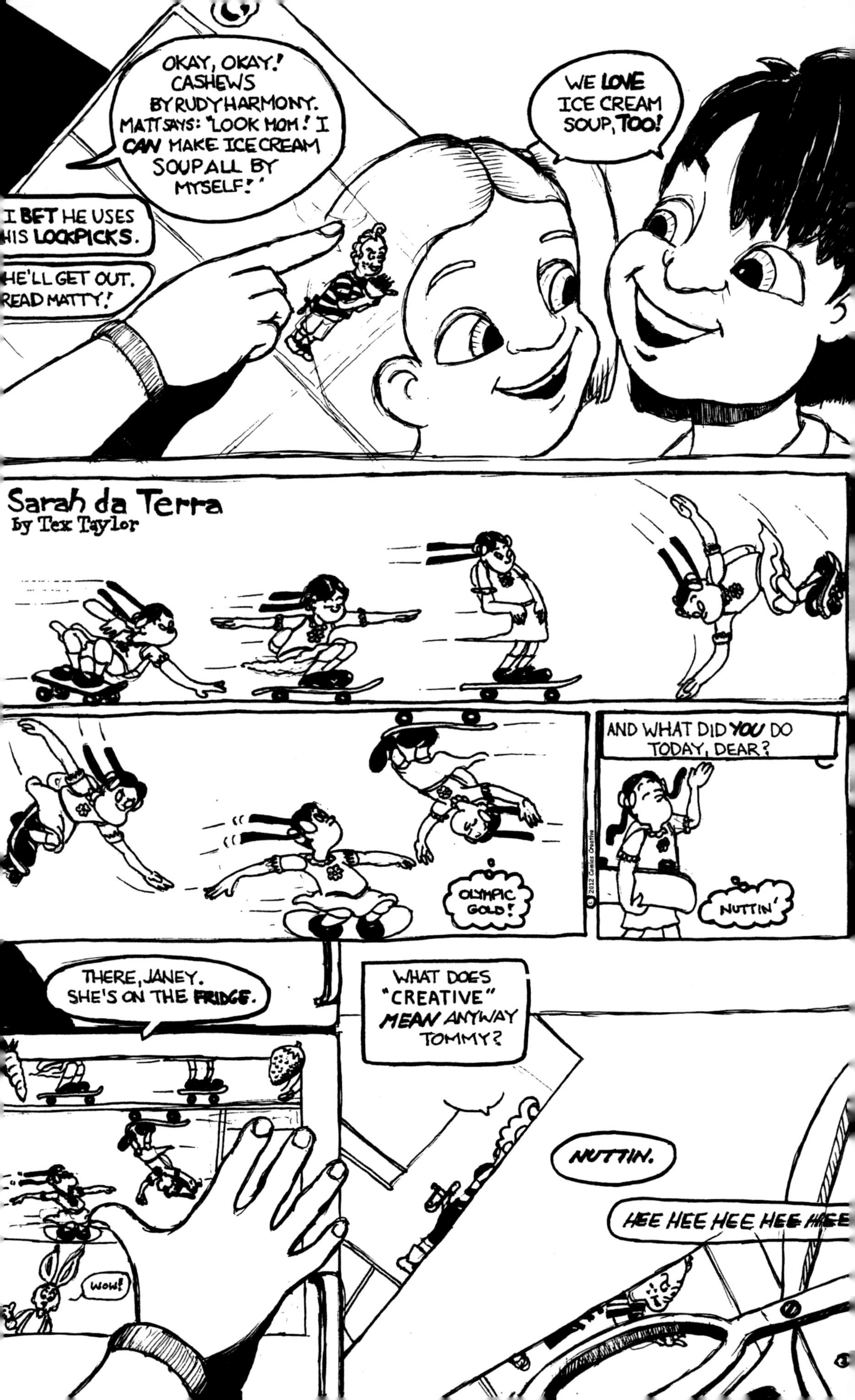
OKAY, OKAY! CASHEWS BY RUDY HARMONY. MATT SAYS: "LOOK MOM! I CAN MAKE ICE CREAM SOUP ALL BY MYSELF!"
WE LOVE ICE CREAM SOUP, TOO!
I BET HE USES HIS LOCKPICKS.
HE'LL GET OUT. READ MATTY!
Sarah da Terra
by Tex Taylor
AND WHAT DID YOU DO TODAY, DEAR?
OLYMPIC GOLD!
© 2012 Comics Creative
NUTTIN'
THERE, JANEY. SHE'S ON THE FRIDGE.
WOW!
WHAT DOES "CREATIVE" MEAN ANYWAY TOMMY?
NUTTIN.
HEE HEE HEE HEE HEE

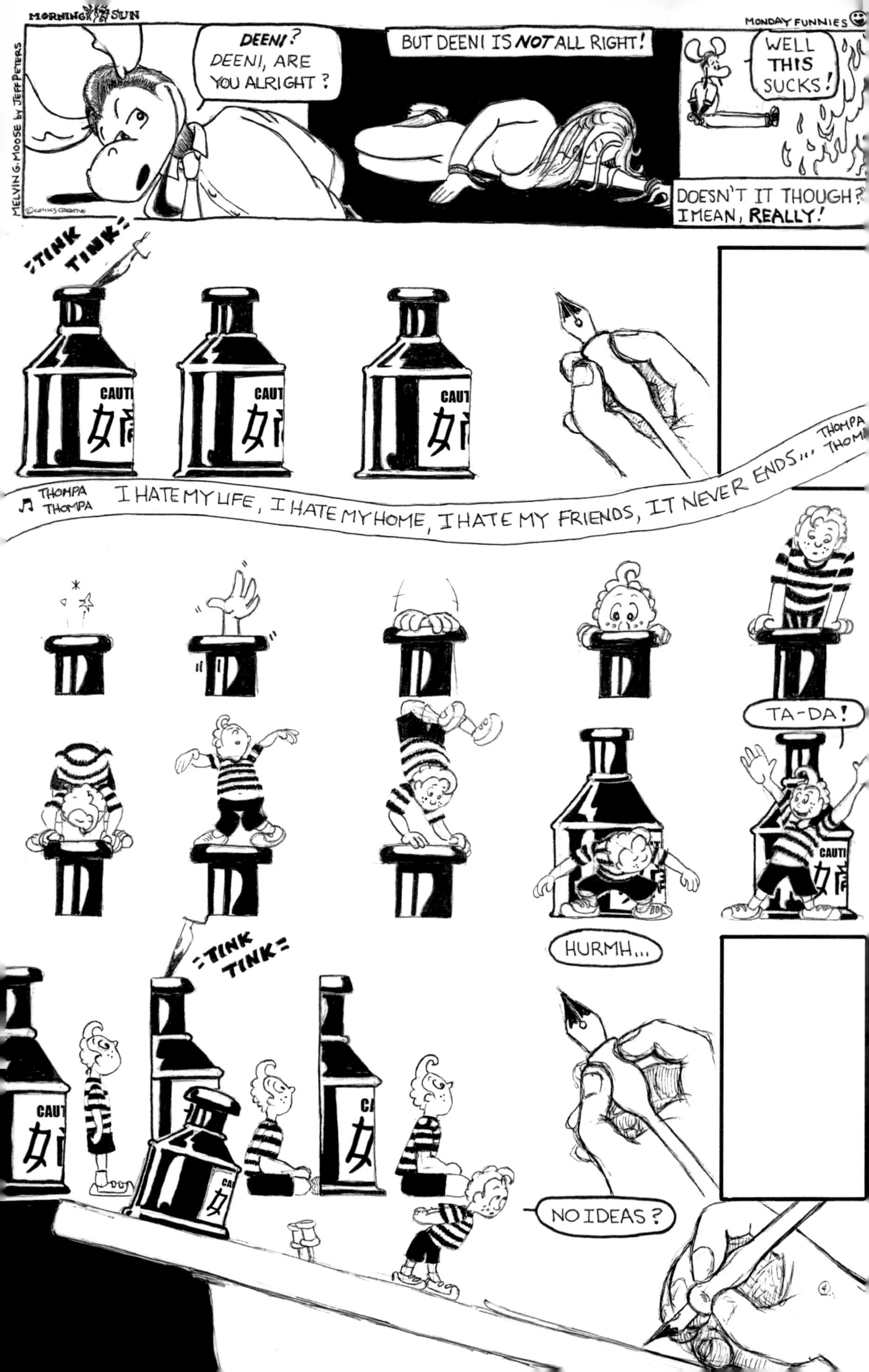
MORNING SUN
MONDAY FUNNIES
MELVIN G. MOOSE by JEFF PETERS
DEENI? DEENI, ARE YOU ALRIGHT?
BUT DEENI IS NOT ALL RIGHT!
WELL THIS SUCKS!
DOESN'T IT THOUGH? I MEAN, REALLY!
TINK TINK
THOMPA THOMPA
I HATE MY LIFE, I HATE MY HOME, I HATE MY FRIENDS, IT NEVER ENDS...
THOMPA THOM
TA-DA!
HURMH...
TINK TINK
NO IDEAS?

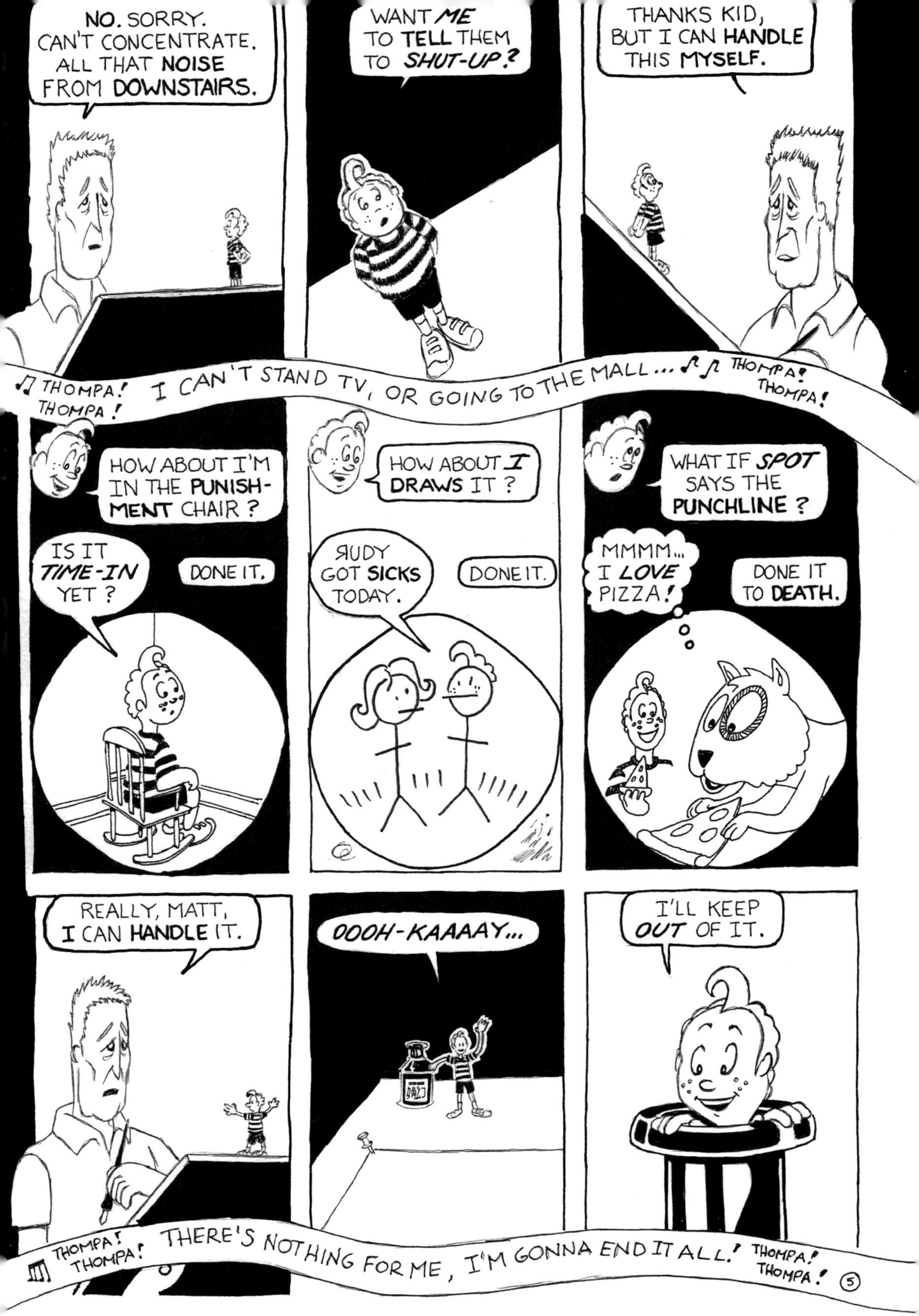
NO. SORRY. CAN'T CONCENTRATE. ALL THAT NOISE FROM DOWNSTAIRS.
WANT ME TO TELL THEM TO SHUT-UP?
THANKS KID, BUT I CAN HANDLE THIS MYSELF.
♫ THOMPA! THOMPA! I CAN'T STAND TV, OR GOING TO THE MALL... ♪♫ THOMPA! THOMPA!
HOW ABOUT I'M IN THE PUNISH-MENT CHAIR?
IS IT TIME-IN YET?
DONE IT.
HOW ABOUT I DRAWS IT?
ЯUDY GOT SICKS TODAY.
DONE IT.
WHAT IF SPOT SAYS THE PUNCHLINE?
MMMM... I LOVE PIZZA!
DONE IT TO DEATH.
REALLY, MATT, I CAN HANDLE IT.
OOOH-KAAAAY...
I'LL KEEP OUT OF IT.
♫ THOMPA! THOMPA! THERE'S NOTHING FOR ME, I'M GONNA END IT ALL! THOMPA! THOMPA!

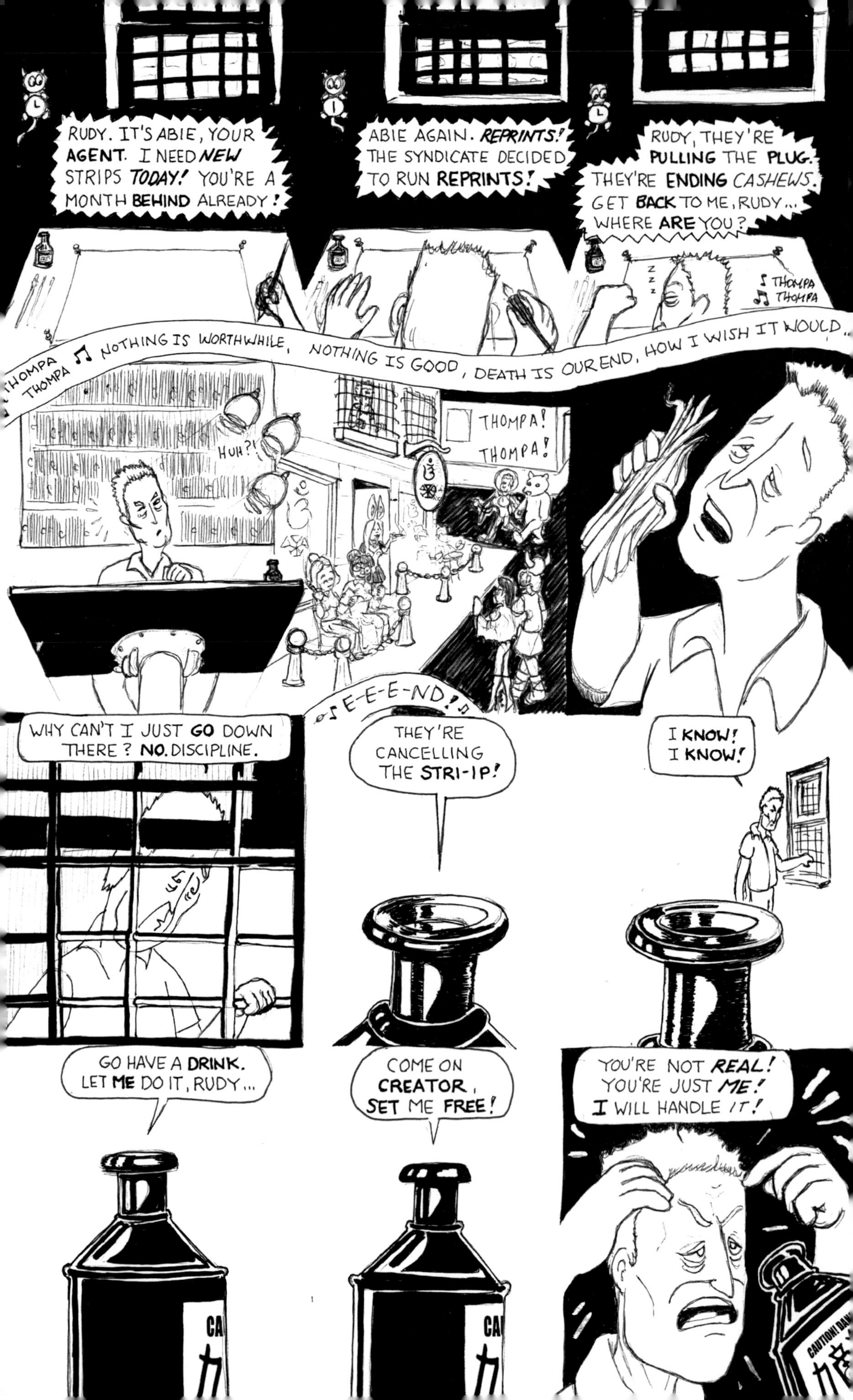

RUDY. IT'S ABIE, YOUR AGENT. I NEED NEW STRIPS TODAY! YOU'RE A MONTH BEHIND ALREADY!
ABIE AGAIN. REPRINTS! THE SYNDICATE DECIDED TO RUN REPRINTS!
RUDY, THEY'RE PULLING THE PLUG. THEY'RE ENDING CASHEWS. GET BACK TO ME, RUDY... WHERE ARE YOU?
Z Z Z
THOMPA THOMPA
THOMPA THOMPA NOTHING IS WORTHWHILE, NOTHING IS GOOD, DEATH IS OUR END, HOW I WISH IT WOULD...
HUH?!
THOMPA! THOMPA!
E-E-E-ND!
WHY CAN'T I JUST GO DOWN THERE? NO. DISCIPLINE.
THEY'RE CANCELLING THE STRI-IP!
I KNOW! I KNOW!
GO HAVE A DRINK. LET ME DO IT, RUDY...
COME ON CREATOR, SET ME FREE!
YOU'RE NOT REAL! YOU'RE JUST ME! I WILL HANDLE IT!

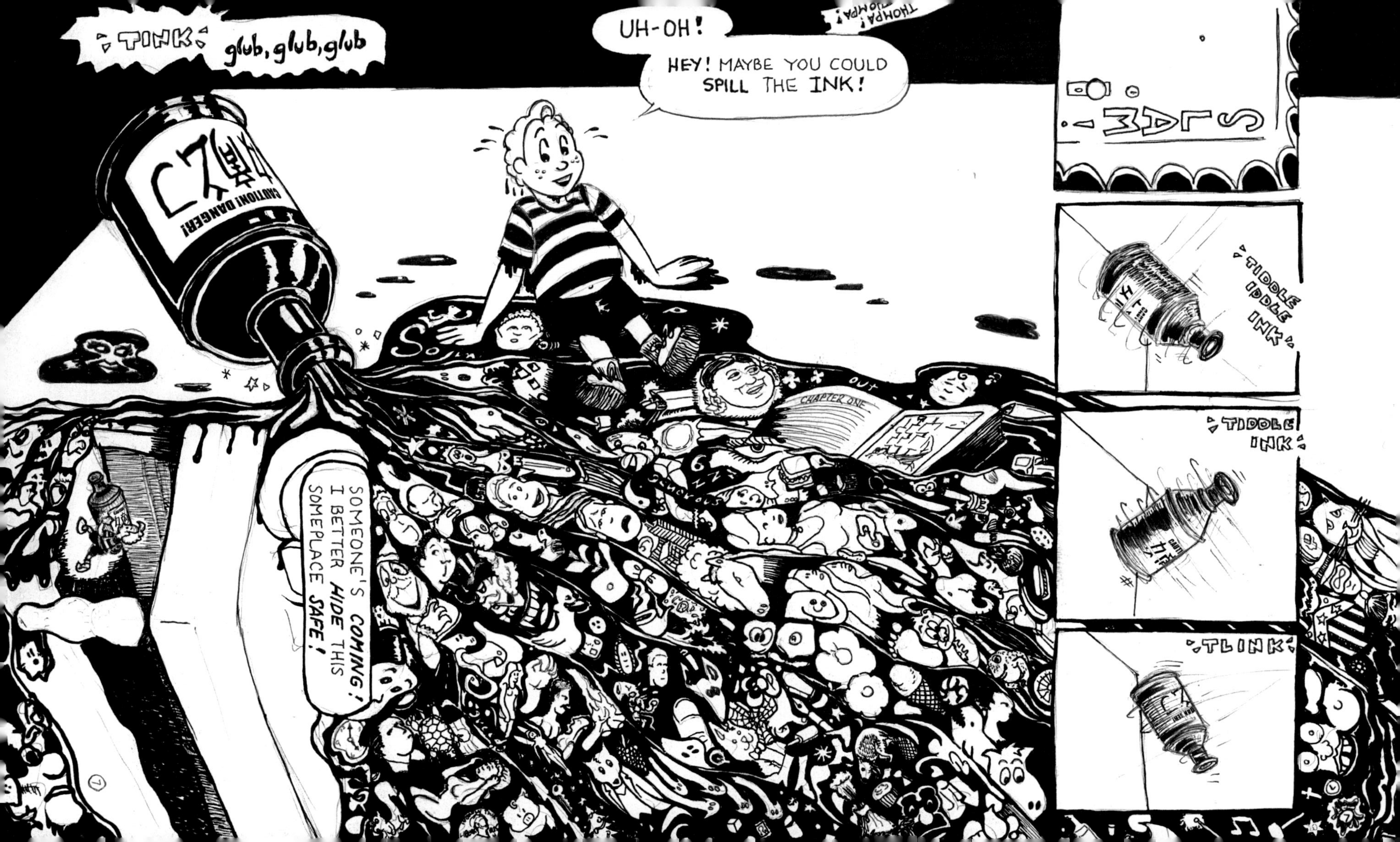
SLAM!
TIDDLE IDDLE INK
TIDDLE INK
TLINK
TINK glub, glub, glub
CAUTION! DANGER!
THOMPA! THOMPA!
UH-OH!
HEY! MAYBE YOU COULD SPILL THE INK!
CHAPTER ONE
OUT
SOMEONE'S COMING! I BETTER HIDE THIS SOMEPLACE SAFE!

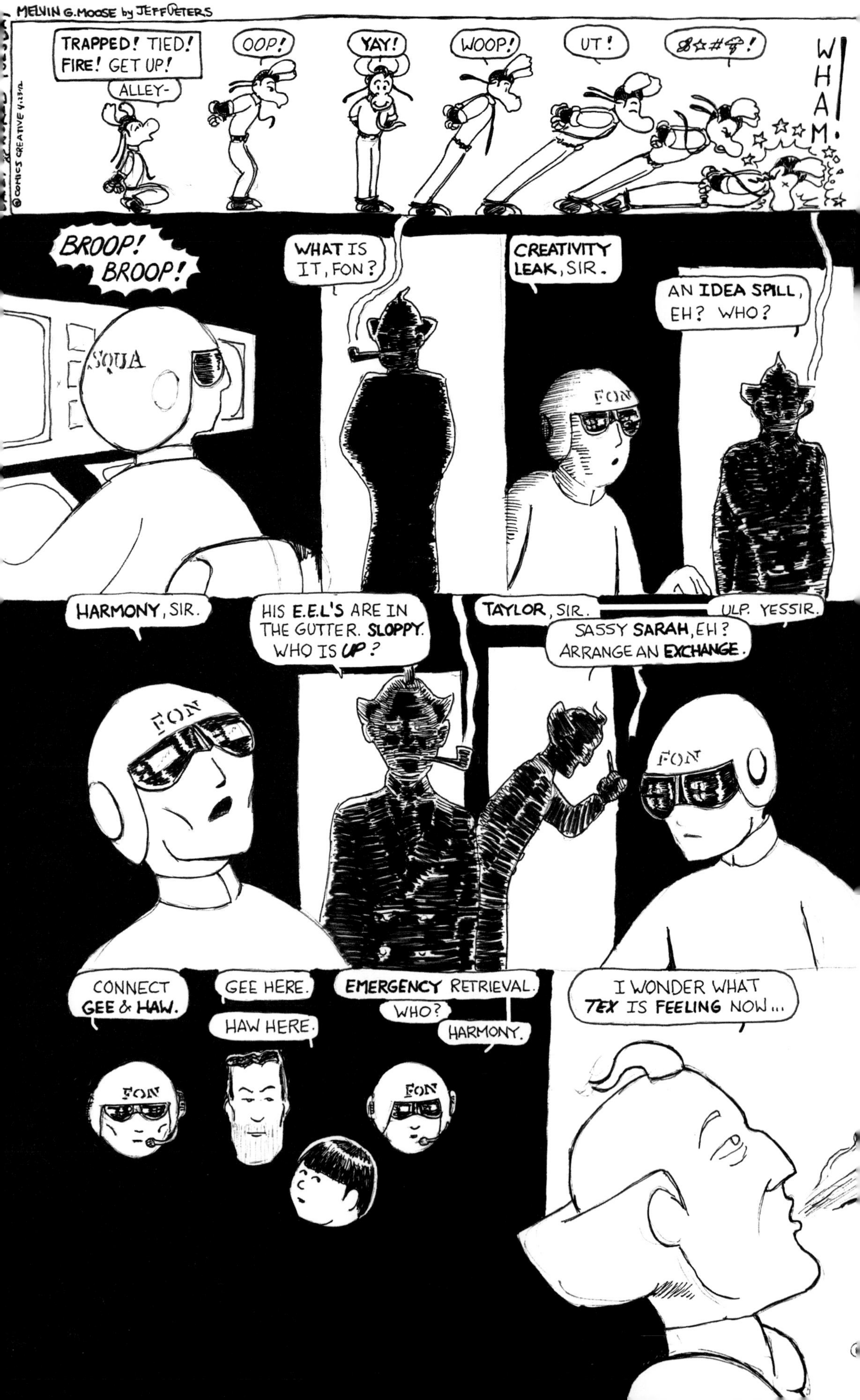
MELVIN G. MOOSE by JEFF PETERS
©COMICS CREATIVE 4.23.12
TRAPPED! TIED! FIRE! GET UP!
ALLEY-
OOP!
YAY!
WOOP!
UT!
WHAM!
BROOP! BROOP!
WHAT IS IT, FON?
CREATIVITY LEAK, SIR.
AN IDEA SPILL, EH? WHO?
HARMONY, SIR.
HIS E.E.L'S ARE IN THE GUTTER. SLOPPY. WHO IS UP?
TAYLOR, SIR.
SASSY SARAH, EH? ARRANGE AN EXCHANGE.
ULP. YESSIR.
CONNECT GEE & HAW.
GEE HERE.
HAW HERE.
EMERGENCY RETRIEVAL.
WHO?
HARMONY.
I WONDER WHAT TEX IS FEELING NOW...

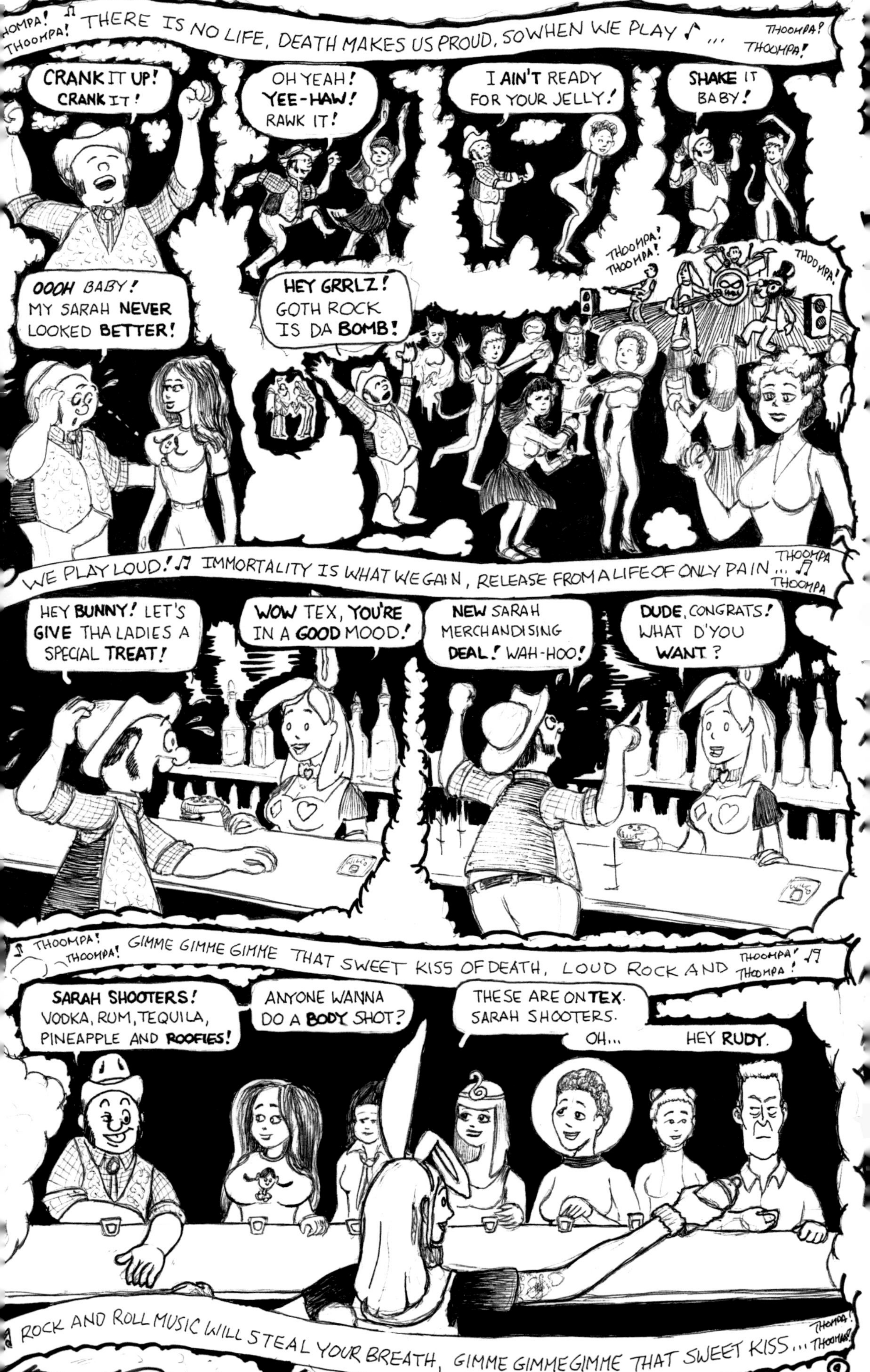
THOOMPA! THOOMPA! THERE IS NO LIFE, DEATH MAKES US PROUD, SO WHEN WE PLAY ... THOOMPA! THOOMPA!
CRANK IT UP! CRANK IT!
OH YEAH! YEE-HAW! RAWK IT!
I AIN'T READY FOR YOUR JELLY!
SHAKE IT BABY!
OOOH BABY! MY SARAH NEVER LOOKED BETTER!
HEY GRRLZ! GOTH ROCK IS DA BOMB!
THOOMPA! THOOMPA!
THOOMPA!
WE PLAY LOUD! IMMORTALITY IS WHAT WE GAIN, RELEASE FROM A LIFE OF ONLY PAIN... THOOMPA THOOMPA
HEY BUNNY! LET'S GIVE THA LADIES A SPECIAL TREAT!
WOW TEX, YOU'RE IN A GOOD MOOD!
NEW SARAH MERCHANDISING DEAL! WAH-HOO!
DUDE, CONGRATS! WHAT D'YOU WANT?
THOOMPA! THOOMPA! GIMME GIMME GIMME THAT SWEET KISS OF DEATH, LOUD ROCK AND THOOMPA! THOOMPA!
SARAH SHOOTERS! VODKA, RUM, TEQUILA, PINEAPPLE AND ROOFIES!
ANYONE WANNA DO A BODY SHOT?
THESE ARE ON TEX. SARAH SHOOTERS.
OH... HEY RUDY.
ROCK AND ROLL MUSIC WILL STEAL YOUR BREATH, GIMME GIMME GIMME THAT SWEET KISS... THOOMPA! THOOMPA!

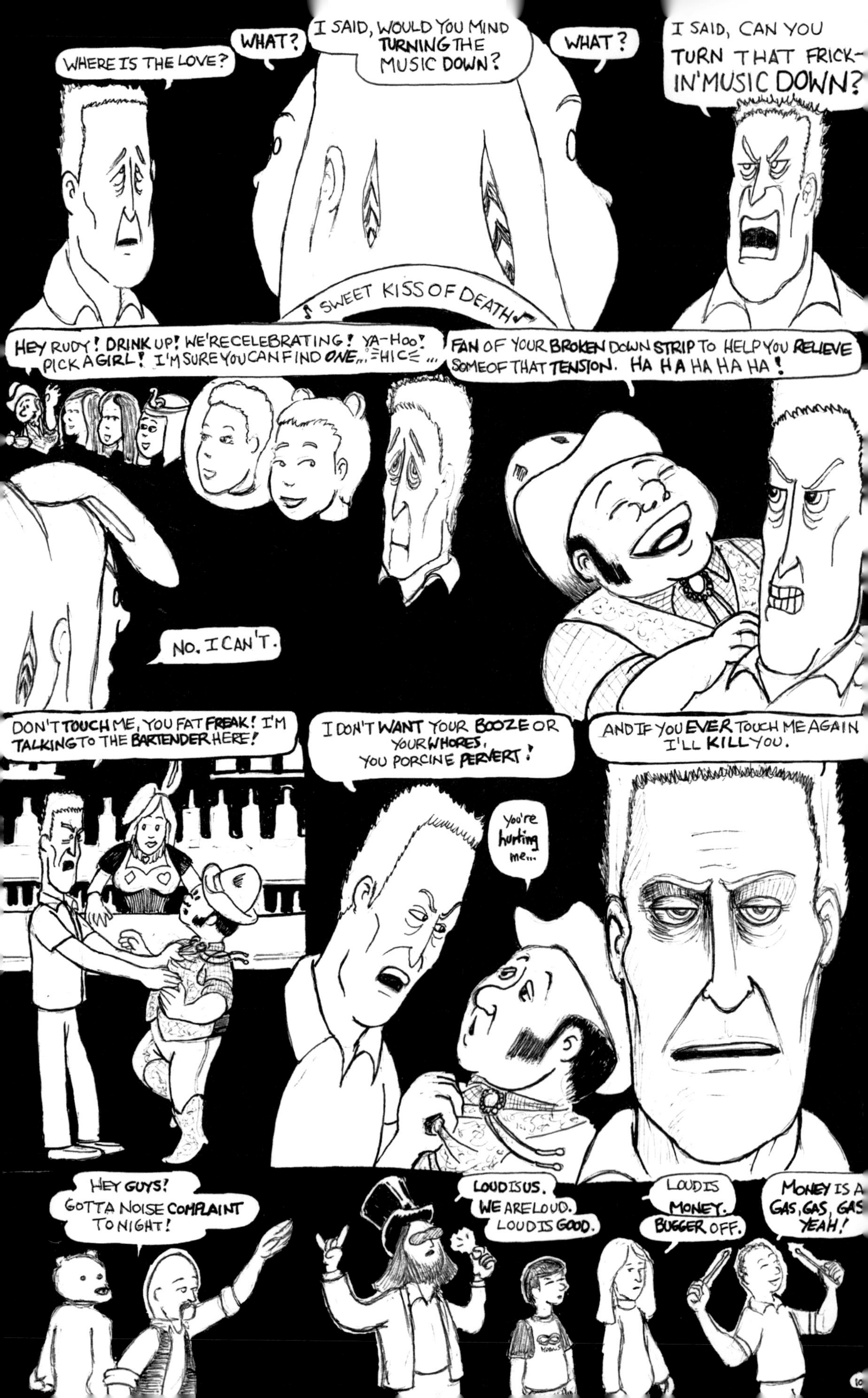

WHERE IS THE LOVE?
WHAT?
I SAID, WOULD YOU MIND TURNING THE MUSIC DOWN?
WHAT?
I SAID, CAN YOU TURN THAT FRICKIN' MUSIC DOWN?
SWEET KISS OF DEATH
HEY RUDY! DRINK UP! WE'RE CELEBRATING! YA-HOO! PICK A GIRL! I'M SURE YOU CAN FIND ONE... HIC...
NO. I CAN'T.
FAN OF YOUR BROKEN DOWN STRIP TO HELP YOU RELIEVE SOME OF THAT TENSION. HA HA HA HA HA!
DON'T TOUCH ME, YOU FAT FREAK! I'M TALKING TO THE BARTENDER HERE!
I DON'T WANT YOUR BOOZE OR YOUR WHORES, YOU PORCINE PERVERT!
You're hurting me...
AND IF YOU EVER TOUCH ME AGAIN I'LL KILL YOU.
HEY GUYS! GOTTA NOISE COMPLAINT TONIGHT!
LOUD IS US. WE ARE LOUD. LOUD IS GOOD.
LOUD IS MONEY. BUGGER OFF.
MONEY IS A GAS, GAS, GAS YEAH!

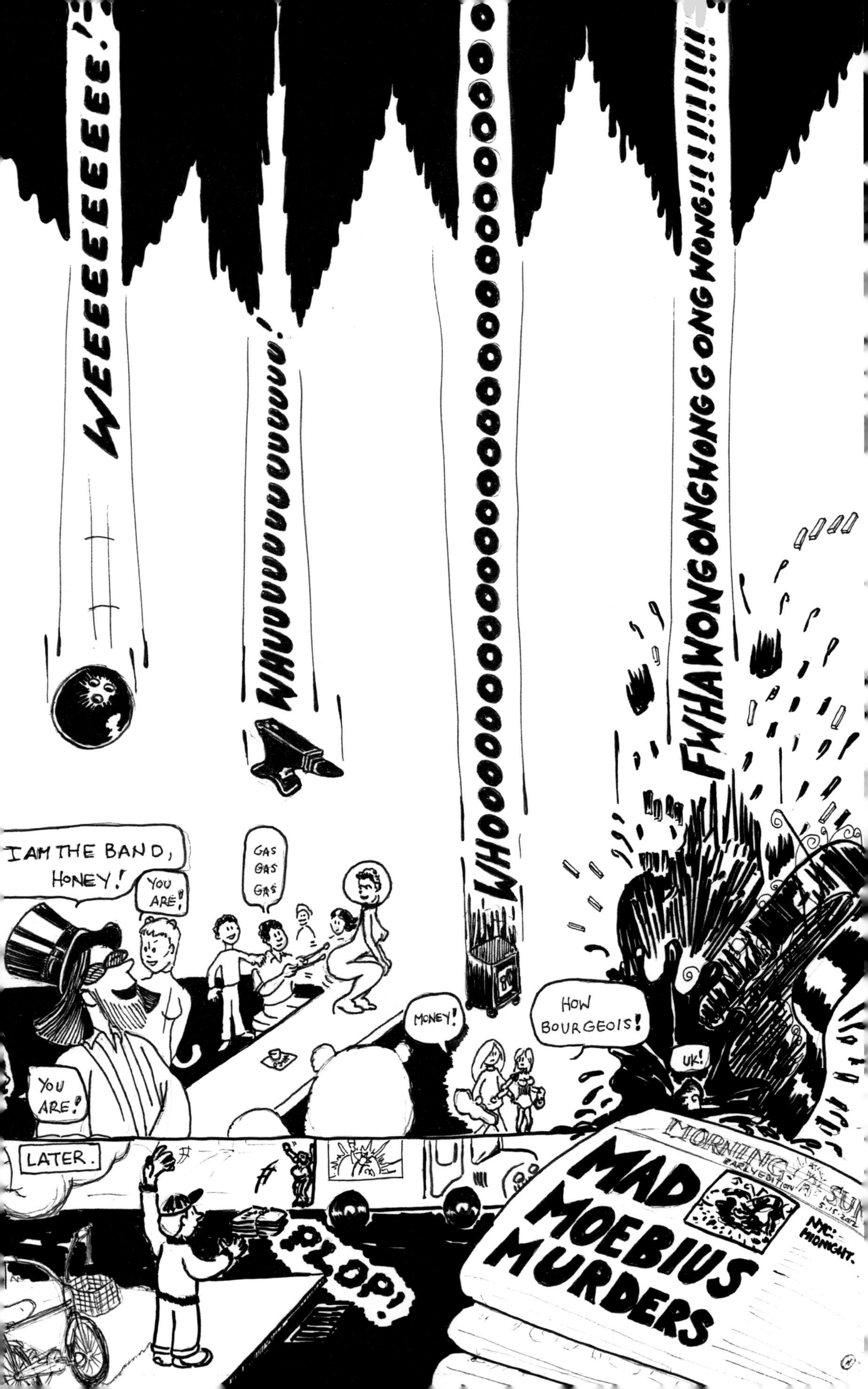
WEEEEEEEEEEEE!
WHUUUUUUUUUUUUUUU!
WHOOOOOOOOOOOOOOOOOOO
FWHAWONGGONGWONGGONGWONG!!!!!!!!!
I AM THE BAND, HONEY!
YOU ARE!
GAS GAS GAS
MONEY!
HOW BOURGEOIS!
UK!
YOU ARE!
LATER.
PLOP!
MORNING SUN
EARLY EDITION
5.15.2012
MAD MOEBIUS MURDERS
NYC: MIDNIGHT.

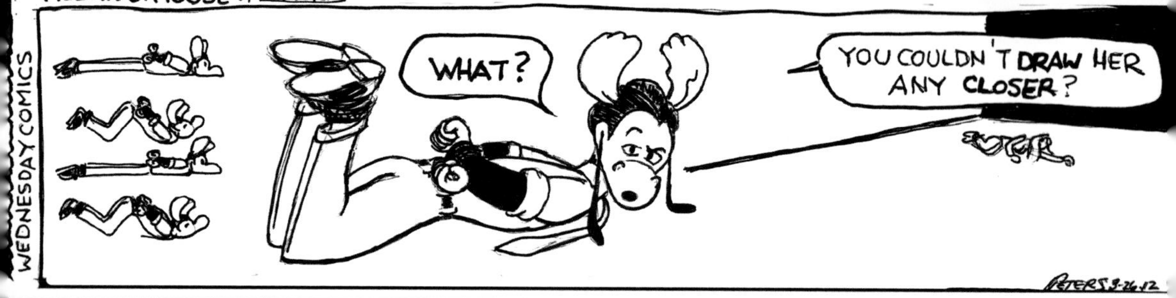
WEDNESDAY COMICS
WHAT?
YOU COULDN'T DRAW HER ANY CLOSER?
PETERS 9-26-12

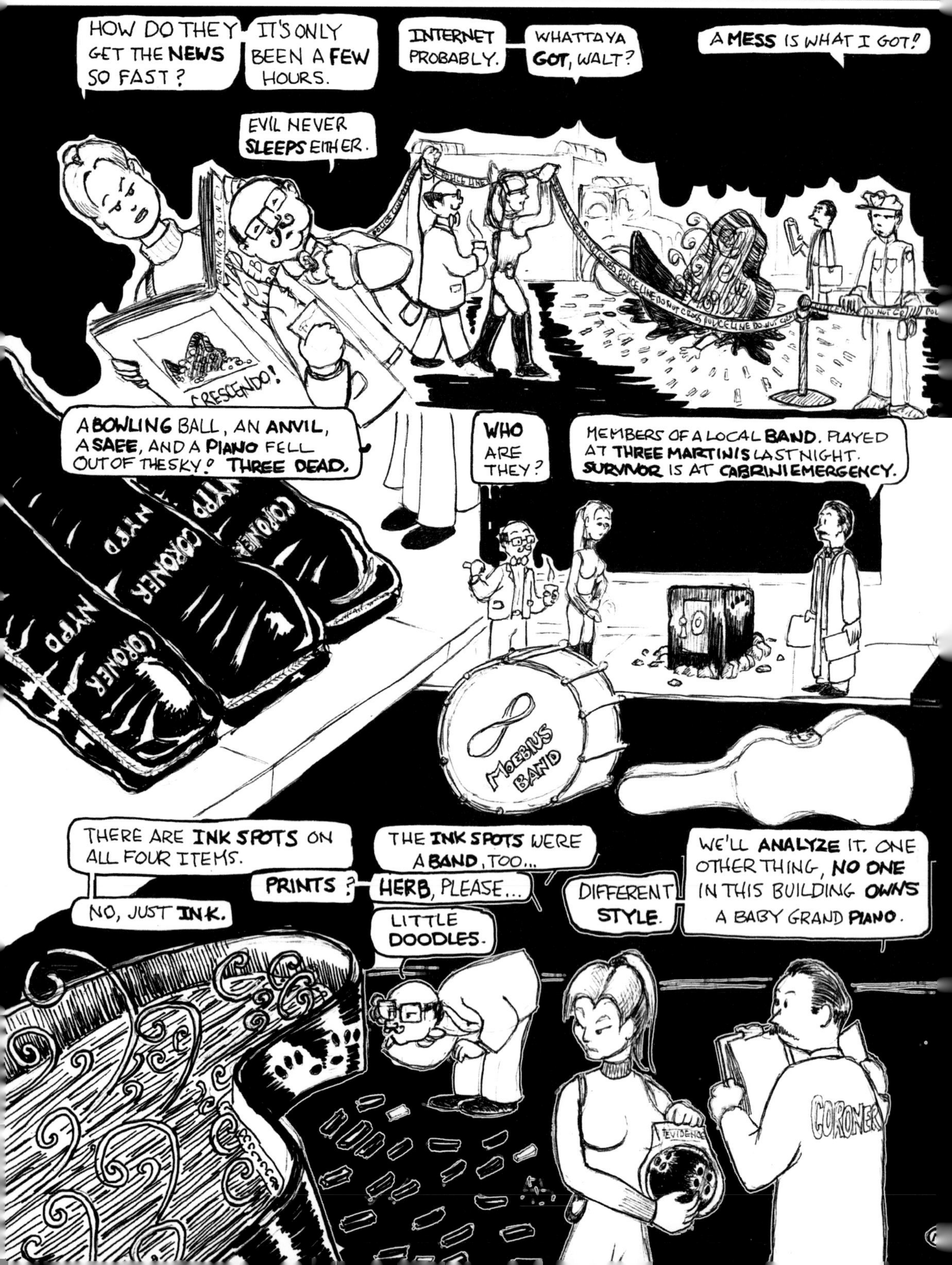
HOW DO THEY GET THE NEWS SO FAST?
IT'S ONLY BEEN A FEW HOURS.
INTERNET PROBABLY.
WHATTAYA GOT, WALT?
A MESS IS WHAT I GOT!
EVIL NEVER SLEEPS EITHER.
CRESCENDO!
A BOWLING BALL, AN ANVIL, A SAFE, AND A PIANO FELL OUT OF THE SKY! THREE DEAD.
WHO ARE THEY?
MEMBERS OF A LOCAL BAND. PLAYED AT THREE MARTINIS LAST NIGHT. SURVIVOR IS AT CABRINI EMERGENCY.
NYPD CORONER
MOEBIUS BAND
THERE ARE INK SPOTS ON ALL FOUR ITEMS.
PRINTS?
NO, JUST INK.
THE INK SPOTS WERE A BAND, TOO...
HERB, PLEASE...
LITTLE DOODLES.
DIFFERENT STYLE.
WE'LL ANALYZE IT. ONE OTHER THING, NO ONE IN THIS BUILDING OWNS A BABY GRAND PIANO.
EVIDENCE
CORONER

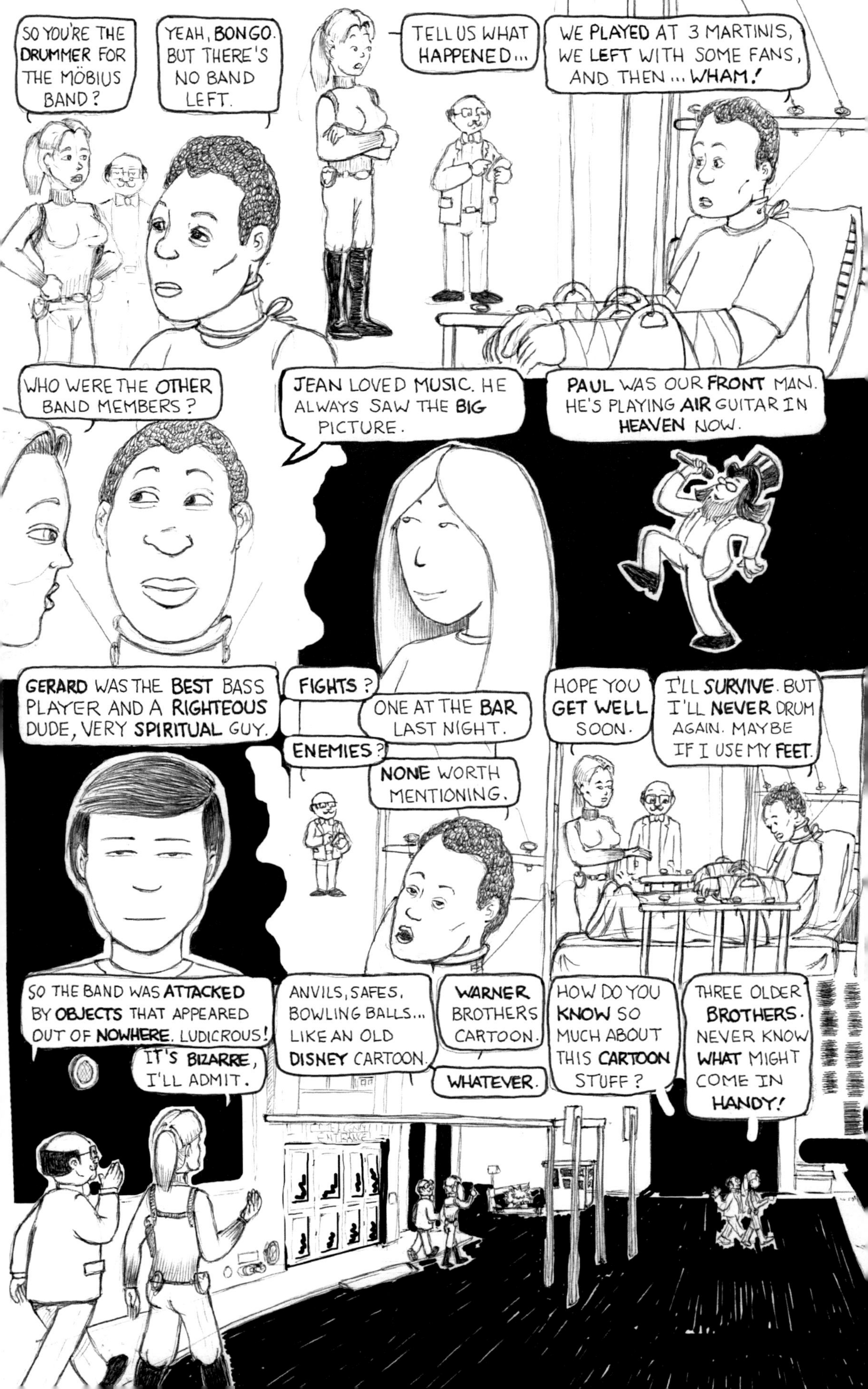
SO YOU'RE THE DRUMMER FOR THE MÖBIUS BAND?
YEAH, BONGO. BUT THERE'S NO BAND LEFT.
TELL US WHAT HAPPENED...
WE PLAYED AT 3 MARTINIS, WE LEFT WITH SOME FANS, AND THEN ... WHAM!
WHO WERE THE OTHER BAND MEMBERS?
JEAN LOVED MUSIC. HE ALWAYS SAW THE BIG PICTURE.
PAUL WAS OUR FRONT MAN. HE'S PLAYING AIR GUITAR IN HEAVEN NOW.
GERARD WAS THE BEST BASS PLAYER AND A RIGHTEOUS DUDE, VERY SPIRITUAL GUY.
FIGHTS?
ONE AT THE BAR LAST NIGHT.
ENEMIES?
NONE WORTH MENTIONING.
HOPE YOU GET WELL SOON.
I'LL SURVIVE. BUT I'LL NEVER DRUM AGAIN. MAYBE IF I USE MY FEET.
SO THE BAND WAS ATTACKED BY OBJECTS THAT APPEARED OUT OF NOWHERE. LUDICROUS!
IT'S BIZARRE, I'LL ADMIT.
ANVILS, SAFES, BOWLING BALLS... LIKE AN OLD DISNEY CARTOON.
WARNER BROTHERS CARTOON.
WHATEVER.
HOW DO YOU KNOW SO MUCH ABOUT THIS CARTOON STUFF?
THREE OLDER BROTHERS. NEVER KNOW WHAT MIGHT COME IN HANDY!

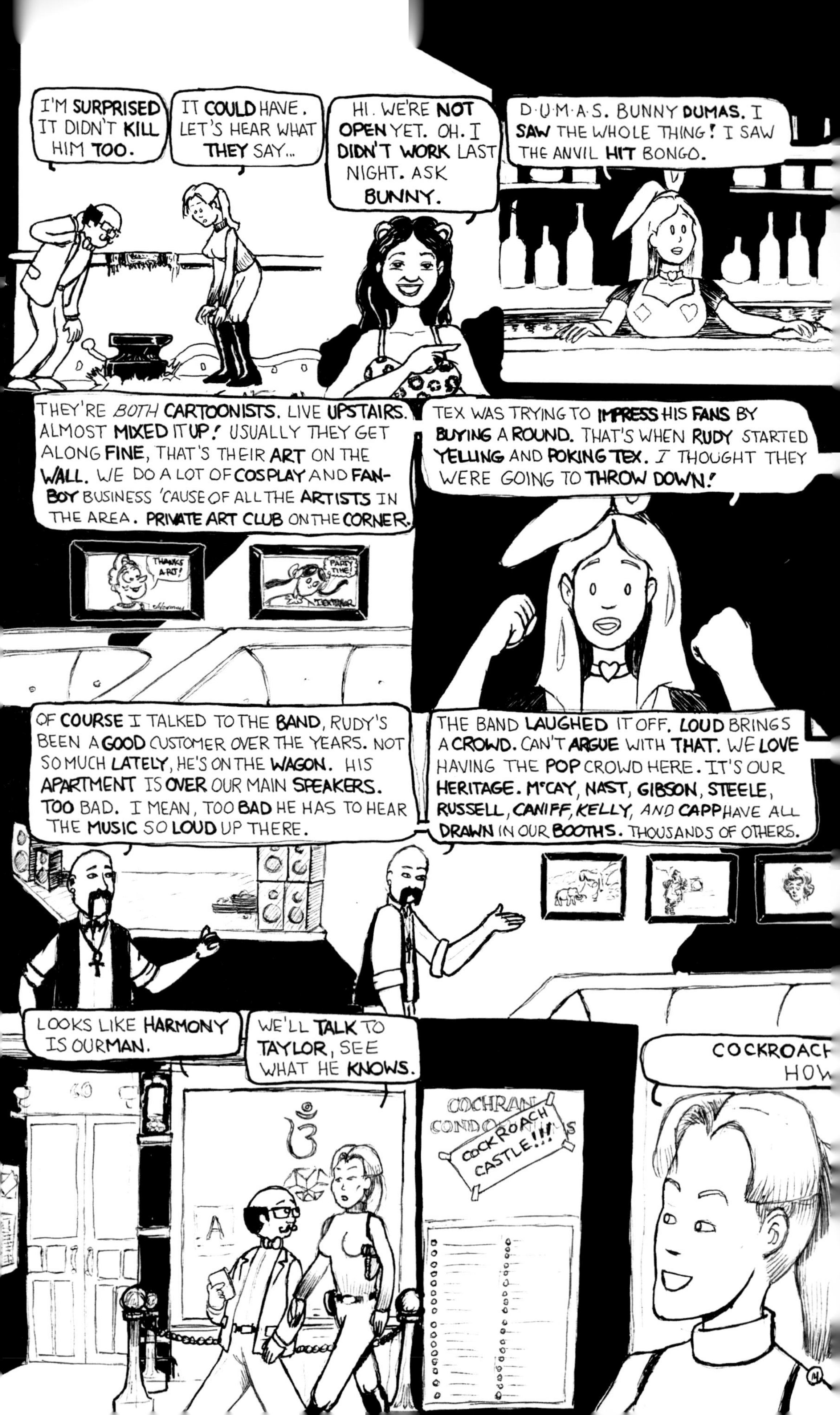
I'M SURPRISED IT DIDN'T KILL HIM TOO.
IT COULD HAVE. LET'S HEAR WHAT THEY SAY...
HI. WE'RE NOT OPEN YET. OH. I DIDN'T WORK LAST NIGHT. ASK BUNNY.
D·U·M·A·S. BUNNY DUMAS. I SAW THE WHOLE THING! I SAW THE ANVIL HIT BONGO.
THEY'RE BOTH CARTOONISTS. LIVE UPSTAIRS. ALMOST MIXED IT UP! USUALLY THEY GET ALONG FINE, THAT'S THEIR ART ON THE WALL. WE DO A LOT OF COSPLAY AND FAN-BOY BUSINESS 'CAUSE OF ALL THE ARTISTS IN THE AREA. PRIVATE ART CLUB ON THE CORNER.
THANKS ART!
PARTY TIME!
TEX WAS TRYING TO IMPRESS HIS FANS BY BUYING A ROUND. THAT'S WHEN RUDY STARTED YELLING AND POKING TEX. I THOUGHT THEY WERE GOING TO THROW DOWN!
OF COURSE I TALKED TO THE BAND, RUDY'S BEEN A GOOD CUSTOMER OVER THE YEARS. NOT SO MUCH LATELY, HE'S ON THE WAGON. HIS APARTMENT IS OVER OUR MAIN SPEAKERS. TOO BAD. I MEAN, TOO BAD HE HAS TO HEAR THE MUSIC SO LOUD UP THERE.
THE BAND LAUGHED IT OFF. LOUD BRINGS A CROWD. CAN'T ARGUE WITH THAT. WE LOVE HAVING THE POP CROWD HERE. IT'S OUR HERITAGE. MᶜCAY, NAST, GIBSON, STEELE, RUSSELL, CANIFF, KELLY, AND CAPP HAVE ALL DRAWN IN OUR BOOTHS. THOUSANDS OF OTHERS.
LOOKS LIKE HARMONY IS OUR MAN.
WE'LL TALK TO TAYLOR, SEE WHAT HE KNOWS.
60
COCHRAN CONDO
COCKROACH CASTLE!!!
COCKROACH
HOW
14

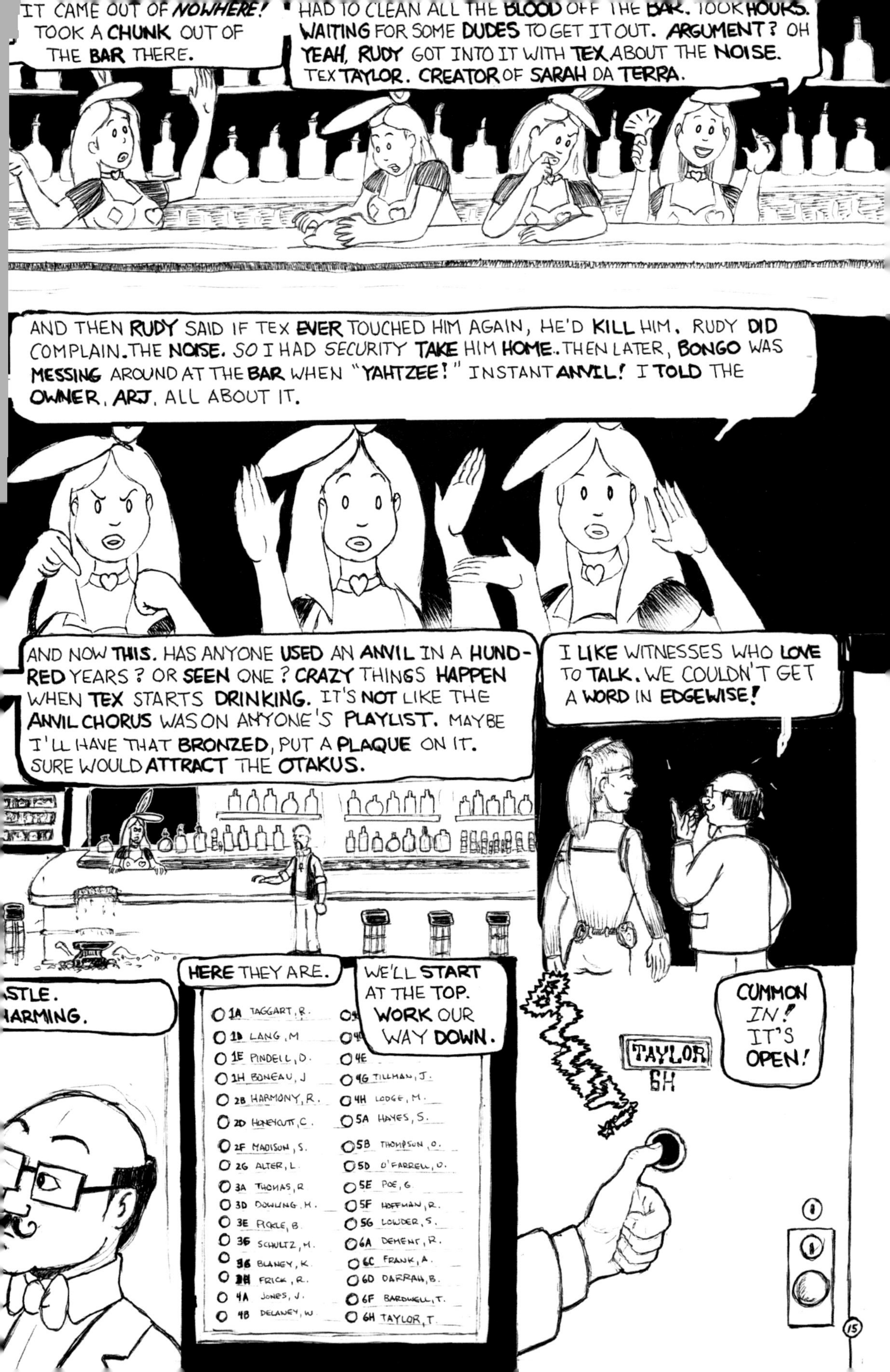
IT CAME OUT OF NOWHERE! TOOK A CHUNK OUT OF THE BAR THERE.
HAD TO CLEAN ALL THE BLOOD OFF THE BAR. TOOK HOURS. WAITING FOR SOME DUDES TO GET IT OUT. ARGUMENT? OH YEAH, RUDY GOT INTO IT WITH TEX ABOUT THE NOISE. TEX TAYLOR. CREATOR OF SARAH DA TERRA.
AND THEN RUDY SAID IF TEX EVER TOUCHED HIM AGAIN, HE'D KILL HIM. RUDY DID COMPLAIN. THE NOISE. SO I HAD SECURITY TAKE HIM HOME. THEN LATER, BONGO WAS MESSING AROUND AT THE BAR WHEN "YAHTZEE!" INSTANT ANVIL! I TOLD THE OWNER, ARJ, ALL ABOUT IT.
AND NOW THIS. HAS ANYONE USED AN ANVIL IN A HUNDRED YEARS? OR SEEN ONE? CRAZY THINGS HAPPEN WHEN TEX STARTS DRINKING. IT'S NOT LIKE THE ANVIL CHORUS WAS ON ANYONE'S PLAYLIST. MAYBE I'LL HAVE THAT BRONZED, PUT A PLAQUE ON IT. SURE WOULD ATTRACT THE OTAKUS.
I LIKE WITNESSES WHO LOVE TO TALK. WE COULDN'T GET A WORD IN EDGEWISE!
STLE.
HARMING.
HERE THEY ARE.
WE'LL START AT THE TOP. WORK OUR WAY DOWN.
1A TAGGART, R.
1D LANG, M
1E PINDELL, D.
1H BONEAU, J
2B HARMONY, R.
2D HONEYCUTT, C.
2F MADISON, S.
2G ALTER, L.
3A THOMAS, R
3D DOWLING, M.
3E PICKLE, B
3G SCHULTZ, M.
BLANEY, K.
FRICK, R.
4A JONES, J.
4B DELANEY, W
4E
4G TILLMAN, J.
4H LODGE, M.
5A HAYES, S.
5B THOMPSON, O.
5D O'FARRELL, O.
5E POE, G.
5F HOFFMAN, R.
5G LOWDER, S.
6A DEMENT, R.
6C FRANK, A.
6D DARRAH, B.
6F BARDWELL, T.
6H TAYLOR, T.
TAYLOR
6H
CUMMON IN! IT'S OPEN!

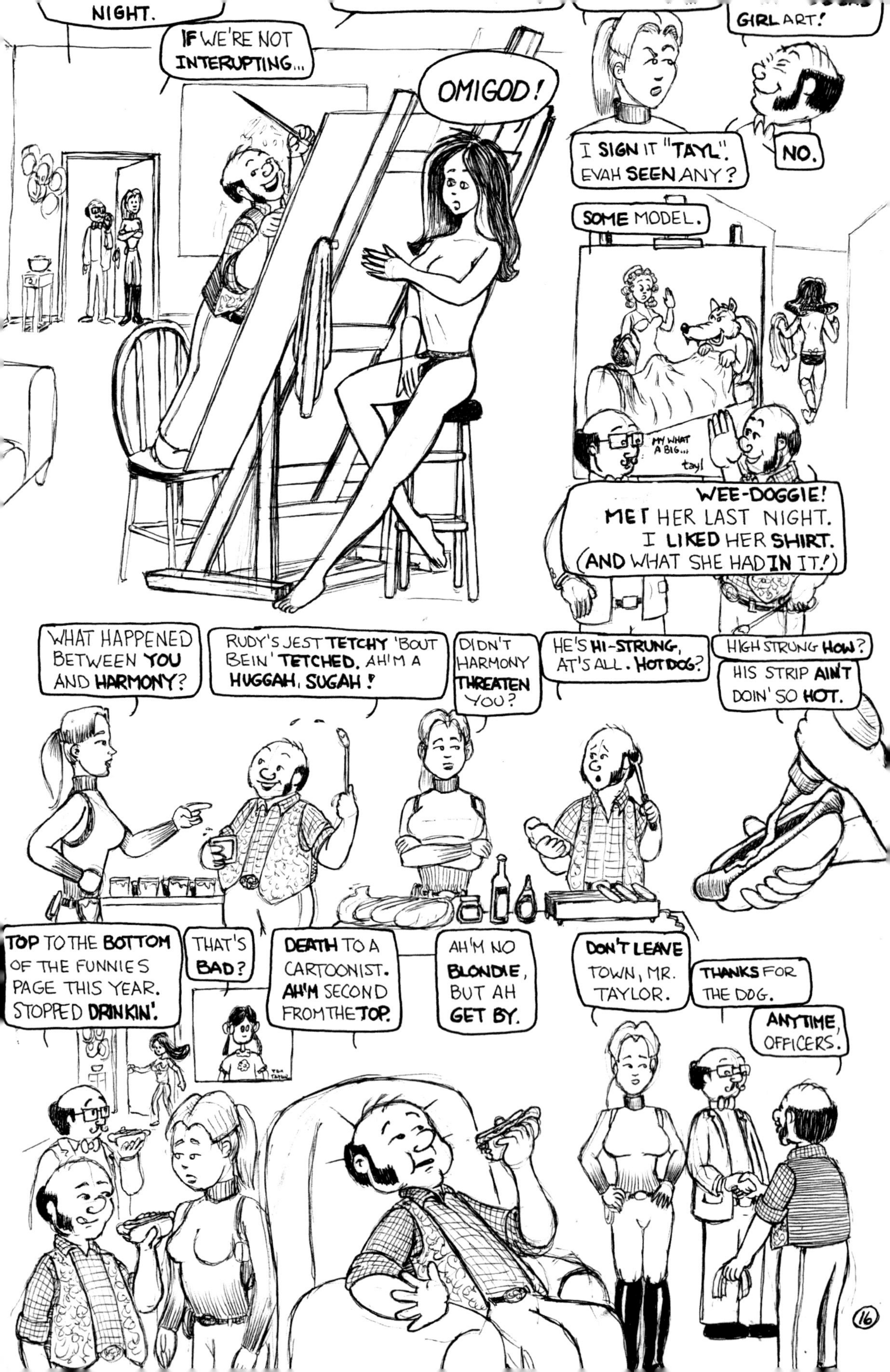
NIGHT.
IF WE'RE NOT INTERUPTING...
OMIGOD!
GIRL ART!
I SIGN IT "TAYL". EVAH SEEN ANY?
NO.
SOME MODEL.
MY WHAT A BIG...
tayl
WEE-DOGGIE! MET HER LAST NIGHT. I LIKED HER SHIRT. (AND WHAT SHE HAD IN IT!)
WHAT HAPPENED BETWEEN YOU AND HARMONY?
RUDY'S JEST TETCHY 'BOUT BEIN' TETCHED. AH'M A HUGGAH, SUGAH!
DIDN'T HARMONY THREATEN YOU?
HE'S HI-STRUNG, AT'S ALL. HOT DOG?
HIGH STRUNG HOW?
HIS STRIP AIN'T DOIN' SO HOT.
TOP TO THE BOTTOM OF THE FUNNIES PAGE THIS YEAR. STOPPED DRINKIN'.
THAT'S BAD?
DEATH TO A CARTOONIST. AH'M SECOND FROM THE TOP.
AH'M NO BLONDIE, BUT AH GET BY.
DON'T LEAVE TOWN, MR. TAYLOR.
THANKS FOR THE DOG.
ANYTIME, OFFICERS.

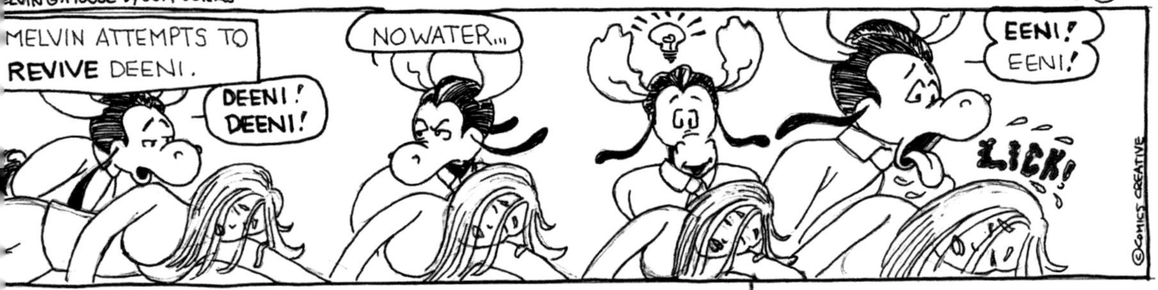
MELVIN ATTEMPTS TO REVIVE DEENI.
DEENI! DEENI!
NO WATER...
EENI! EENI!
LICK!
©COMICS CREATIVE

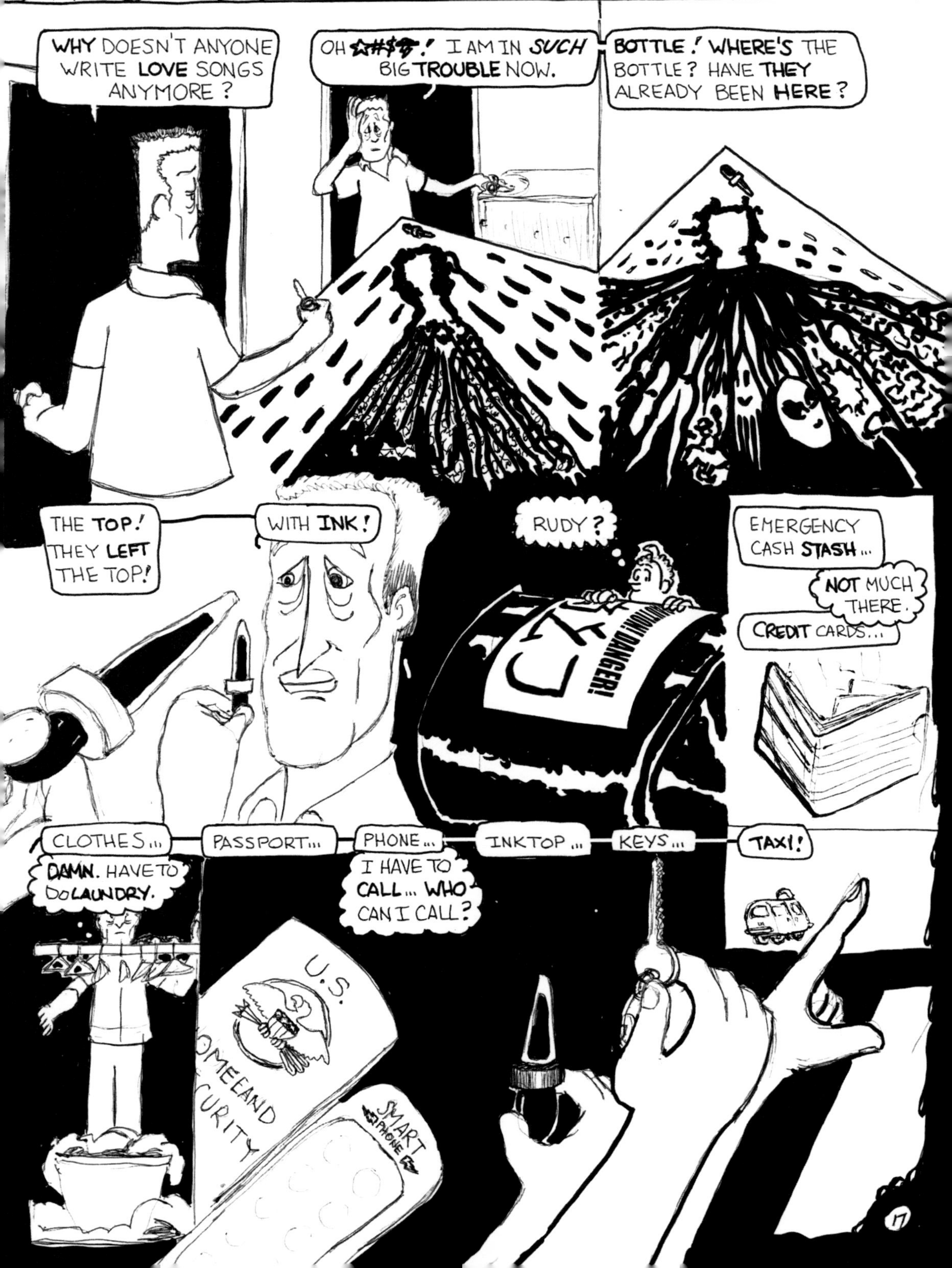
WHY DOESN'T ANYONE WRITE LOVE SONGS ANYMORE?
OH ☆#$%! I AM IN SUCH BIG TROUBLE NOW.
BOTTLE! WHERE'S THE BOTTLE? HAVE THEY ALREADY BEEN HERE?
THE TOP! THEY LEFT THE TOP!
WITH INK!
RUDY?
DANGER!
EMERGENCY CASH STASH...
NOT MUCH THERE.
CREDIT CARDS...
CLOTHES...
DAMN. HAVE TO DO LAUNDRY.
PASSPORT...
PHONE...
I HAVE TO CALL... WHO CAN I CALL?
INKTOP...
KEYS...
TAXI!
U.S.
OMELAND SECURITY
SMART PHONE

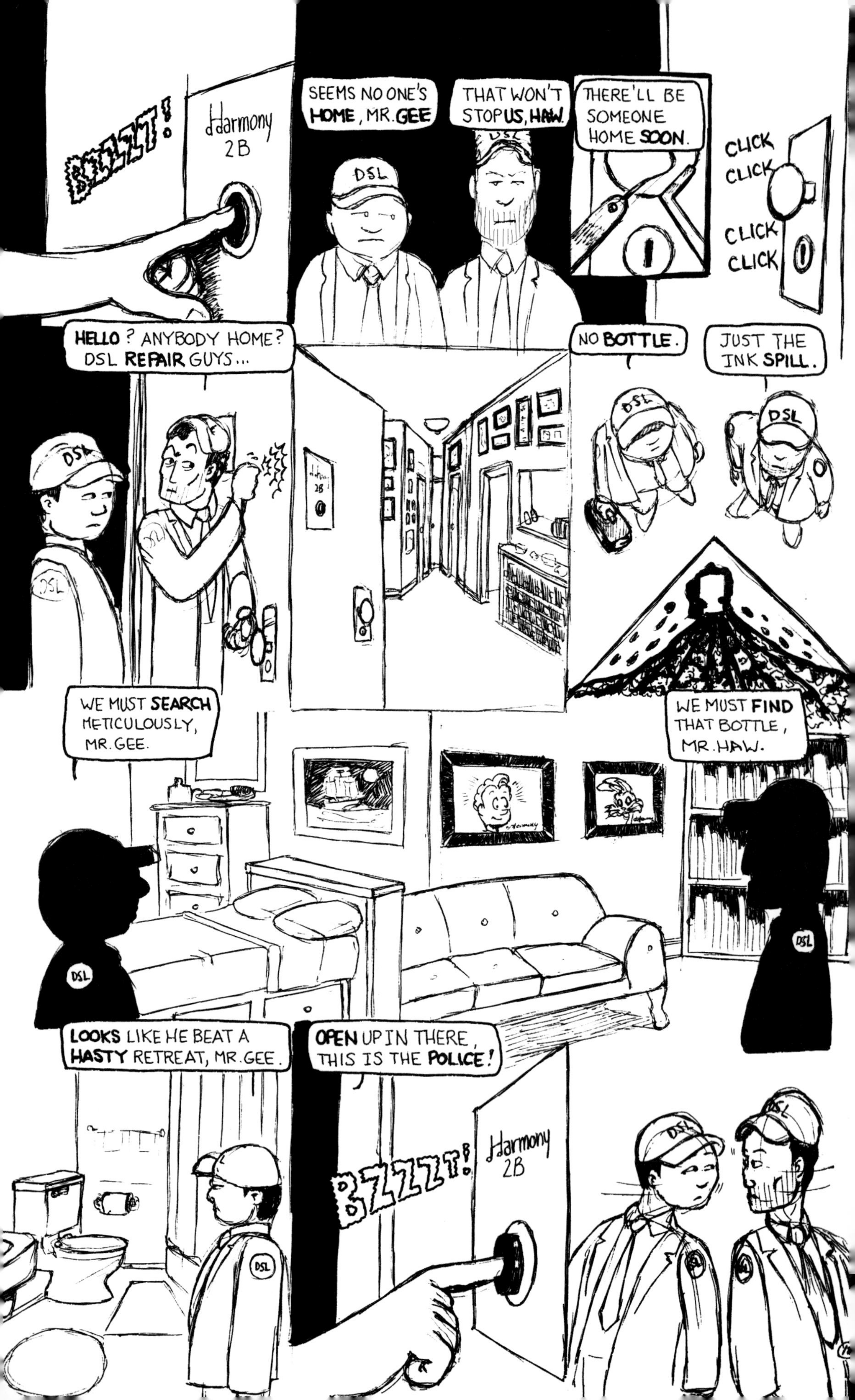
BZZZT!
Harmony
2B
SEEMS NO ONE'S HOME, MR. GEE
THAT WON'T STOP US, HAW.
THERE'LL BE SOMEONE HOME SOON.
CLICK
CLICK
CLICK
CLICK
HELLO? ANYBODY HOME? DSL REPAIR GUYS...
NO BOTTLE.
JUST THE INK SPILL.
WE MUST SEARCH METICULOUSLY, MR. GEE.
WE MUST FIND THAT BOTTLE, MR. HAW.
LOOKS LIKE HE BEAT A HASTY RETREAT, MR. GEE.
OPEN UP IN THERE, THIS IS THE POLICE!
BZZZZT!
Harmony
2B

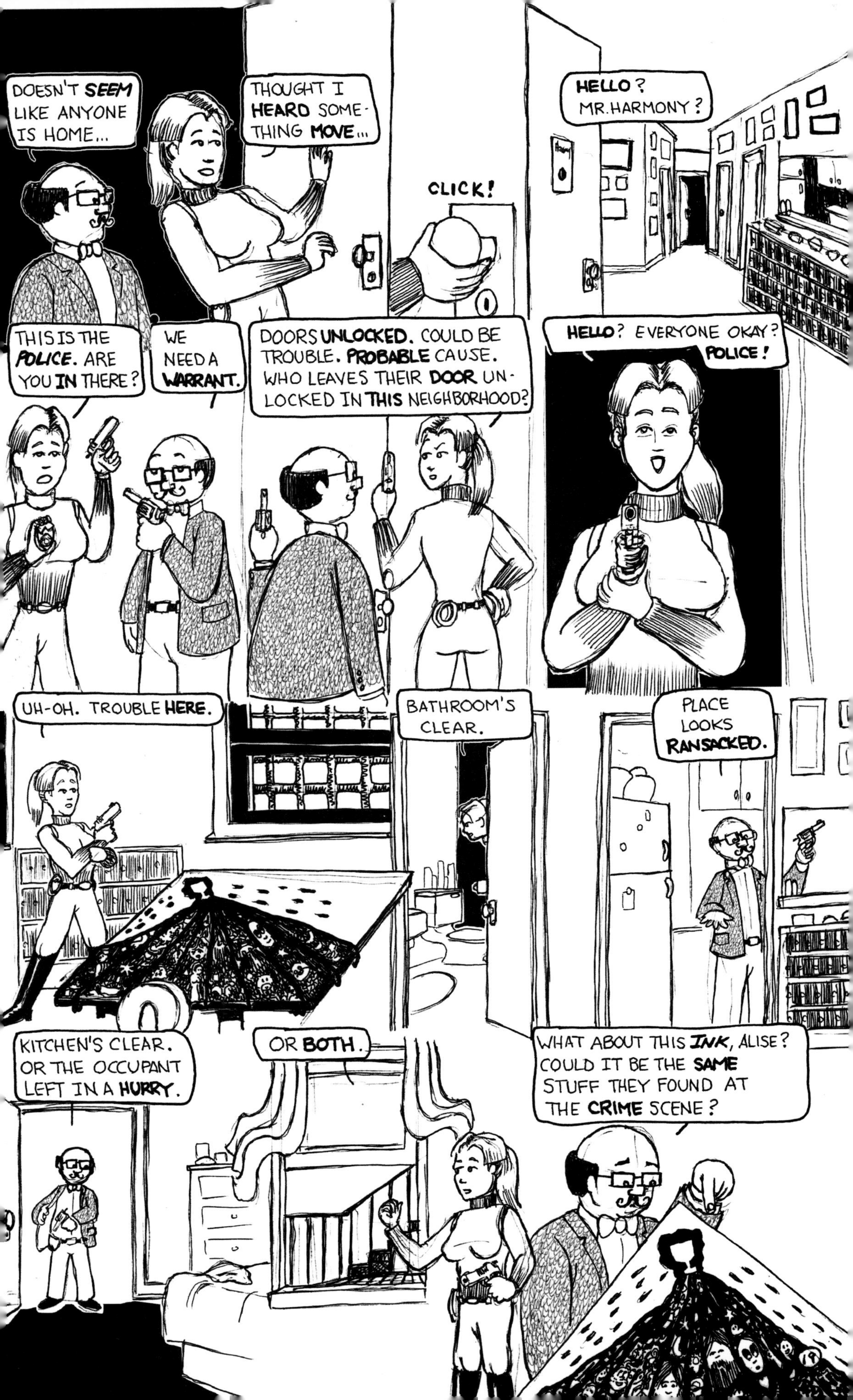
DOESN'T SEEM LIKE ANYONE IS HOME...
THOUGHT I HEARD SOME-THING MOVE...
CLICK!
HELLO? MR. HARMONY?
THIS IS THE POLICE. ARE YOU IN THERE?
WE NEED A WARRANT.
DOORS UNLOCKED. COULD BE TROUBLE. PROBABLE CAUSE. WHO LEAVES THEIR DOOR UN-LOCKED IN THIS NEIGHBORHOOD?
HELLO? EVERYONE OKAY? POLICE!
UH-OH. TROUBLE HERE.
BATHROOM'S CLEAR.
PLACE LOOKS RANSACKED.
KITCHEN'S CLEAR. OR THE OCCUPANT LEFT IN A HURRY.
OR BOTH.
WHAT ABOUT THIS INK, ALISE? COULD IT BE THE SAME STUFF THEY FOUND AT THE CRIME SCENE?

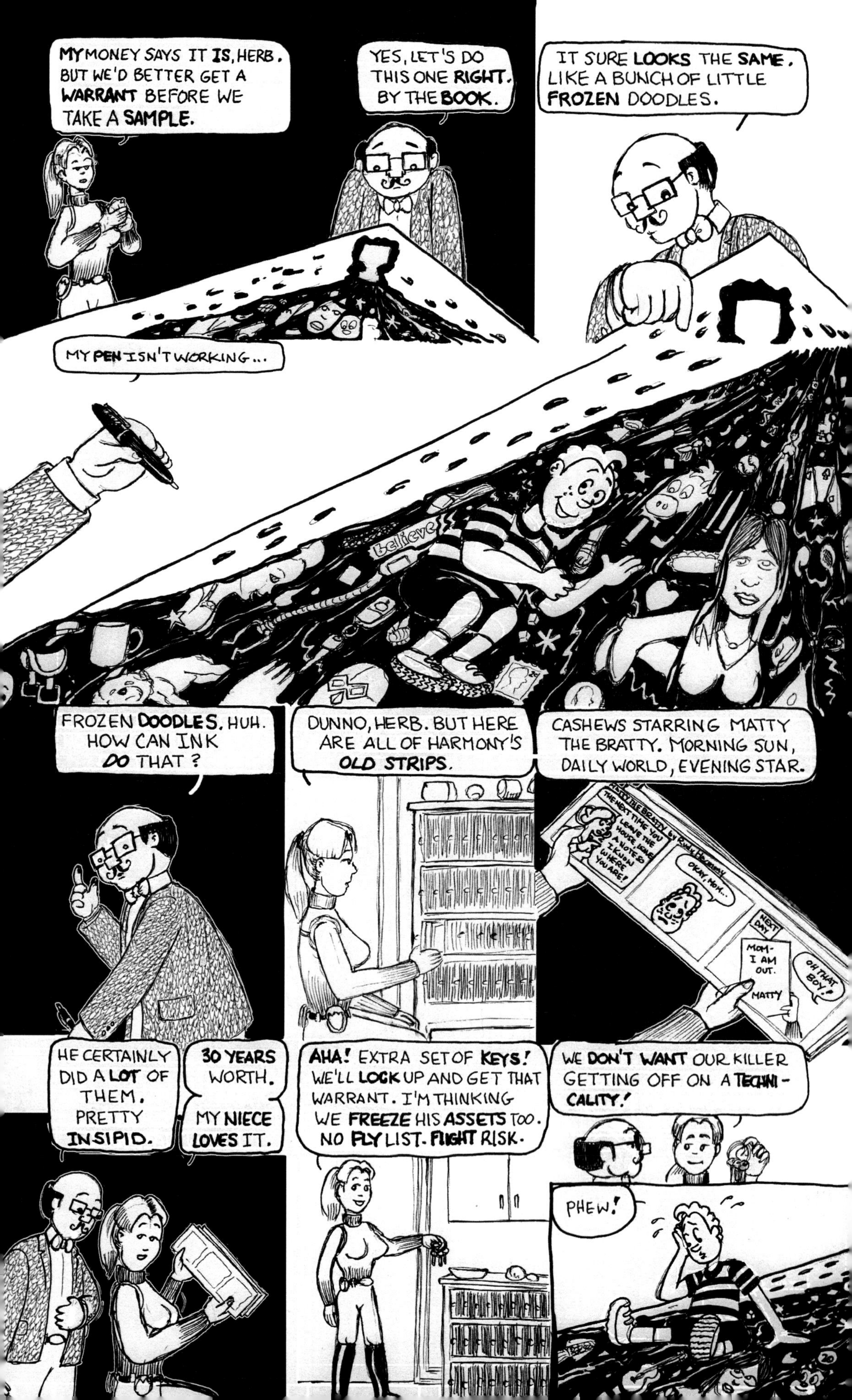

MY MONEY SAYS IT IS, HERB. BUT WE'D BETTER GET A WARRANT BEFORE WE TAKE A SAMPLE.
YES, LET'S DO THIS ONE RIGHT. BY THE BOOK.
IT SURE LOOKS THE SAME. LIKE A BUNCH OF LITTLE FROZEN DOODLES.
MY PEN ISN'T WORKING...
believe
FROZEN DOODLES, HUH. HOW CAN INK DO THAT?
DUNNO, HERB. BUT HERE ARE ALL OF HARMONY'S OLD STRIPS.
CASHEWS STARRING MATTY THE BRATTY. MORNING SUN, DAILY WORLD, EVENING STAR.
MATTY THE BRATTY by Rudy Harmony
THE NEXT TIME YOU LEAVE THE HOUSE, LEAVE A NOTE SO I KNOW WHERE YOU ARE!
OKAY, MOM...
NEXT DAY
MOM- I AM OUT. MATTY
OH THAT BOY!
HE CERTAINLY DID A LOT OF THEM. PRETTY INSIPID.
30 YEARS WORTH.
MY NIECE LOVES IT.
AHA! EXTRA SET OF KEYS! WE'LL LOCK UP AND GET THAT WARRANT. I'M THINKING WE FREEZE HIS ASSETS TOO. NO FLY LIST. FLIGHT RISK.
WE DON'T WANT OUR KILLER GETTING OFF ON A TECHNI-CALITY!
PHEW!
20

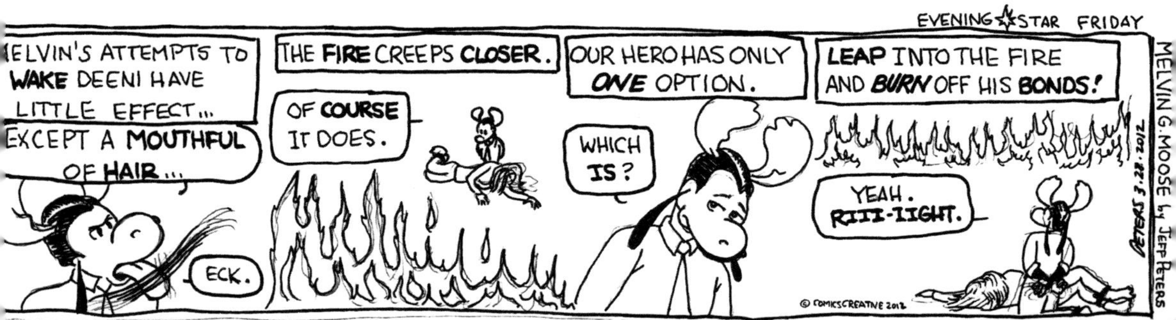
EVENING STAR FRIDAY
MELVIN G. MOOSE by JEFF PETERS
MELVIN'S ATTEMPTS TO WAKE DEENI HAVE LITTLE EFFECT...
EXCEPT A MOUTHFUL OF HAIR...
ECK.
THE FIRE CREEPS CLOSER.
OF COURSE IT DOES.
OUR HERO HAS ONLY ONE OPTION.
WHICH IS?
LEAP INTO THE FIRE AND BURN OFF HIS BONDS!
YEAH. RIII-IIGHT.
PETERS 3.28.2012
© COMICSCREATIVE 2012

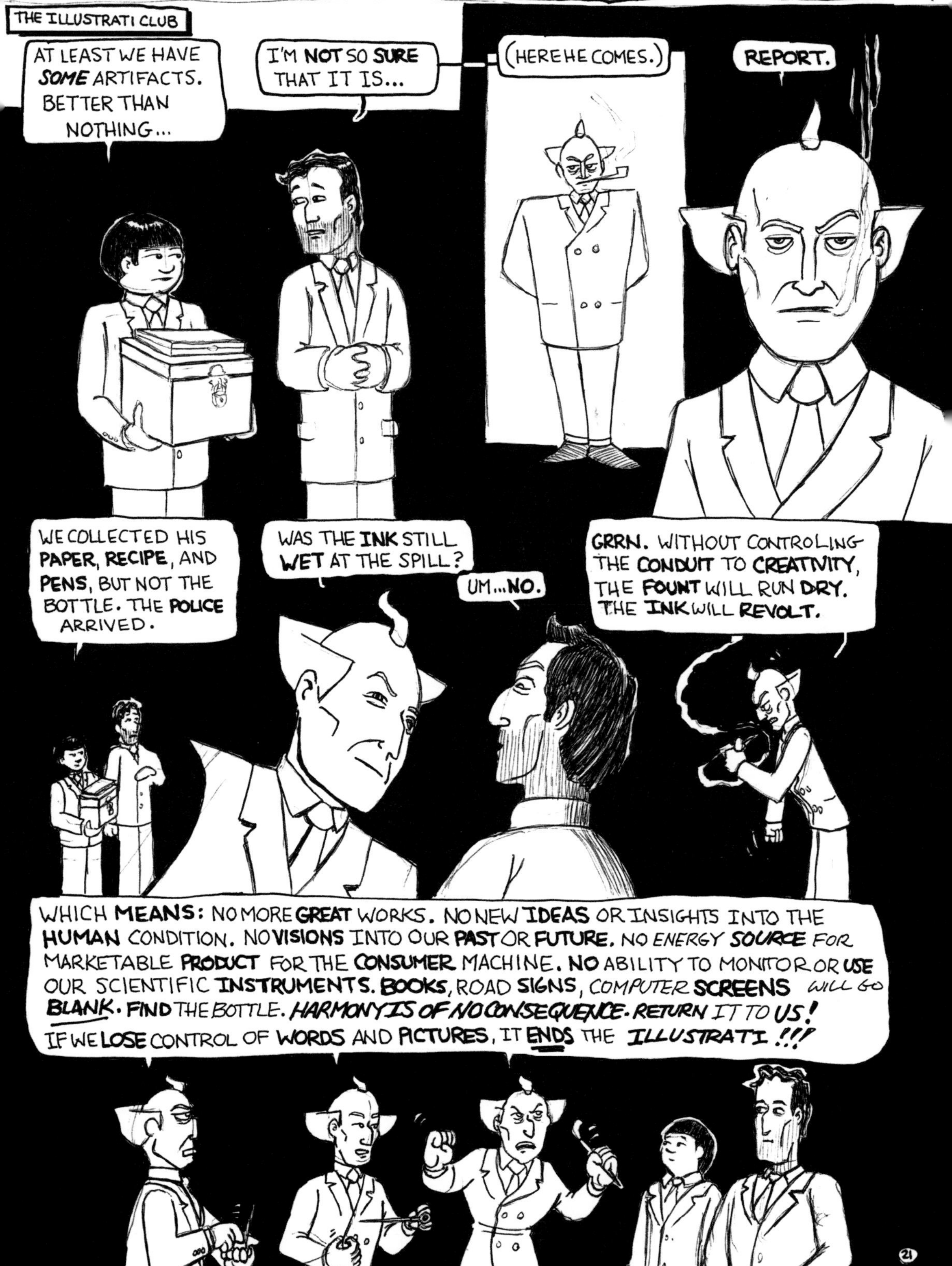
THE ILLUSTRATI CLUB
AT LEAST WE HAVE SOME ARTIFACTS. BETTER THAN NOTHING...
I'M NOT SO SURE THAT IT IS...
(HERE HE COMES.)
REPORT.
WE COLLECTED HIS PAPER, RECIPE, AND PENS, BUT NOT THE BOTTLE. THE POLICE ARRIVED.
WAS THE INK STILL WET AT THE SPILL?
UM...NO.
GRRN. WITHOUT CONTROLING THE CONDUIT TO CREATIVITY, THE FOUNT WILL RUN DRY. THE INK WILL REVOLT.
WHICH MEANS: NO MORE GREAT WORKS. NO NEW IDEAS OR INSIGHTS INTO THE HUMAN CONDITION. NO VISIONS INTO OUR PAST OR FUTURE. NO ENERGY SOURCE FOR MARKETABLE PRODUCT FOR THE CONSUMER MACHINE. NO ABILITY TO MONITOR OR USE OUR SCIENTIFIC INSTRUMENTS. BOOKS, ROAD SIGNS, COMPUTER SCREENS WILL GO BLANK. FIND THE BOTTLE. HARMONY IS OF NO CONSEQUENCE. RETURN IT TO US! IF WE LOSE CONTROL OF WORDS AND PICTURES, IT ENDS THE ILLUSTRATI!!!

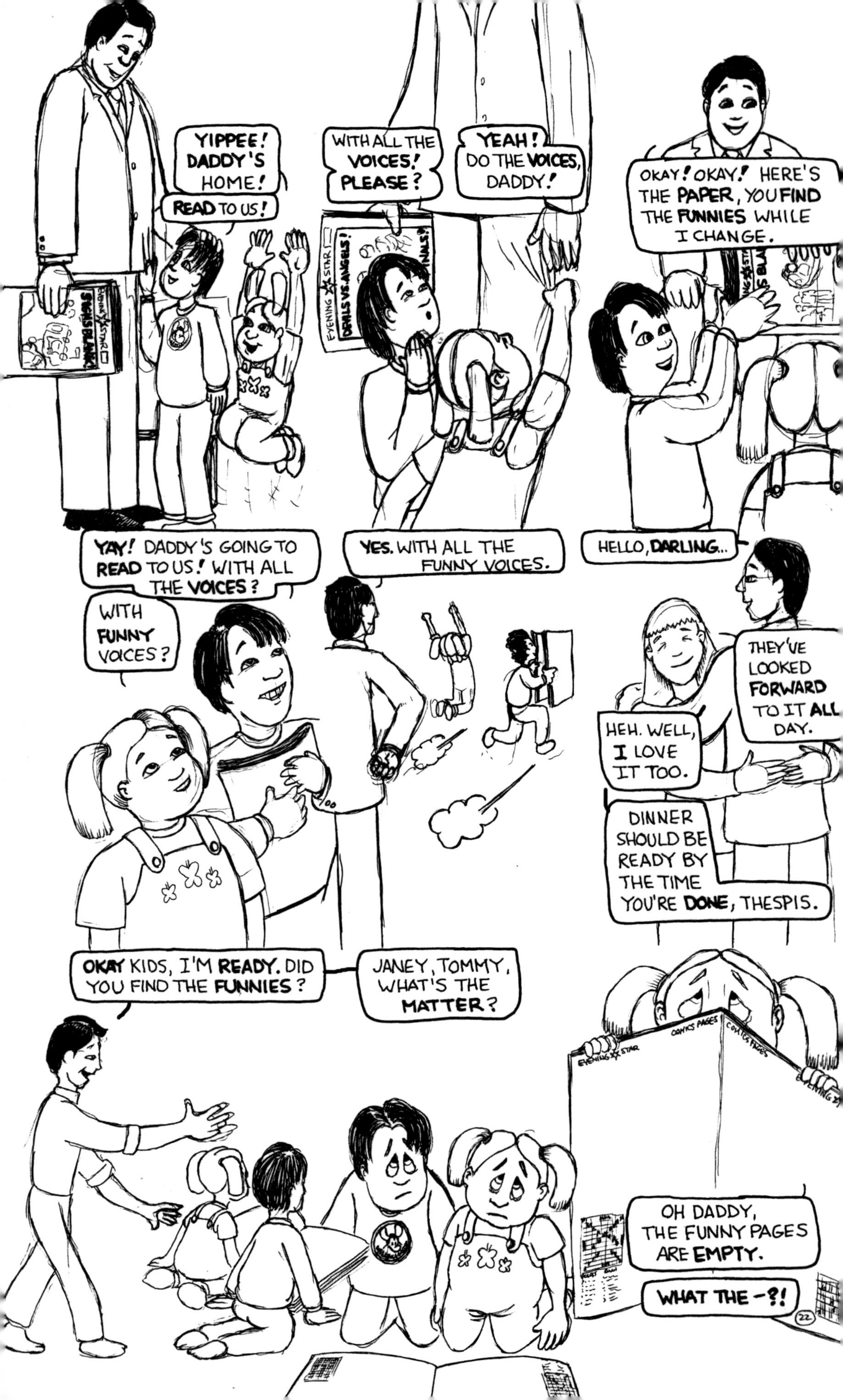
YIPPEE! DADDY'S HOME!
READ TO US!
WITH ALL THE VOICES! PLEASE?
YEAH! DO THE VOICES, DADDY!
OKAY! OKAY! HERE'S THE PAPER, YOU FIND THE FUNNIES WHILE I CHANGE.
YAY! DADDY'S GOING TO READ TO US! WITH ALL THE VOICES?
WITH FUNNY VOICES?
YES. WITH ALL THE FUNNY VOICES.
HELLO, DARLING...
THEY'VE LOOKED FORWARD TO IT ALL DAY.
HEH. WELL, I LOVE IT TOO.
DINNER SHOULD BE READY BY THE TIME YOU'RE DONE, THESPIS.
OKAY KIDS, I'M READY. DID YOU FIND THE FUNNIES?
JANEY, TOMMY, WHAT'S THE MATTER?
OH DADDY, THE FUNNY PAGES ARE EMPTY.
WHAT THE -?!
EVENING STAR
DEVILS VS. ANGELS!
COMICS PAGES

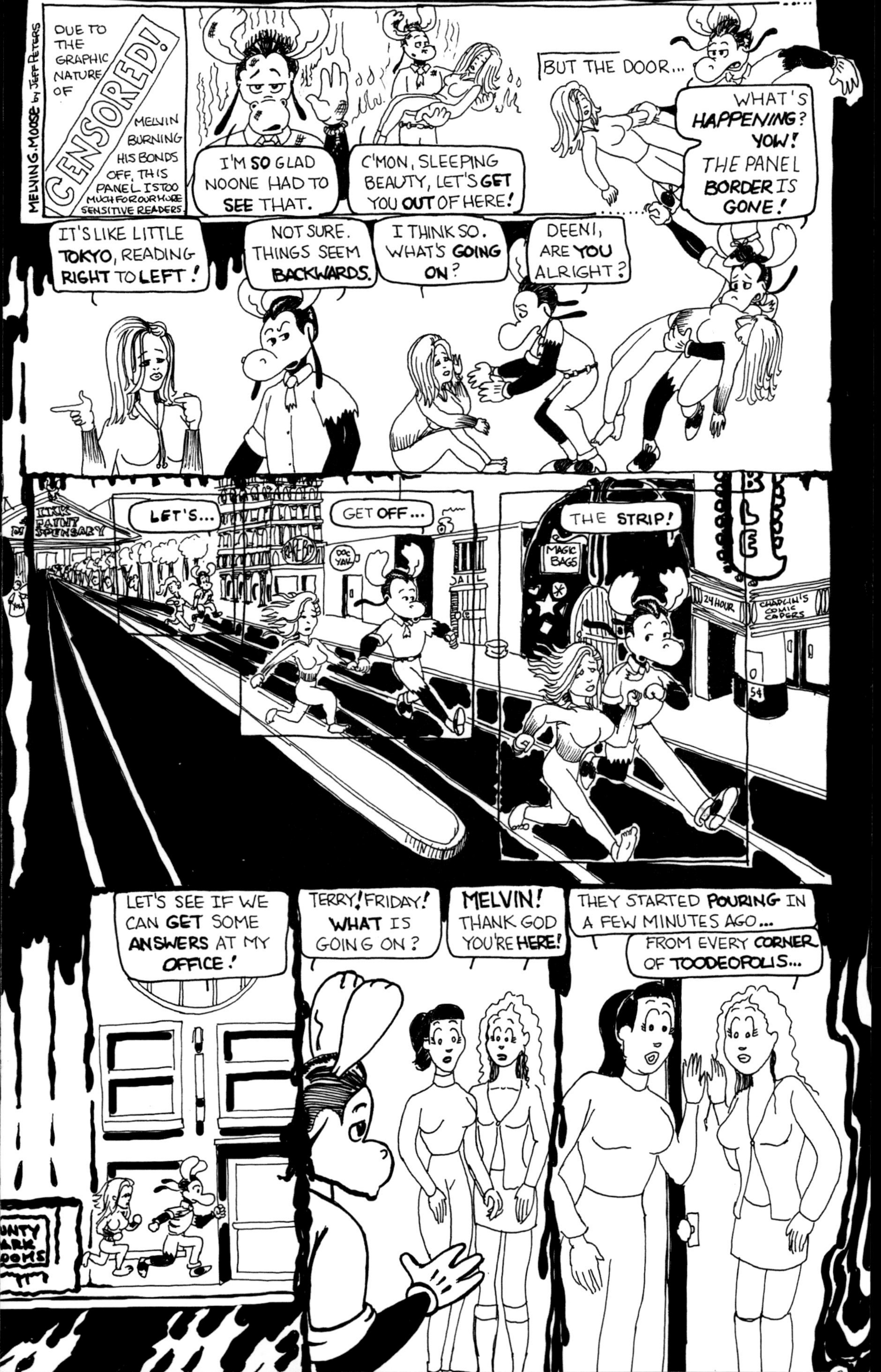
MELVIN.MOOSE by JEFF PETERS
DUE TO THE GRAPHIC NATURE OF MELVIN BURNING HIS BONDS OFF, THIS PANEL IS TOO MUCH FOR OUR MORE SENSITIVE READERS
CENSORED!
I'M SO GLAD NOONE HAD TO SEE THAT.
C'MON, SLEEPING BEAUTY, LET'S GET YOU OUT OF HERE!
BUT THE DOOR...
WHAT'S HAPPENING? YOW! THE PANEL BORDER IS GONE!
DEENI, ARE YOU ALRIGHT?
I THINK SO. WHAT'S GOING ON?
NOT SURE. THINGS SEEM BACKWARDS.
IT'S LIKE LITTLE TOKYO, READING RIGHT TO LEFT!
LET'S...
GET OFF...
THE STRIP!
MAGIC BAGS
24 HOUR
CHAPLIN'S COMIC CAPERS
LET'S SEE IF WE CAN GET SOME ANSWERS AT MY OFFICE!
TERRY! FRIDAY! WHAT IS GOING ON?
MELVIN! THANK GOD YOU'RE HERE!
THEY STARTED POURING IN A FEW MINUTES AGO...
FROM EVERY CORNER OF TOODEOPOLIS...

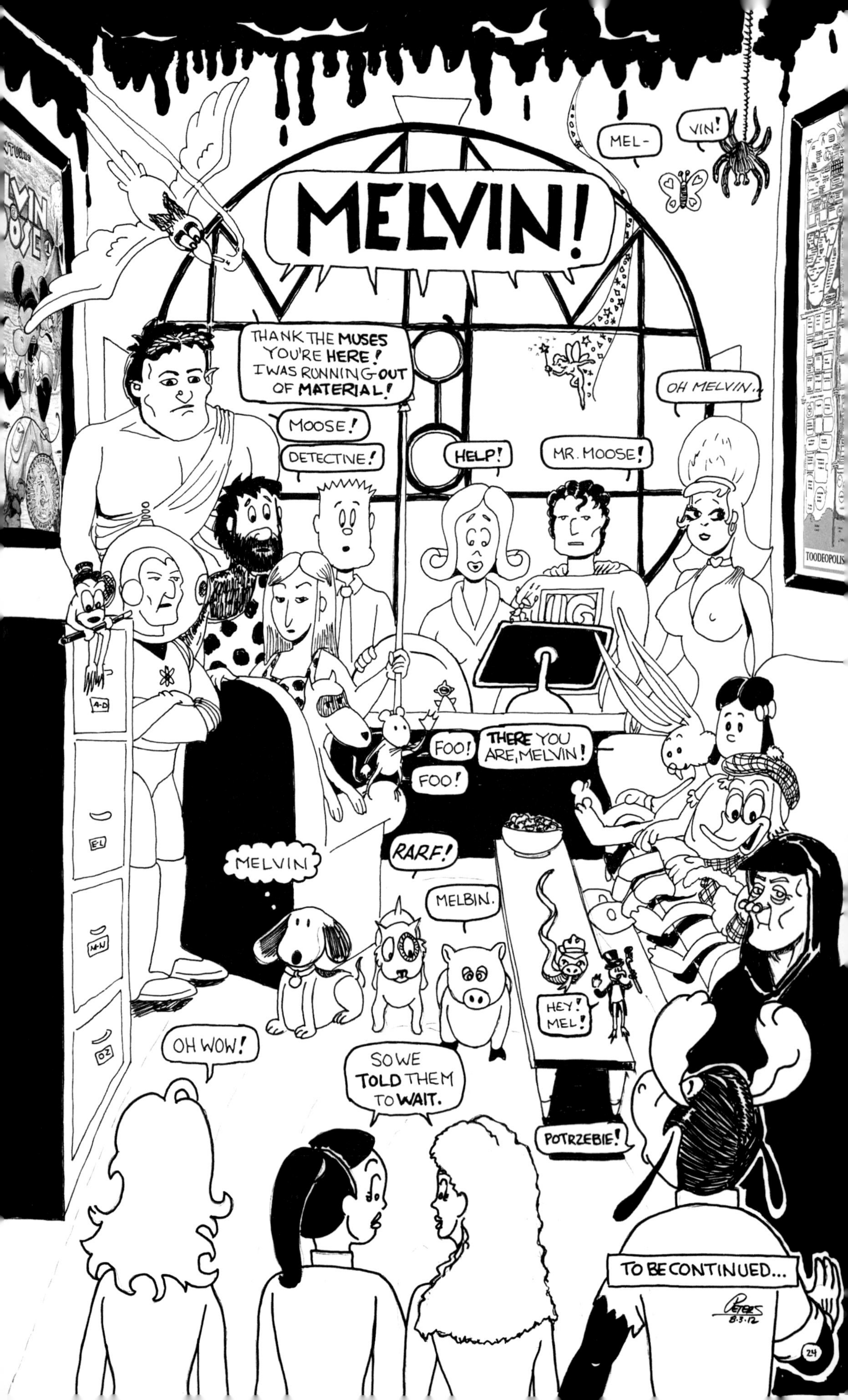
MEL-
VIN!
MELVIN!
THANK THE MUSES YOU'RE HERE! I WAS RUNNING OUT OF MATERIAL!
MOOSE!
DETECTIVE!
HELP!
MR. MOOSE!
OH MELVIN...
FOO!
FOO!
THERE YOU ARE, MELVIN!
MELVIN
RARF!
MELBIN.
HEY! MEL!
OH WOW!
SO WE TOLD THEM TO WAIT.
POTRZEBIE!
TO BE CONTINUED...
TOODEOPOLIS

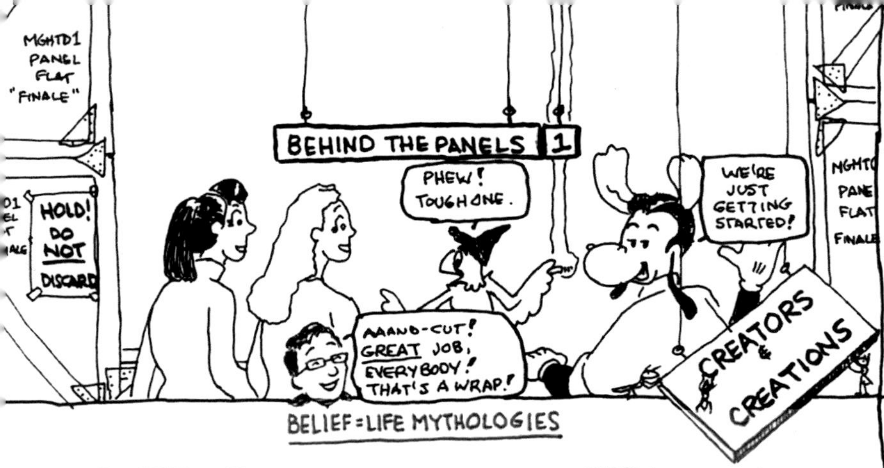
MGMTD1 PANEL FLAT "FINALE"
BEHIND THE PANELS 1
HOLD! DO NOT DISCARD
PHEW! TOUGH ONE.
WE'RE JUST GETTING STARTED!
AAAND-CUT! GREAT JOB, EVERYBODY! THAT'S A WRAP!
CREATORS & CREATIONS

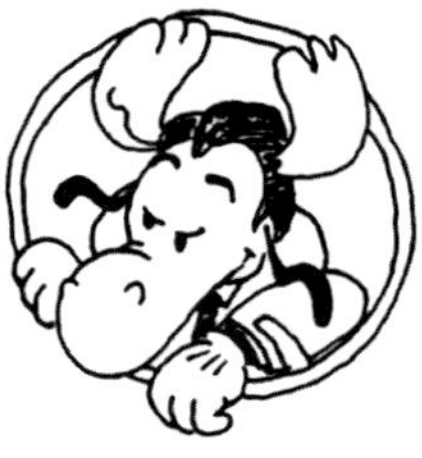

re: SOURCES

BELIEF = LIFE MYTHOLOGIES

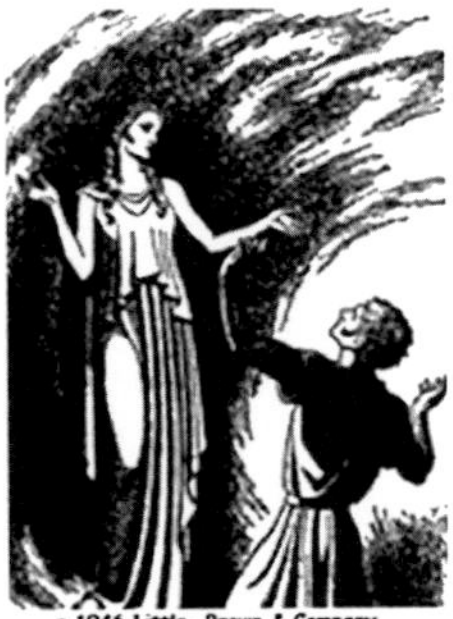
c 1946 Little, Brown & Company

PYGMALION SO **LOVED** HIS **STATUE** OF GALATEA, THAT **VENUS** BROUGHT HER TO **LIFE!** ADAPTATIONS OF THIS CLASSIC **MYTH** INCLUDE MY FAIR LADY, PRETTY WOMAN, EDUCATING RITA, MANNEQUIN, AND **DOZENS** OF OTHERS.

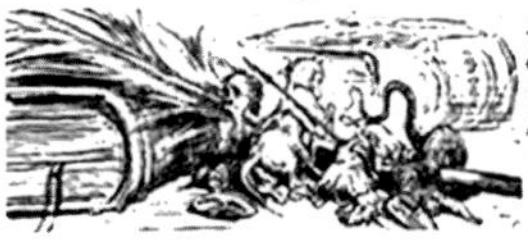
c Dover Books

ARTIST GUSTAVE **DORE** DEPICTS **MADNESS** RESULTS FROM READING IN CERVANTES' "**DON QUIXOTE**". DORE SHOWS **DEMONS** ALIVE IN **BOOKS** FROM "LES CONTES DROLATIQUES."

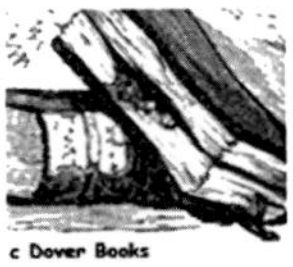
c Dover Books

Public Domain Image

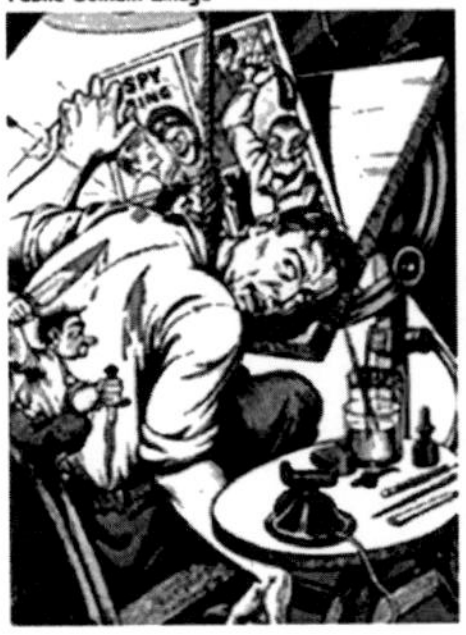

Public Domain Image

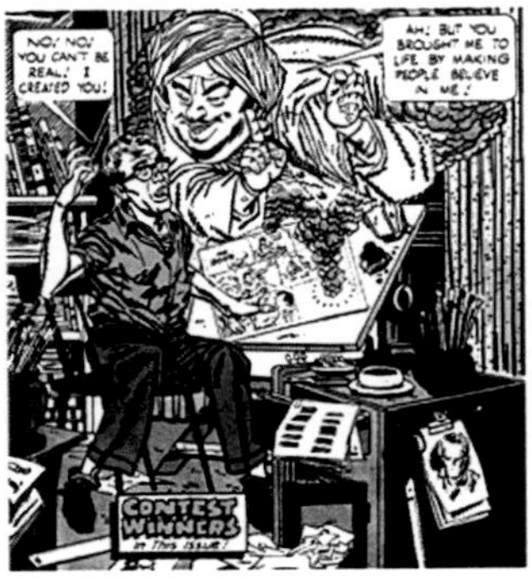
NO! NO! YOU CAN'T BE REAL! I CREATED YOU!
AH! BUT YOU BROUGHT ME TO LIFE BY MAKING PEOPLE BELIEVE IN ME!
CONTEST WINNERS in this issue!

Public Domain Image

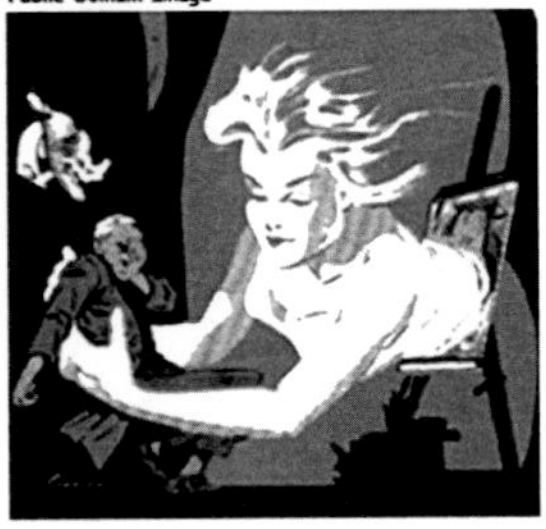

IN 1941, **PUNCH COMICS** ARTIST FALLS **AFOUL** OF HIS OWN SPY RING. FROM SCOTT SHAW'S ODDBALLCOMICS.COM

1955'S *SURPRISE ADVENTURES* **COVER** CLEARLY **STATES** THAT "**BELIEF EQUALS LIFE**." NO STORY INSIDE, THOUGH!

1957'S MAN IN BLACK #1 DEPICTS THE **ARTIST** BEING **COMFORTED** BY THE **SPIRIT** OF HIS **CREATION**.

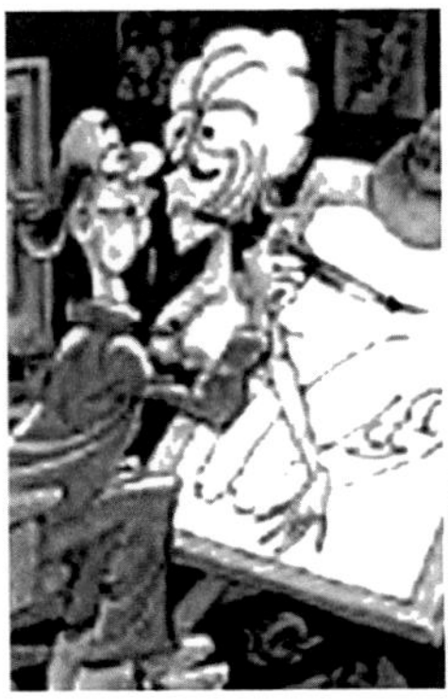
c1976 Kitchen Sink Press

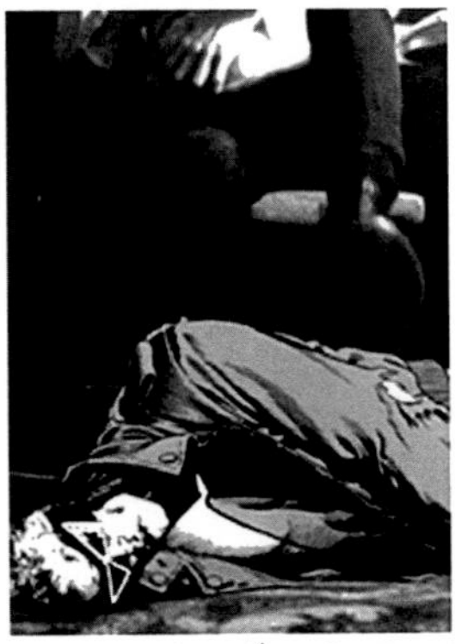
c2003 DC Entertainment

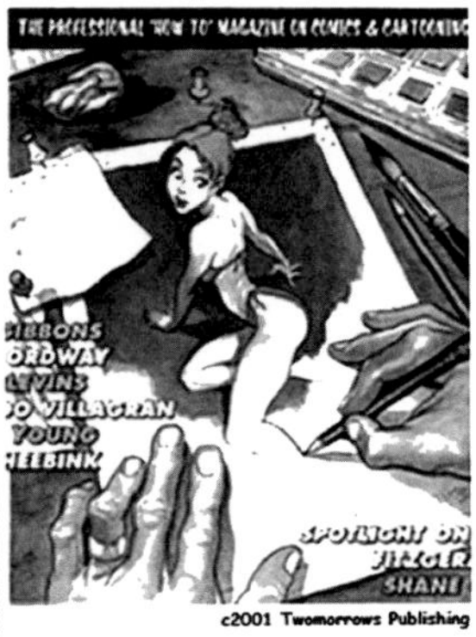
THE PROFESSIONAL "HOW TO" MAGAZINE ON COMICS & CARTOONING
c2001 Twomorrows Publishing

KURTZ KOMIX #1 HAS CREATOR HARVEY KURTZMAN **KISSED** BY HIS GALATEA, LITTLE ANNIE FANNY.

ANIMAL MAN #26 CONTAINS A **MEETING** BETWEEN THE CHARACTER AND HIS AUTHOR/CREATOR, GRANT MORRISON.

DRAW #1 SHOWS ARTIST BRET BLEVINS' FEMME **RISING** FROM THE **PAGE** UNDER HIS PROLIFIC CREATOR'S HAND.

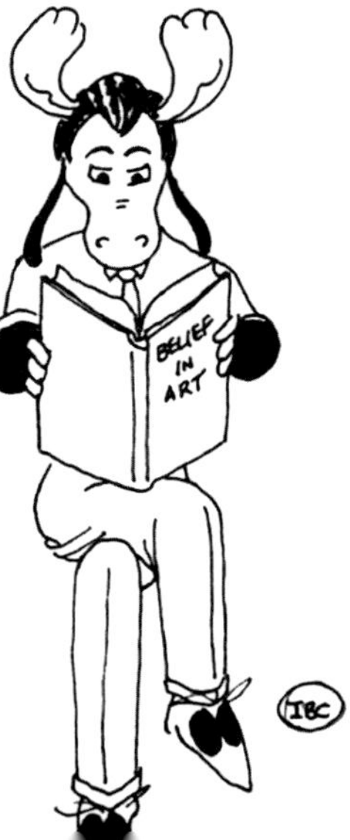
BELIEF IN ART
IBC

NEXT ISSUE

- OUR SECOND CHAPTER
- "TOODES"

or: "FUNNIES BUSINESS"

or: "WHEN ALL SEEMS LOST, IT'S GOOD TO HAVE A MAP."

or: "NEVER POKE A MAD MUSE."

LOOK FOR THE COMPLETE MELVIN G. MOOSE TOODE DICK GRAPHIC NOVEL ONLINE AND IN BOOK STORES AND COMIC SHOPS OF EXQUISITE TASTE.

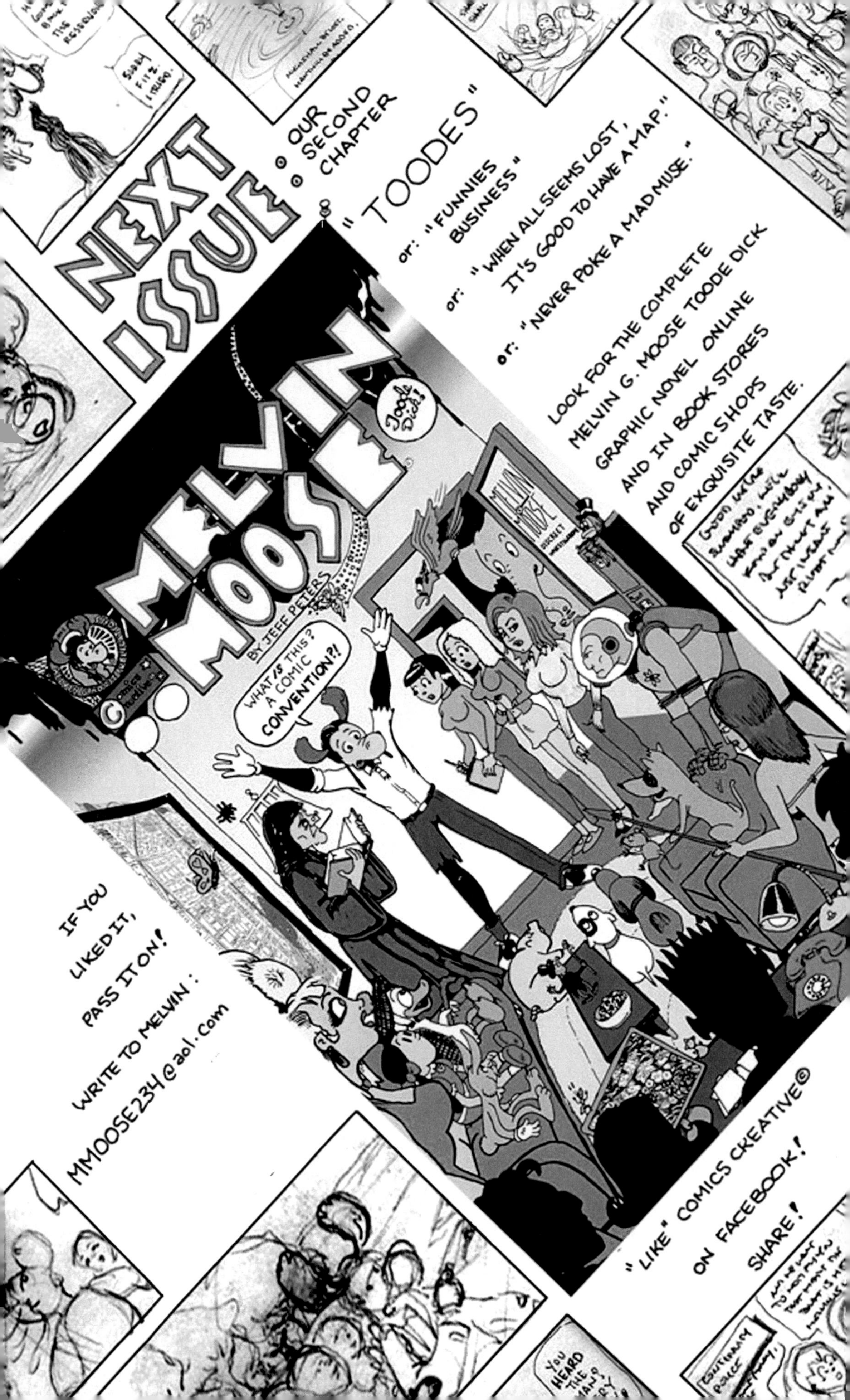
MELVIN MOOSE
BY JEFF PETERS
Toode Dick!
WHAT IS THIS? A COMIC CONVENTION?!

IF YOU LIKED IT, PASS IT ON!

WRITE TO MELVIN: MMOOSE234@aol.com

"LIKE" COMICS CREATIVE© ON FACEBOOK! SHARE!

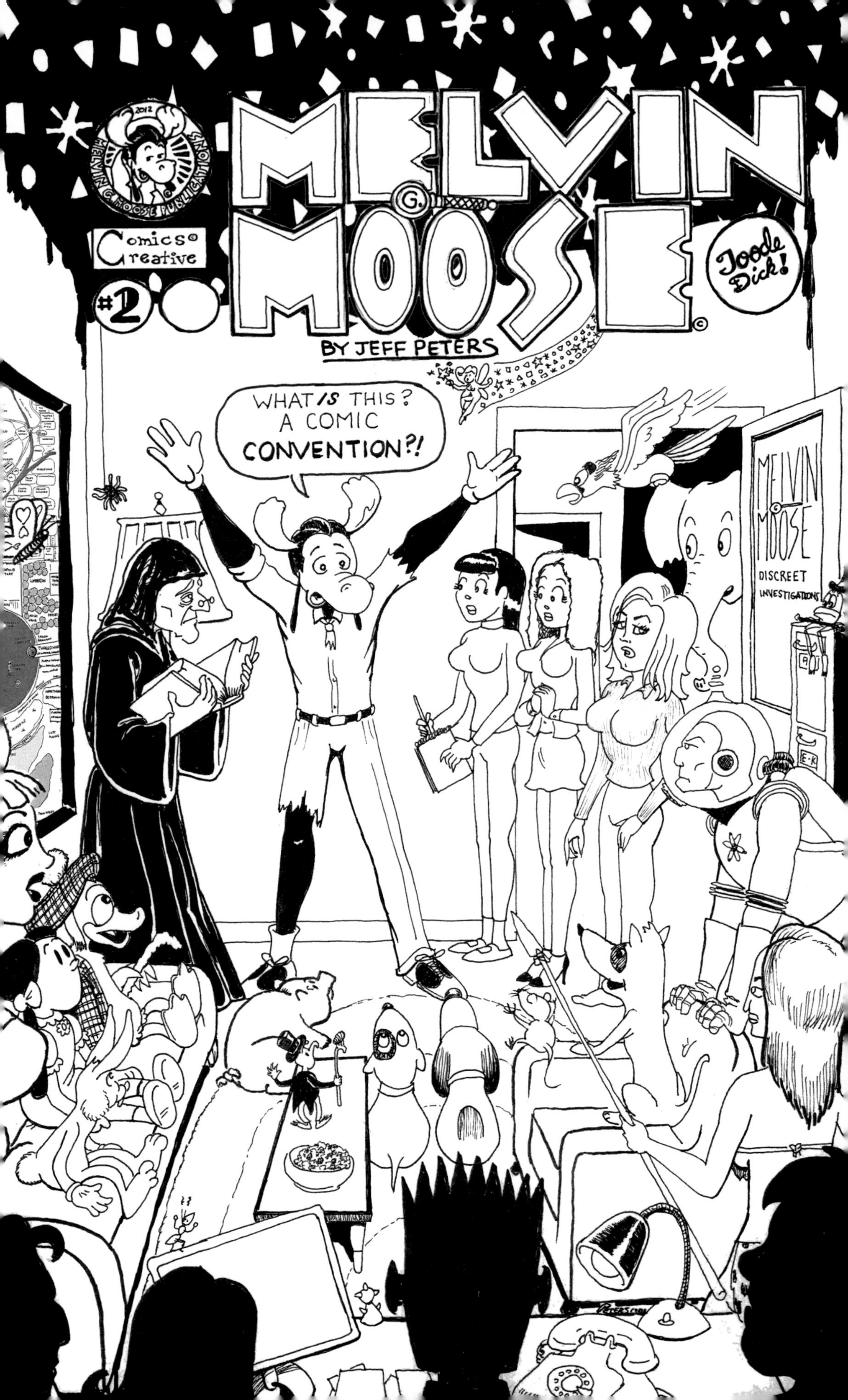
MELVIN G. MOOSE PUBLICATIONS 2012
Comics Creative
#2
MELVIN G. MOOSE
Toodle Dick!
BY JEFF PETERS
WHAT IS THIS? A COMIC CONVENTION?!
MELVIN G. MOOSE DISCREET INVESTIGATIONS

TOODES.

MELVIN G. MOOSE
TOODE DICK!
CHAPTER (2) TWO
FIRST ISSUE © 2012
JEFFREY
EDWARD
PETERS
ALL RIGHTS
RESERVED.

"THE TREACHERY
OF IMAGES"

"THIS IS NOT
A PIPE."
— MAGRITTE

NO PORTION(S)
OF THE WORDS
AND IMAGES
CONTAINED
WITHIN
MAY BE REPRO-
DUCED IN ANY
MEDIUM
WITHOUT THE
EXPRESS
WRITTEN CONSENT
OF THE
AUTHOR
OR HIS ASSIGNEES.
— FILL YOUR PIPE
AND SUCK ON THAT.!

BUT, SERIOUSLY,
ASK ME FIRST.
Mrmoose234@aol.com

TO ED, JIM, &
NADE
FOR THE SCIENCE,
ENGINEERING,
NATURE & COMICS!

WHAT THE *&%#@.! IS A TOODE? HOW DO YOU PRONOUNCE IT? WHY SO SURREAL? WHY SHOULD I CARE? THESE ARE THE QUESTIONS YOUR ERSTWHILE CREATOR IS OFTEN ASKED. PLEASE ALLOW ME TO EXPLAIN. OPEN YOUR MIND.

A TOODE (TWO-DIMENSIONAL BEING) IS CREATED BY ONE OF US, THE THREEDS (THREE-DIMENSIONAL BEINGS). USUALLY PRONOUNCED "TWO-DEE" OR "TUDE" FOR SHORT, ALL TOODES LIVE IN TOODEOPOLIS. FROM THE PAINTED CAVES TO THE FOURTH ESTATES AND SNOB HILL, THROUGH THE DARK WOOD OF WORDS IN LITERATURE, THE SPECTRUM OF ALL MANKIND'S WORDS AND PICTURES GLOWS ACROSS THE CITY. ALL TWO-DIMENSIONAL CREATIONS, IDEAS, CONCEPTS AND CHARACTERS EXIST IN TOODEOPOLIS FOREVER AS A PART OF OUR SHARED COMMON CONSCIOUSNESS.

MOST TOODES OUTLIVE THEIR THREED CREATORS, BUT CONTINUE TO BE PART OF OUR CULTURE, REPRESENTING THEM FOR HUNDREDS OR EVEN THOUSANDS OF YEARS AFTER THEIR DEATHS. GAEA, ZEUS, ODIN, VENUS, MOSES, MOHAMMED, BUDDHA, KRISHNA, JESUS, ODYSSEUS, BEOWULF, DON QUIXOTE, HAMLET, JANE EYRE, SHERLOCK HOLMES, MONA LISA, PETER PAN, GANDALF, FELIX THE CAT, THE COWARDLY LION, MICKEY MOUSE, BATMAN, CAPTAIN AMERICA, SALLY FORTH, CALVIN & HOBBES, BUZZ AND WOODY, MAO AND MARX AND BILLIONS OF OTHERS TOO LONG TO LIST ALL CO-EXIST HAPPILY IN TOODEOPOLIS.

IMAGINE WITH ME, IF YOU WILL, ANOTHER PLANE OF CONSCIOUNESS DEEP WITHIN OURS, WHERE ANYTHING THAT ALL OF MANKIND HAS WRITTEN OR DRAWN IS ALIVE AND YOU WILL BEGIN TO ENVISION THE SCOPE AND RANGE OF TOODEOPOLIS.

IN THIS CHAPTER, WE BEGIN TO EXPLORE THE INFINITE WORLD OF TOODEOPOLIS, BEGINNING ON THE NEW STRIP, THE HEART OF POPULAR CULTURE. YOU'LL HOPEFULLY RECOGNIZE A NUMBER OF ARCHETYPES FROM COMIC STRIPS, COMIC BOOKS, AND ANIMATION. HOPEFULLY THESE DENIZENS WILL APPEAR FAMILIAR RATHER THAN ALIEN. BUT AS VISITORS FROM ANOTHER DIMENSION, I SUPPOSE WE'RE AS ALIEN TO THEM AS THEY ARE TO US. WAIT! I'M GETTING AHEAD OF MYSELF. I DON'T MEAN TO TRIGGER YOUR REPTILIAN FLIGHT RESPONSE (NOT UNTIL ISSUE 5, ANYWAY). I HOPE INSTEAD THAT YOU EMBRACE OUR CITIZENS WITH OPEN AND WELCOMING HEARTS, FOR THEY ARE NOT ALIEN, THEY'VE BEEN HERE WITH US ALL ALONG.

— JEFF PETERS 3/30/2012

RIGHT NOW, MUCH HAS GONE WRONG IN TOODEOPOLIS...

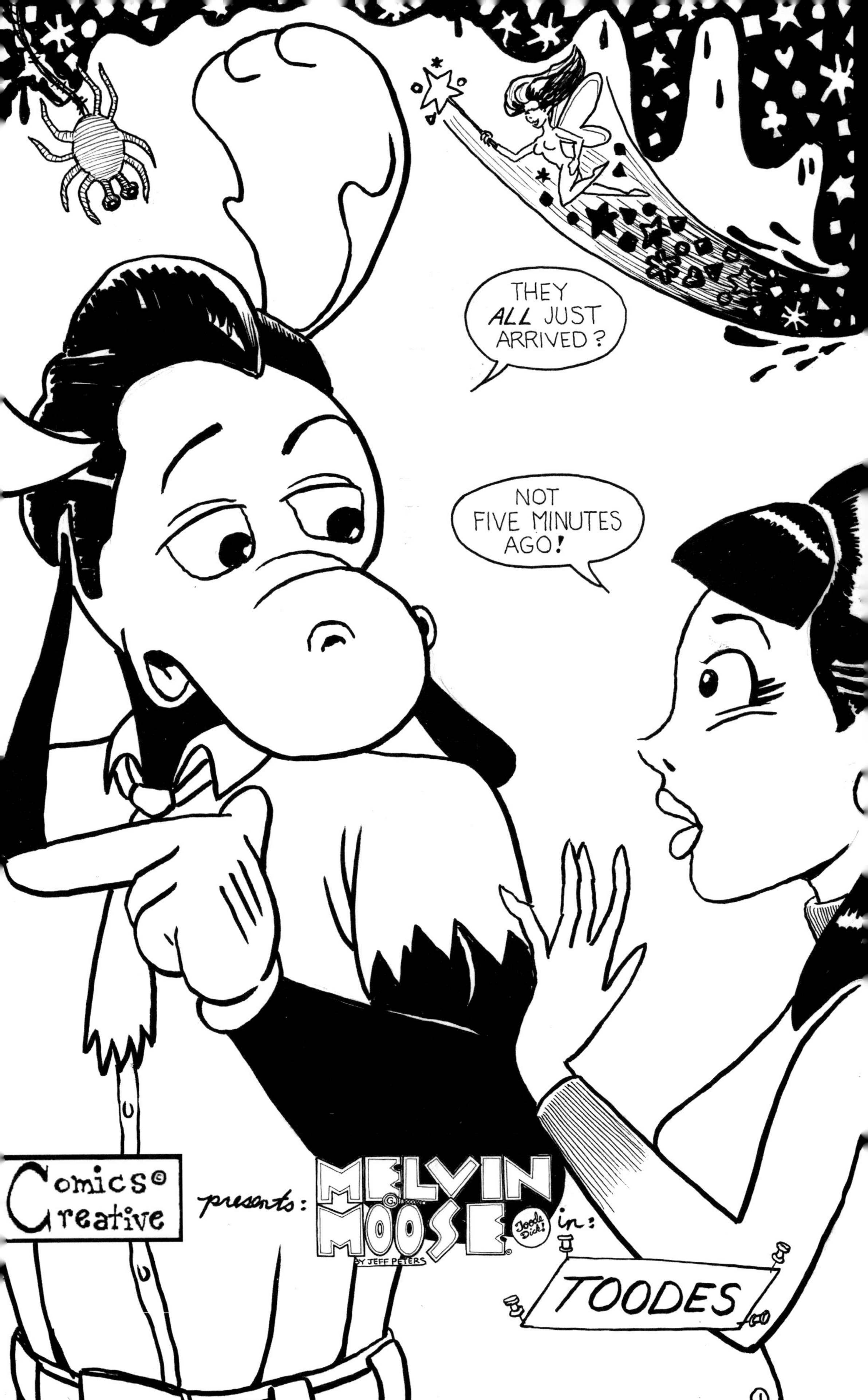
THEY ALL JUST ARRIVED?
NOT FIVE MINUTES AGO!
Comics© Creative
presents:
MELVIN MOOSE©
BY JEFF PETERS
in:
TOODES

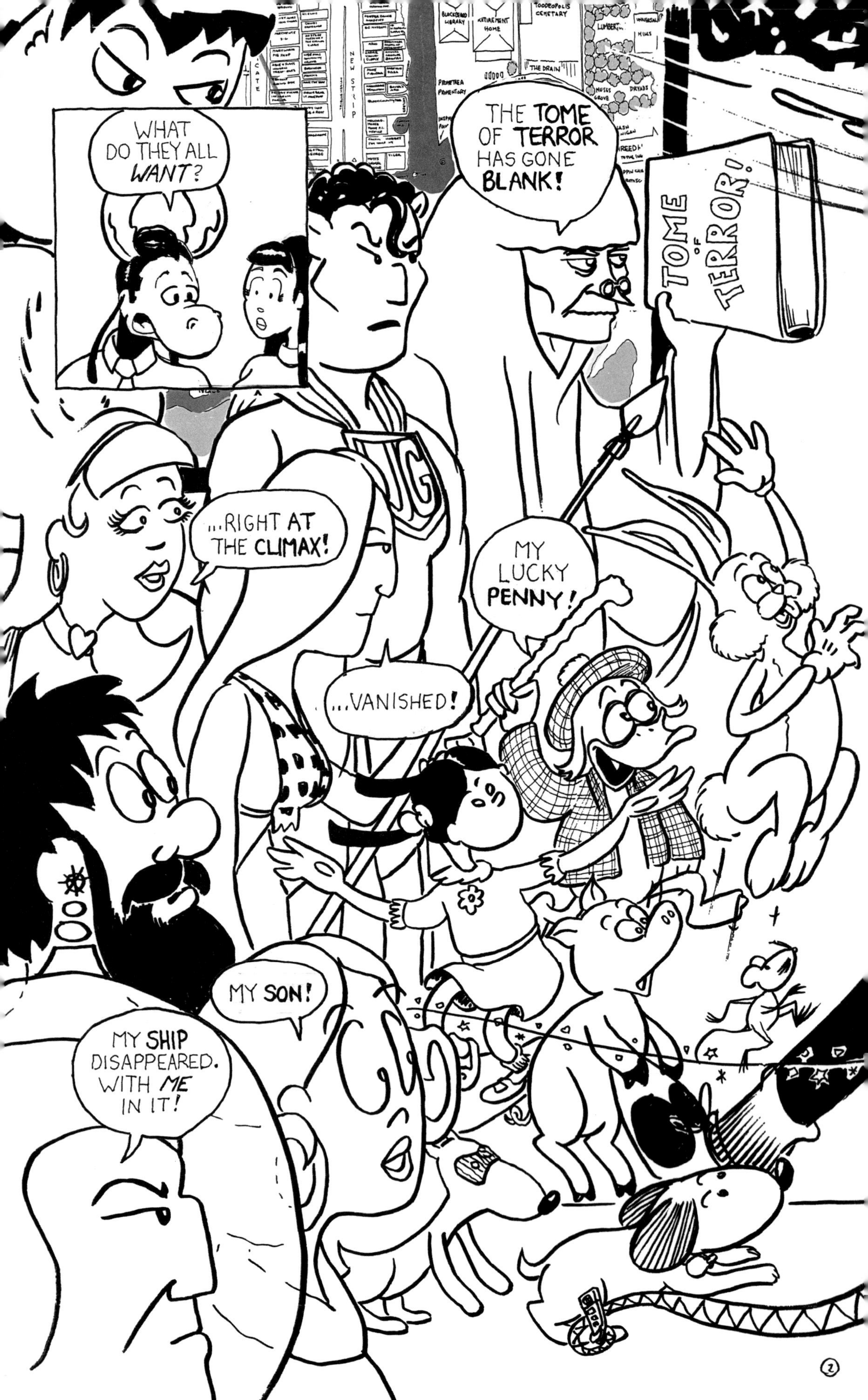
WHAT DO THEY ALL WANT?
THE TOME OF TERROR HAS GONE BLANK!
TOME OF TERROR!
...RIGHT AT THE CLIMAX!
MY LUCKY PENNY!
...VANISHED!
MY SON!
MY SHIP DISAPPEARED. WITH ME IN IT!

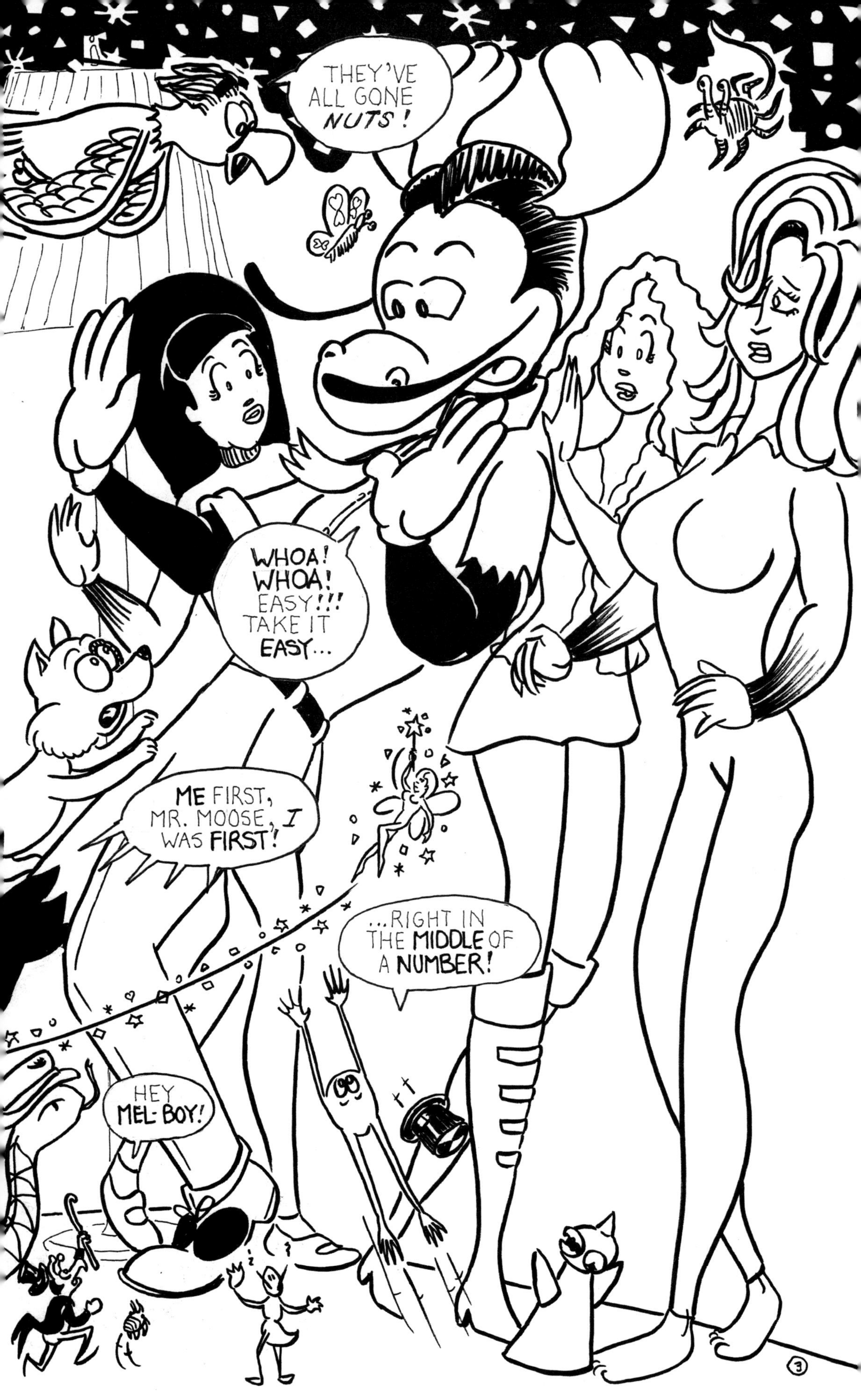
THEY'VE ALL GONE NUTS!
WHOA! WHOA! EASY!!! TAKE IT EASY...
ME FIRST, MR. MOOSE, I WAS FIRST!
...RIGHT IN THE MIDDLE OF A NUMBER!
HEY MEL-BOY!

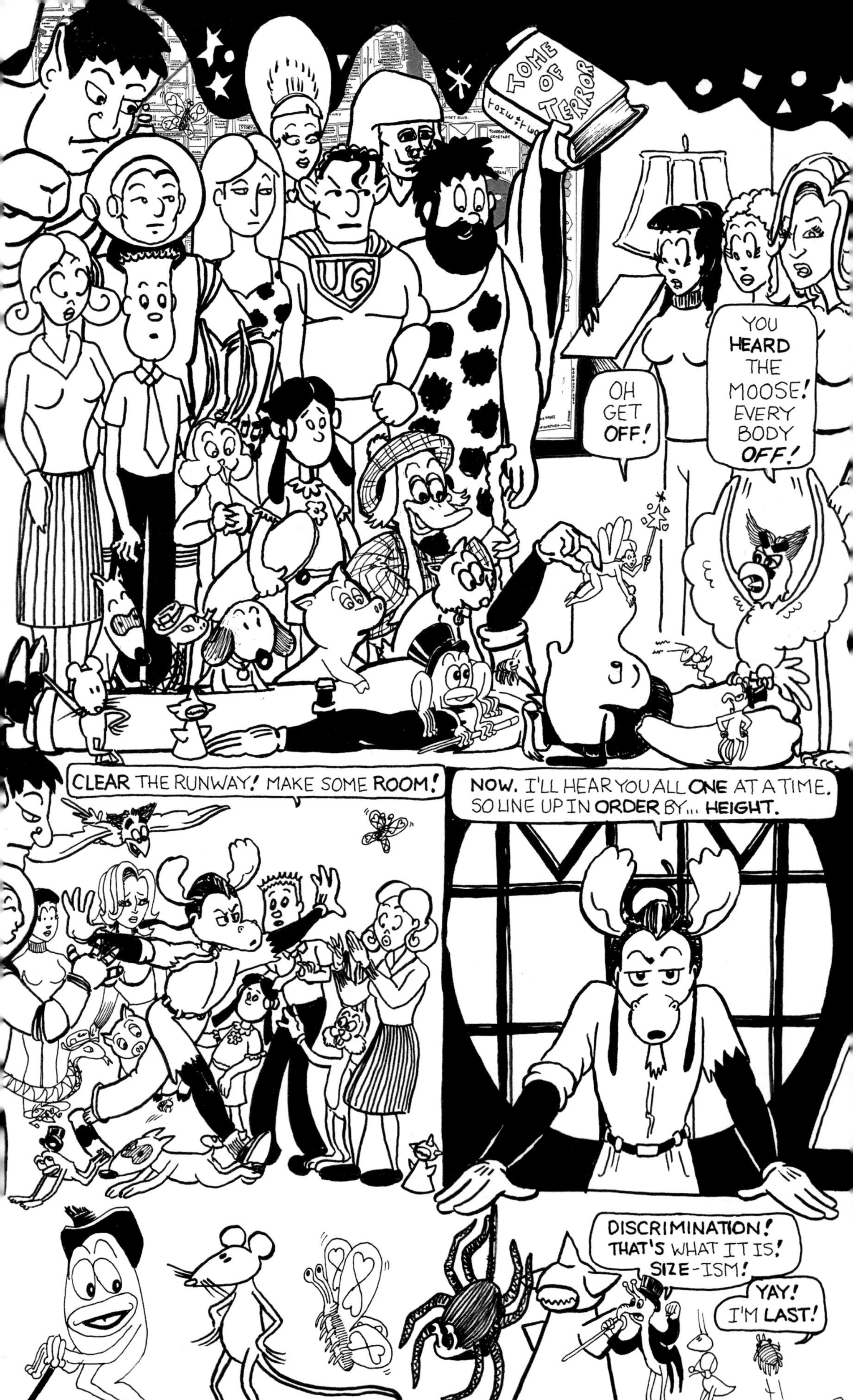
TOME OF TERROR
UG
OH GET OFF!
YOU HEARD THE MOOSE! EVERY BODY OFF!
CLEAR THE RUNWAY! MAKE SOME ROOM!
NOW. I'LL HEAR YOU ALL ONE AT A TIME. SO LINE UP IN ORDER BY... HEIGHT.
DISCRIMINATION! THAT'S WHAT IT IS! SIZE-ISM!
YAY! I'M LAST!

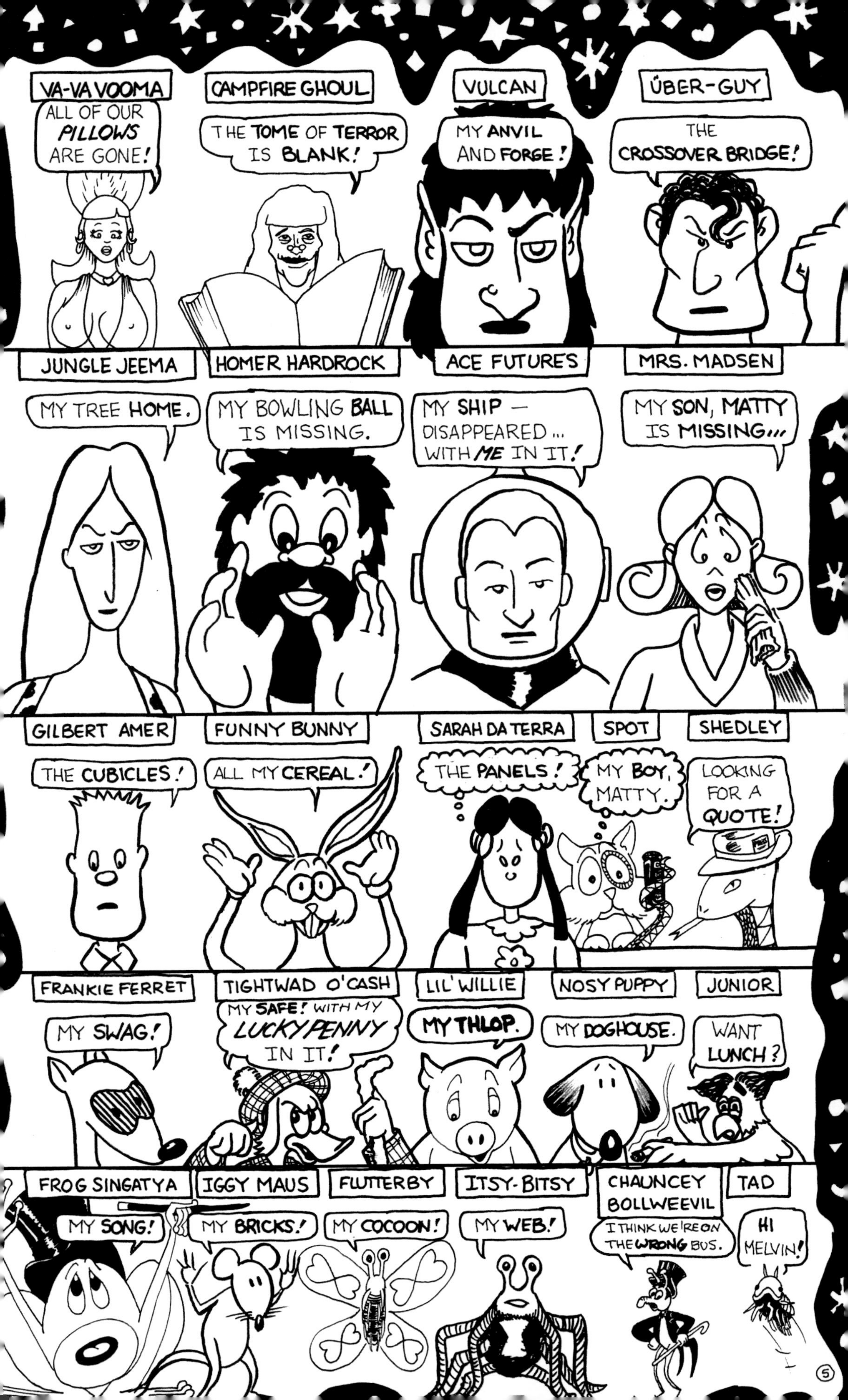

VA-VA VOOMA
ALL OF OUR PILLOWS ARE GONE!
CAMPFIRE GHOUL
THE TOME OF TERROR IS BLANK!
VULCAN
MY ANVIL AND FORGE!
ÜBER-GUY
THE CROSSOVER BRIDGE!
JUNGLE JEEMA
MY TREE HOME.
HOMER HARDROCK
MY BOWLING BALL IS MISSING.
ACE FUTURES
MY SHIP — DISAPPEARED... WITH ME IN IT!
MRS. MADSEN
MY SON, MATTY IS MISSING...
GILBERT AMER
THE CUBICLES!
FUNNY BUNNY
ALL MY CEREAL!
SARAH DA TERRA
THE PANELS!
SPOT
MY BOY, MATTY.
SHEDLEY
LOOKING FOR A QUOTE!
FRANKIE FERRET
MY SWAG!
TIGHTWAD O'CASH
MY SAFE! WITH MY LUCKY PENNY IN IT!
LIL' WILLIE
MY THLOP.
NOSY PUPPY
MY DOGHOUSE.
JUNIOR
WANT LUNCH?
FROG SINGATYA
MY SONG!
IGGY MAUS
MY BRICKS!
FLUTTERBY
MY COCOON!
ITSY-BITSY
MY WEB!
CHAUNCEY BOLLWEEVIL
I THINK WE'RE ON THE WRONG BUS.
TAD
HI MELVIN!

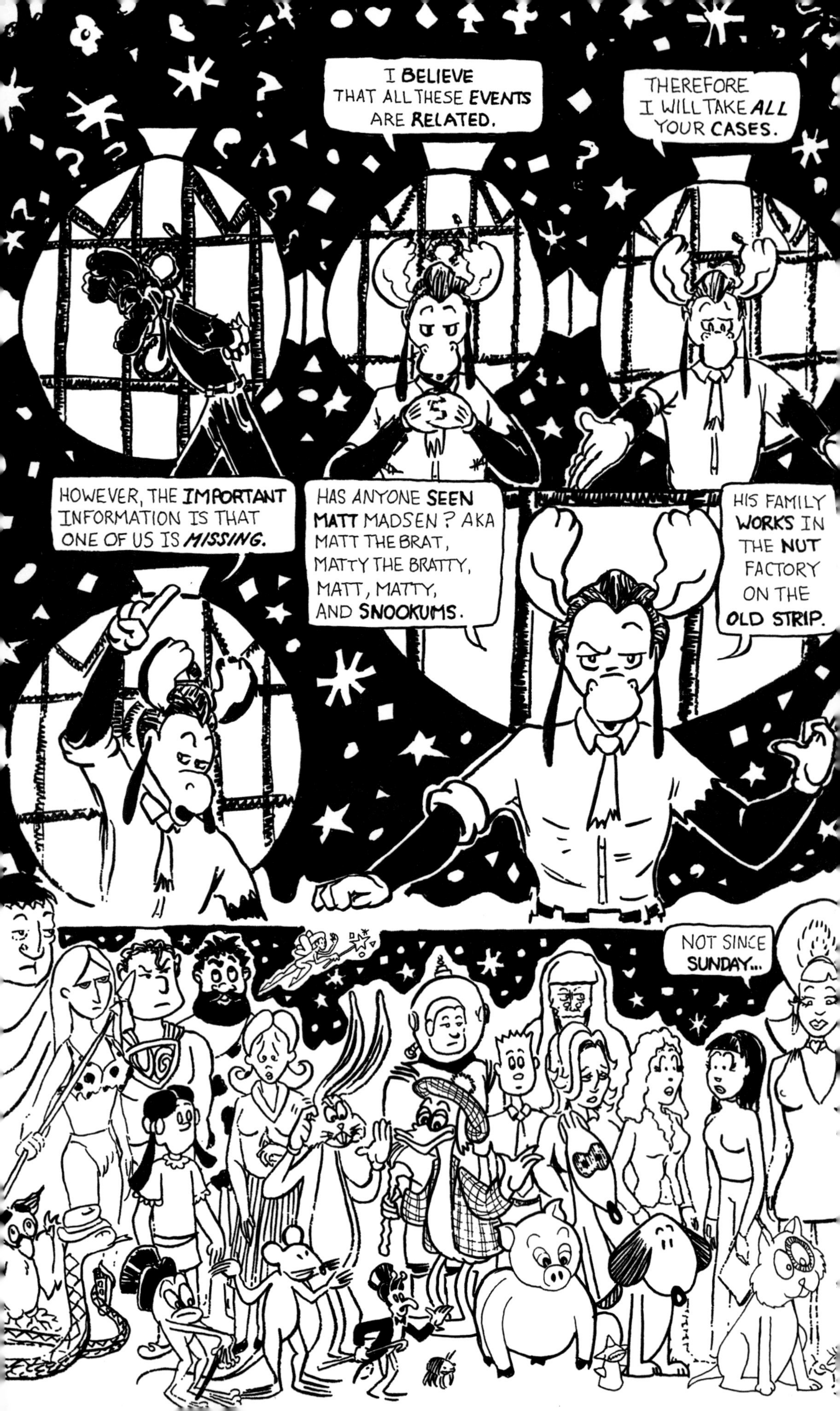
I BELIEVE THAT ALL THESE EVENTS ARE RELATED.
THEREFORE I WILL TAKE ALL YOUR CASES.
HOWEVER, THE IMPORTANT INFORMATION IS THAT ONE OF US IS MISSING.
HAS ANYONE SEEN MATT MADSEN? AKA MATT THE BRAT, MATTY THE BRATTY, MATT, MATTY, AND SNOOKUMS.
HIS FAMILY WORKS IN THE NUT FACTORY ON THE OLD STRIP.
NOT SINCE SUNDAY...

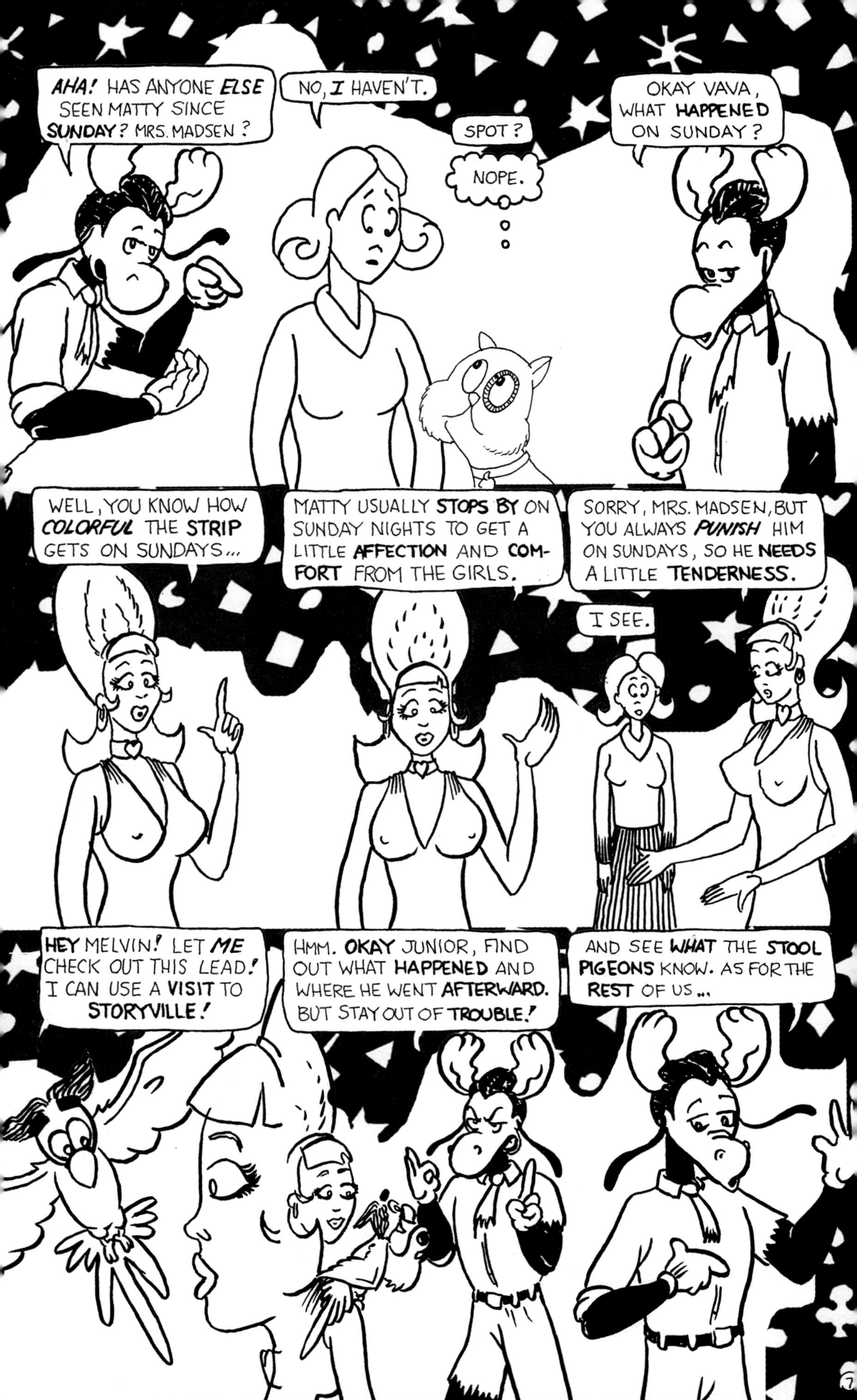
AHA! HAS ANYONE ELSE SEEN MATTY SINCE SUNDAY? MRS. MADSEN?
NO, I HAVEN'T.
SPOT?
NOPE.
OKAY VAVA, WHAT HAPPENED ON SUNDAY?
WELL, YOU KNOW HOW COLORFUL THE STRIP GETS ON SUNDAYS...
MATTY USUALLY STOPS BY ON SUNDAY NIGHTS TO GET A LITTLE AFFECTION AND COMFORT FROM THE GIRLS.
SORRY, MRS. MADSEN, BUT YOU ALWAYS PUNISH HIM ON SUNDAYS, SO HE NEEDS A LITTLE TENDERNESS.
I SEE.
HEY MELVIN! LET ME CHECK OUT THIS LEAD! I CAN USE A VISIT TO STORYVILLE!
HMM. OKAY JUNIOR, FIND OUT WHAT HAPPENED AND WHERE HE WENT AFTERWARD. BUT STAY OUT OF TROUBLE!
AND SEE WHAT THE STOOL PIGEONS KNOW. AS FOR THE REST OF US...

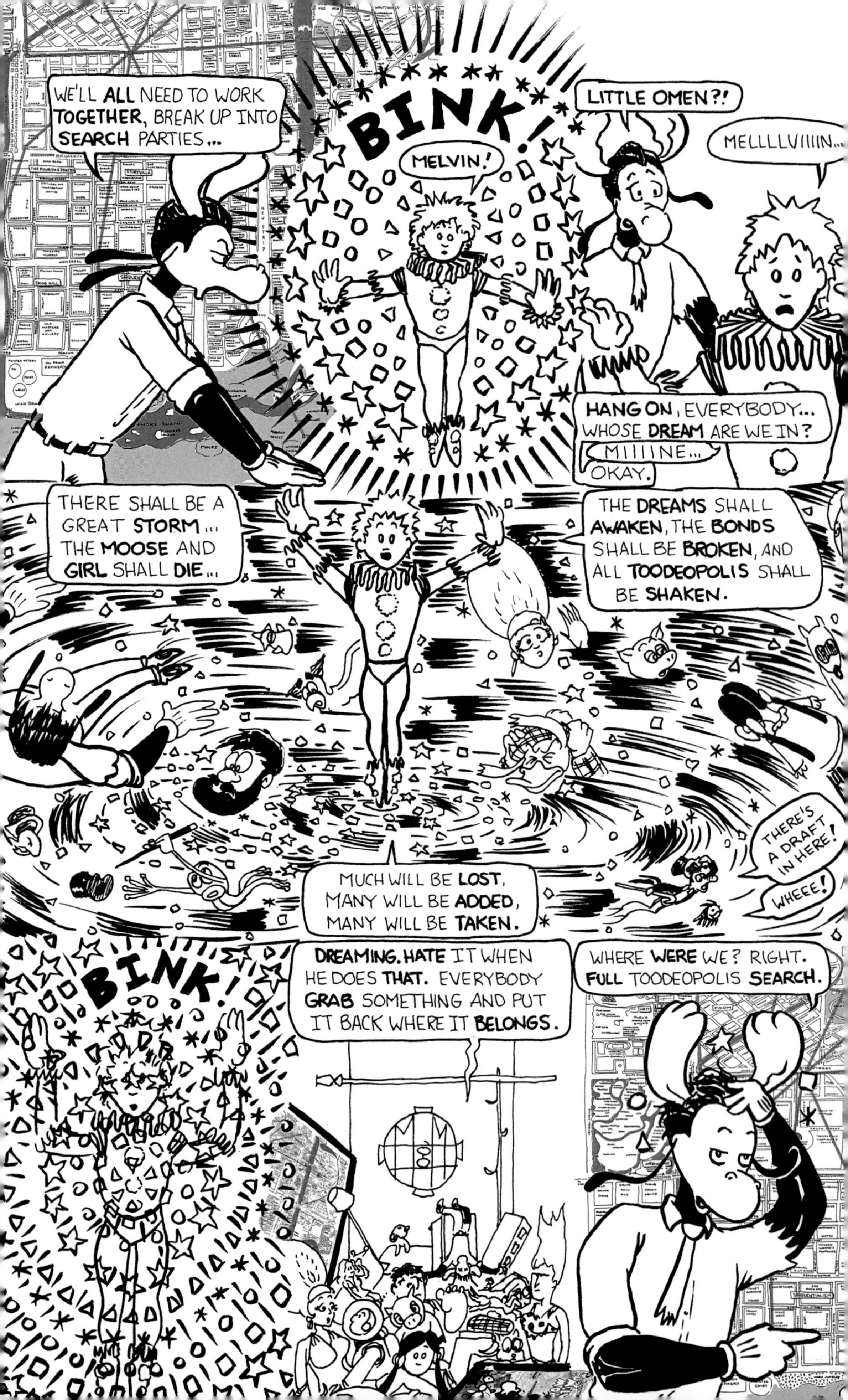
WE'LL ALL NEED TO WORK TOGETHER, BREAK UP INTO SEARCH PARTIES...
BINK!
MELVIN!
LITTLE OMEN?!
MELLLLVIIIIN...
HANG ON, EVERYBODY... WHOSE DREAM ARE WE IN?
MIIIINE...
OKAY.
THERE SHALL BE A GREAT STORM... THE MOOSE AND GIRL SHALL DIE...
THE DREAMS SHALL AWAKEN, THE BONDS SHALL BE BROKEN, AND ALL TOODEOPOLIS SHALL BE SHAKEN.
MUCH WILL BE LOST, MANY WILL BE ADDED, MANY WILL BE TAKEN.
THERE'S A DRAFT IN HERE!
WHEEE!
BINK!
DREAMING. HATE IT WHEN HE DOES THAT. EVERYBODY GRAB SOMETHING AND PUT IT BACK WHERE IT BELONGS.
WHERE WERE WE? RIGHT. FULL TOODEOPOLIS SEARCH.

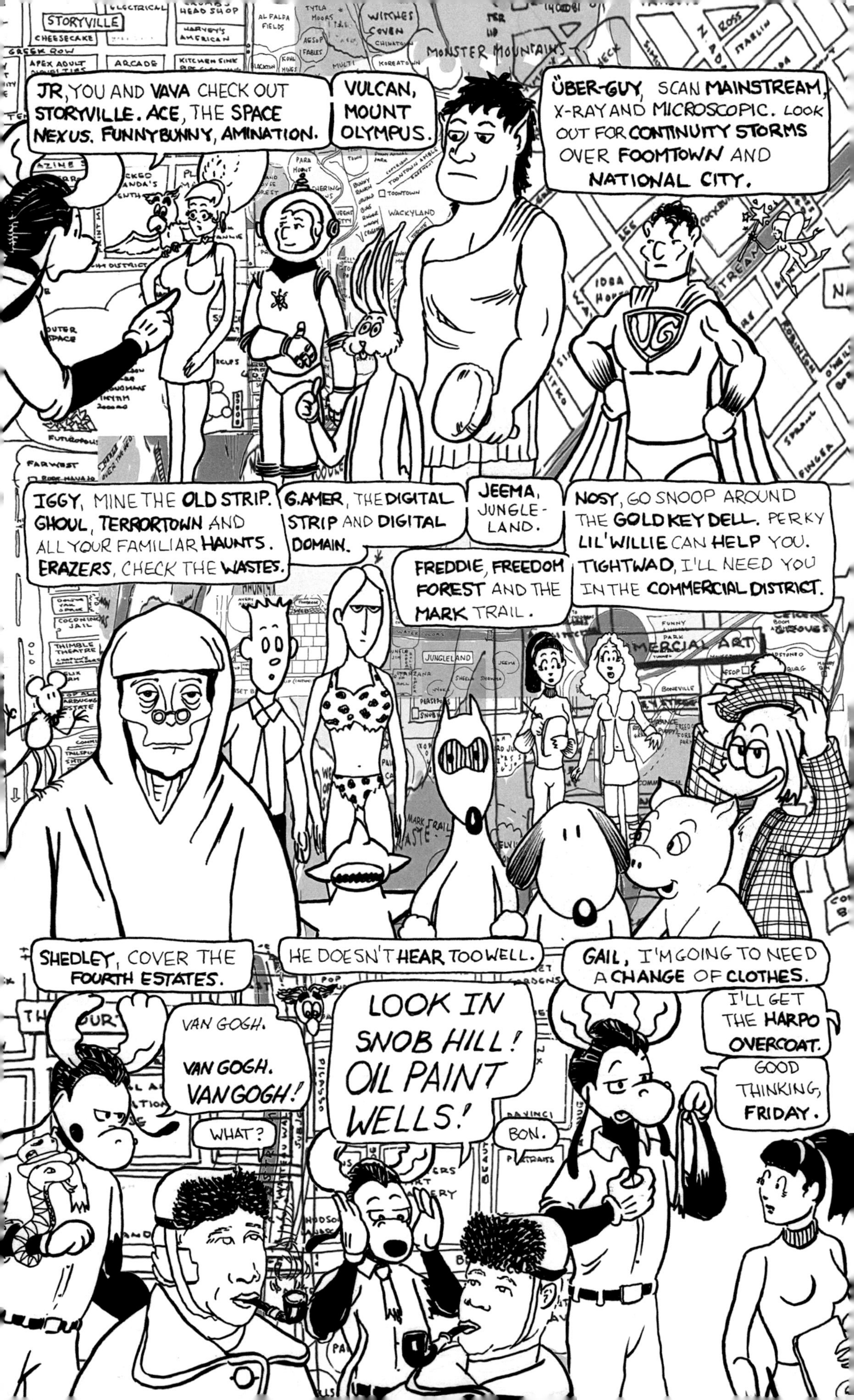
JR, YOU AND VAVA CHECK OUT STORYVILLE. ACE, THE SPACE NEXUS. FUNNYBUNNY, AMINATION.
VULCAN, MOUNT OLYMPUS.
ÜBER-GUY, SCAN MAINSTREAM, X-RAY AND MICROSCOPIC. LOOK OUT FOR CONTINUITY STORMS OVER FOOMTOWN AND NATIONAL CITY.
IGGY, MINE THE OLD STRIP. GHOUL, TERRORTOWN AND ALL YOUR FAMILIAR HAUNTS. ERAZERS, CHECK THE WASTES.
G.AMER, THE DIGITAL STRIP AND DIGITAL DOMAIN.
JEEMA, JUNGLE-LAND.
FREDDIE, FREEDOM FOREST AND THE MARK TRAIL.
NOSY, GO SNOOP AROUND THE GOLD KEY DELL. PERKY LIL'WILLIE CAN HELP YOU. TIGHTWAD, I'LL NEED YOU IN THE COMMERCIAL DISTRICT.
SHEDLEY, COVER THE FOURTH ESTATES.
HE DOESN'T HEAR TOO WELL.
GAIL, I'M GOING TO NEED A CHANGE OF CLOTHES.
VAN GOGH. VAN GOGH. VAN GOGH!
WHAT?
LOOK IN SNOB HILL! OIL PAINT WELLS!
BON.
I'LL GET THE HARPO OVERCOAT.
GOOD THINKING, FRIDAY.

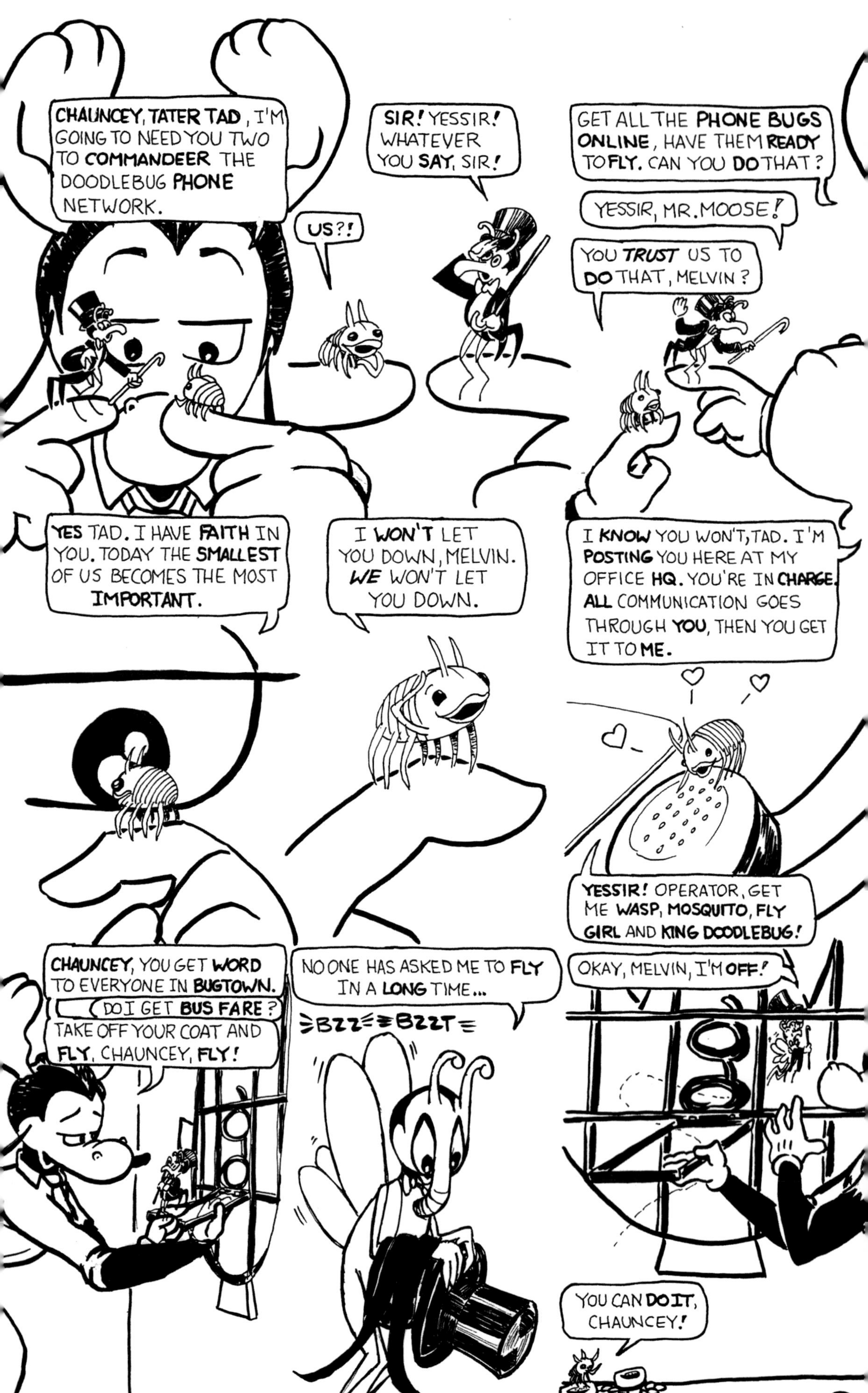
CHAUNCEY, TATER TAD, I'M GOING TO NEED YOU TWO TO COMMANDEER THE DOODLEBUG PHONE NETWORK.
US?!
SIR! YESSIR! WHATEVER YOU SAY, SIR!
GET ALL THE PHONE BUGS ONLINE, HAVE THEM READY TO FLY. CAN YOU DO THAT?
YESSIR, MR. MOOSE!
YOU TRUST US TO DO THAT, MELVIN?
YES TAD. I HAVE FAITH IN YOU. TODAY THE SMALLEST OF US BECOMES THE MOST IMPORTANT.
I WON'T LET YOU DOWN, MELVIN. WE WON'T LET YOU DOWN.
I KNOW YOU WON'T, TAD. I'M POSTING YOU HERE AT MY OFFICE HQ. YOU'RE IN CHARGE. ALL COMMUNICATION GOES THROUGH YOU, THEN YOU GET IT TO ME.
YESSIR! OPERATOR, GET ME WASP, MOSQUITO, FLY GIRL AND KING DOODLEBUG!
CHAUNCEY, YOU GET WORD TO EVERYONE IN BUGTOWN.
DO I GET BUS FARE?
TAKE OFF YOUR COAT AND FLY, CHAUNCEY, FLY!
NO ONE HAS ASKED ME TO FLY IN A LONG TIME...
BZZ BZZT
OKAY, MELVIN, I'M OFF!
YOU CAN DO IT, CHAUNCEY!

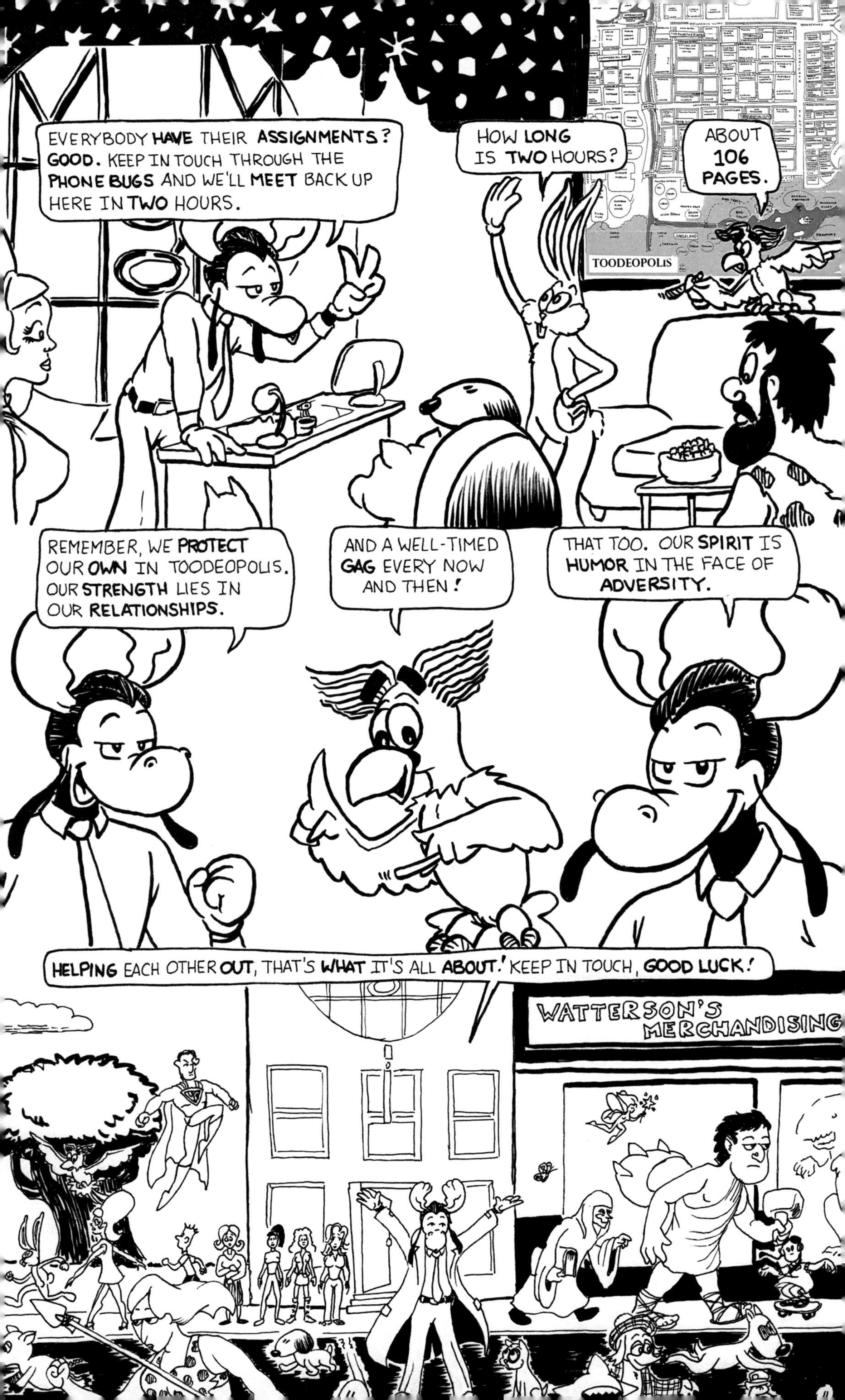
EVERYBODY HAVE THEIR ASSIGNMENTS? GOOD. KEEP IN TOUCH THROUGH THE PHONE BUGS AND WE'LL MEET BACK UP HERE IN TWO HOURS.
HOW LONG IS TWO HOURS?
ABOUT 106 PAGES.
TOODEOPOLIS
REMEMBER, WE PROTECT OUR OWN IN TOODEOPOLIS. OUR STRENGTH LIES IN OUR RELATIONSHIPS.
AND A WELL-TIMED GAG EVERY NOW AND THEN!
THAT TOO. OUR SPIRIT IS HUMOR IN THE FACE OF ADVERSITY.
HELPING EACH OTHER OUT, THAT'S WHAT IT'S ALL ABOUT! KEEP IN TOUCH, GOOD LUCK!
WATTERSON'S MERCHANDISING

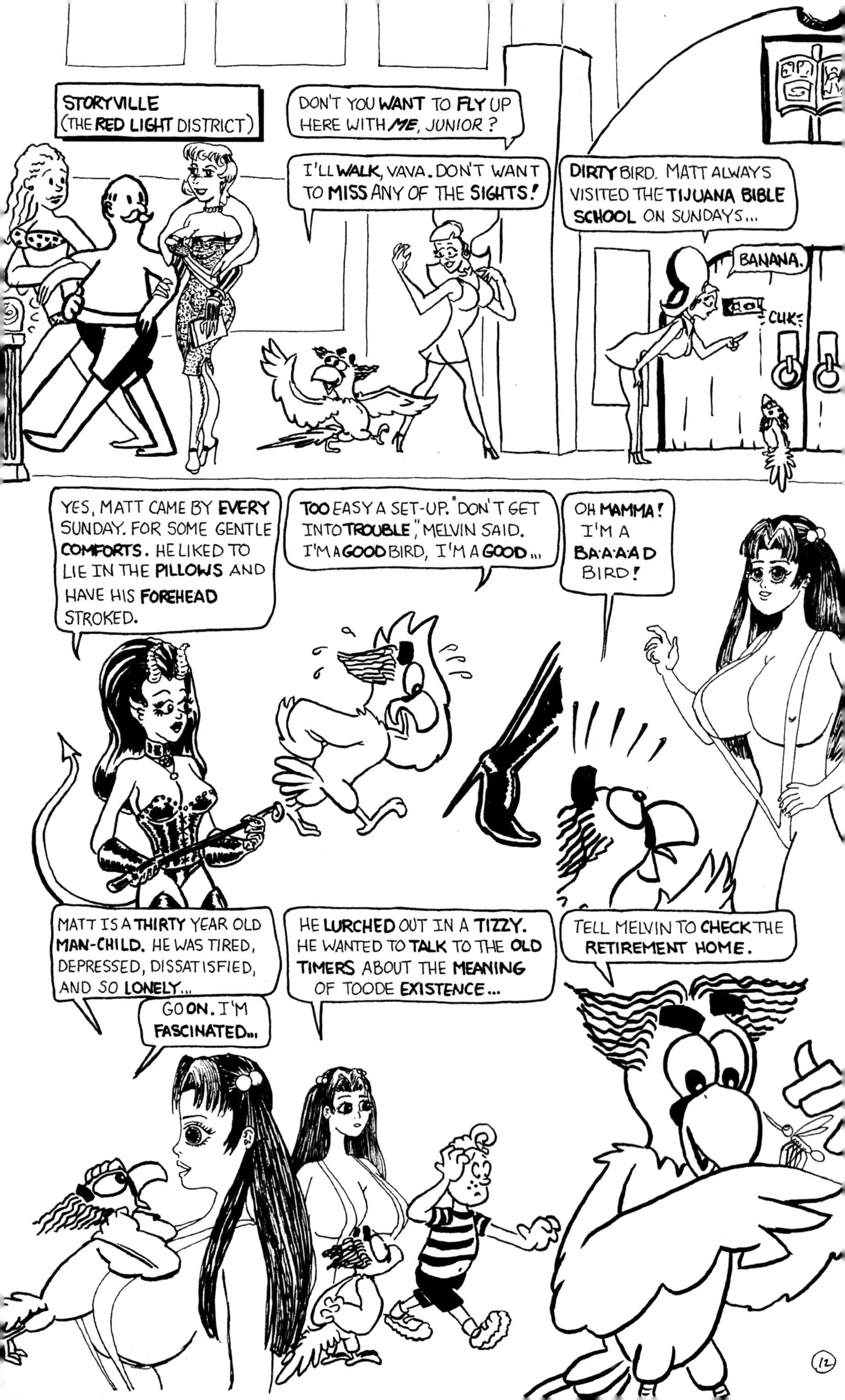
STORYVILLE (THE RED LIGHT DISTRICT)
DON'T YOU WANT TO FLY UP HERE WITH ME, JUNIOR?
I'LL WALK, VAVA. DON'T WANT TO MISS ANY OF THE SIGHTS!
DIRTY BIRD. MATT ALWAYS VISITED THE TIJUANA BIBLE SCHOOL ON SUNDAYS...
BANANA.
CUK
YES, MATT CAME BY EVERY SUNDAY. FOR SOME GENTLE COMFORTS. HE LIKED TO LIE IN THE PILLOWS AND HAVE HIS FOREHEAD STROKED.
TOO EASY A SET-UP. "DON'T GET INTO TROUBLE," MELVIN SAID. I'M A GOOD BIRD, I'M A GOOD...
OH MAMMA! I'M A BA-A-A-A-D BIRD!
MATT IS A THIRTY YEAR OLD MAN-CHILD. HE WAS TIRED, DEPRESSED, DISSATISFIED, AND SO LONELY...
GO ON. I'M FASCINATED...
HE LURCHED OUT IN A TIZZY. HE WANTED TO TALK TO THE OLD TIMERS ABOUT THE MEANING OF TOODE EXISTENCE...
TELL MELVIN TO CHECK THE RETIREMENT HOME.

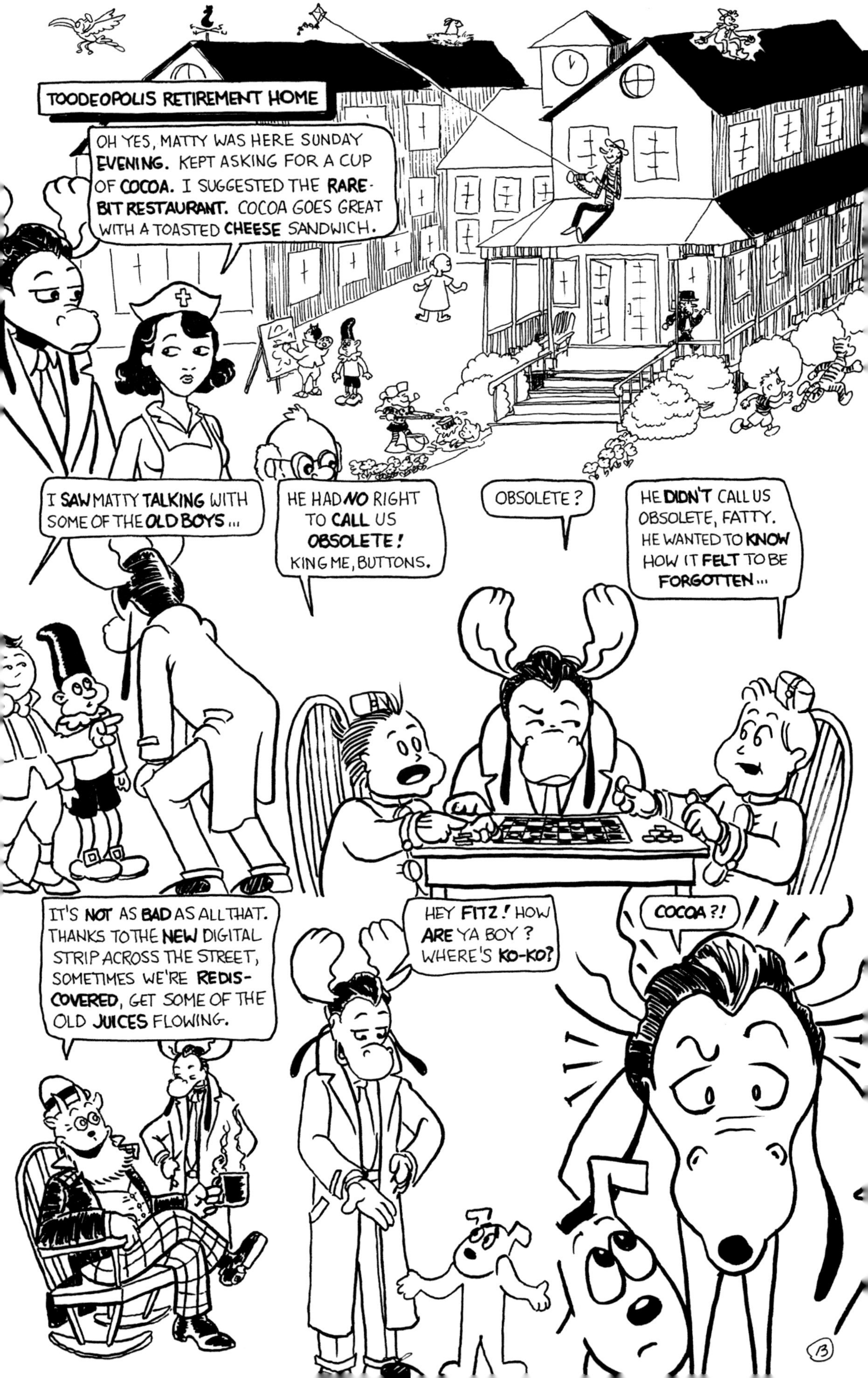
TOODEOPOLIS RETIREMENT HOME
OH YES, MATTY WAS HERE SUNDAY EVENING. KEPT ASKING FOR A CUP OF COCOA. I SUGGESTED THE RARE-BIT RESTAURANT. COCOA GOES GREAT WITH A TOASTED CHEESE SANDWICH.
I SAW MATTY TALKING WITH SOME OF THE OLD BOYS...
HE HAD NO RIGHT TO CALL US OBSOLETE! KING ME, BUTTONS.
OBSOLETE?
HE DIDN'T CALL US OBSOLETE, FATTY. HE WANTED TO KNOW HOW IT FELT TO BE FORGOTTEN...
IT'S NOT AS BAD AS ALL THAT. THANKS TO THE NEW DIGITAL STRIP ACROSS THE STREET, SOMETIMES WE'RE REDIS-COVERED, GET SOME OF THE OLD JUICES FLOWING.
HEY FITZ! HOW ARE YA BOY? WHERE'S KO-KO?
COCOA?!

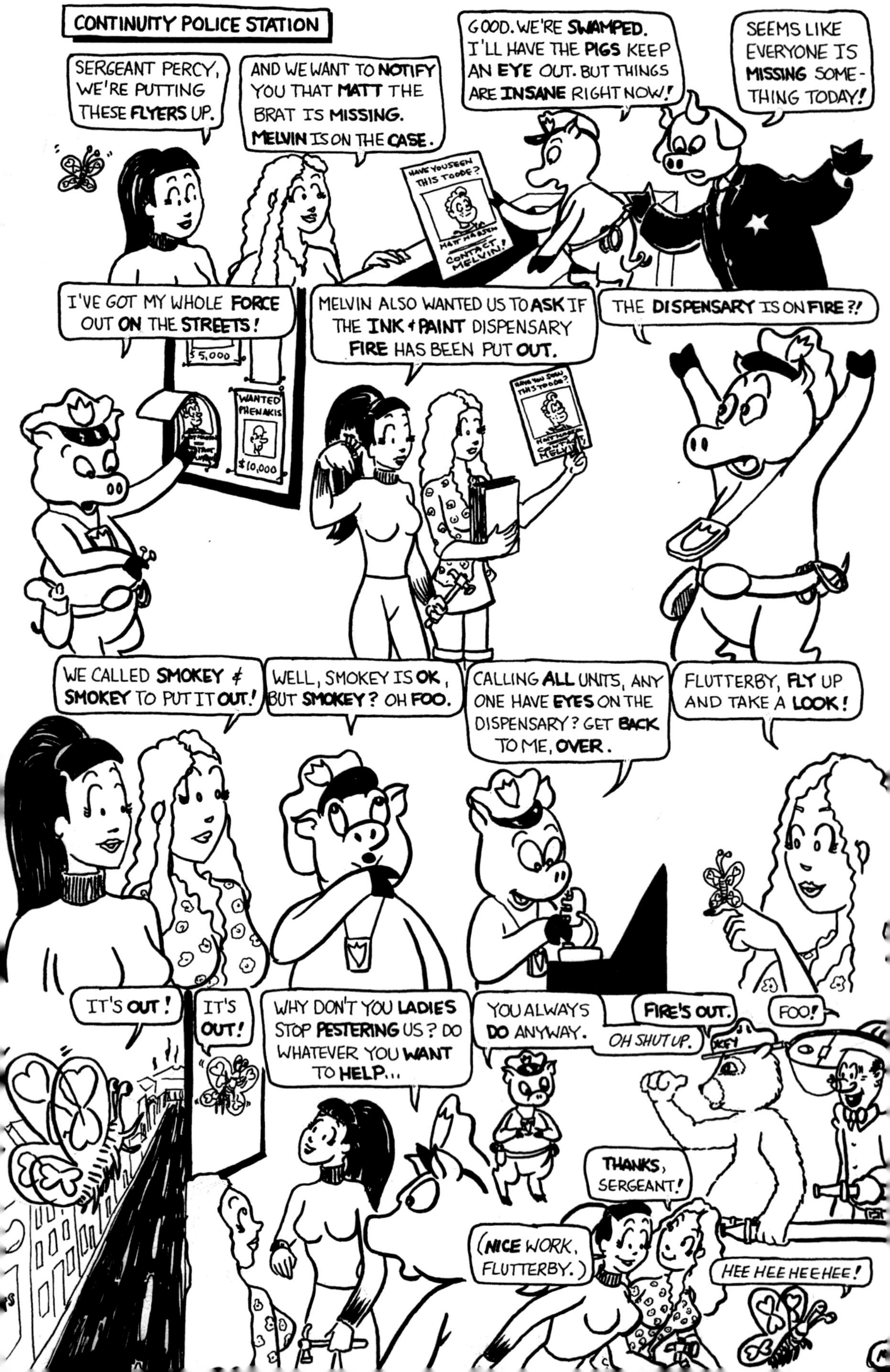
CONTINUITY POLICE STATION
SERGEANT PERCY, WE'RE PUTTING THESE FLYERS UP.
AND WE WANT TO NOTIFY YOU THAT MATT THE BRAT IS MISSING. MELVIN IS ON THE CASE.
GOOD. WE'RE SWAMPED. I'LL HAVE THE PIGS KEEP AN EYE OUT. BUT THINGS ARE INSANE RIGHT NOW!
SEEMS LIKE EVERYONE IS MISSING SOMETHING TODAY!
I'VE GOT MY WHOLE FORCE OUT ON THE STREETS!
$5,000
WANTED
$10,000
MELVIN ALSO WANTED US TO ASK IF THE INK & PAINT DISPENSARY FIRE HAS BEEN PUT OUT.
THE DISPENSARY IS ON FIRE?!
WE CALLED SMOKEY & SMOKEY TO PUT IT OUT!
WELL, SMOKEY IS OK, BUT SMOKEY? OH FOO.
CALLING ALL UNITS, ANY ONE HAVE EYES ON THE DISPENSARY? GET BACK TO ME, OVER.
FLUTTERBY, FLY UP AND TAKE A LOOK!
IT'S OUT!
IT'S OUT!
WHY DON'T YOU LADIES STOP PESTERING US? DO WHATEVER YOU WANT TO HELP...
YOU ALWAYS DO ANYWAY.
FIRE'S OUT.
OH SHUT UP.
FOO!
THANKS, SERGEANT!
(NICE WORK, FLUTTERBY.)
HEE HEE HEE HEE!

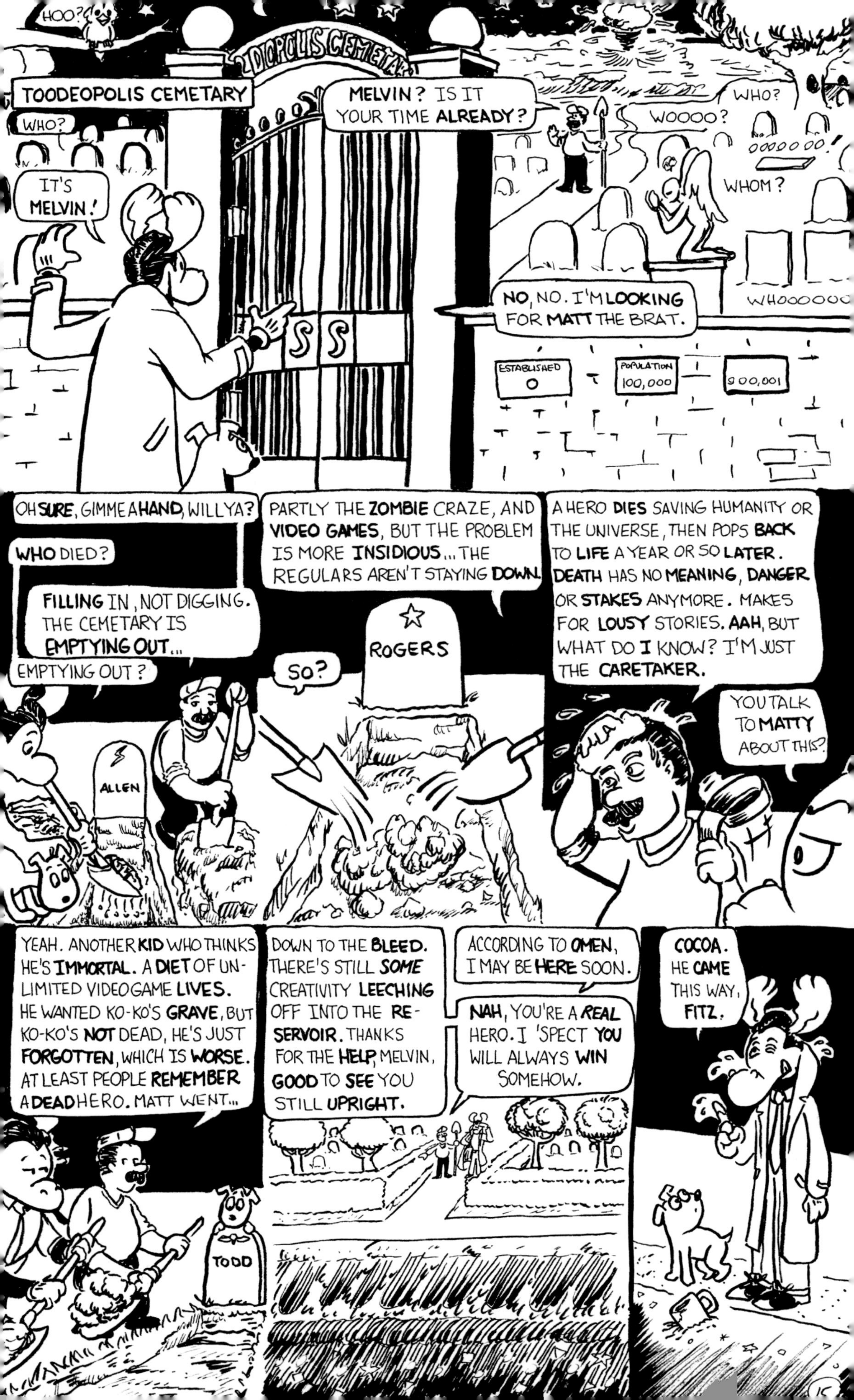
HOO?
TOODEOPOLIS CEMETARY
WHO?
IT'S MELVIN!
MELVIN? IS IT YOUR TIME ALREADY?
WHO?
WOOOO?
OOOOOOO!
WHOM?
NO, NO. I'M LOOKING FOR MATT THE BRAT.
WHOOOOOO
ESTABLISHED 0
POPULATION 100,000
900,001
OH SURE, GIMME A HAND, WILLYA?
WHO DIED?
FILLING IN, NOT DIGGING. THE CEMETARY IS EMPTYING OUT...
EMPTYING OUT?
ALLEN
PARTLY THE ZOMBIE CRAZE, AND VIDEO GAMES, BUT THE PROBLEM IS MORE INSIDIOUS... THE REGULARS AREN'T STAYING DOWN.
SO?
ROGERS
A HERO DIES SAVING HUMANITY OR THE UNIVERSE, THEN POPS BACK TO LIFE A YEAR OR SO LATER. DEATH HAS NO MEANING, DANGER OR STAKES ANYMORE. MAKES FOR LOUSY STORIES. AAH, BUT WHAT DO I KNOW? I'M JUST THE CARETAKER.
YOU TALK TO MATTY ABOUT THIS?
YEAH. ANOTHER KID WHO THINKS HE'S IMMORTAL. A DIET OF UNLIMITED VIDEOGAME LIVES. HE WANTED KO-KO'S GRAVE, BUT KO-KO'S NOT DEAD, HE'S JUST FORGOTTEN, WHICH IS WORSE. AT LEAST PEOPLE REMEMBER A DEAD HERO. MATT WENT...
TODD
DOWN TO THE BLEED. THERE'S STILL SOME CREATIVITY LEECHING OFF INTO THE RESERVOIR. THANKS FOR THE HELP, MELVIN, GOOD TO SEE YOU STILL UPRIGHT.
ACCORDING TO OMEN, I MAY BE HERE SOON.
NAH, YOU'RE A REAL HERO. I 'SPECT YOU WILL ALWAYS WIN SOMEHOW.
COCOA. HE CAME THIS WAY, FITZ.

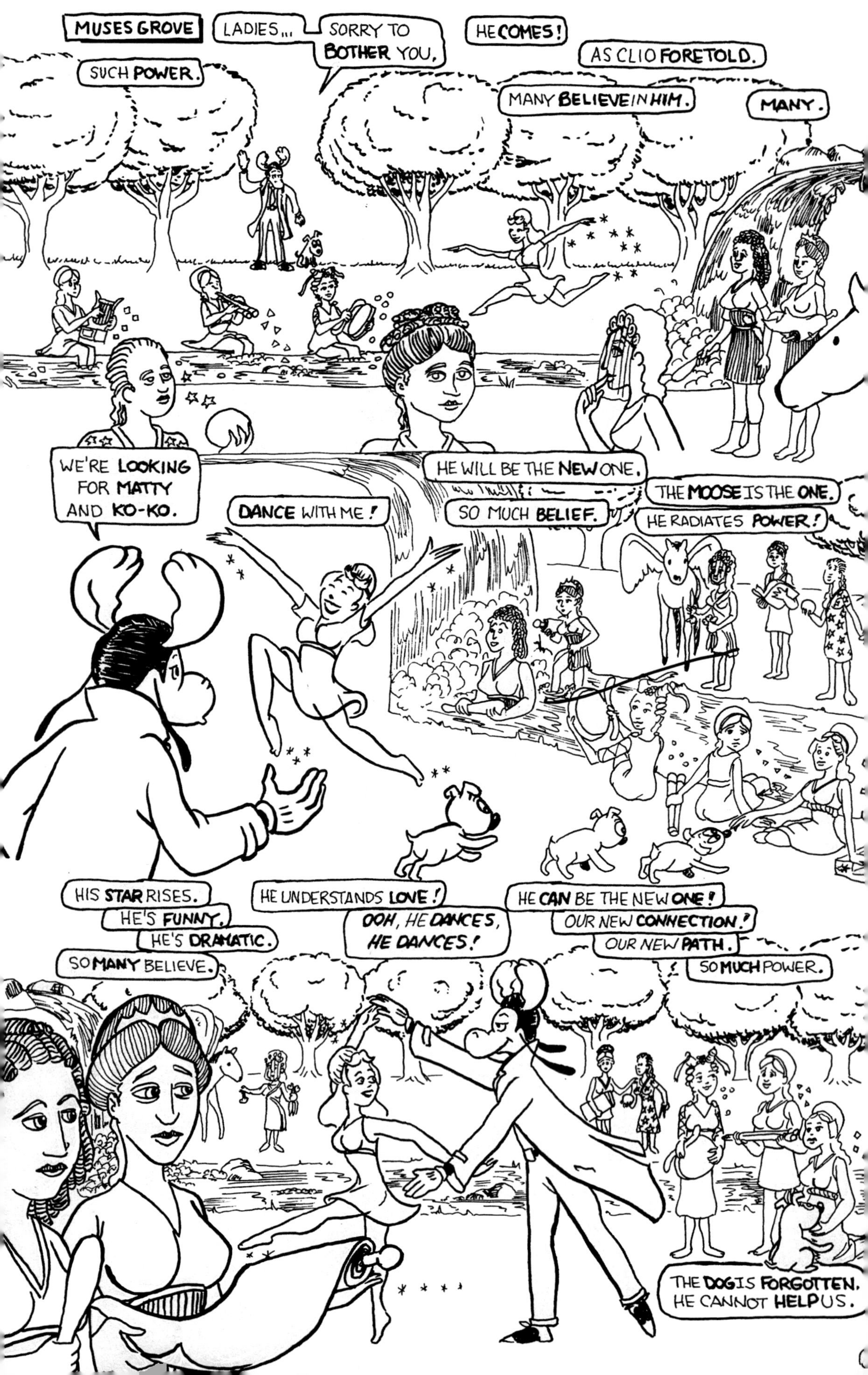

MUSES GROVE
LADIES...
SORRY TO BOTHER YOU,
HE COMES!
AS CLIO FORETOLD.
SUCH POWER.
MANY BELIEVE IN HIM.
MANY.
WE'RE LOOKING FOR MATTY AND KO-KO.
HE WILL BE THE NEW ONE.
THE MOOSE IS THE ONE.
DANCE WITH ME!
SO MUCH BELIEF.
HE RADIATES POWER!
HIS STAR RISES.
HE'S FUNNY.
HE'S DRAMATIC.
SO MANY BELIEVE.
HE UNDERSTANDS LOVE!
OOH, HE DANCES, HE DANCES!
HE CAN BE THE NEW ONE!
OUR NEW CONNECTION!
OUR NEW PATH.
SO MUCH POWER.
THE DOG IS FORGOTTEN. HE CANNOT HELP US.

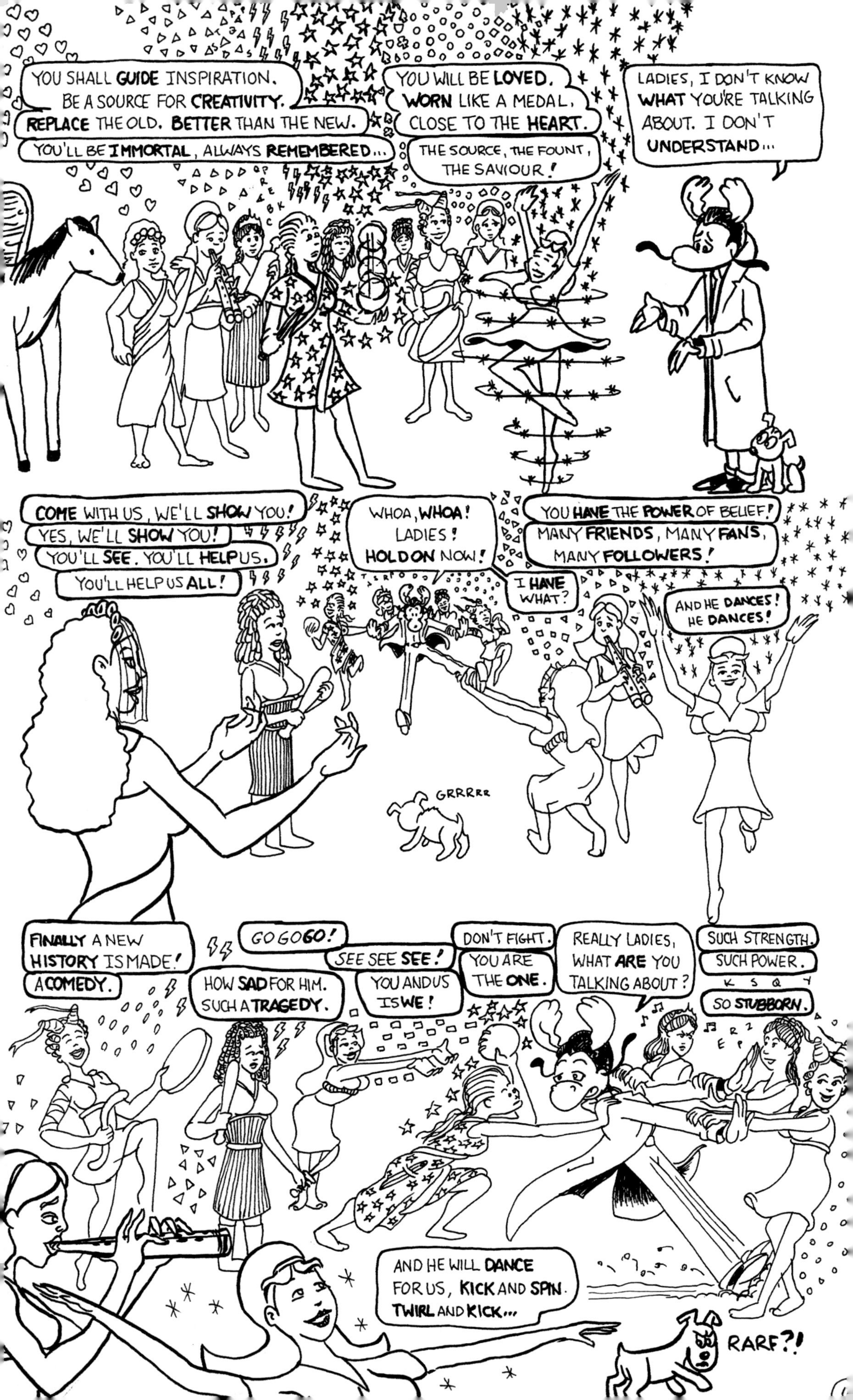
YOU SHALL GUIDE INSPIRATION. BE A SOURCE FOR CREATIVITY.
REPLACE THE OLD. BETTER THAN THE NEW.
YOU'LL BE IMMORTAL, ALWAYS REMEMBERED...
YOU WILL BE LOVED. WORN LIKE A MEDAL, CLOSE TO THE HEART.
THE SOURCE, THE FOUNT, THE SAVIOUR!
LADIES, I DON'T KNOW WHAT YOU'RE TALKING ABOUT. I DON'T UNDERSTAND...
COME WITH US, WE'LL SHOW YOU!
YES, WE'LL SHOW YOU!
YOU'LL SEE. YOU'LL HELP US.
YOU'LL HELP US ALL!
WHOA, WHOA! LADIES! HOLD ON NOW!
YOU HAVE THE POWER OF BELIEF!
MANY FRIENDS, MANY FANS, MANY FOLLOWERS!
I HAVE WHAT?
AND HE DANCES! HE DANCES!
GRRRRR
FINALLY A NEW HISTORY IS MADE!
A COMEDY.
GO GO GO!
HOW SAD FOR HIM. SUCH A TRAGEDY.
SEE SEE SEE!
YOU AND US IS WE!
DON'T FIGHT.
YOU ARE THE ONE.
REALLY LADIES, WHAT ARE YOU TALKING ABOUT?
SUCH STRENGTH.
SUCH POWER.
SO STUBBORN.
AND HE WILL DANCE FOR US, KICK AND SPIN. TWIRL AND KICK...
RARF?!

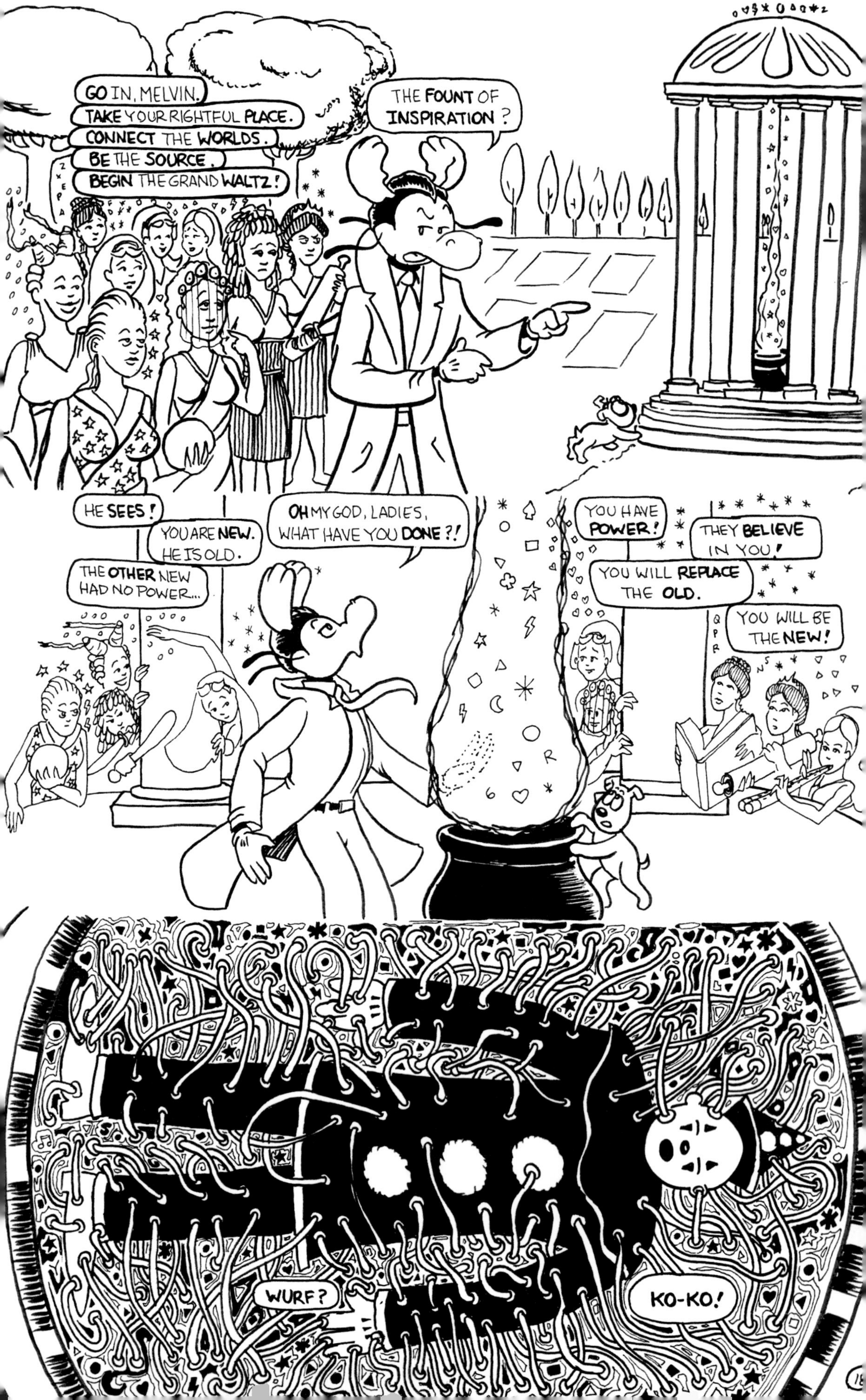
GO IN, MELVIN.
TAKE YOUR RIGHTFUL PLACE.
CONNECT THE WORLDS.
BE THE SOURCE.
BEGIN THE GRAND WALTZ!
THE FOUNT OF INSPIRATION?
HE SEES!
YOU ARE NEW. HE IS OLD.
THE OTHER NEW HAD NO POWER...
OH MY GOD, LADIES, WHAT HAVE YOU DONE?!
YOU HAVE POWER!
THEY BELIEVE IN YOU!
YOU WILL REPLACE THE OLD.
YOU WILL BE THE NEW!
WURF?
KO-KO!

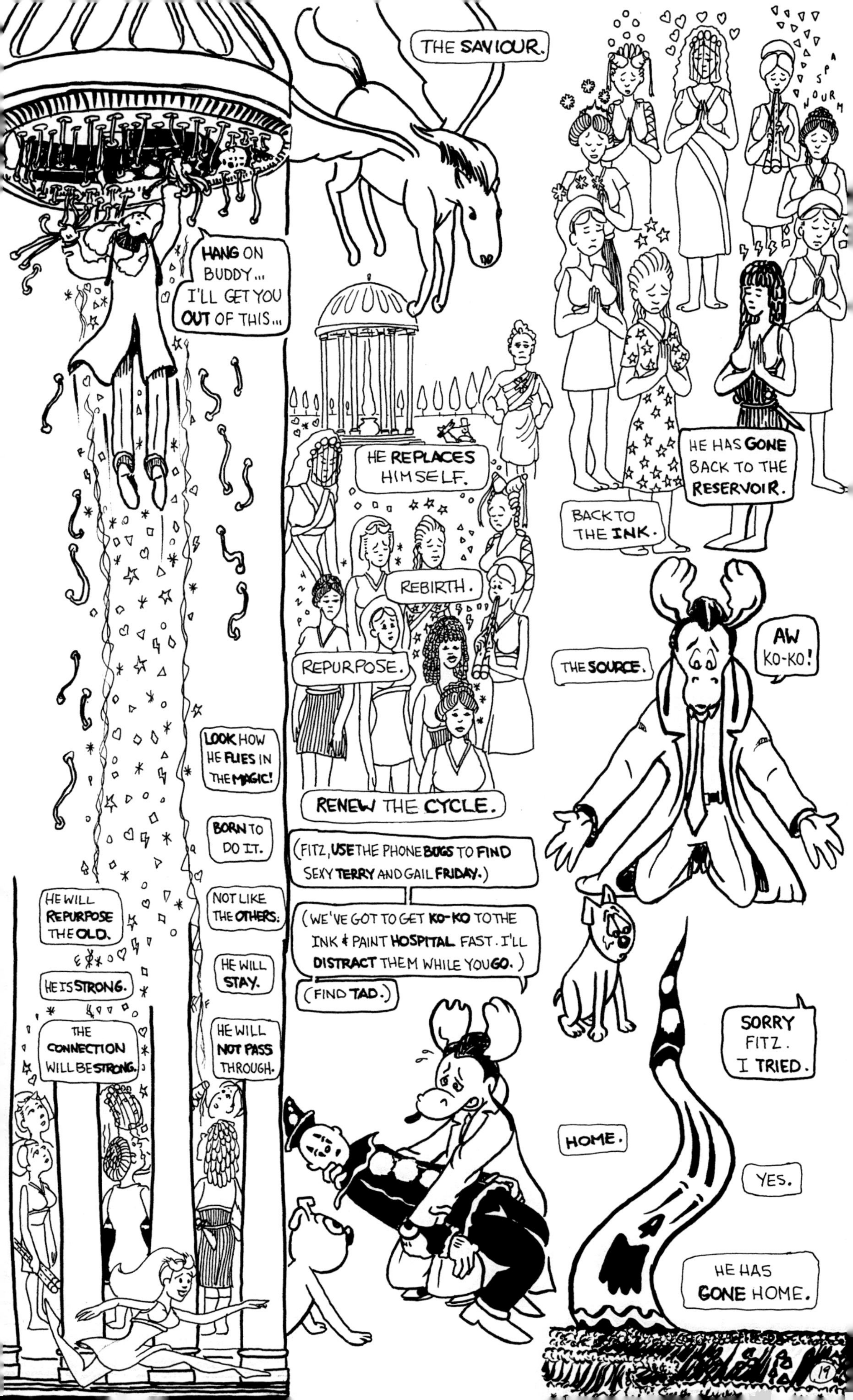
HANG ON BUDDY... I'LL GET YOU OUT OF THIS...
LOOK HOW HE FLIES IN THE MAGIC!
BORN TO DO IT.
NOT LIKE THE OTHERS.
HE WILL STAY.
HE WILL NOT PASS THROUGH.
HE WILL REPURPOSE THE OLD.
HE IS STRONG.
THE CONNECTION WILL BE STRONG.
THE SAVIOUR.
HE REPLACES HIMSELF.
REBIRTH.
REPURPOSE.
RENEW THE CYCLE.
(FITZ, USE THE PHONE BUGS TO FIND SEXY TERRY AND GAIL FRIDAY.)
(WE'VE GOT TO GET KO-KO TO THE INK & PAINT HOSPITAL FAST. I'LL DISTRACT THEM WHILE YOU GO.)
(FIND TAD.)
HE HAS GONE BACK TO THE RESERVOIR.
BACK TO THE INK.
THE SOURCE.
AW KO-KO!
SORRY FITZ. I TRIED.
HOME.
YES.
HE HAS GONE HOME.

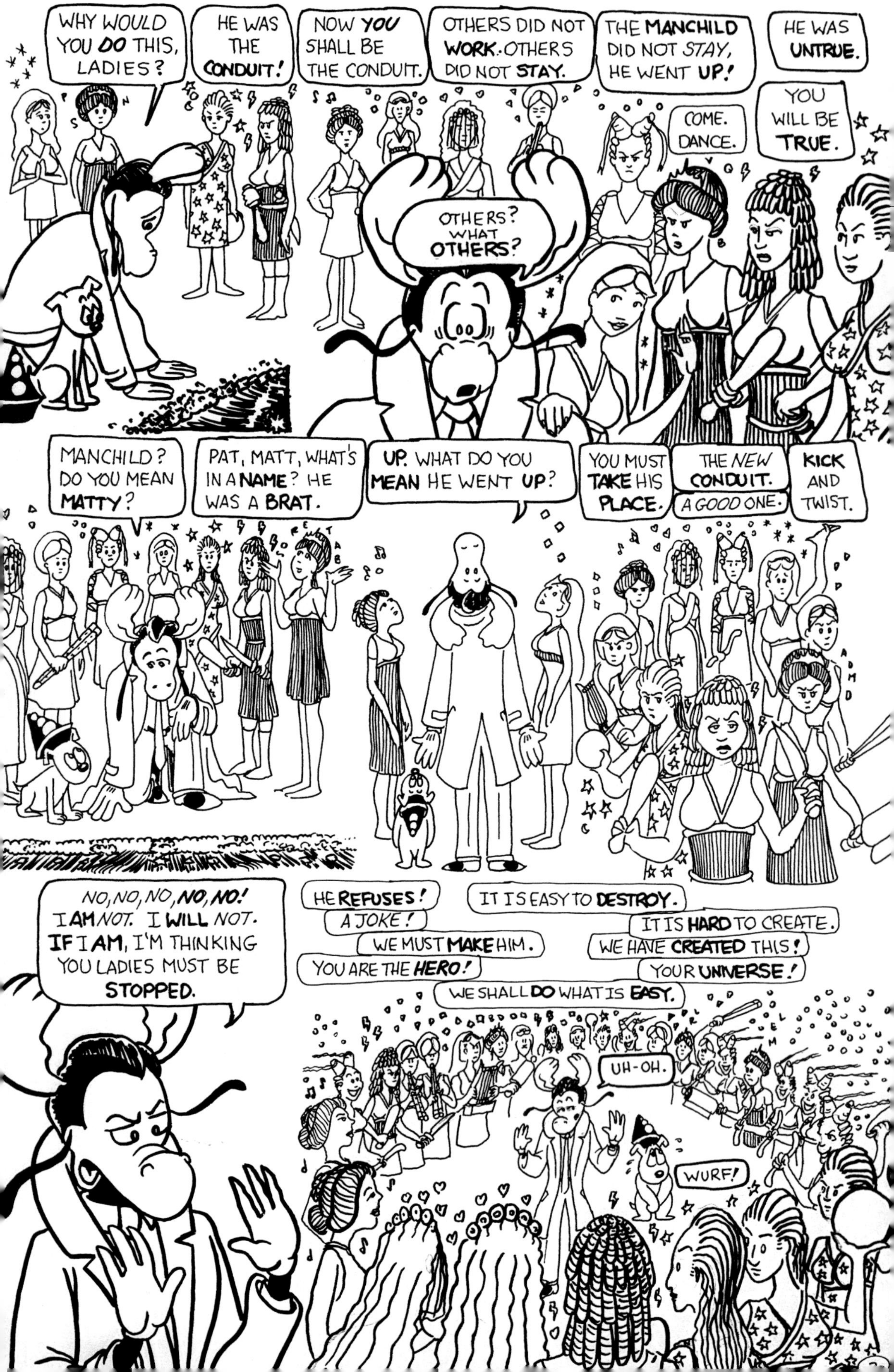
WHY WOULD YOU DO THIS, LADIES?
HE WAS THE CONDUIT!
NOW YOU SHALL BE THE CONDUIT.
OTHERS DID NOT WORK. OTHERS DID NOT STAY.
THE MANCHILD DID NOT STAY, HE WENT UP!
HE WAS UNTRUE.
COME. DANCE.
YOU WILL BE TRUE.
OTHERS? WHAT OTHERS?
MANCHILD? DO YOU MEAN MATTY?
PAT, MATT, WHAT'S IN A NAME? HE WAS A BRAT.
UP. WHAT DO YOU MEAN HE WENT UP?
YOU MUST TAKE HIS PLACE.
THE NEW CONDUIT.
A GOOD ONE.
KICK AND TWIST.
NO, NO, NO, NO, NO! I AM NOT. I WILL NOT. IF I AM, I'M THINKING YOU LADIES MUST BE STOPPED.
HE REFUSES!
A JOKE!
WE MUST MAKE HIM.
YOU ARE THE HERO!
IT IS EASY TO DESTROY.
IT IS HARD TO CREATE.
WE HAVE CREATED THIS!
YOUR UNIVERSE!
WE SHALL DO WHAT IS EASY.
UH-OH.
WURF!

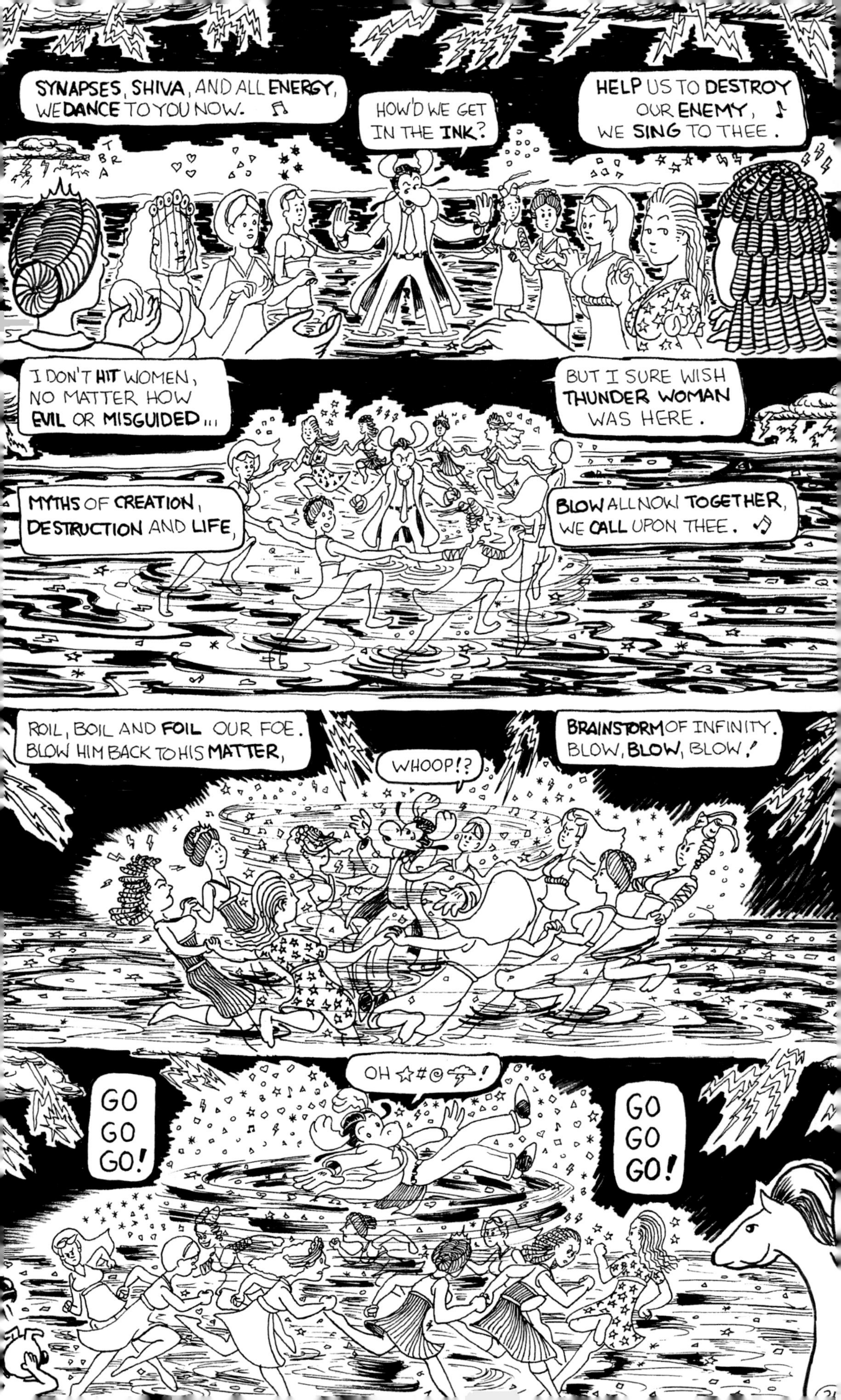
SYNAPSES, SHIVA, AND ALL ENERGY, WE DANCE TO YOU NOW.
HOW'D WE GET IN THE INK?
HELP US TO DESTROY OUR ENEMY, WE SING TO THEE.
I DON'T HIT WOMEN, NO MATTER HOW EVIL OR MISGUIDED...
BUT I SURE WISH THUNDER WOMAN WAS HERE.
MYTHS OF CREATION, DESTRUCTION AND LIFE,
BLOW ALL NOW TOGETHER, WE CALL UPON THEE.
ROIL, BOIL AND FOIL OUR FOE. BLOW HIM BACK TO HIS MATTER,
WHOOP!?
BRAINSTORM OF INFINITY. BLOW, BLOW, BLOW!
OH ☆#@!
GO GO GO!
GO GO GO!

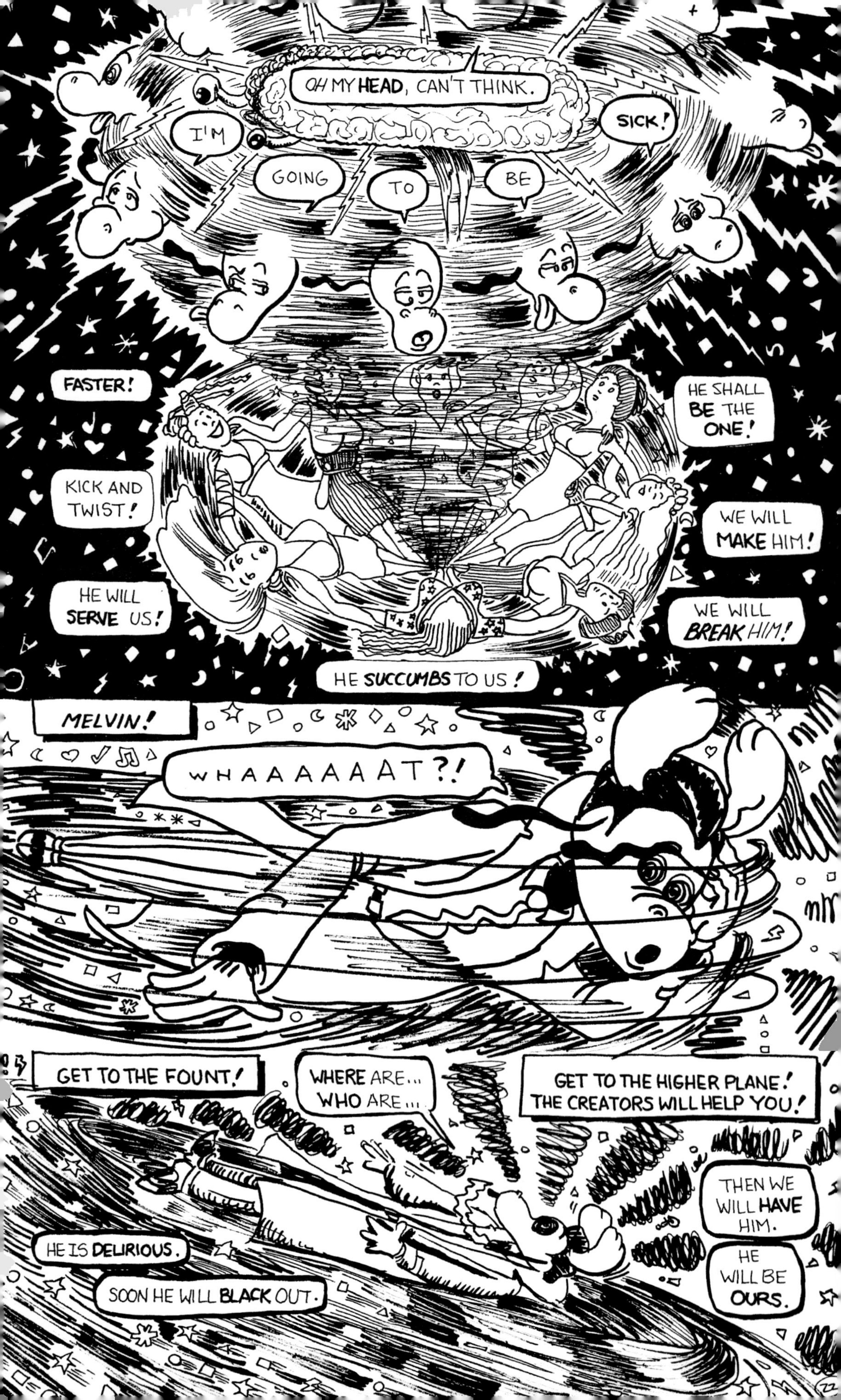

OH MY HEAD, CAN'T THINK.
I'M
GOING
TO
BE
SICK!
FASTER!
KICK AND TWIST!
HE WILL SERVE US!
HE SHALL BE THE ONE!
WE WILL MAKE HIM!
WE WILL BREAK HIM!
HE SUCCUMBS TO US!
MELVIN!
WHAAAAAAT?!
GET TO THE FOUNT!
WHERE ARE... WHO ARE...
GET TO THE HIGHER PLANE! THE CREATORS WILL HELP YOU!
THEN WE WILL HAVE HIM.
HE WILL BE OURS.
HE IS DELIRIOUS.
SOON HE WILL BLACK OUT.

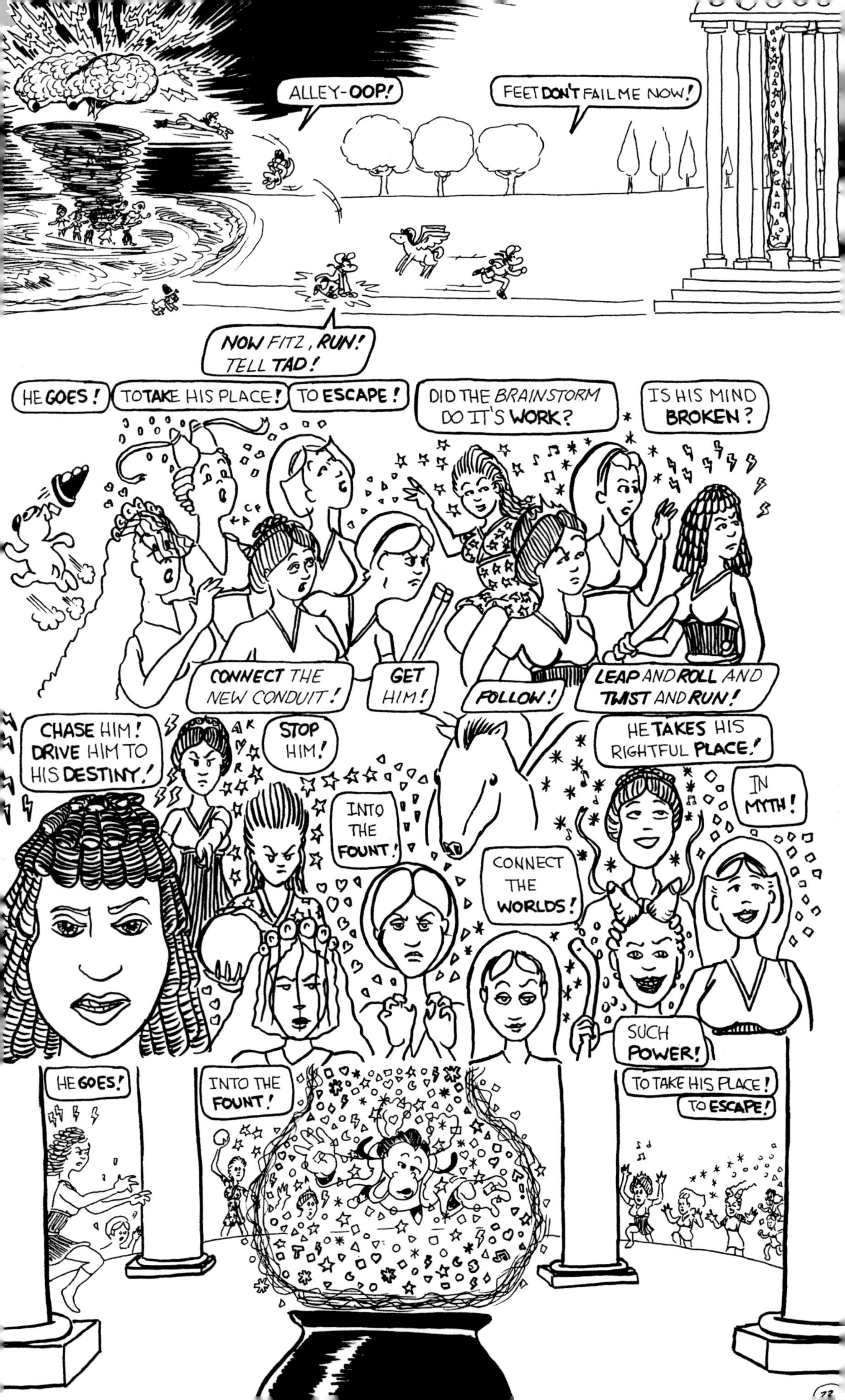

ALLEY-OOP!
FEET DON'T FAIL ME NOW!
NOW FITZ, RUN! TELL TAD!
HE GOES!
TO TAKE HIS PLACE!
TO ESCAPE!
DID THE BRAINSTORM DO IT'S WORK?
IS HIS MIND BROKEN?
CONNECT THE NEW CONDUIT!
GET HIM!
FOLLOW!
LEAP AND ROLL AND TWIST AND RUN!
CHASE HIM! DRIVE HIM TO HIS DESTINY!
STOP HIM!
HE TAKES HIS RIGHTFUL PLACE!
IN MYTH!
INTO THE FOUNT!
CONNECT THE WORLDS!
SUCH POWER!
HE GOES!
INTO THE FOUNT!
TO TAKE HIS PLACE!
TO ESCAPE!

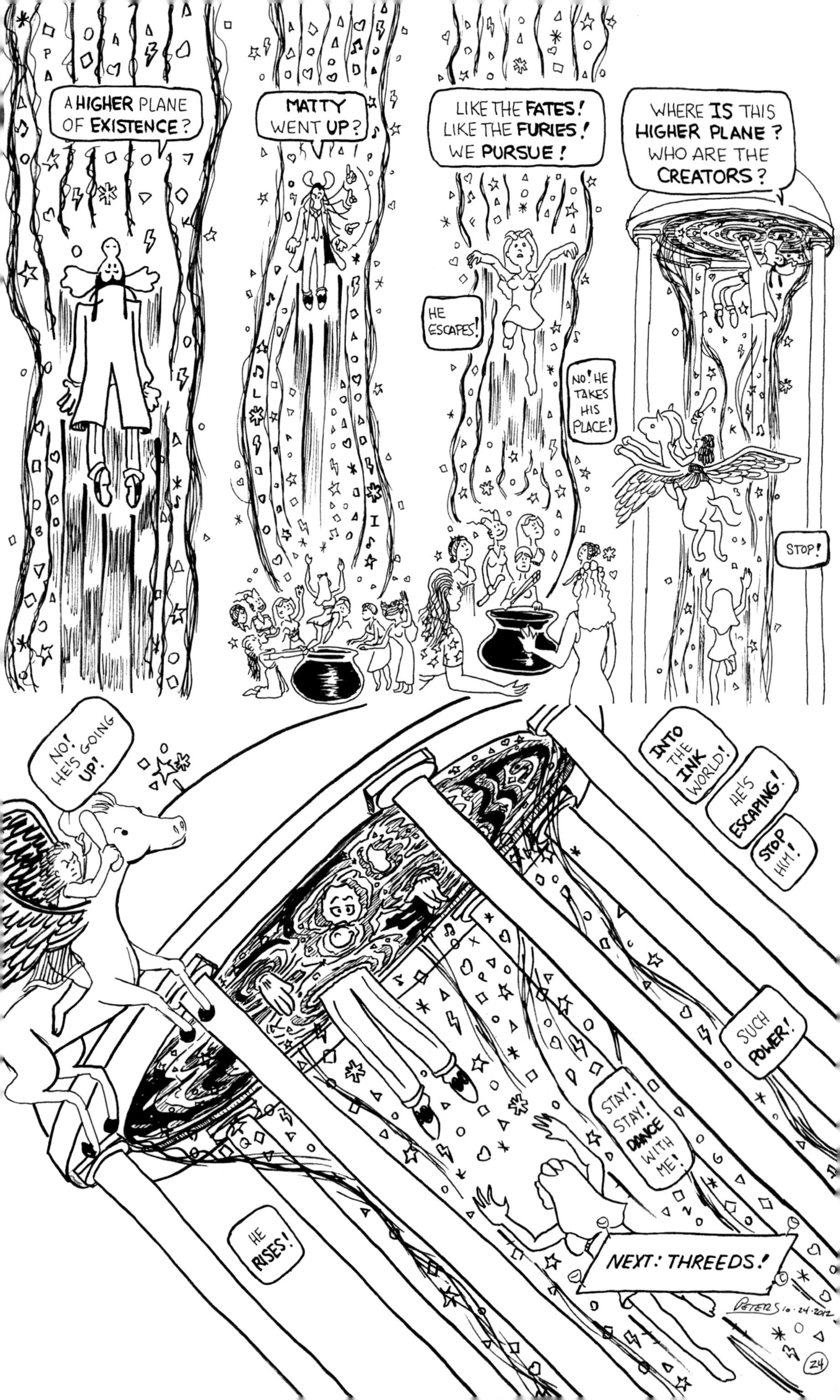
A HIGHER PLANE OF EXISTENCE?
MATTY WENT UP?
LIKE THE FATES! LIKE THE FURIES! WE PURSUE!
HE ESCAPES!
NO! HE TAKES HIS PLACE!
WHERE IS THIS HIGHER PLANE? WHO ARE THE CREATORS?
STOP!
NO! HE'S GOING UP!
INTO THE INK WORLD!
HE'S ESCAPING!
STOP HIM!
SUCH POWER!
STAY! STAY! DANCE WITH ME!
HE RISES!
NEXT: THREEDS!
PETERS 10·24·2012

BEHIND THE PANELS 2

THE
WORLD
TD 2
.24
OLD!

MGMTD 2 #24
MUSES SEQUENCE HOLD!

HOLD FLAT!
MGMTD 2
MUSES SEQ.

WOW! I'M STARVED.

ME THREE!

CHECK CRAFTY!

LUNCH!

I'M GLAD YOU FINALLY GOT AROUND TO IT.

YEAH, ME TOO. I MISSED YOU.

I MISSED YOU TOO, BUDDY.

MEMBER MELVIN G. MOOSE FAN CLUB ©

re: SOURCES

INK WORLD

ONE OF THE **CONNECTIONS** BETWEEN **OUR** REALITY (THE THREED WORLD) AND THE **TWO-DIMENSIONAL** REALITY (TOODEOPOLIS) IS THROUGH THE **INKWORLD**. INKWORLD CONTAINS AN INSPIRED **MIXTURE** OF ALL IDEAS, WORDS, AND PICTURES THAT HAVE EVER BEEN CONCIEVED, IMAGINED OR CREATED BY HUMANKIND. INKWORLD ALSO CONTAINS THE **COLLECTIVE UNCONSCIOUS** OF THE FLORA AND FAUNA USED THROUGHOUT HISTORY TO **MAKE** THE INK ITSELF. THE FOUNT OF INSPIRATION FLOWS **DIRECTLY** INTO INKWORLD, AWAITING DISCOVERY BY THREED IMAGINATIONS.

BLACK MAGIC INK.

KO-KO

KO-KO THE CLOWN WAS ONE OF THE **FIRST** TOODES TO EMERGE FROM THE INKWORLD AND BECOME A MAJOR THREED WORLD ANIMATION **STAR**. HIS EARLIEST FORAYS INTO THE THREED WORLD WERE CAPTURED ON **FILM** BY DAVE & MAX **FLEISHER**, PIONEERS IN EARLY ANIMATION. MANY OF THESE **DOCUMENTARIES** ARE ON THE INTERNET. KO-KO FIRST CAME OUT OF THE INKWELL IN 1917. HE MOST RECENTLY MADE A **CAMEO** APPEARANCE IN 1988'S "WHO FRAMED ROGER RABBIT?" AND HAS **NOT** BEEN **SEEN** SINCE. OTHER CELEBRITY TOODES IN INKWORLD INCLUDE: BETTY BOOP, BIMBO, HOLLI WOULD AND SPLASH BRANNIGAN.

THE MUSES

IN GREEK MYTHOLOGY, THE MUSES ARE **GODDESSES** OF **INSPIRATION**, ESPECIALLY IN THE FIELDS OF **SCIENCE**, THE **ARTS**, AND **LITERATURE**. IN TOODEOPOLIS THEY CAN BE FOUND IN **MUSES GROVE**, FEEDING THE CREATIVE FLOW, CREATIVE RESERVOIR, AND FOUNT OF INSPIRATION WITH THEIR IDEAS, CONCEPTS AND SCHEMES. THEY'RE ACCOMPANIED BY **PEGASUS**, THE FLYING HORSE WHO CREATED THEIR INSPIRATIONAL SPRING WITH HIS HOOVES. THE MUSES ARE: **CALLIOPE**: EPIC POETRY **CLIO**: HISTORY **ERATO**: LOVE & EROTIC POETRY **EUTERPE**: MUSIC **MELPOMENE**: TRAGEDY **POLYHYMNIA**: SACRED POETRY **TERPSICHORE**: DANCE **THALIA**: COMEDY **URANIA**: ASTRONOMY

BRAINSTORMS

THE **GENESIS** OF **IDEA** CREATION, **BRAINSTORMS** ARE FOUND OVER THE **CREATIVE RESERVOIR**. WILD, UNPREDICTABLE **WHIRLWINDS** OF HALF-BAKED IDEAS, CONCEPTS, SUGGESTIONS, WHIMS, AND FANCIES, BRAINSTORMS ARE A METHOD OF **EXPLORING** AND **CLEARING** THE CREATIVE AIR, GENERALLY RESULTING IN THE DISTILLATION OF A MOST WORKABLE **SOLUTION** TO A CREATIVE **CHALLENGE**. BRAINSTORMS ARE INITIALLY **DANGEROUS** AND CAN DESTROY ALL **MENTAL FUNCTIONS**. HOWEVER, BY EXAMINING, PROCESSING, AND DISCARDING ALL INPUT **USELESS** TO ACHIEVING CORE CREATIVE **GOALS**, BRAINSTORMS CAN ULTIMATELY **TRANSFORM** CONCEPTS INTO PURE CREATIVE **GENIUS**.

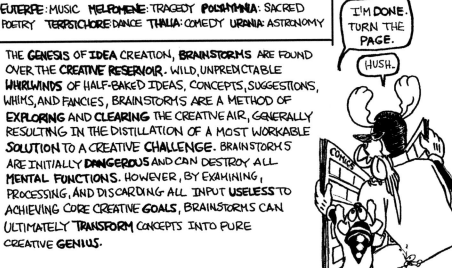

I'M DONE. TURN THE PAGE.

HUSH.

COMICS

Peters 10-25-2012

IBC

NEXT ISSUE: OUR THIRD CHAPTER

"THREEDS"

or: "THE MOEBIUS McGUFFIN"

or: "WHICH DIMENSION IS THIS?"

or: "EVERYBODY OUT OF THE INK POOL, I WANT TO TAKE A DRINK!"

DO YOU LIKE MELVIN? BUY A COPY FOR YOUR FRIENDS, OR FAVORITE COMIC FAN! THE COMPLETE SAGA IS AVAILABLE AT AMAZON.COM!

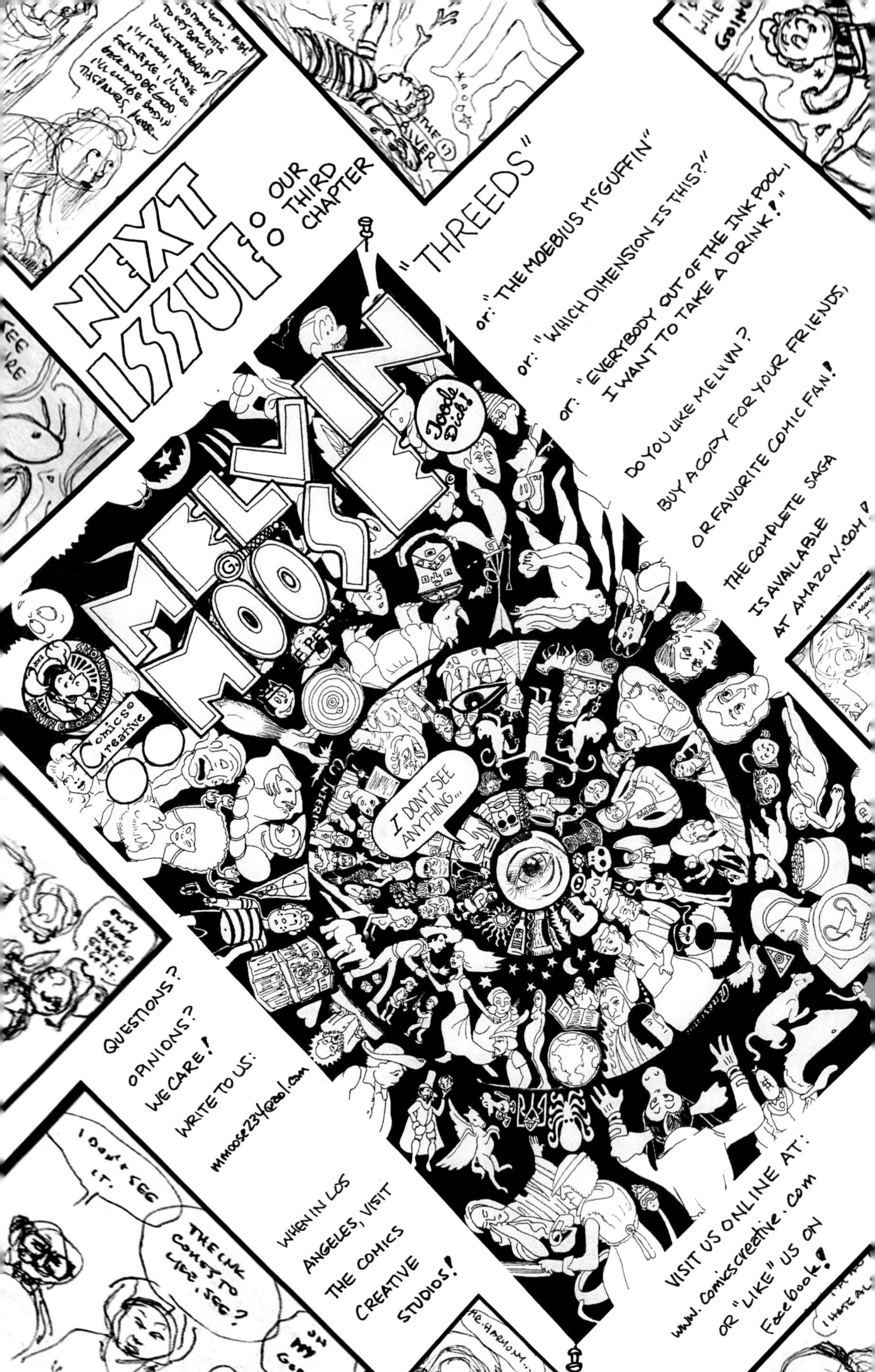
MELVIN G. MOOSE
Joodle Dick!
I DON'T SEE ANYTHING...
Comics Creative

QUESTIONS? OPINIONS? WE CARE! WRITE TO US: mmoose234@aol.com

WHEN IN LOS ANGELES, VISIT THE COMICS CREATIVE STUDIOS!

VISIT US ONLINE AT: www.comicscreative.com OR "LIKE" US ON Facebook!

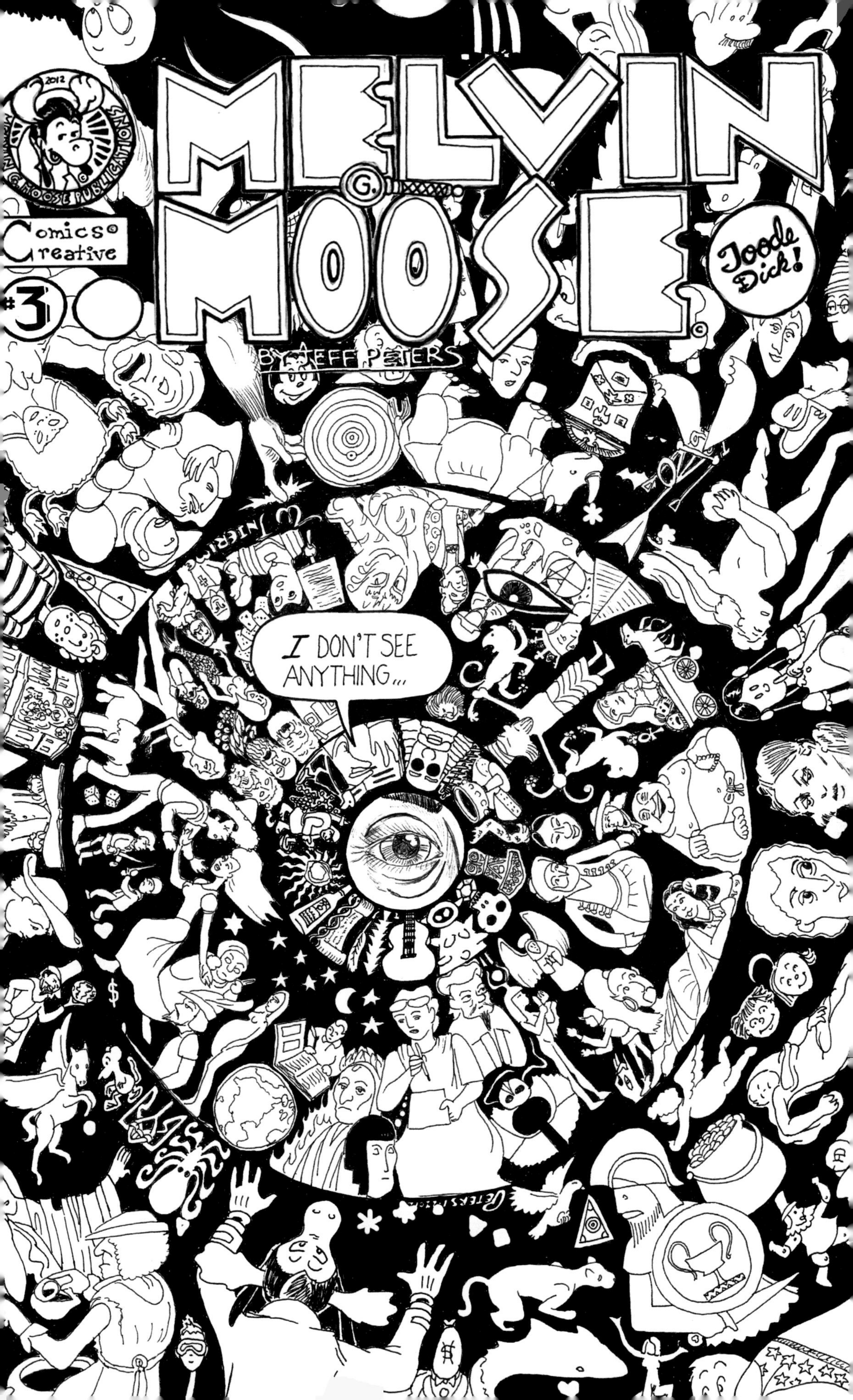
MELVIN G. MOOSE
BY JEFF PETERS
Comics Creative
#3
Joode Dick!
I DON'T SEE ANYTHING...

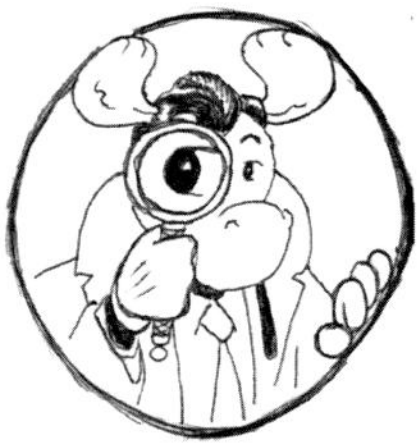

PERCEPTIONS:

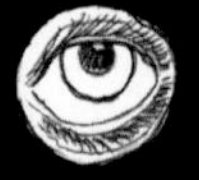

MELVIN G. MOOSE
TOODE DICK
CHAPTER (3) THREE
"THREEDS"

"OPENING
THE THREED
EYE"

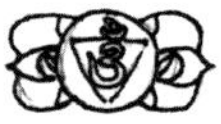

or:
"NOT ASLEEP,
JUST RESTING
MY THIRD EYE."

THIS ONE IS **FOR:**
IZA, JANE, ART,
JENNY, DRU, STEVEN
CLAIRE & HOMER;
MY **FAMILY**
WHO ENCOURAGE
AND SUPPORT MY
CREATIVE
LIFE AND WHIMS.
MANY HEARTFELT
THANKS.

THREEDS

HOW MANY **DIMENSIONS** ARE THERE? DEPENDS ON WHETHER WE'RE DISCUSSING **STRING THEORY.** **5, 10, 26**? NOT TO WORRY, WE'LL ONLY BE **DEALING** WITH THE FIRST **FEW.** 26 DIMENSIONS, MATH, **ASPECT RATIOS**? **THEMES** ARE GETTING **HEADY** IN HERE. I'VE PUT ON SOME GOOD **ROCK** AND **ROLL** FOR THIS **ISSUE**, SO I'LL SUGGEST YOU DO THE **SAME** BEFORE YOU JOIN US IN OUR **WORLD.** GRAB A **BEVERAGE** AND **COMFY** READING SPOT. IF YOU HAVE ONE, GET YOUR **MAGNIFYING GLASS,** YOU MIGHT FIND IT HANDY, AS **CLUES** ARE **EVERYWHERE**, THREED SLEUTHER.

WHEN WE **LEFT** OUR THREED ADVENTURERS, THE MEMBERS OF THE **MÖBIUS BAND** (JEAN, PAUL, GERARD & BONGO) HAD BEEN **ATTACKED**, CAUSING THREE **FATALITIES.** NYPD DETECTIVES **ALISE ADAMS** AND **HERBERT MIGGS** INVESTIGATED, MEETING CARTOONISTS **TEX TAYLOR & RUDY HARMONY**, THE REGULARS AT THE **3 MARTINIS BAR** AND NIGHT CLUB, AND MANY OTHERS. ALISE AND HERB SEARCH FOR A **KILLER** WHO PREFERS BOWLING BALLS, SAFES, ANVILS, AND PIANOS AS HIS **WEAPONS** OF CHOICE. THERE ARE **OTHERS** INTERESTED IN THIS CRIME. **MR. GEE** AND **MR. HAW** REPRESENT THE SECRET SOCIETY KNOWN AS THE **ILLUSTRATI**, WHOSE MYSTERIOUS **LEADER** IS KEEN ON LOCATING RUDY HARMONY AND A CERTAIN BOTTLE OF **INK.**

WHY ALL THIS **FUSS** OVER SPILLED **INK**? PERHAPS BECAUSE IT **CONTAINS** THE TWO DIMENSIONAL WORLD, WHERE EVERYTHING WE THREEDERS WRITE AND EVERYTHING WE DRAW **ACHIEVES** AND MAINTAINS **CONSCIOUSNESS.** A STATE OF BEING QUICKLY BECOMING **OBSOLETE** AND ANTIQUATED BY THE EVER WIDENING SCOPE OF THE **DIGITAL** DOMAIN.

HOW MANY **DIMENSIONS** ARE THERE? FOR THE MOMENT, EXACTLY AS MANY AS I **NEED** TO TELL YOU THIS **STORY**, DEAREST THREEDER. JOHN LENNON'S "**IMAGINE**" JUST POPPED ON THE RADIO, SO LET'S **TAKE** HIS ADVICE AND **RE-ENTER** THE WORLD OF **THREEDS.**

SEARCH **WARRANT** OBTAINED, **ALISE** AND **HERB** GATHER **EVIDENCE** FROM RUDY HARMONY'S STUDIO...

— JEFF PETERS 4/3/2012

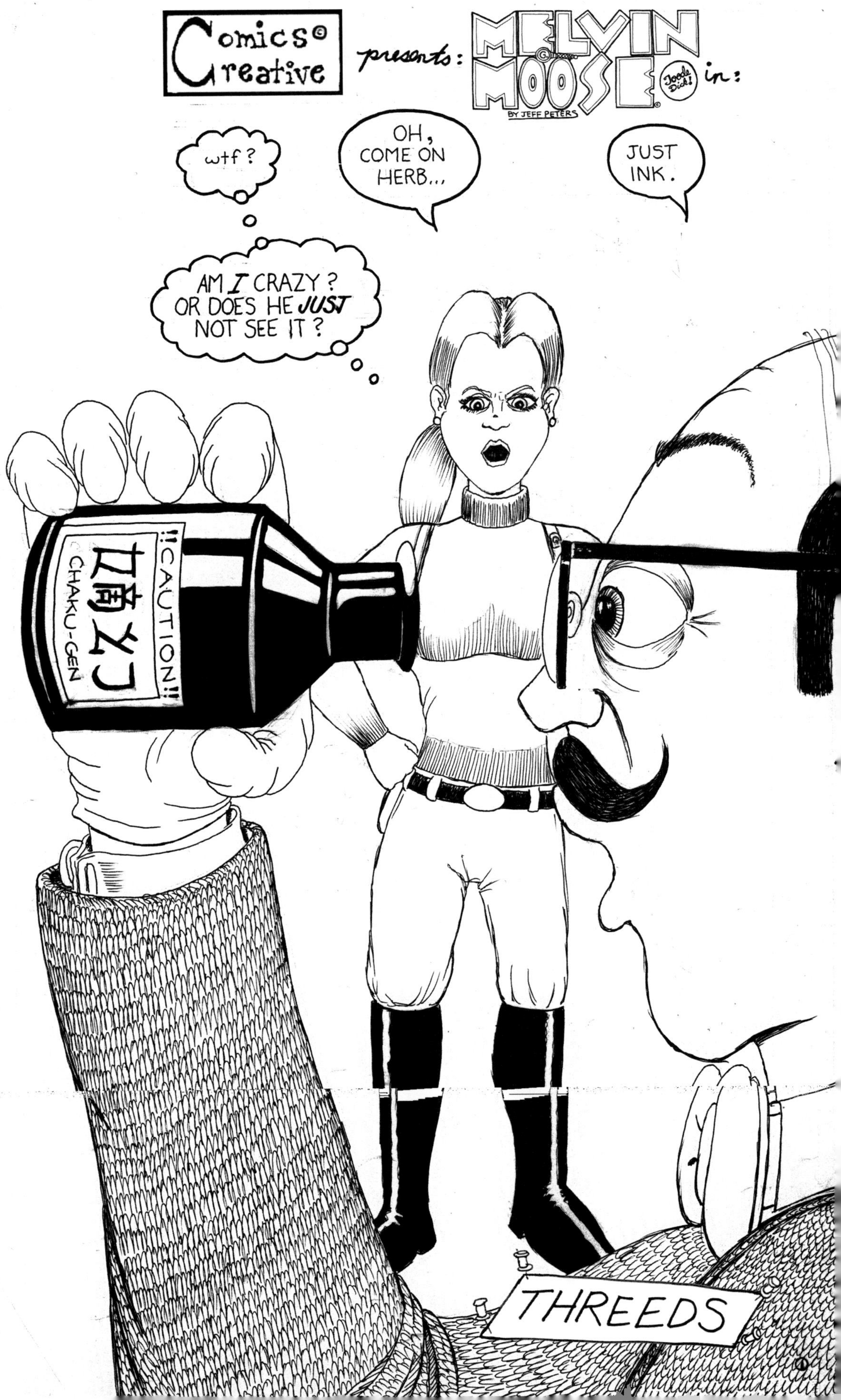

Comics© Creative
presents:
MELVIN MOOSE© in:
BY JEFF PETERS
wtf?
OH, COME ON HERB...
JUST INK.
AM I CRAZY? OR DOES HE JUST NOT SEE IT?
!!CAUTION!!
CHAKU-GEN
THREEDS

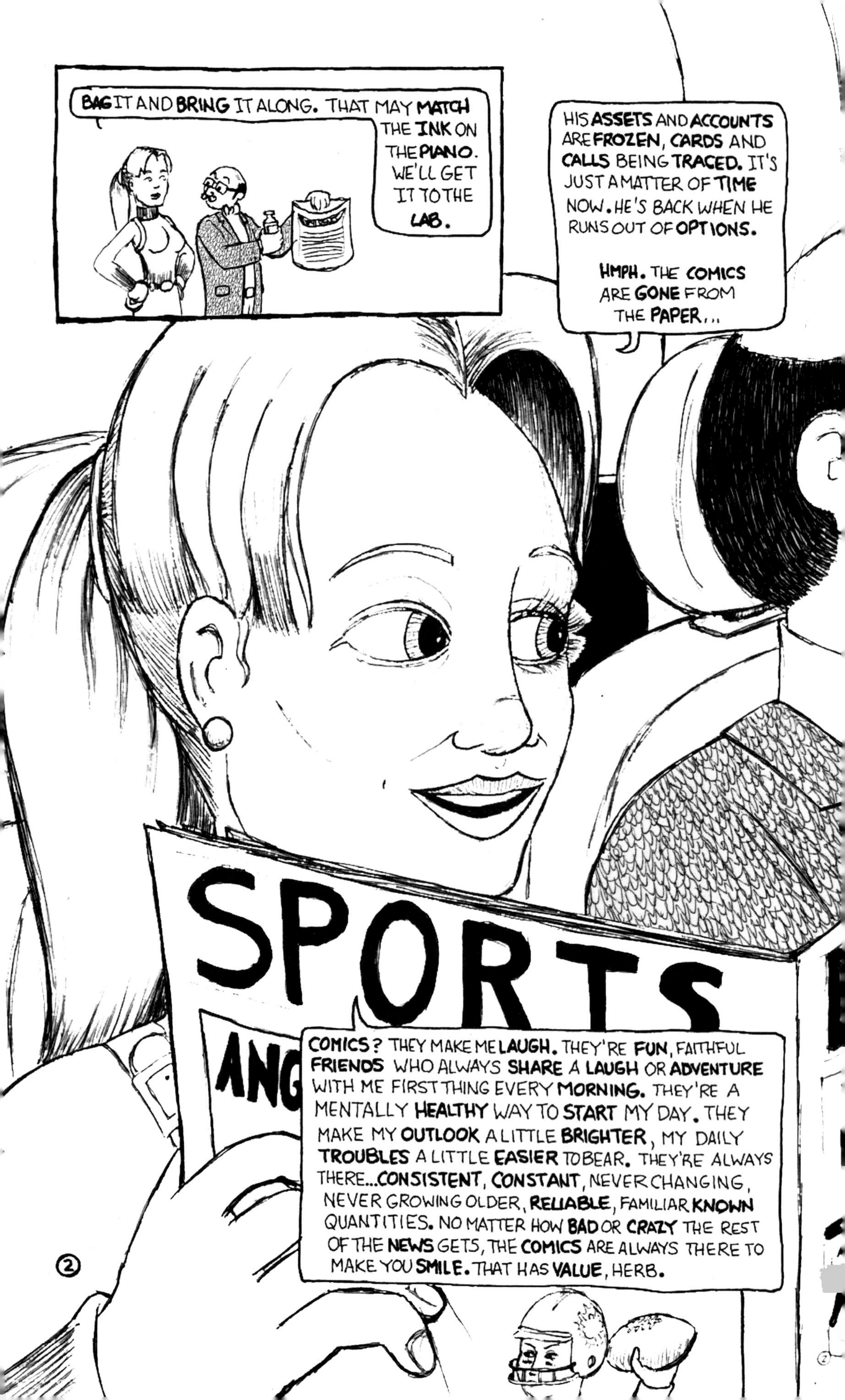
BAG IT AND BRING IT ALONG. THAT MAY MATCH THE INK ON THE PIANO. WE'LL GET IT TO THE LAB.
HIS ASSETS AND ACCOUNTS ARE FROZEN, CARDS AND CALLS BEING TRACED. IT'S JUST A MATTER OF TIME NOW. HE'S BACK WHEN HE RUNS OUT OF OPTIONS.
HMPH. THE COMICS ARE GONE FROM THE PAPER...
SPORTS
COMICS? THEY MAKE ME LAUGH. THEY'RE FUN, FAITHFUL FRIENDS WHO ALWAYS SHARE A LAUGH OR ADVENTURE WITH ME FIRST THING EVERY MORNING. THEY'RE A MENTALLY HEALTHY WAY TO START MY DAY. THEY MAKE MY OUTLOOK A LITTLE BRIGHTER, MY DAILY TROUBLES A LITTLE EASIER TO BEAR. THEY'RE ALWAYS THERE...CONSISTENT, CONSTANT, NEVER CHANGING, NEVER GROWING OLDER, RELIABLE, FAMILIAR KNOWN QUANTITIES. NO MATTER HOW BAD OR CRAZY THE REST OF THE NEWS GETS, THE COMICS ARE ALWAYS THERE TO MAKE YOU SMILE. THAT HAS VALUE, HERB.

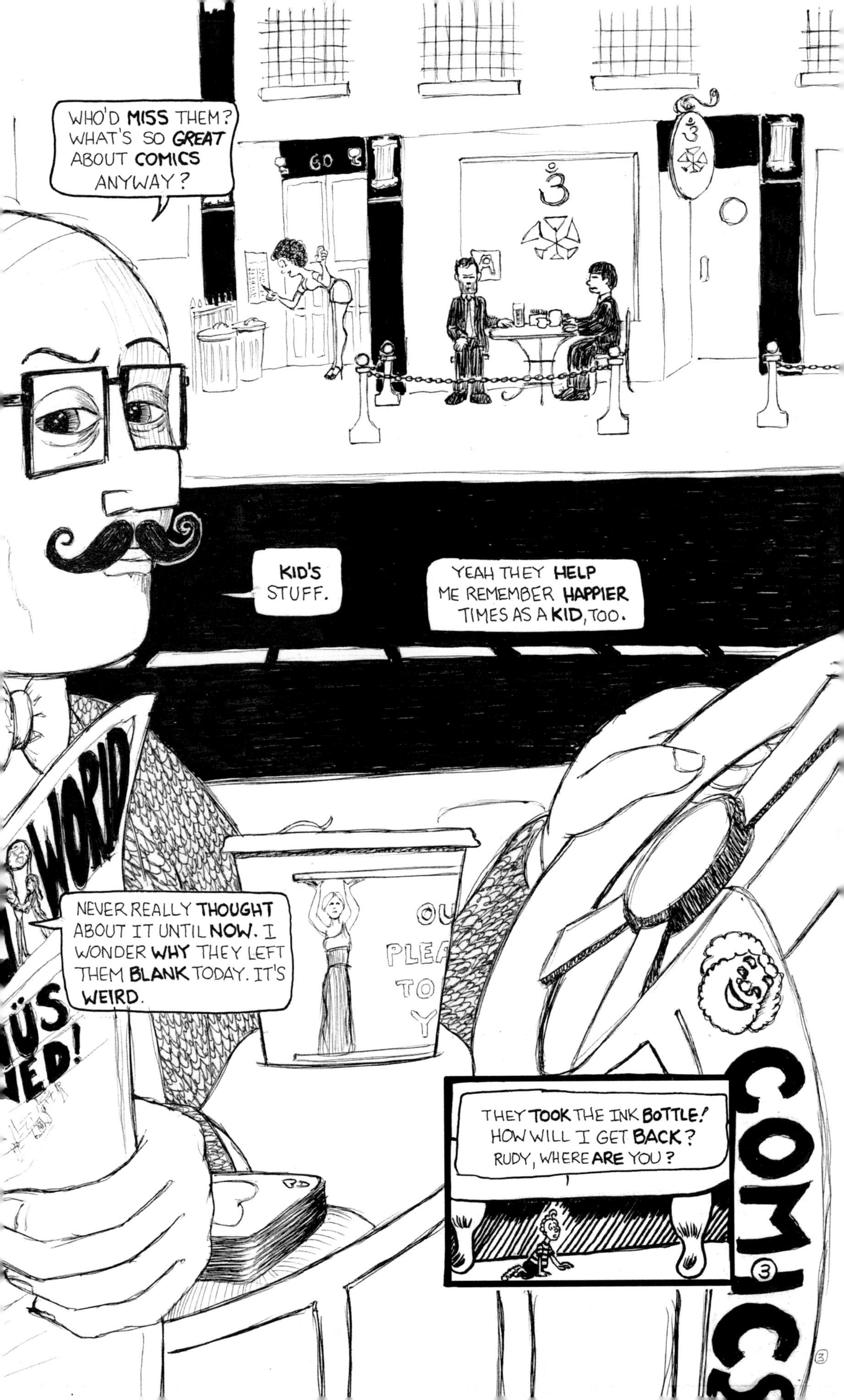
WHO'D MISS THEM? WHAT'S SO GREAT ABOUT COMICS ANYWAY?
GO
KID'S STUFF.
YEAH THEY HELP ME REMEMBER HAPPIER TIMES AS A KID, TOO.
WORLD
NEVER REALLY THOUGHT ABOUT IT UNTIL NOW. I WONDER WHY THEY LEFT THEM BLANK TODAY. IT'S WEIRD.
THEY TOOK THE INK BOTTLE! HOW WILL I GET BACK? RUDY, WHERE ARE YOU?
COMICS
3

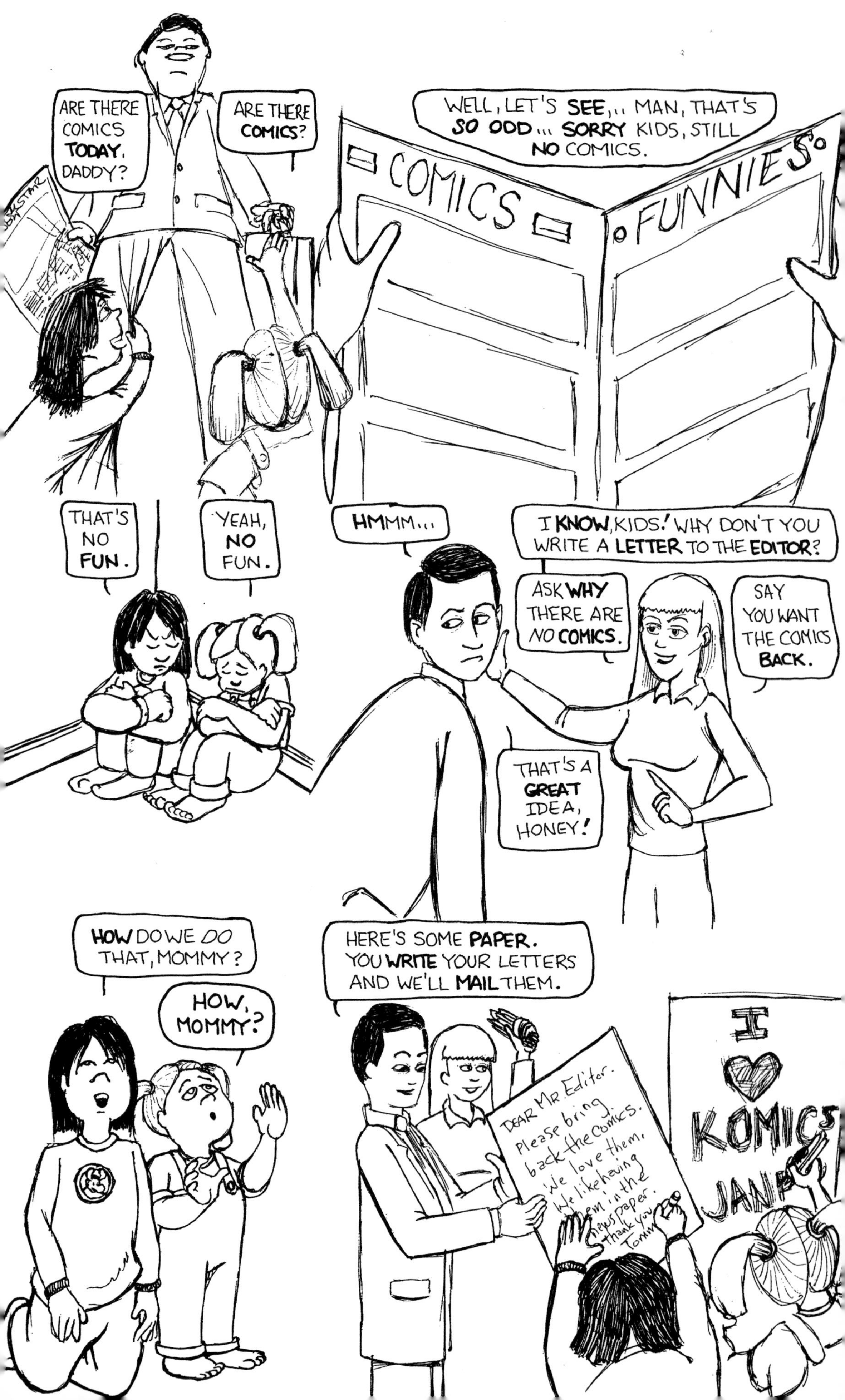
ARE THERE COMICS TODAY, DADDY?
ARE THERE COMICS?
WELL, LET'S SEE,.. MAN, THAT'S SO ODD... SORRY KIDS, STILL NO COMICS.
COMICS
FUNNIES
THAT'S NO FUN.
YEAH, NO FUN.
HMMM...
I KNOW, KIDS! WHY DON'T YOU WRITE A LETTER TO THE EDITOR?
ASK WHY THERE ARE NO COMICS.
SAY YOU WANT THE COMICS BACK.
THAT'S A GREAT IDEA, HONEY!
HOW DO WE DO THAT, MOMMY?
HOW, MOMMY?
HERE'S SOME PAPER. YOU WRITE YOUR LETTERS AND WE'LL MAIL THEM.
DEAR Mr Editor. Please bring back the comics. We love them. We like having them in the newspaper. thank you
I
KOMICS

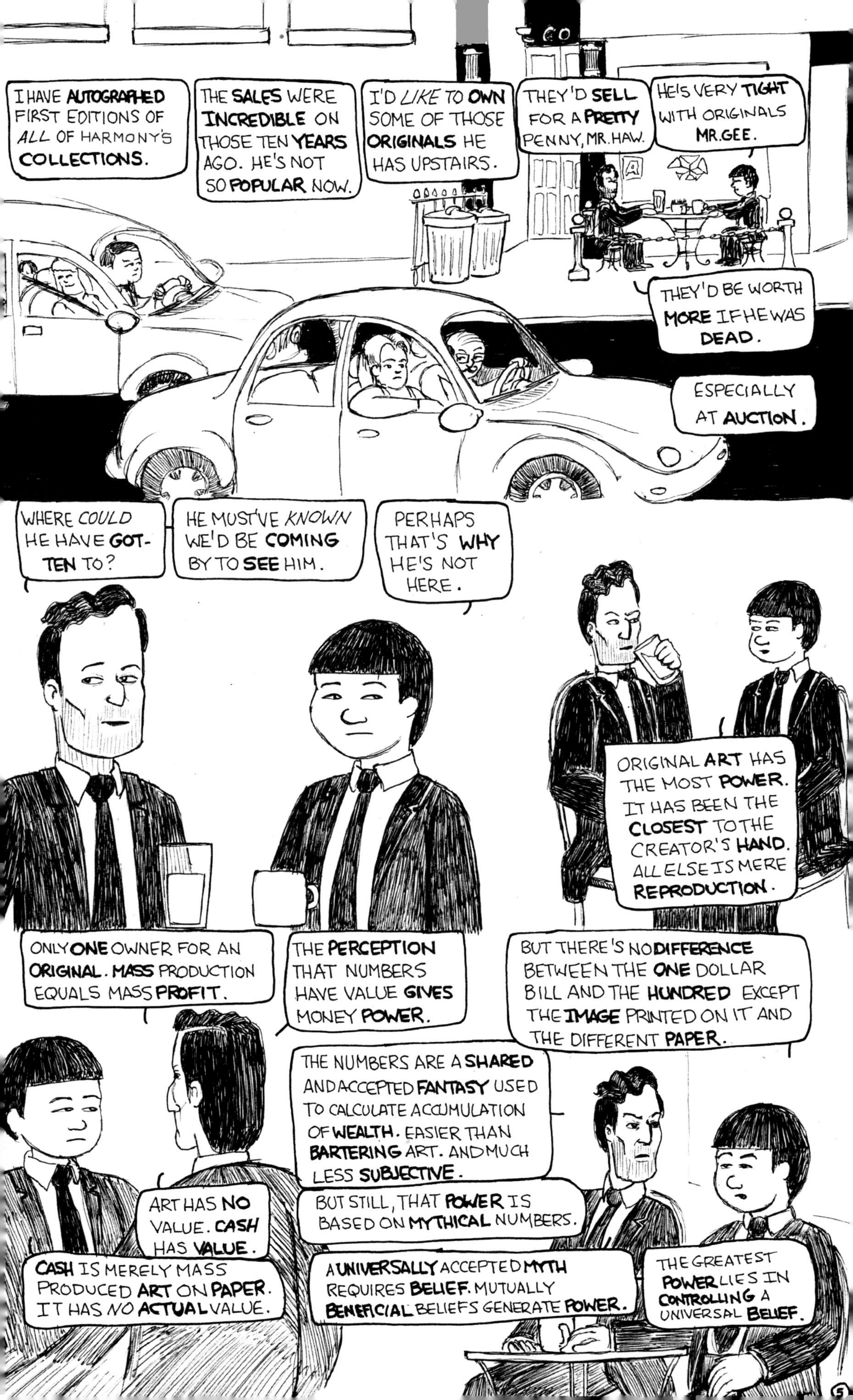
I HAVE AUTOGRAPHED FIRST EDITIONS OF ALL OF HARMONY'S COLLECTIONS.
THE SALES WERE INCREDIBLE ON THOSE TEN YEARS AGO. HE'S NOT SO POPULAR NOW.
I'D LIKE TO OWN SOME OF THOSE ORIGINALS HE HAS UPSTAIRS.
THEY'D SELL FOR A PRETTY PENNY, MR. HAW.
HE'S VERY TIGHT WITH ORIGINALS MR. GEE.
THEY'D BE WORTH MORE IF HE WAS DEAD.
ESPECIALLY AT AUCTION.
WHERE COULD HE HAVE GOTTEN TO?
HE MUST'VE KNOWN WE'D BE COMING BY TO SEE HIM.
PERHAPS THAT'S WHY HE'S NOT HERE.
ORIGINAL ART HAS THE MOST POWER. IT HAS BEEN THE CLOSEST TO THE CREATOR'S HAND. ALL ELSE IS MERE REPRODUCTION.
ONLY ONE OWNER FOR AN ORIGINAL. MASS PRODUCTION EQUALS MASS PROFIT.
THE PERCEPTION THAT NUMBERS HAVE VALUE GIVES MONEY POWER.
BUT THERE'S NO DIFFERENCE BETWEEN THE ONE DOLLAR BILL AND THE HUNDRED EXCEPT THE IMAGE PRINTED ON IT AND THE DIFFERENT PAPER.
THE NUMBERS ARE A SHARED AND ACCEPTED FANTASY USED TO CALCULATE ACCUMULATION OF WEALTH. EASIER THAN BARTERING ART. AND MUCH LESS SUBJECTIVE.
ART HAS NO VALUE. CASH HAS VALUE.
BUT STILL, THAT POWER IS BASED ON MYTHICAL NUMBERS.
CASH IS MERELY MASS PRODUCED ART ON PAPER. IT HAS NO ACTUAL VALUE.
A UNIVERSALLY ACCEPTED MYTH REQUIRES BELIEF. MUTUALLY BENEFICIAL BELIEFS GENERATE POWER.
THE GREATEST POWER LIES IN CONTROLLING A UNIVERSAL BELIEF.

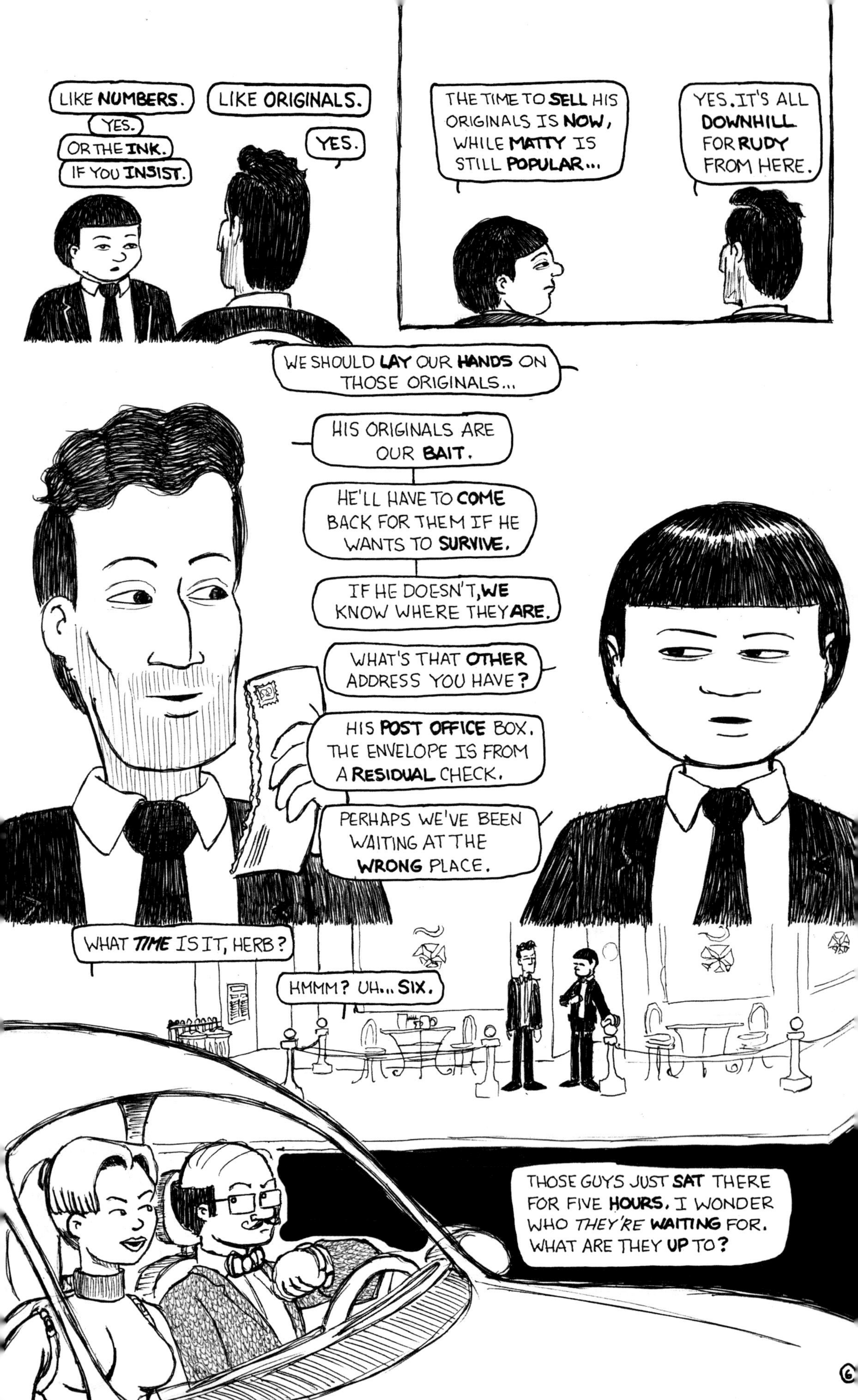
LIKE NUMBERS.
YES.
OR THE INK.
IF YOU INSIST.
LIKE ORIGINALS.
YES.
THE TIME TO SELL HIS ORIGINALS IS NOW, WHILE MATTY IS STILL POPULAR...
YES. IT'S ALL DOWNHILL FOR RUDY FROM HERE.
WE SHOULD LAY OUR HANDS ON THOSE ORIGINALS...
HIS ORIGINALS ARE OUR BAIT.
HE'LL HAVE TO COME BACK FOR THEM IF HE WANTS TO SURVIVE.
IF HE DOESN'T, WE KNOW WHERE THEY ARE.
WHAT'S THAT OTHER ADDRESS YOU HAVE?
HIS POST OFFICE BOX. THE ENVELOPE IS FROM A RESIDUAL CHECK.
PERHAPS WE'VE BEEN WAITING AT THE WRONG PLACE.
WHAT TIME IS IT, HERB?
HMMM? UH... SIX.
THOSE GUYS JUST SAT THERE FOR FIVE HOURS. I WONDER WHO THEY'RE WAITING FOR. WHAT ARE THEY UP TO?

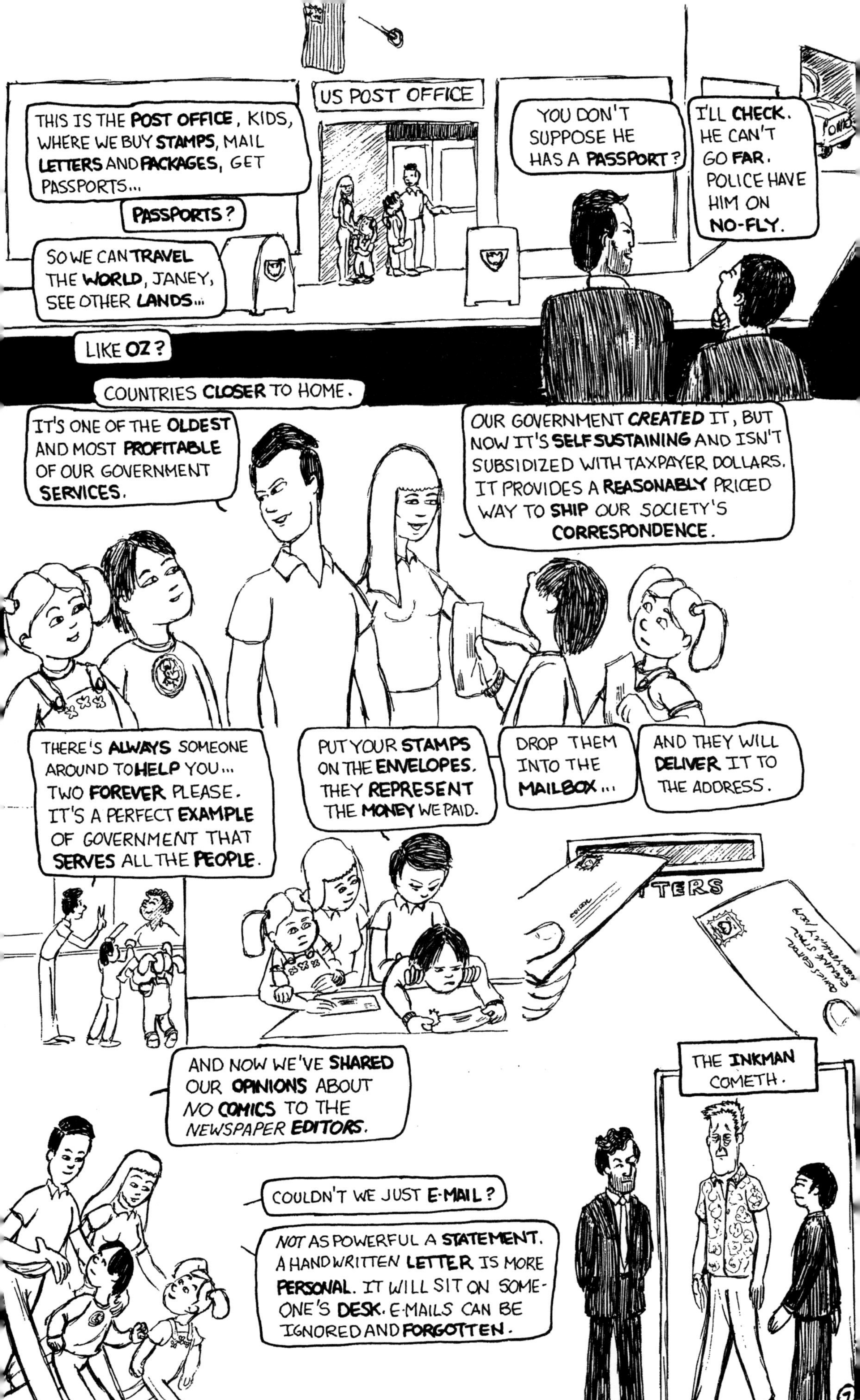

US POST OFFICE
THIS IS THE POST OFFICE, KIDS, WHERE WE BUY STAMPS, MAIL LETTERS AND PACKAGES, GET PASSPORTS...
PASSPORTS?
SO WE CAN TRAVEL THE WORLD, JANEY, SEE OTHER LANDS...
LIKE OZ?
COUNTRIES CLOSER TO HOME.
YOU DON'T SUPPOSE HE HAS A PASSPORT?
I'LL CHECK. HE CAN'T GO FAR. POLICE HAVE HIM ON NO-FLY.
IT'S ONE OF THE OLDEST AND MOST PROFITABLE OF OUR GOVERNMENT SERVICES.
OUR GOVERNMENT CREATED IT, BUT NOW IT'S SELF SUSTAINING AND ISN'T SUBSIDIZED WITH TAXPAYER DOLLARS. IT PROVIDES A REASONABLY PRICED WAY TO SHIP OUR SOCIETY'S CORRESPONDENCE.
THERE'S ALWAYS SOMEONE AROUND TO HELP YOU... TWO FOREVER PLEASE. IT'S A PERFECT EXAMPLE OF GOVERNMENT THAT SERVES ALL THE PEOPLE.
PUT YOUR STAMPS ON THE ENVELOPES. THEY REPRESENT THE MONEY WE PAID.
DROP THEM INTO THE MAILBOX...
AND THEY WILL DELIVER IT TO THE ADDRESS.
AND NOW WE'VE SHARED OUR OPINIONS ABOUT NO COMICS TO THE NEWSPAPER EDITORS.
COULDN'T WE JUST E-MAIL?
NOT AS POWERFUL A STATEMENT. A HANDWRITTEN LETTER IS MORE PERSONAL. IT WILL SIT ON SOMEONE'S DESK. E-MAILS CAN BE IGNORED AND FORGOTTEN.
THE INKMAN COMETH.

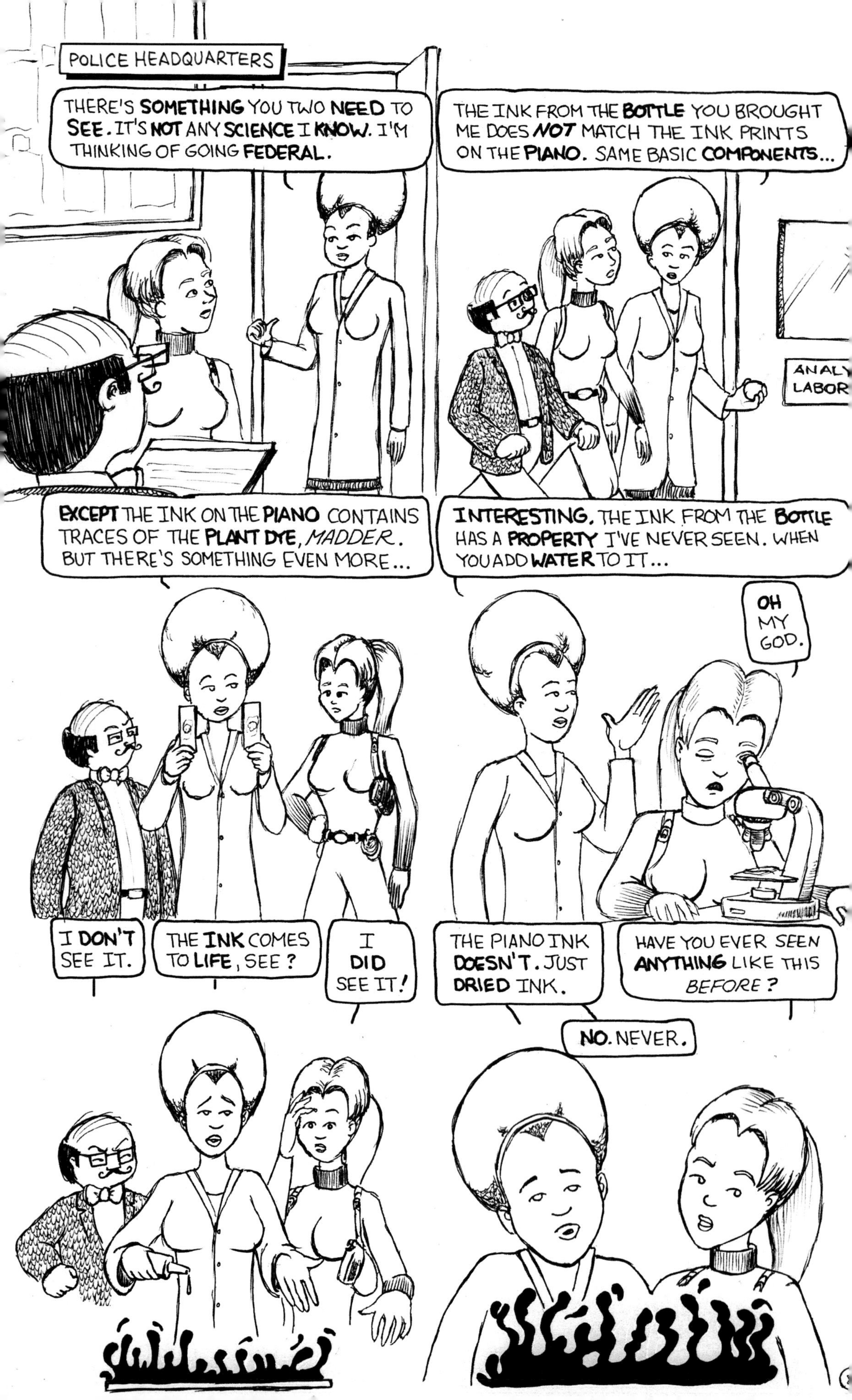
POLICE HEADQUARTERS
THERE'S SOMETHING YOU TWO NEED TO SEE. IT'S NOT ANY SCIENCE I KNOW. I'M THINKING OF GOING FEDERAL.
THE INK FROM THE BOTTLE YOU BROUGHT ME DOES NOT MATCH THE INK PRINTS ON THE PIANO. SAME BASIC COMPONENTS...
ANALY
LABOR
EXCEPT THE INK ON THE PIANO CONTAINS TRACES OF THE PLANT DYE, MADDER. BUT THERE'S SOMETHING EVEN MORE...
I DON'T SEE IT.
THE INK COMES TO LIFE, SEE?
I DID SEE IT!
INTERESTING. THE INK FROM THE BOTTLE HAS A PROPERTY I'VE NEVER SEEN. WHEN YOU ADD WATER TO IT...
OH MY GOD.
THE PIANO INK DOESN'T. JUST DRIED INK.
HAVE YOU EVER SEEN ANYTHING LIKE THIS BEFORE?
NO. NEVER.

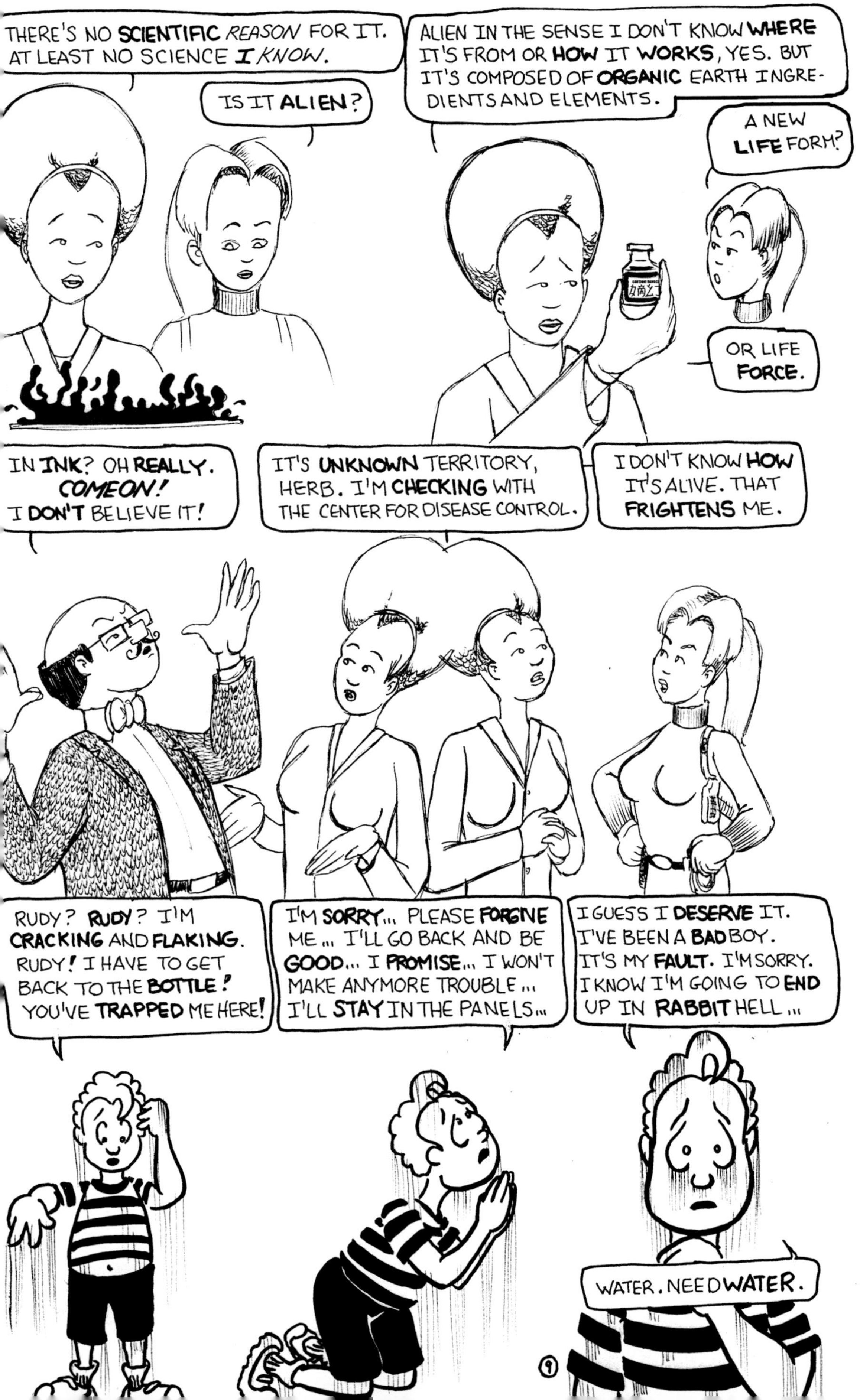
THERE'S NO SCIENTIFIC REASON FOR IT. AT LEAST NO SCIENCE I KNOW.
IS IT ALIEN?
ALIEN IN THE SENSE I DON'T KNOW WHERE IT'S FROM OR HOW IT WORKS, YES. BUT IT'S COMPOSED OF ORGANIC EARTH INGREDIENTS AND ELEMENTS.
A NEW LIFE FORM?
OR LIFE FORCE.
IN INK? OH REALLY. COMEON! I DON'T BELIEVE IT!
IT'S UNKNOWN TERRITORY, HERB. I'M CHECKING WITH THE CENTER FOR DISEASE CONTROL.
I DON'T KNOW HOW IT'S ALIVE. THAT FRIGHTENS ME.
RUDY? RUDY? I'M CRACKING AND FLAKING. RUDY! I HAVE TO GET BACK TO THE BOTTLE! YOU'VE TRAPPED ME HERE!
I'M SORRY... PLEASE FORGIVE ME... I'LL GO BACK AND BE GOOD... I PROMISE... I WON'T MAKE ANYMORE TROUBLE... I'LL STAY IN THE PANELS...
I GUESS I DESERVE IT. I'VE BEEN A BAD BOY. IT'S MY FAULT. I'M SORRY. I KNOW I'M GOING TO END UP IN RABBIT HELL...
WATER. NEED WATER.
9

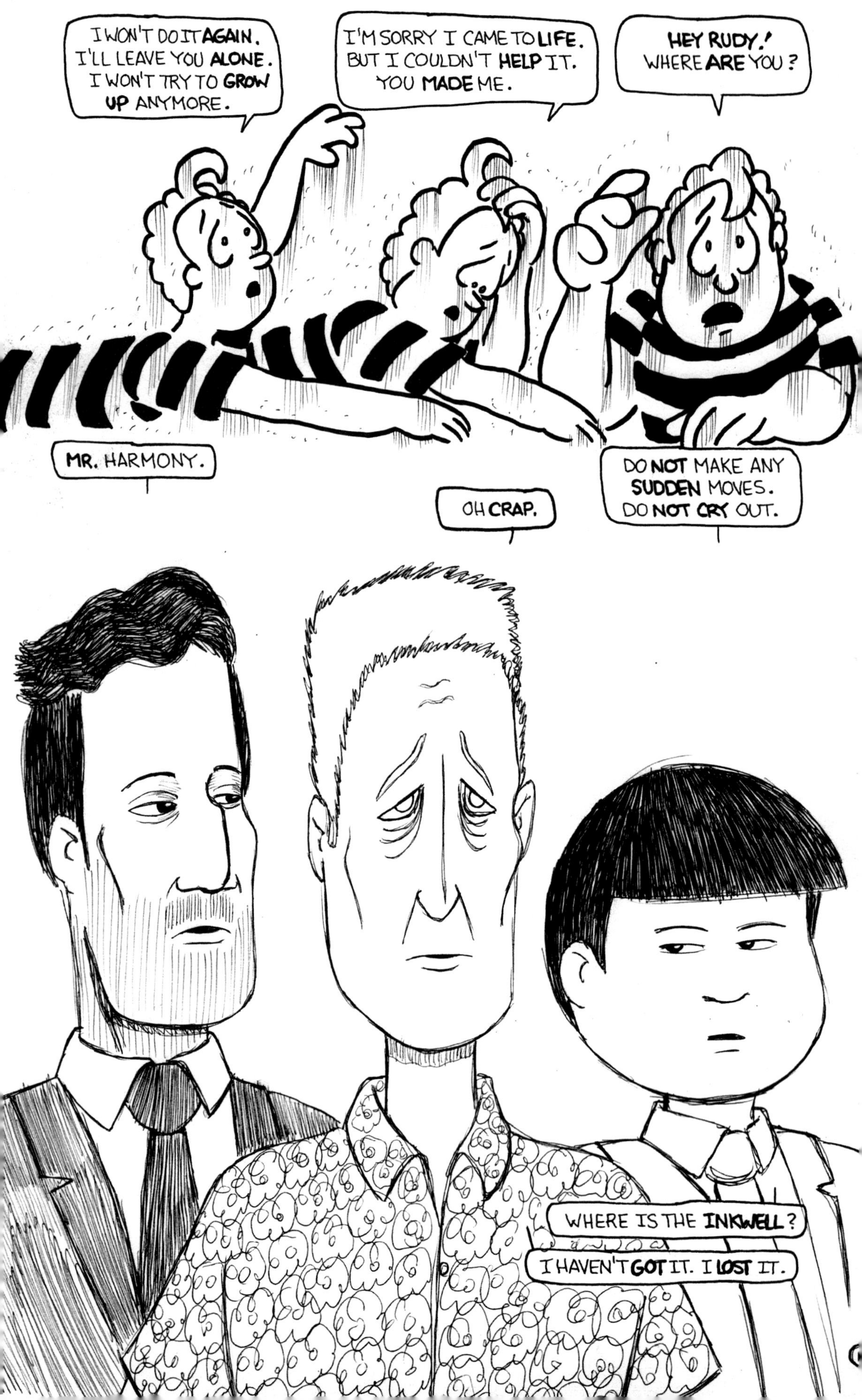
I WON'T DO IT AGAIN. I'LL LEAVE YOU ALONE. I WON'T TRY TO GROW UP ANYMORE.
I'M SORRY I CAME TO LIFE. BUT I COULDN'T HELP IT. YOU MADE ME.
HEY RUDY! WHERE ARE YOU?
MR. HARMONY.
OH CRAP.
DO NOT MAKE ANY SUDDEN MOVES. DO NOT CRY OUT.
WHERE IS THE INKWELL?
I HAVEN'T GOT IT. I LOST IT.

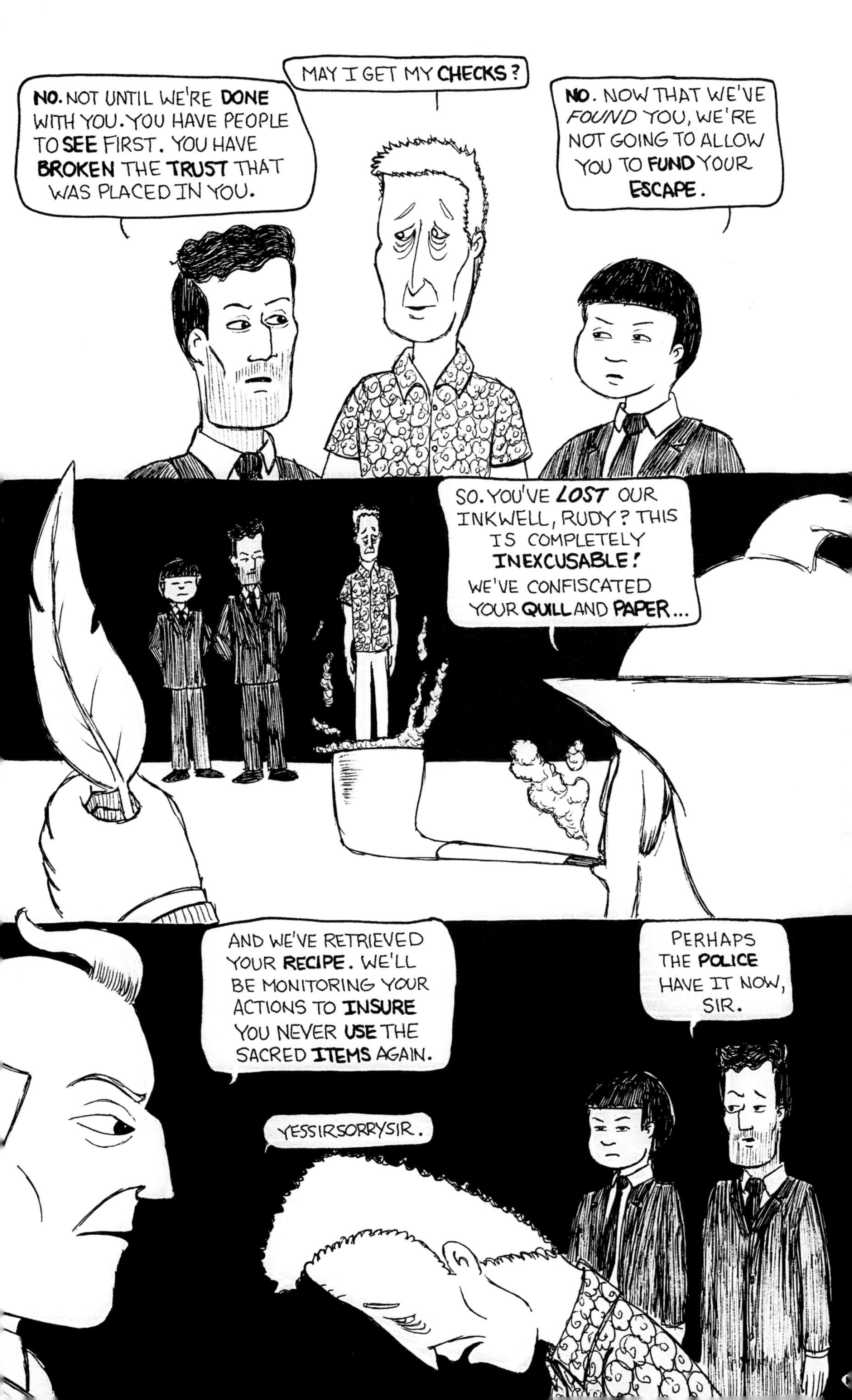
MAY I GET MY CHECKS?
NO. NOT UNTIL WE'RE DONE WITH YOU. YOU HAVE PEOPLE TO SEE FIRST. YOU HAVE BROKEN THE TRUST THAT WAS PLACED IN YOU.
NO. NOW THAT WE'VE FOUND YOU, WE'RE NOT GOING TO ALLOW YOU TO FUND YOUR ESCAPE.
SO. YOU'VE LOST OUR INKWELL, RUDY? THIS IS COMPLETELY INEXCUSABLE! WE'VE CONFISCATED YOUR QUILL AND PAPER...
AND WE'VE RETRIEVED YOUR RECIPE. WE'LL BE MONITORING YOUR ACTIONS TO INSURE YOU NEVER USE THE SACRED ITEMS AGAIN.
PERHAPS THE POLICE HAVE IT NOW, SIR.
YESSIRSORRYSIR.

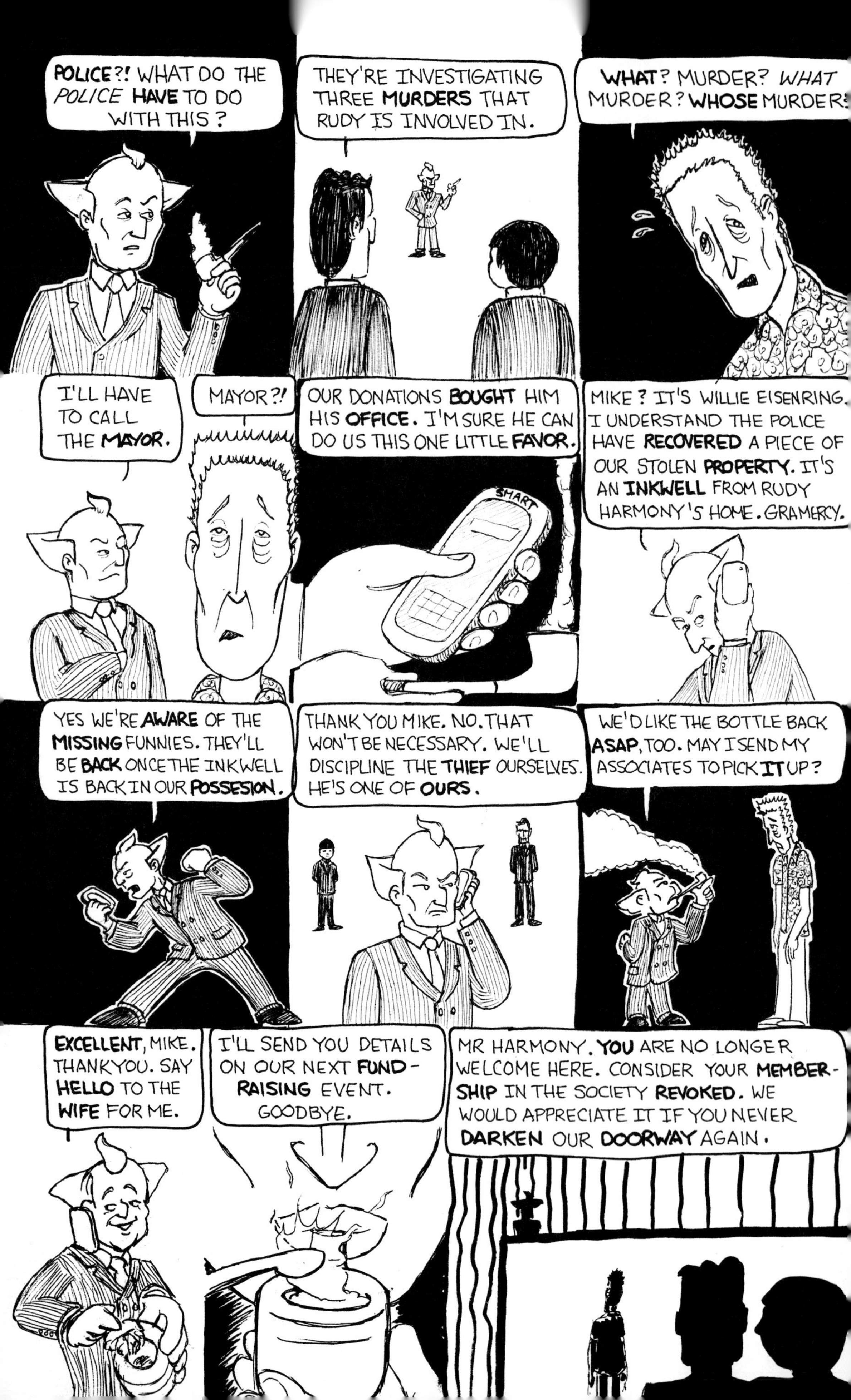
POLICE?! WHAT DO THE POLICE HAVE TO DO WITH THIS?
THEY'RE INVESTIGATING THREE MURDERS THAT RUDY IS INVOLVED IN.
WHAT? MURDER? WHAT MURDER? WHOSE MURDER?
I'LL HAVE TO CALL THE MAYOR.
MAYOR?!
OUR DONATIONS BOUGHT HIM HIS OFFICE. I'M SURE HE CAN DO US THIS ONE LITTLE FAVOR.
SMART
MIKE? IT'S WILLIE EISENRING. I UNDERSTAND THE POLICE HAVE RECOVERED A PIECE OF OUR STOLEN PROPERTY. IT'S AN INKWELL FROM RUDY HARMONY'S HOME. GRAMERCY.
YES WE'RE AWARE OF THE MISSING FUNNIES. THEY'LL BE BACK ONCE THE INKWELL IS BACK IN OUR POSSESION.
THANK YOU MIKE. NO. THAT WON'T BE NECESSARY. WE'LL DISCIPLINE THE THIEF OURSELVES. HE'S ONE OF OURS.
WE'D LIKE THE BOTTLE BACK ASAP, TOO. MAY I SEND MY ASSOCIATES TO PICK IT UP?
EXCELLENT, MIKE. THANKYOU. SAY HELLO TO THE WIFE FOR ME.
I'LL SEND YOU DETAILS ON OUR NEXT FUND-RAISING EVENT. GOODBYE.
MR HARMONY. YOU ARE NO LONGER WELCOME HERE. CONSIDER YOUR MEMBERSHIP IN THE SOCIETY REVOKED. WE WOULD APPRECIATE IT IF YOU NEVER DARKEN OUR DOORWAY AGAIN.

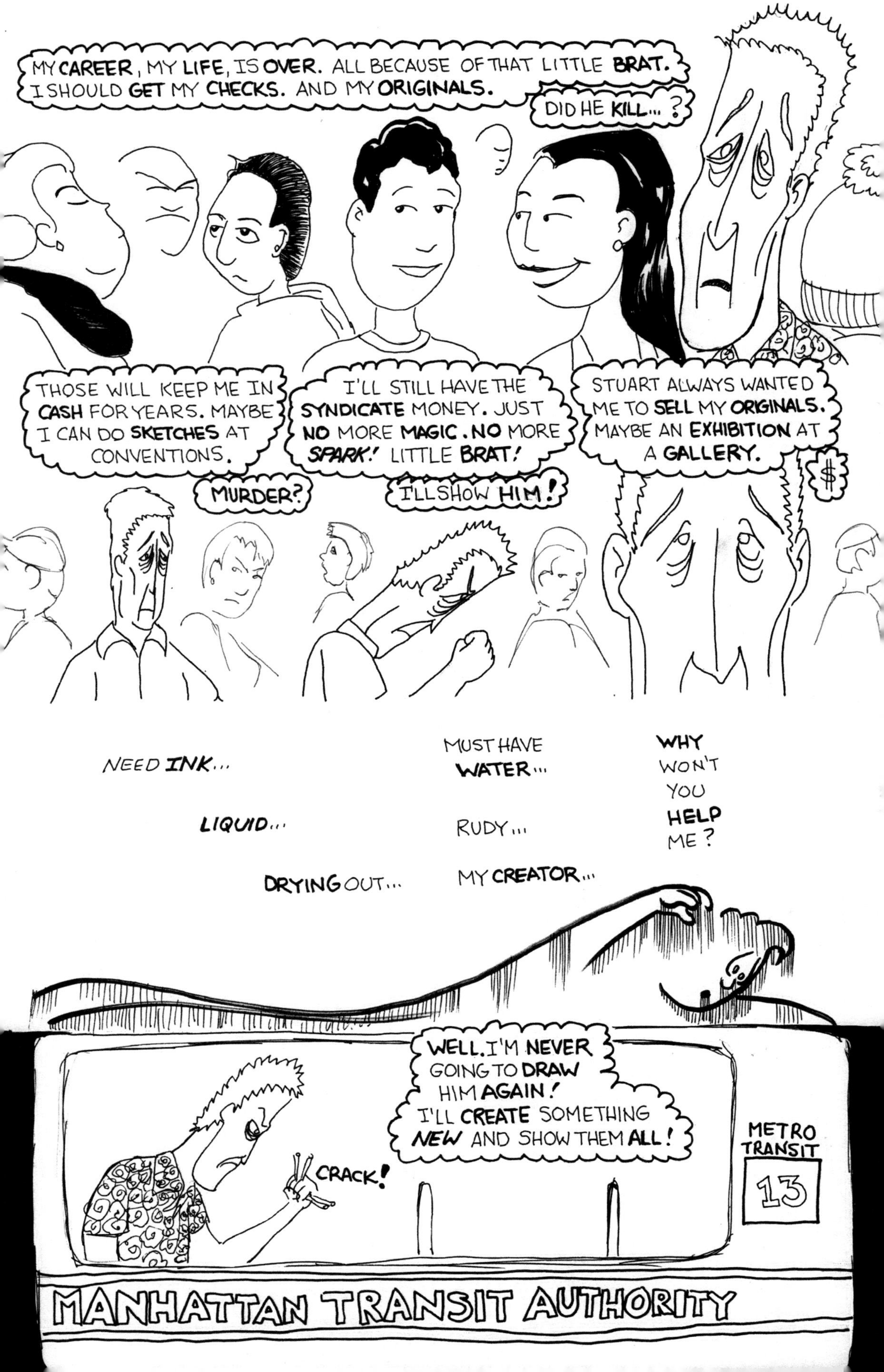
MY CAREER, MY LIFE, IS OVER. ALL BECAUSE OF THAT LITTLE BRAT.
I SHOULD GET MY CHECKS. AND MY ORIGINALS.
DID HE KILL...?
THOSE WILL KEEP ME IN CASH FOR YEARS. MAYBE I CAN DO SKETCHES AT CONVENTIONS.
MURDER?
I'LL STILL HAVE THE SYNDICATE MONEY. JUST NO MORE MAGIC. NO MORE SPARK! LITTLE BRAT!
I'LL SHOW HIM!
STUART ALWAYS WANTED ME TO SELL MY ORIGINALS. MAYBE AN EXHIBITION AT A GALLERY.
$
NEED INK...
LIQUID...
DRYING OUT...
MUST HAVE WATER...
RUDY...
MY CREATOR...
WHY WON'T YOU HELP ME?
WELL. I'M NEVER GOING TO DRAW HIM AGAIN! I'LL CREATE SOMETHING NEW AND SHOW THEM ALL!
CRACK!
METRO TRANSIT
13
MANHATTAN TRANSIT AUTHORITY

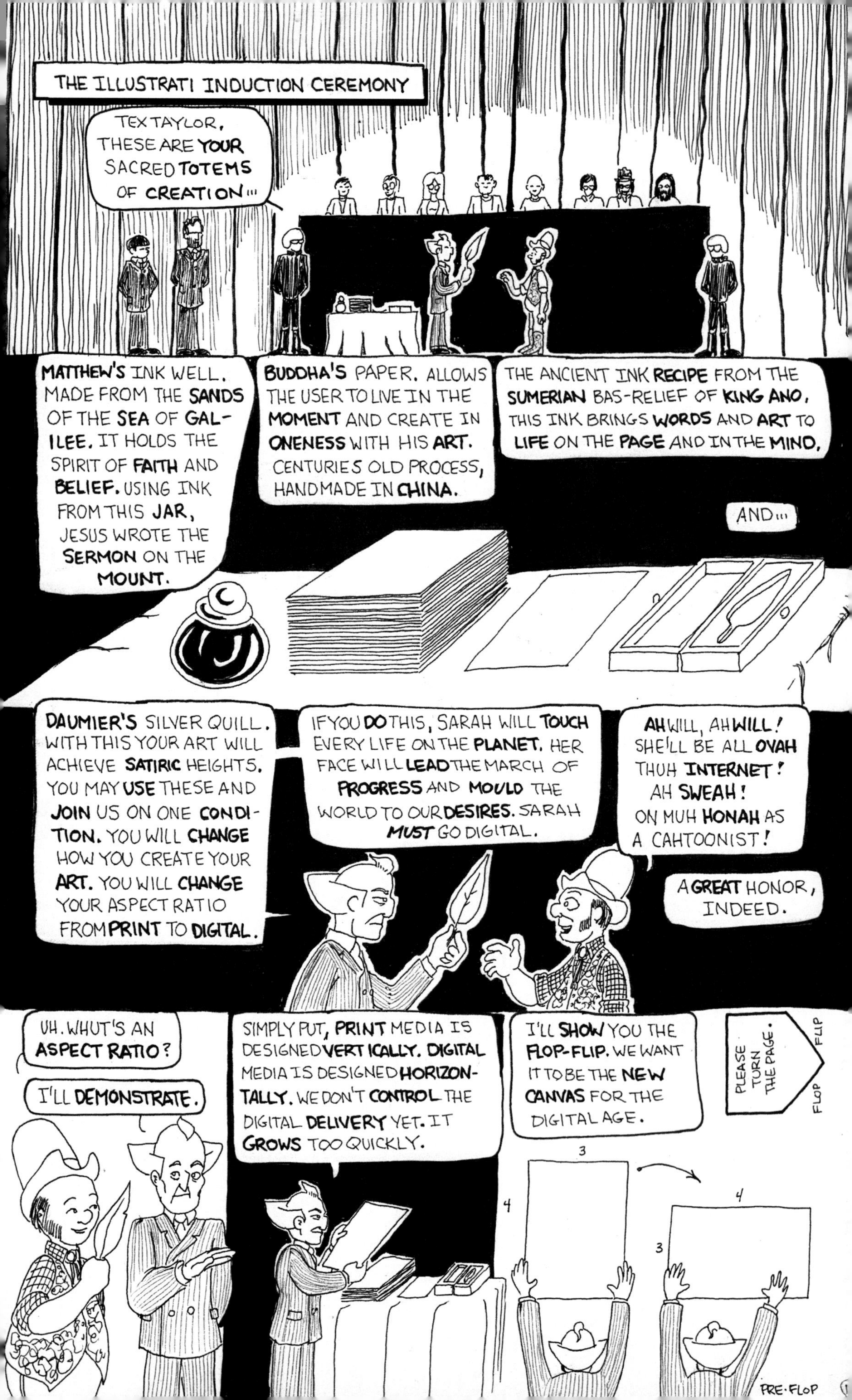
THE ILLUSTRATI INDUCTION CEREMONY
TEX TAYLOR, THESE ARE YOUR SACRED TOTEMS OF CREATION...
MATTHEW'S INK WELL. MADE FROM THE SANDS OF THE SEA OF GALILEE. IT HOLDS THE SPIRIT OF FAITH AND BELIEF. USING INK FROM THIS JAR, JESUS WROTE THE SERMON ON THE MOUNT.
BUDDHA'S PAPER. ALLOWS THE USER TO LIVE IN THE MOMENT AND CREATE IN ONENESS WITH HIS ART. CENTURIES OLD PROCESS, HANDMADE IN CHINA.
THE ANCIENT INK RECIPE FROM THE SUMERIAN BAS-RELIEF OF KING ANO. THIS INK BRINGS WORDS AND ART TO LIFE ON THE PAGE AND IN THE MIND.
AND...
DAUMIER'S SILVER QUILL. WITH THIS YOUR ART WILL ACHIEVE SATIRIC HEIGHTS. YOU MAY USE THESE AND JOIN US ON ONE CONDITION. YOU WILL CHANGE HOW YOU CREATE YOUR ART. YOU WILL CHANGE YOUR ASPECT RATIO FROM PRINT TO DIGITAL.
IF YOU DO THIS, SARAH WILL TOUCH EVERY LIFE ON THE PLANET. HER FACE WILL LEAD THE MARCH OF PROGRESS AND MOULD THE WORLD TO OUR DESIRES. SARAH MUST GO DIGITAL.
AH WILL, AH WILL! SHE'LL BE ALL OVAH THUH INTERNET! AH SWEAH! ON MUH HONAH AS A CAHTOONIST!
A GREAT HONOR, INDEED.
UH. WHUT'S AN ASPECT RATIO?
I'LL DEMONSTRATE.
SIMPLY PUT, PRINT MEDIA IS DESIGNED VERTICALLY. DIGITAL MEDIA IS DESIGNED HORIZONTALLY. WE DON'T CONTROL THE DIGITAL DELIVERY YET. IT GROWS TOO QUICKLY.
I'LL SHOW YOU THE FLOP-FLIP. WE WANT IT TO BE THE NEW CANVAS FOR THE DIGITAL AGE.
PLEASE TURN THE PAGE.
FLOP
FLIP
3
4
4
3
PRE-FLOP

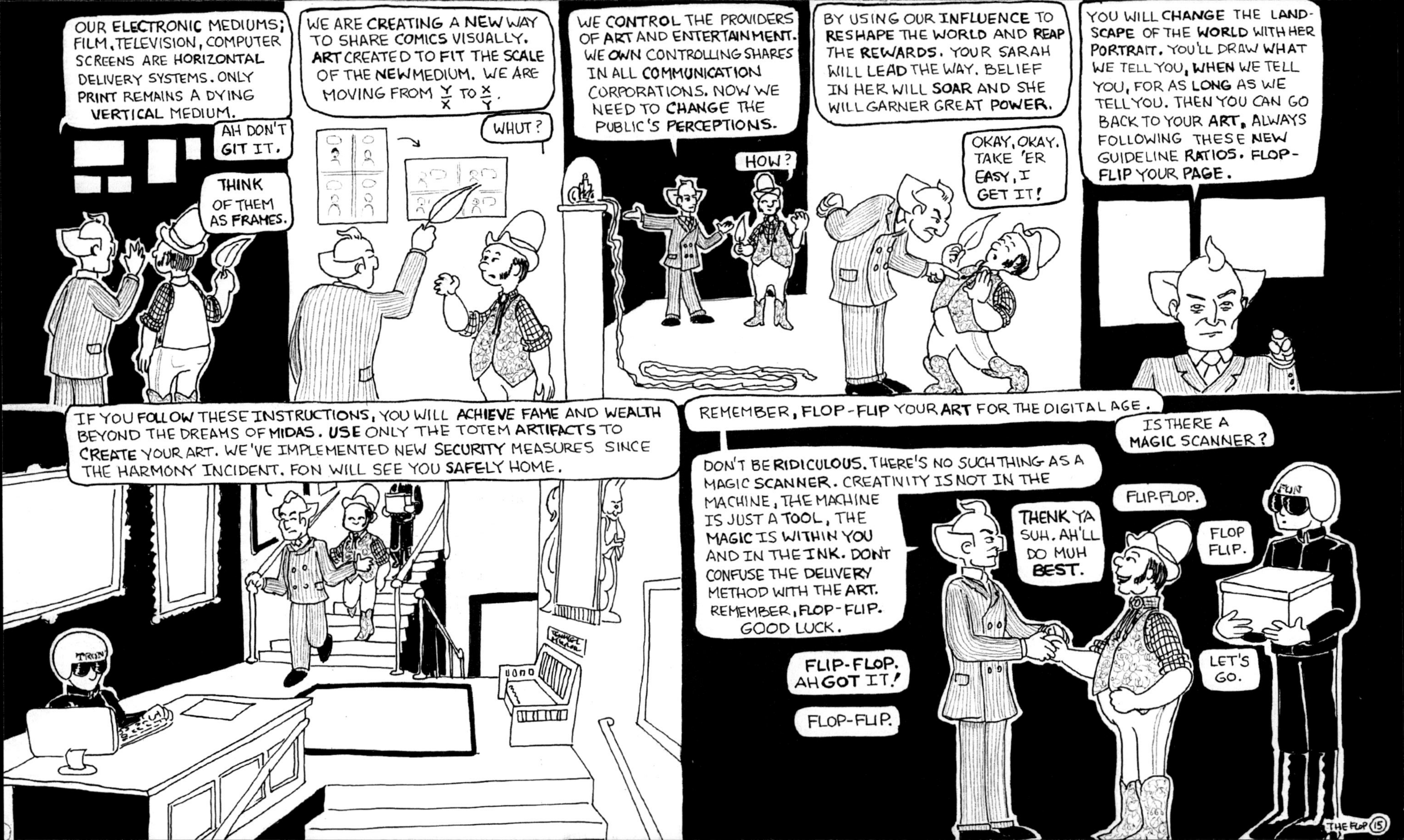
OUR ELECTRONIC MEDIUMS; FILM, TELEVISION, COMPUTER SCREENS ARE HORIZONTAL DELIVERY SYSTEMS. ONLY PRINT REMAINS A DYING VERTICAL MEDIUM.
AH DON'T GIT IT.
THINK OF THEM AS FRAMES.
WE ARE CREATING A NEW WAY TO SHARE COMICS VISUALLY. ART CREATED TO FIT THE SCALE OF THE NEW MEDIUM. WE ARE MOVING FROM Y/X TO X/Y.
WHUT?
WE CONTROL THE PROVIDERS OF ART AND ENTERTAINMENT. WE OWN CONTROLLING SHARES IN ALL COMMUNICATION CORPORATIONS. NOW WE NEED TO CHANGE THE PUBLIC'S PERCEPTIONS.
HOW?
BY USING OUR INFLUENCE TO RESHAPE THE WORLD AND REAP THE REWARDS. YOUR SARAH WILL LEAD THE WAY. BELIEF IN HER WILL SOAR AND SHE WILL GARNER GREAT POWER.
OKAY, OKAY. TAKE 'ER EASY, I GET IT!
YOU WILL CHANGE THE LANDSCAPE OF THE WORLD WITH HER PORTRAIT. YOU'LL DRAW WHAT WE TELL YOU, WHEN WE TELL YOU, FOR AS LONG AS WE TELL YOU. THEN YOU CAN GO BACK TO YOUR ART, ALWAYS FOLLOWING THESE NEW GUIDELINE RATIOS. FLOP-FLIP YOUR PAGE.
IF YOU FOLLOW THESE INSTRUCTIONS, YOU WILL ACHIEVE FAME AND WEALTH BEYOND THE DREAMS OF MIDAS. USE ONLY THE TOTEM ARTIFACTS TO CREATE YOUR ART. WE'VE IMPLEMENTED NEW SECURITY MEASURES SINCE THE HARMONY INCIDENT. FON WILL SEE YOU SAFELY HOME.
TRON
REMEMBER, FLOP-FLIP YOUR ART FOR THE DIGITAL AGE.
IS THERE A MAGIC SCANNER?
DON'T BE RIDICULOUS. THERE'S NO SUCH THING AS A MAGIC SCANNER. CREATIVITY IS NOT IN THE MACHINE, THE MACHINE IS JUST A TOOL, THE MAGIC IS WITHIN YOU AND IN THE INK. DON'T CONFUSE THE DELIVERY METHOD WITH THE ART. REMEMBER, FLOP-FLIP. GOOD LUCK.
THENK YA SUH. AH'LL DO MUH BEST.
FLIP-FLOP.
FLOP FLIP.
FON
FLIP-FLOP. AH GOT IT!
FLOP-FLIP.
LET'S GO.
THE FLOP 15

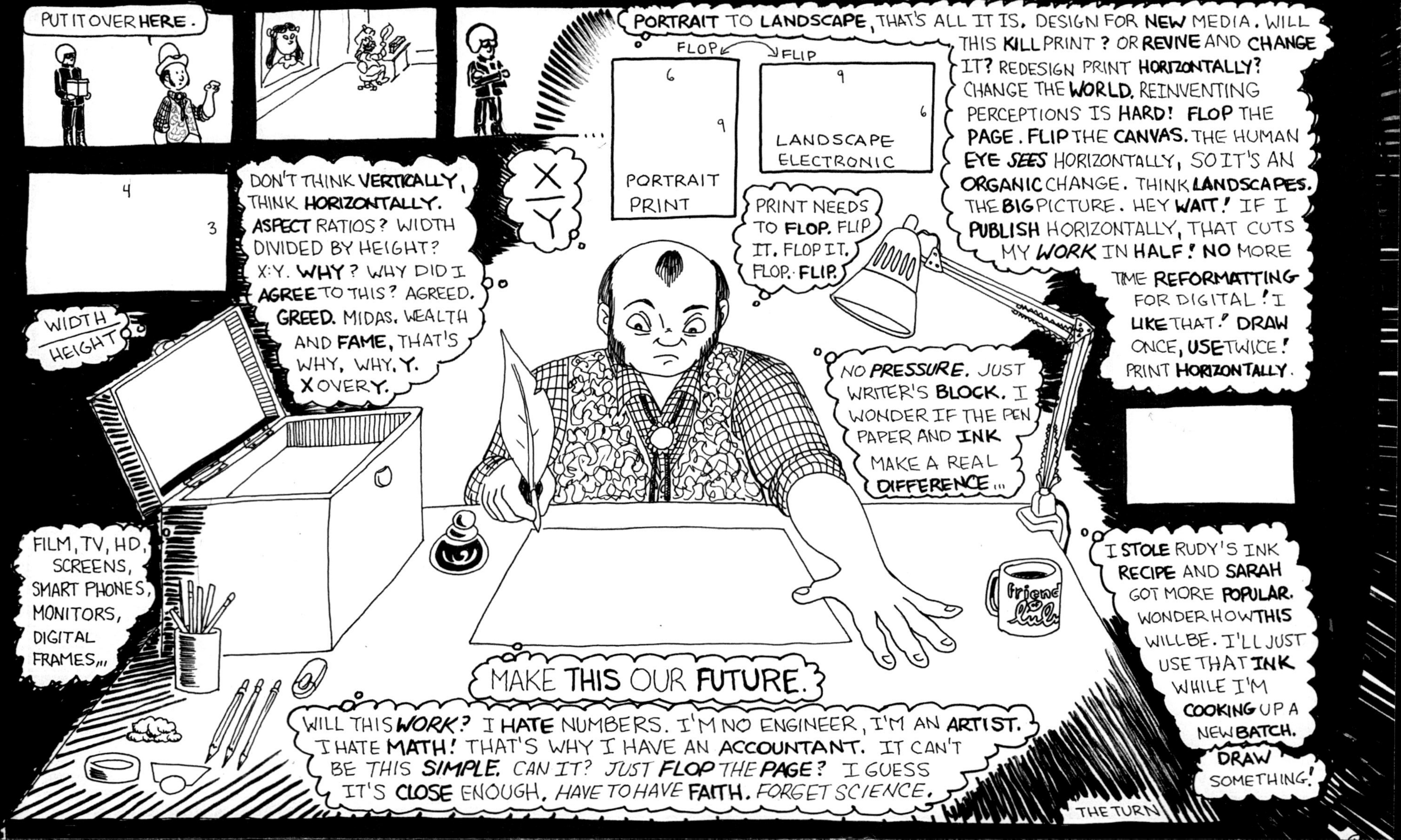
PUT IT OVER HERE.
PORTRAIT TO LANDSCAPE, THAT'S ALL IT IS. DESIGN FOR NEW MEDIA. WILL THIS KILL PRINT? OR REVIVE AND CHANGE IT? REDESIGN PRINT HORIZONTALLY? CHANGE THE WORLD. REINVENTING PERCEPTIONS IS HARD! FLOP THE PAGE. FLIP THE CANVAS. THE HUMAN EYE SEES HORIZONTALLY, SO IT'S AN ORGANIC CHANGE. THINK LANDSCAPES. THE BIG PICTURE. HEY WAIT! IF I PUBLISH HORIZONTALLY, THAT CUTS MY WORK IN HALF! NO MORE TIME REFORMATTING FOR DIGITAL! I LIKE THAT! DRAW ONCE, USE TWICE! PRINT HORIZONTALLY.
FLOP
FLIP
6
9
PORTRAIT
PRINT
9
6
LANDSCAPE
ELECTRONIC
4
3
X
Y
DON'T THINK VERTICALLY, THINK HORIZONTALLY. ASPECT RATIOS? WIDTH DIVIDED BY HEIGHT? X:Y. WHY? WHY DID I AGREE TO THIS? AGREED. GREED. MIDAS. WEALTH AND FAME, THAT'S WHY, WHY, Y. X OVER Y.
WIDTH
HEIGHT
PRINT NEEDS TO FLOP. FLIP IT. FLOP IT. FLOP. FLIP.
NO PRESSURE. JUST WRITER'S BLOCK. I WONDER IF THE PEN PAPER AND INK MAKE A REAL DIFFERENCE...
FILM, TV, HD, SCREENS, SMART PHONES, MONITORS, DIGITAL FRAMES...
friend ink
I STOLE RUDY'S INK RECIPE AND SARAH GOT MORE POPULAR. WONDER HOW THIS WILL BE. I'LL JUST USE THAT INK WHILE I'M COOKING UP A NEW BATCH.
DRAW SOMETHING!
MAKE THIS OUR FUTURE.
WILL THIS WORK? I HATE NUMBERS. I'M NO ENGINEER, I'M AN ARTIST. I HATE MATH! THAT'S WHY I HAVE AN ACCOUNTANT. IT CAN'T BE THIS SIMPLE. CAN IT? JUST FLOP THE PAGE? I GUESS IT'S CLOSE ENOUGH. HAVE TO HAVE FAITH. FORGET SCIENCE.
THE TURN

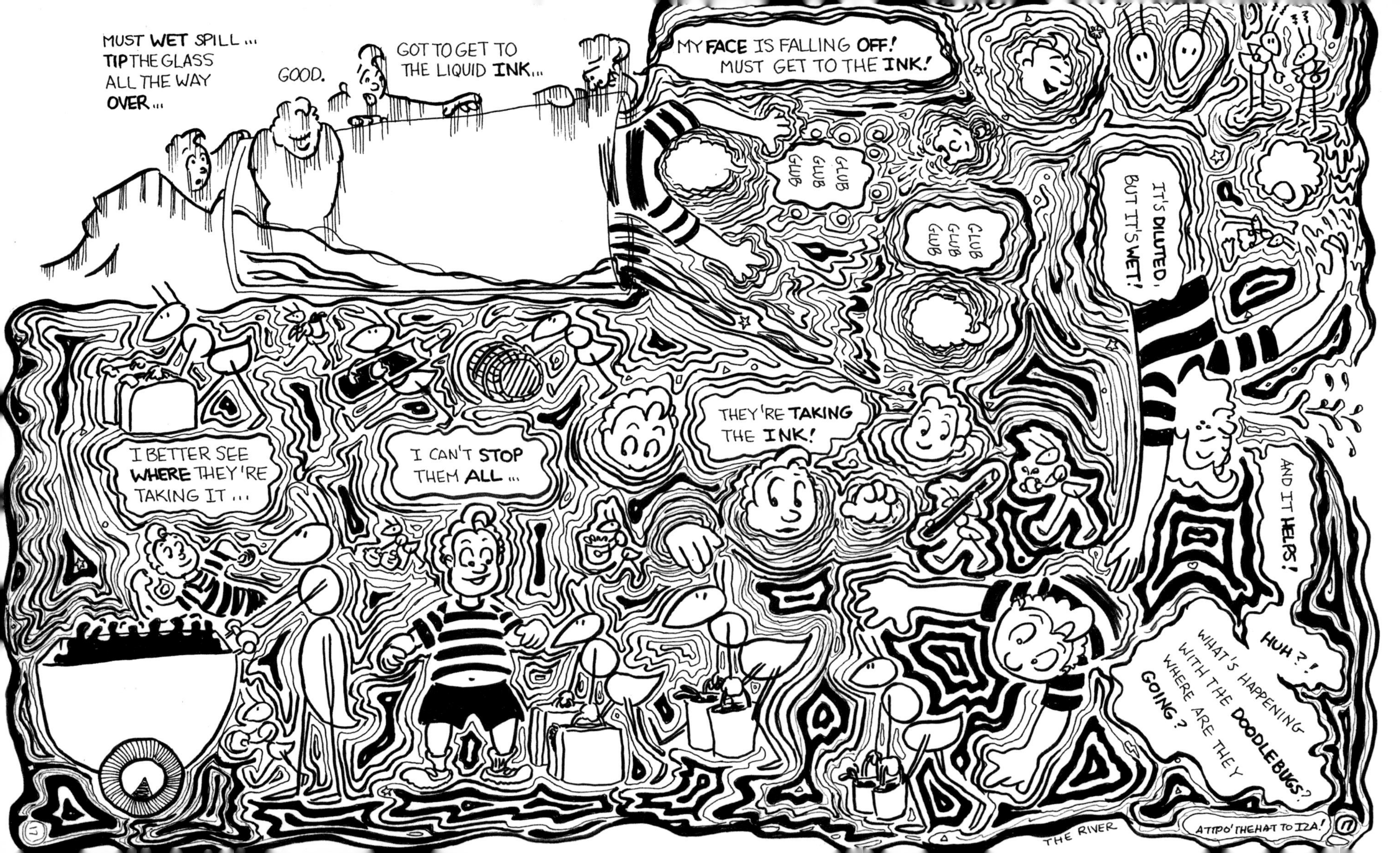
MUST WET SPILL ... TIP THE GLASS ALL THE WAY OVER ...
GOOD.
GOT TO GET TO THE LIQUID INK ...
MY FACE IS FALLING OFF! MUST GET TO THE INK!
GLUB GLUB GLUB
GLUB GLUB GLUB
IT'S DILUTED, BUT IT'S WET!
AND IT HELPS!
HUH?!
WHAT'S HAPPENING WITH THE DOODLEBUGS? WHERE ARE THEY GOING?
THEY'RE TAKING THE INK!
I CAN'T STOP THEM ALL ...
I BETTER SEE WHERE THEY'RE TAKING IT ...
THE RIVER
A TIP O' THE HAT TO IZA!

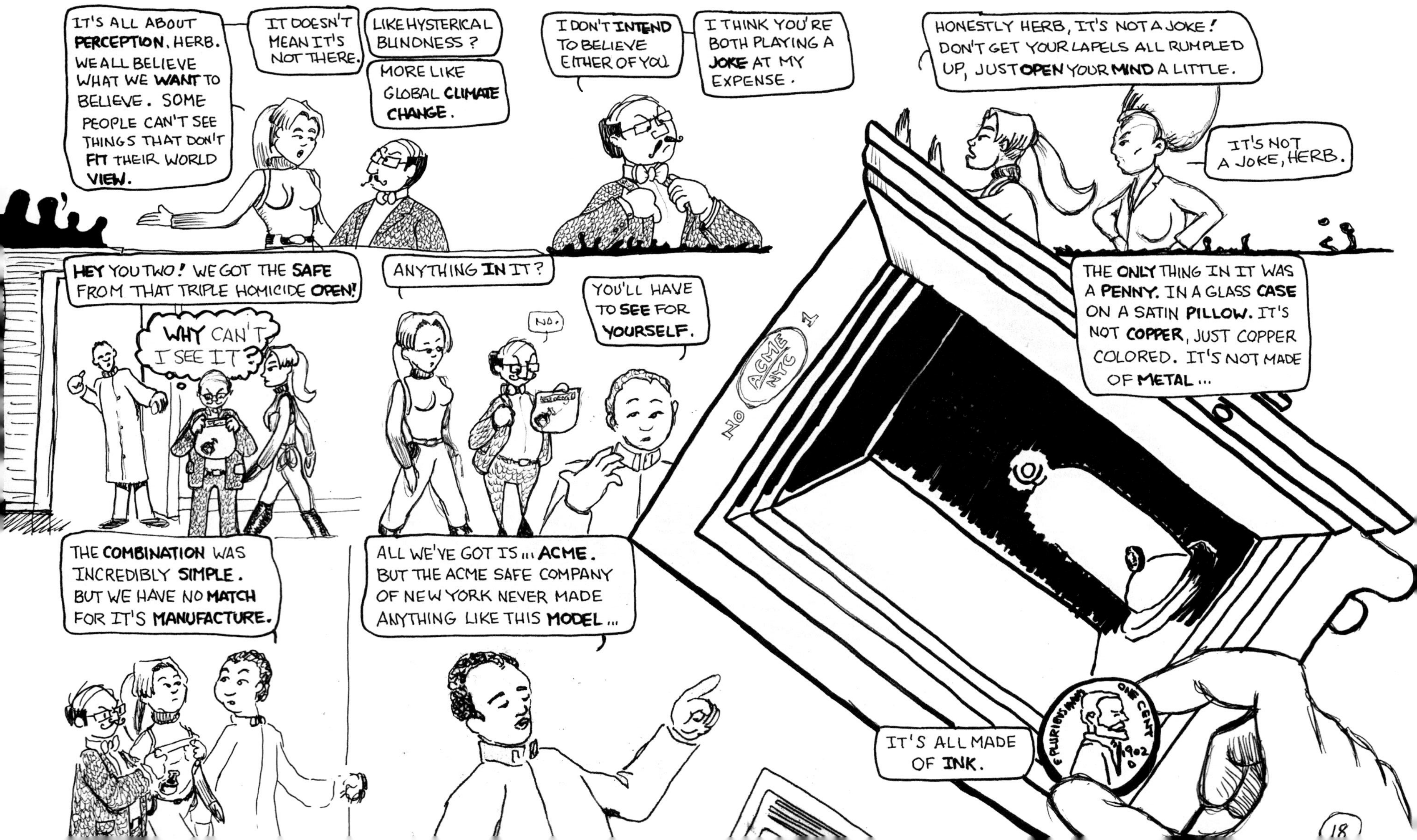

IT'S ALL ABOUT **PERCEPTION**, HERB. WE ALL BELIEVE WHAT WE **WANT** TO BELIEVE. SOME PEOPLE CAN'T SEE THINGS THAT DON'T **FIT** THEIR WORLD **VIEW**.
IT DOESN'T MEAN IT'S NOT THERE.
LIKE HYSTERICAL BLINDNESS?
MORE LIKE GLOBAL **CLIMATE CHANGE**.
I DON'T **INTEND** TO BELIEVE EITHER OF YOU.
I THINK YOU'RE BOTH PLAYING A **JOKE** AT MY EXPENSE.
HONESTLY HERB, IT'S NOT A JOKE! DON'T GET YOUR LAPELS ALL RUMPLED UP, JUST **OPEN** YOUR **MIND** A LITTLE.
IT'S NOT A JOKE, HERB.
HEY YOU TWO! WE GOT THE **SAFE** FROM THAT TRIPLE HOMICIDE **OPEN**!
WHY CAN'T I SEE IT?
ANYTHING **IN** IT?
NO.
YOU'LL HAVE TO **SEE** FOR **YOURSELF**.
NO ACME NYC 1
THE **ONLY** THING IN IT WAS A **PENNY**. IN A GLASS **CASE** ON A SATIN **PILLOW**. IT'S NOT **COPPER**, JUST COPPER COLORED. IT'S NOT MADE OF **METAL**...
THE **COMBINATION** WAS INCREDIBLY **SIMPLE**. BUT WE HAVE NO **MATCH** FOR IT'S **MANUFACTURE**.
ALL WE'VE GOT IS... **ACME**. BUT THE ACME SAFE COMPANY OF NEW YORK NEVER MADE ANYTHING LIKE THIS **MODEL**...
ONE CENT
E PLURIBUS UNUM
1902
IT'S ALL MADE OF **INK**.

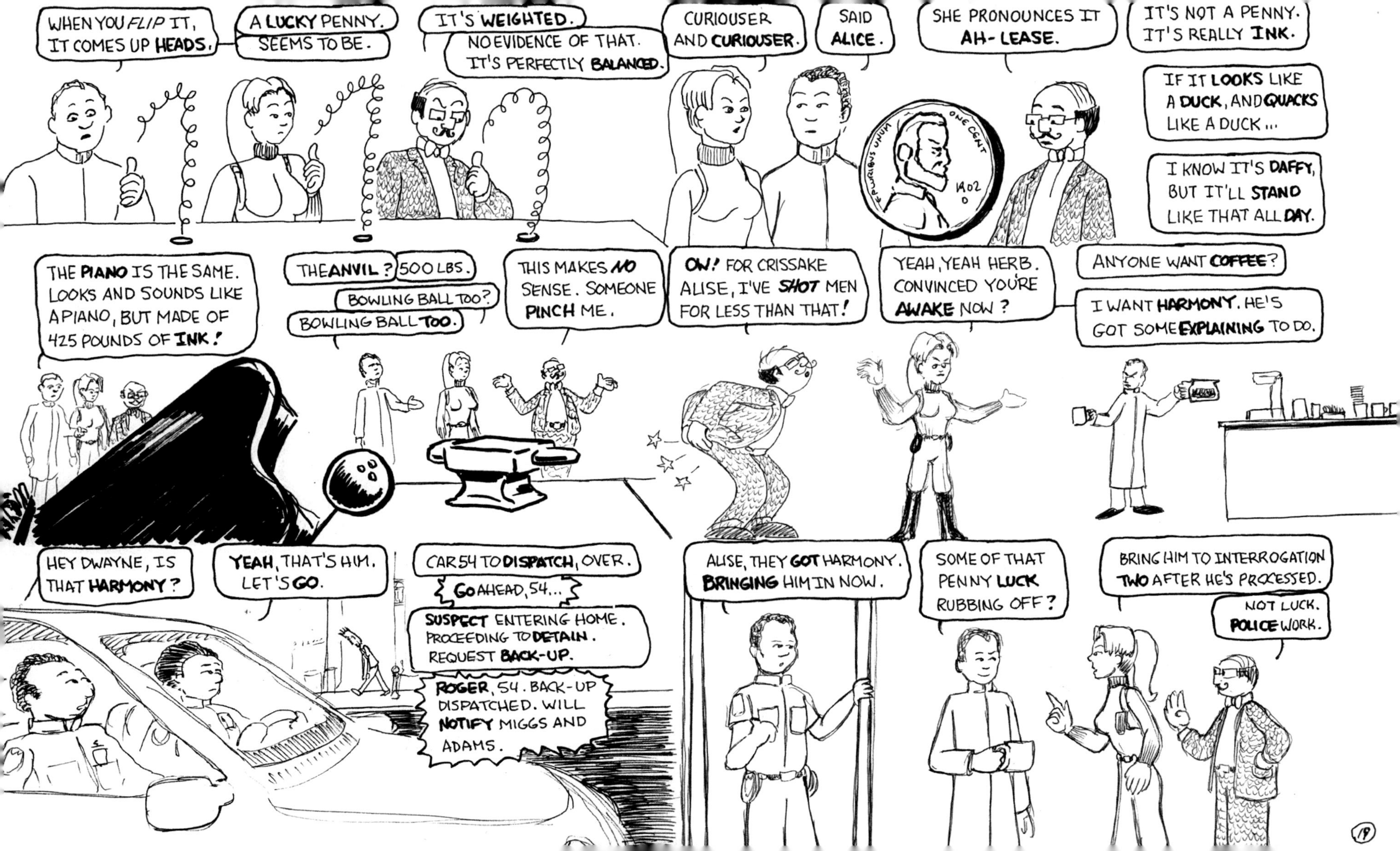
WHEN YOU FLIP IT, IT COMES UP HEADS.
A LUCKY PENNY.
SEEMS TO BE.
IT'S WEIGHTED.
NO EVIDENCE OF THAT. IT'S PERFECTLY BALANCED.
CURIOUSER AND CURIOUSER.
SAID ALICE.
SHE PRONOUNCES IT AH-LEASE.
IT'S NOT A PENNY. IT'S REALLY INK.
IF IT LOOKS LIKE A DUCK, AND QUACKS LIKE A DUCK...
I KNOW IT'S DAFFY, BUT IT'LL STAND LIKE THAT ALL DAY.
ONE CENT
1902
E PLURIBUS UNUM
THE PIANO IS THE SAME. LOOKS AND SOUNDS LIKE A PIANO, BUT MADE OF 425 POUNDS OF INK!
THE ANVIL?
500 LBS.
BOWLING BALL TOO?
BOWLING BALL TOO.
THIS MAKES NO SENSE. SOMEONE PINCH ME.
OW! FOR CRISSAKE ALISE, I'VE SHOT MEN FOR LESS THAN THAT!
YEAH, YEAH HERB. CONVINCED YOU'RE AWAKE NOW?
ANYONE WANT COFFEE?
I WANT HARMONY. HE'S GOT SOME EXPLAINING TO DO.
HEY DWAYNE, IS THAT HARMONY?
YEAH, THAT'S HIM. LET'S GO.
CAR 54 TO DISPATCH, OVER.
GO AHEAD, 54...
SUSPECT ENTERING HOME. PROCEEDING TO DETAIN. REQUEST BACK-UP.
ROGER, 54. BACK-UP DISPATCHED. WILL NOTIFY MIGGS AND ADAMS.
ALISE, THEY GOT HARMONY. BRINGING HIM IN NOW.
SOME OF THAT PENNY LUCK RUBBING OFF?
BRING HIM TO INTERROGATION TWO AFTER HE'S PROCESSED.
NOT LUCK. POLICE WORK.

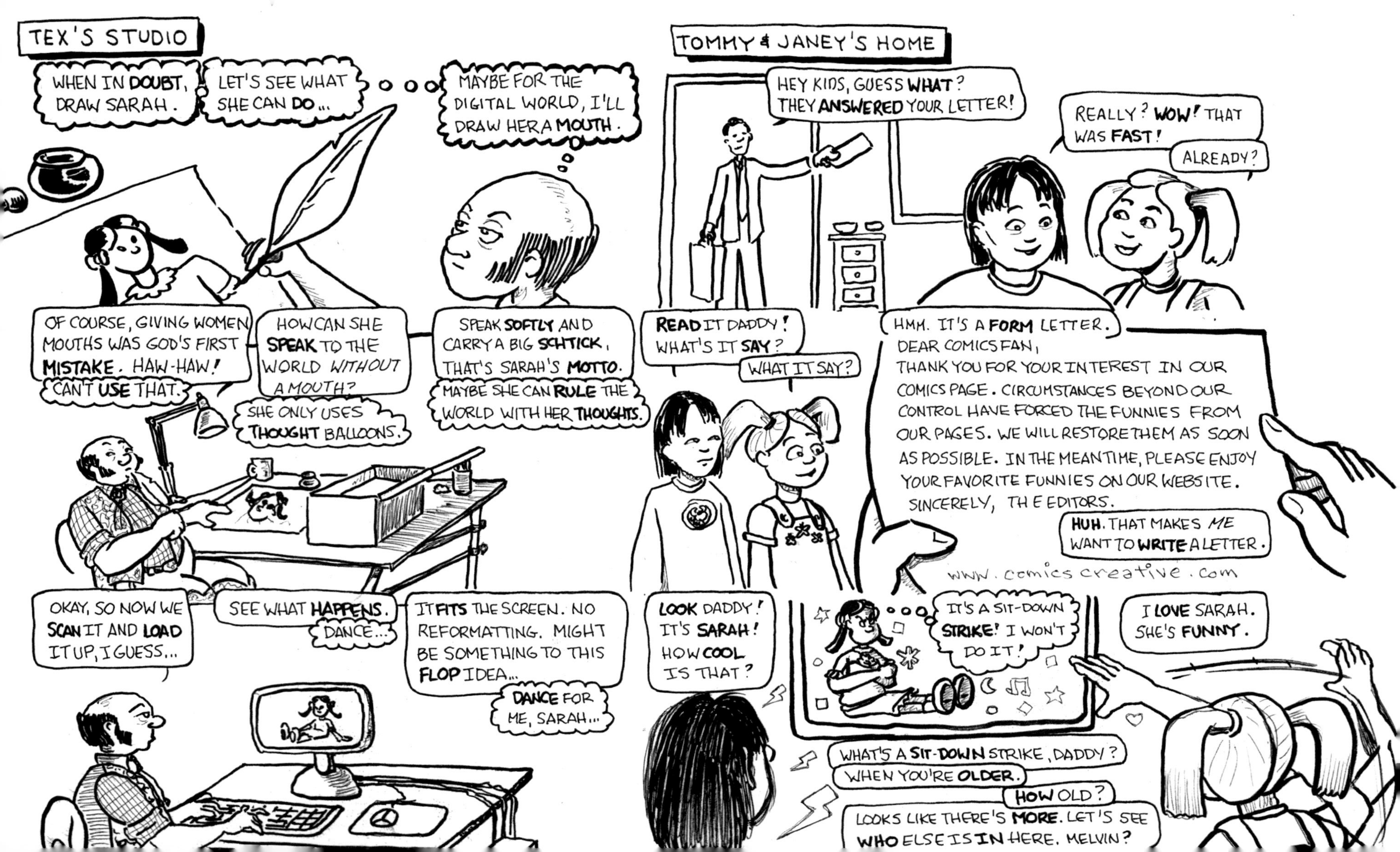
TEX'S STUDIO
WHEN IN DOUBT, DRAW SARAH.
LET'S SEE WHAT SHE CAN DO...
MAYBE FOR THE DIGITAL WORLD, I'LL DRAW HER A MOUTH.
OF COURSE, GIVING WOMEN MOUTHS WAS GOD'S FIRST MISTAKE. HAW-HAW!
CAN'T USE THAT.
HOW CAN SHE SPEAK TO THE WORLD WITHOUT A MOUTH?
SHE ONLY USES THOUGHT BALLOONS.
SPEAK SOFTLY AND CARRY A BIG SCHTICK, THAT'S SARAH'S MOTTO.
MAYBE SHE CAN RULE THE WORLD WITH HER THOUGHTS.
OKAY, SO NOW WE SCAN IT AND LOAD IT UP, I GUESS...
SEE WHAT HAPPENS.
DANCE...
IT FITS THE SCREEN. NO REFORMATTING. MIGHT BE SOMETHING TO THIS FLOP IDEA...
DANCE FOR ME, SARAH...
TOMMY & JANEY'S HOME
HEY KIDS, GUESS WHAT? THEY ANSWERED YOUR LETTER!
REALLY? WOW! THAT WAS FAST!
ALREADY?
READ IT DADDY! WHAT'S IT SAY?
WHAT IT SAY?
HMM. IT'S A FORM LETTER.
DEAR COMICS FAN,
THANK YOU FOR YOUR INTEREST IN OUR COMICS PAGE. CIRCUMSTANCES BEYOND OUR CONTROL HAVE FORCED THE FUNNIES FROM OUR PAGES. WE WILL RESTORE THEM AS SOON AS POSSIBLE. IN THE MEANTIME, PLEASE ENJOY YOUR FAVORITE FUNNIES ON OUR WEBSITE.
SINCERELY, THE EDITORS.
HUH. THAT MAKES ME WANT TO WRITE A LETTER.
www.comicscreative.com
LOOK DADDY! IT'S SARAH! HOW COOL IS THAT?
IT'S A SIT-DOWN STRIKE! I WON'T DO IT!
I LOVE SARAH. SHE'S FUNNY.
WHAT'S A SIT-DOWN STRIKE, DADDY?
WHEN YOU'RE OLDER.
HOW OLD?
LOOKS LIKE THERE'S MORE. LET'S SEE WHO ELSE IS IN HERE. MELVIN?

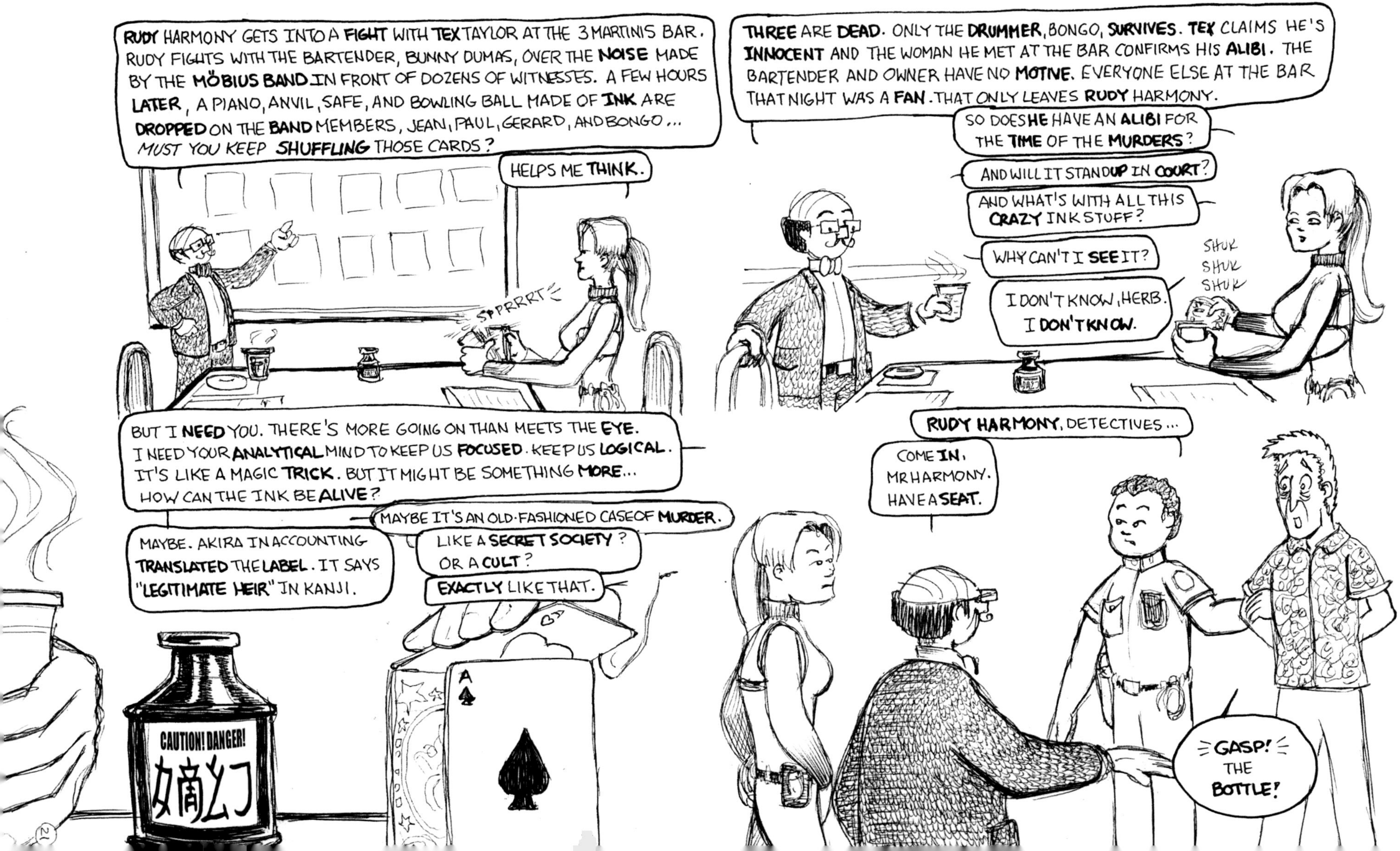
RUDY HARMONY GETS INTO A FIGHT WITH TEX TAYLOR AT THE 3 MARTINIS BAR. RUDY FIGHTS WITH THE BARTENDER, BUNNY DUMAS, OVER THE NOISE MADE BY THE MÖBIUS BAND IN FRONT OF DOZENS OF WITNESSES. A FEW HOURS LATER, A PIANO, ANVIL, SAFE, AND BOWLING BALL MADE OF INK ARE DROPPED ON THE BAND MEMBERS, JEAN, PAUL, GERARD, AND BONGO... MUST YOU KEEP SHUFFLING THOSE CARDS?
HELPS ME THINK.
SPPRRRT
THREE ARE DEAD. ONLY THE DRUMMER, BONGO, SURVIVES. TEX CLAIMS HE'S INNOCENT AND THE WOMAN HE MET AT THE BAR CONFIRMS HIS ALIBI. THE BARTENDER AND OWNER HAVE NO MOTIVE. EVERYONE ELSE AT THE BAR THAT NIGHT WAS A FAN. THAT ONLY LEAVES RUDY HARMONY.
SO DOES HE HAVE AN ALIBI FOR THE TIME OF THE MURDERS?
AND WILL IT STAND UP IN COURT?
AND WHAT'S WITH ALL THIS CRAZY INK STUFF?
WHY CAN'T I SEE IT?
SHUK SHUK SHUK
I DON'T KNOW, HERB. I DON'T KNOW.
BUT I NEED YOU. THERE'S MORE GOING ON THAN MEETS THE EYE. I NEED YOUR ANALYTICAL MIND TO KEEP US FOCUSED. KEEP US LOGICAL. IT'S LIKE A MAGIC TRICK. BUT IT MIGHT BE SOMETHING MORE... HOW CAN THE INK BE ALIVE?
MAYBE IT'S AN OLD-FASHIONED CASE OF MURDER.
MAYBE. AKIRA IN ACCOUNTING TRANSLATED THE LABEL. IT SAYS "LEGITIMATE HEIR" IN KANJI.
LIKE A SECRET SOCIETY? OR A CULT?
EXACTLY LIKE THAT.
CAUTION! DANGER!
RUDY HARMONY, DETECTIVES...
COME IN, MR HARMONY. HAVE A SEAT.
GASP! THE BOTTLE!

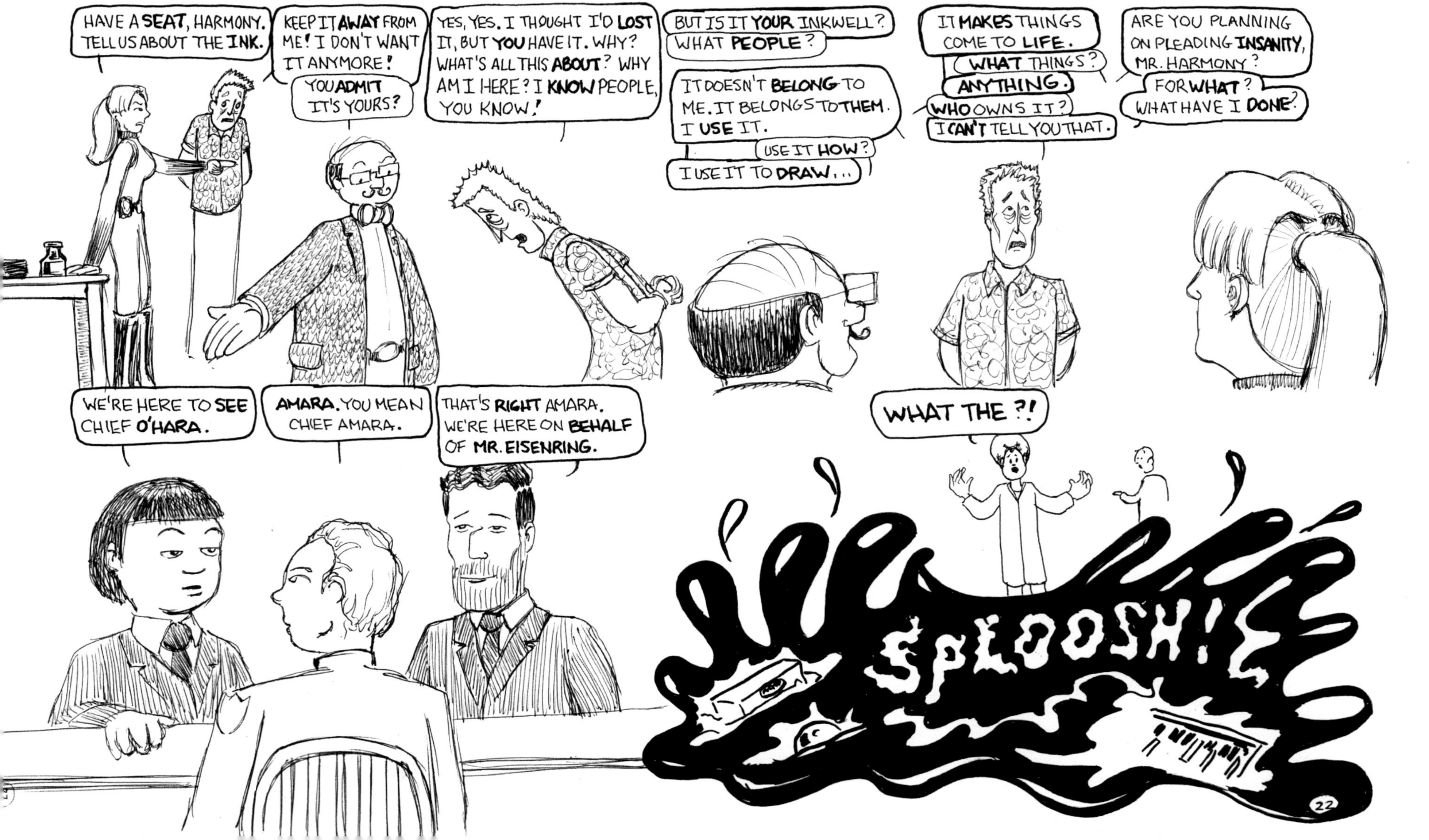
HAVE A SEAT, HARMONY. TELL US ABOUT THE INK.
KEEP IT AWAY FROM ME! I DON'T WANT IT ANYMORE!
YOU ADMIT IT'S YOURS?
YES, YES. I THOUGHT I'D LOST IT, BUT YOU HAVE IT. WHY? WHAT'S ALL THIS ABOUT? WHY AM I HERE? I KNOW PEOPLE, YOU KNOW!
BUT IS IT YOUR INKWELL?
WHAT PEOPLE?
IT DOESN'T BELONG TO ME. IT BELONGS TO THEM. I USE IT.
USE IT HOW?
I USE IT TO DRAW...
IT MAKES THINGS COME TO LIFE.
WHAT THINGS?
ANYTHING.
WHO OWNS IT?
I CAN'T TELL YOU THAT.
ARE YOU PLANNING ON PLEADING INSANITY, MR. HARMONY?
FOR WHAT? WHAT HAVE I DONE?
WE'RE HERE TO SEE CHIEF O'HARA.
AMARA. YOU MEAN CHIEF AMARA.
THAT'S RIGHT AMARA. WE'RE HERE ON BEHALF OF MR. EISENRING.
WHAT THE?!
SPLOOSH!
22

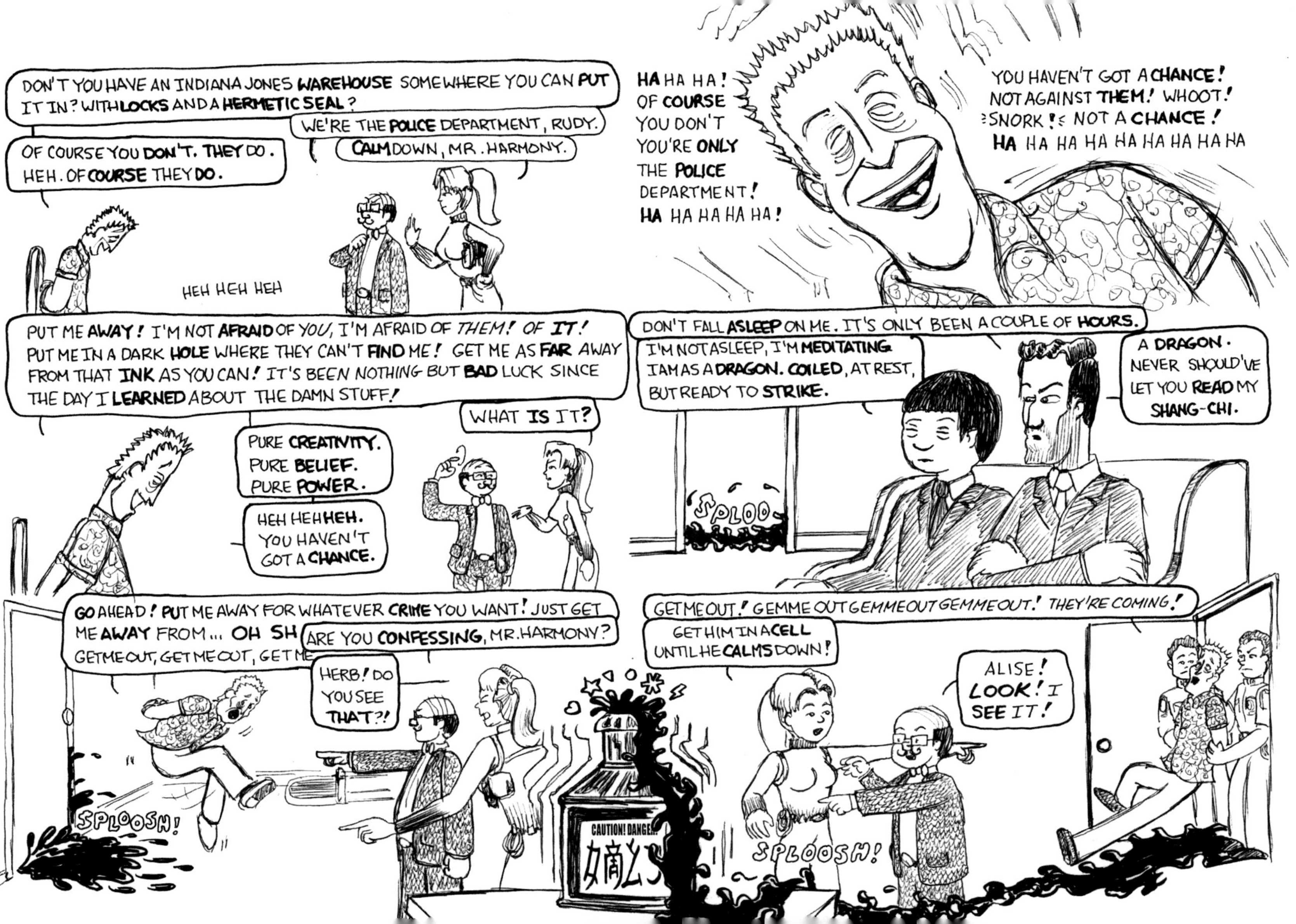
DON'T YOU HAVE AN INDIANA JONES WAREHOUSE SOMEWHERE YOU CAN PUT IT IN? WITH LOCKS AND A HERMETIC SEAL?
WE'RE THE POLICE DEPARTMENT, RUDY.
OF COURSE YOU DON'T. THEY DO. HEH. OF COURSE THEY DO.
CALM DOWN, MR. HARMONY.
HEH HEH HEH
HA HA HA! OF COURSE YOU DON'T YOU'RE ONLY THE POLICE DEPARTMENT! HA HA HA HA HA!
YOU HAVEN'T GOT A CHANCE! NOT AGAINST THEM! WHOOT! SNORK! NOT A CHANCE! HA HA HA HA HA HA HA HA HA
PUT ME AWAY! I'M NOT AFRAID OF YOU, I'M AFRAID OF THEM! OF IT! PUT ME IN A DARK HOLE WHERE THEY CAN'T FIND ME! GET ME AS FAR AWAY FROM THAT INK AS YOU CAN! IT'S BEEN NOTHING BUT BAD LUCK SINCE THE DAY I LEARNED ABOUT THE DAMN STUFF!
WHAT IS IT?
PURE CREATIVITY. PURE BELIEF. PURE POWER.
HEH HEH HEH. YOU HAVEN'T GOT A CHANCE.
DON'T FALL ASLEEP ON ME. IT'S ONLY BEEN A COUPLE OF HOURS.
I'M NOT ASLEEP, I'M MEDITATING. I AM AS A DRAGON. COILED, AT REST, BUT READY TO STRIKE.
A DRAGON. NEVER SHOULD'VE LET YOU READ MY SHANG-CHI.
SPLOO
GO AHEAD! PUT ME AWAY FOR WHATEVER CRIME YOU WANT! JUST GET ME AWAY FROM... OH SH
GET ME OUT, GET ME OUT, GET ME
ARE YOU CONFESSING, MR. HARMONY?
HERB! DO YOU SEE THAT?!
SPLOOSH!
CAUTION! DANGER!
GET ME OUT! GEMME OUT GEMME OUT GEMME OUT! THEY'RE COMING!
GET HIM IN A CELL UNTIL HE CALMS DOWN!
ALISE! LOOK! I SEE IT!
SPLOOSH!

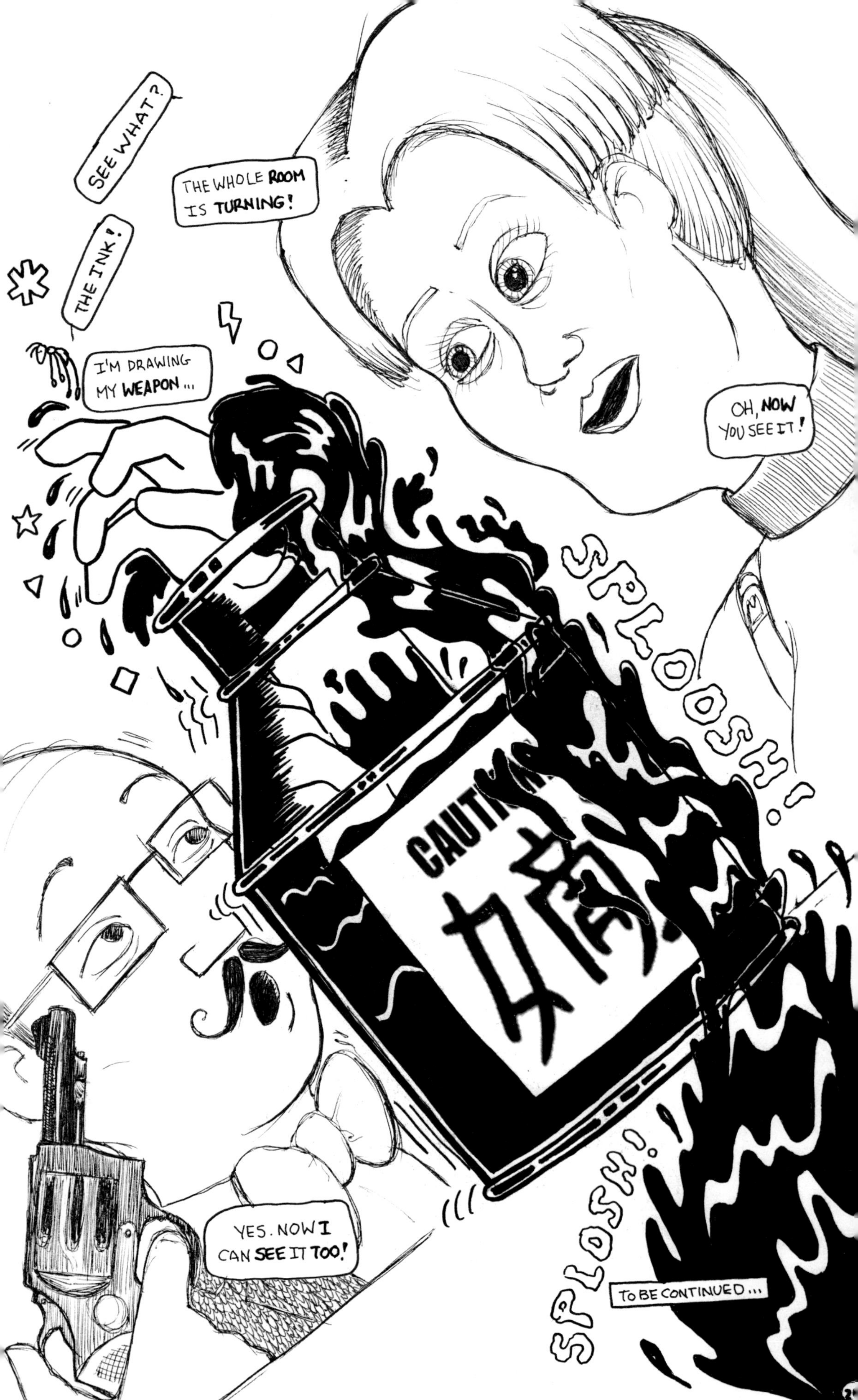
SEE WHAT?
THE WHOLE ROOM IS TURNING!
THE INK!
I'M DRAWING MY WEAPON...
OH, NOW YOU SEE IT!
CAUTION
SPLOOSH!
YES. NOW I CAN SEE IT TOO!
SPLOSH!
TO BE CONTINUED...

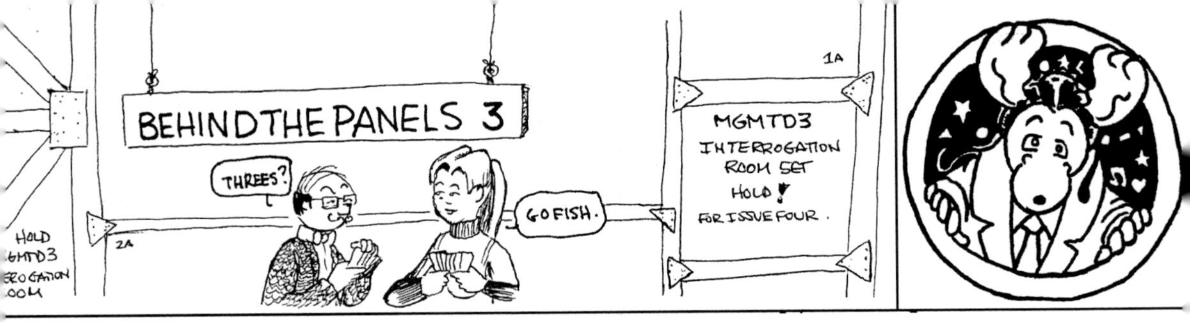
BEHIND THE PANELS 3
THREES?
GO FISH.
1A
MGMTD3 INTERROGATION ROOM SET HOLD! FOR ISSUE FOUR.
2A

THE KEY TO THE COVER. A HISTORY OF THE MAGIC INK. HAVE FUN! GOOD LUCK!

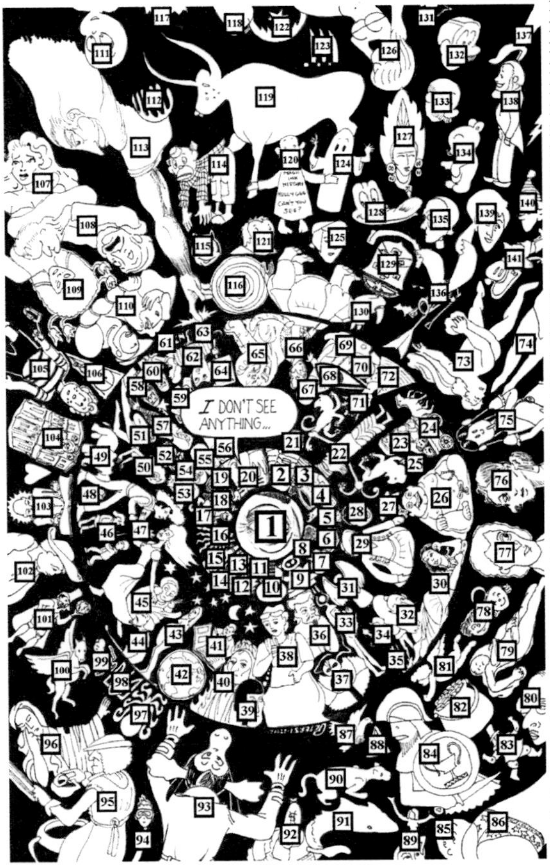
I DON'T SEE ANYTHING...

1. Herbert Miggs
   Threed NYPD Detective
2. Anu
3. Archimedes
4. Dionysus
5. Grendel
6. Poetic Edda
7. Death
8. Treasure
9. Erazer
10. Music
11. Pine Galls
12. Quill Pen
13. Papyrus
14. Hippocrates Caduceus
15. Labels
16. Light
17. Aesop
18. Lo Shu Magic Squares
19. Egyptian Cuneiform
20. Language and Writing
21. King of Beasts
22. Gilgamesh
23. Hroswitha
24. Thespis
25. Eternal Life
26. Laughing Buddha
27. Chaucer
28. Mahabarata
29. Omar Khayyam
30. Shakuntala
31. Illumination
32. Scheherazade
33. Cleopatra
34. Everyman
35. Hamsa
36. Confucious
37. Mask Design
38. Herodutus' Clio
39. Faust
40. Dante Alighieri
41. Guttenberg
42. Cristobol Columbus
43. Birth
44. Robin Hood
45. Gammer Gurton
46. Piccini, Punch and Judy
47. Romeo and Juliet
48. Gambling
49. Native Art
50. Erotica
51. Plautus
52. Math
53. Aristophanes
54. Plato
55. Aristotle
56. Tiahuanaco
57. J.M. Barrie
58. Parables
59. Entertainment
60. Abelard and Heliose
61. Law
62. Machiavelli
63. Declaration of
    Independence
64. Magna Carta
65. Maruyama Okyo
66. Kyoto School
67. Saint Peter
68. Nefertiti eye paint
69. Mapmaking
70. Geometry
71. Portrait painting
72. Architecture
73. Titian
74. Raphael
75. Tex Taylor, Sarah da Terrah
76. Female Pen Sketch
77. El Greco
78. Rudolph Dirks
79. Reclining Figure
80. Pablo Picasso
81. Sandro Botticelli
82. Pot of Luck
83. Marionette
84. One Grecian Urn
85. Herge
86. William Moulton Marston
87. Dioscorides.
88. Mystic Symbols
89. Frans Masereel
90. Panther
91. A Big Fish
92. Thomas Nast
93. Melvin G. Moose, Toode Dick
94. Jack Cole
95. Pieter Bruegel the elder
96. Sorrow
97. Euboean Octopus
98. Ukranian Falcon
99. George Herriman
100. Pegasus
101. Sir Francis Drake
102. Honore Daumier, Miguel de Cervantes
103. William Shakespeare
104. Inigo Jones
105. Rudy Harmony, Matty the Bratty
106. Galileo Galilei
107. Al Capp
108. Violence
109. Aubrey Beardsley
110. The Artist's Dying Breath
111. Seymour Reit, Joe Oriolo
112. Wassily Kandinsky
113. Michelangelo
114. F. B. Opper
115. Otto Messmer
116. Copernicus
117. - 118. Matt Groening
119. Lascaux Caves
120. Richard F. Outcault
121. Winsor McCay
122. Jack Kirby
123. Design
124. Boo!
125. Vincent Van Gogh
126. Mort Walker
127. Inspiration
128. Walt Kelly
129. Heraldry
130. Albrecht Durer
131. Osama Tezuka
132. - 133. Bud Fisher
134. James Swinnerton
135. Max Beerbohm
136. Leonardo Da Vinci
137. Harvey Kurtzman
138. Leslie Ward
139. Amedeo Modigliani
140. Martin Hanford
141. James Gillray
142. The inkwell is
     currently in the hands
     of the Threed NYPD.

re: SOURCES

Every idea that has ever been or ever will be lives in the Magic Ink. The magic inks, magic paints, and magic dyes hold the universe of our collective imagination and global conciousness within them. They have been gifted to many hands throughout the history of the threed world. We have left our mark with them, and they have left their mark on us.

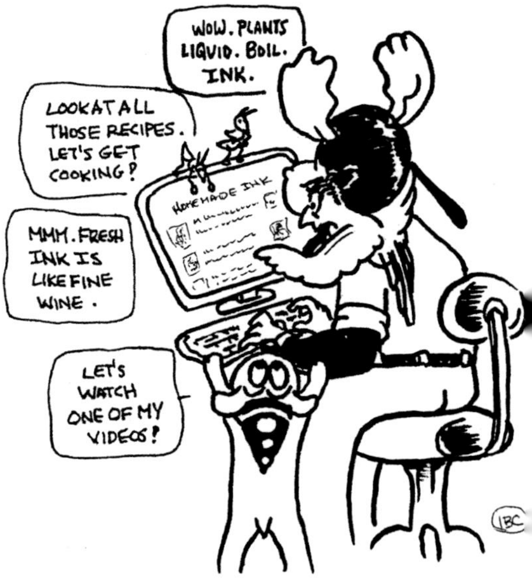
WOW. PLANTS LIQUID. BOIL. INK.
LOOK AT ALL THOSE RECIPES. LET'S GET COOKING!
HOME MADE INK
MMM. FRESH INK IS LIKE FINE WINE.
LET'S WATCH ONE OF MY VIDEOS!
IBC

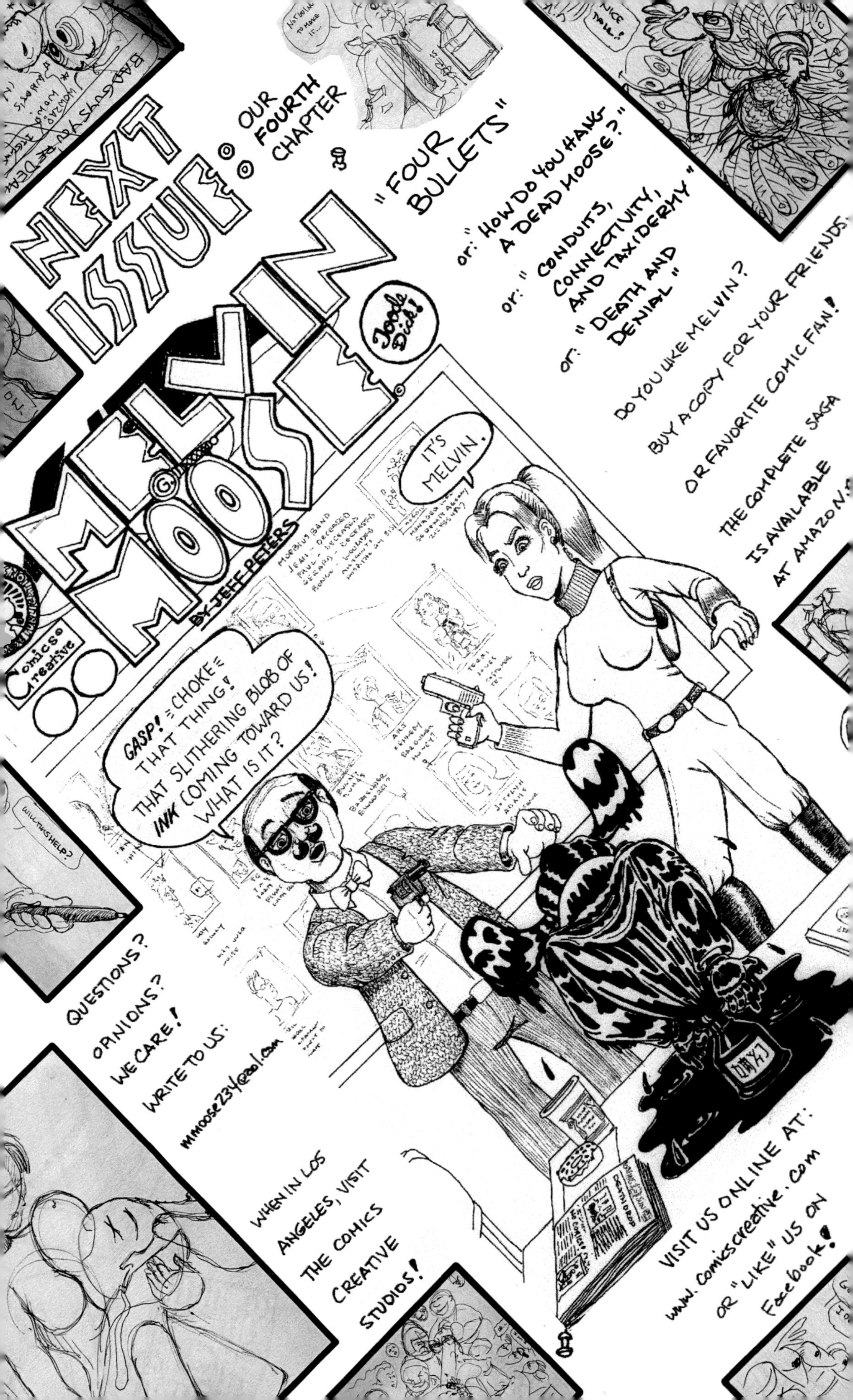
NEXT ISSUE© OUR FOURTH CHAPTER OF
MELVIN G. MOOSE©
BY JEFF PETERS
"FOUR BULLETS"
or: "HOW DO YOU HANG A DEAD MOOSE?"
or: "CONDUITS, CONNECTIVITY, AND TAXIDERMY"
or: "DEATH AND DENIAL"
DO YOU LIKE MELVIN?
BUY A COPY FOR YOUR FRIENDS OR FAVORITE COMIC FAN!
THE COMPLETE SAGA IS AVAILABLE AT AMAZON.
IT'S MELVIN.
GASP! ≡CHOKE≡ THAT THING! THAT SLITHERING BLOB OF INK COMING TOWARD US! WHAT IS IT?
Comics Creative
QUESTIONS? OPINIONS? WE CARE! WRITE TO US: mmoose234@aol.com
WHEN IN LOS ANGELES, VISIT THE COMICS CREATIVE STUDIOS!
VISIT US ONLINE AT: www.comicscreative.com OR "LIKE" US ON Facebook!

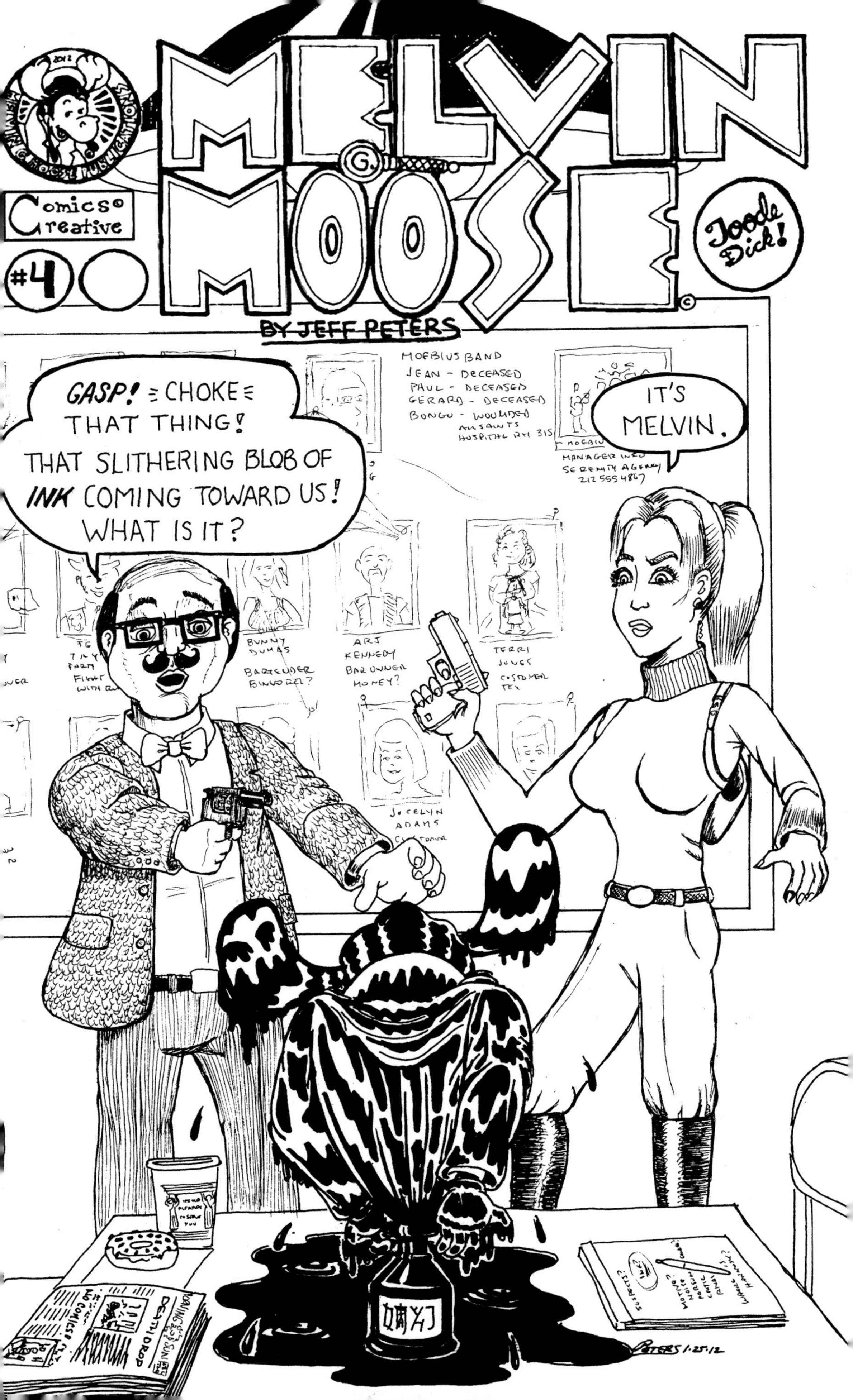

Comics Creative
#4
MELVIN G. MOOSE
Toodle Dick!
BY JEFF PETERS
MOEBIUS BAND
JEAN - DECEASED
PAUL - DECEASED
GERARD - DECEASED
GASP! CHOKE THAT THING! THAT SLITHERING BLOB OF INK COMING TOWARD US! WHAT IS IT?
IT'S MELVIN.
BUNNY DUMAS
ARJ KENNEDY
TERRI JONES
JOCELYN ADAMS
DEATH DROP
PETERS 1.25.12

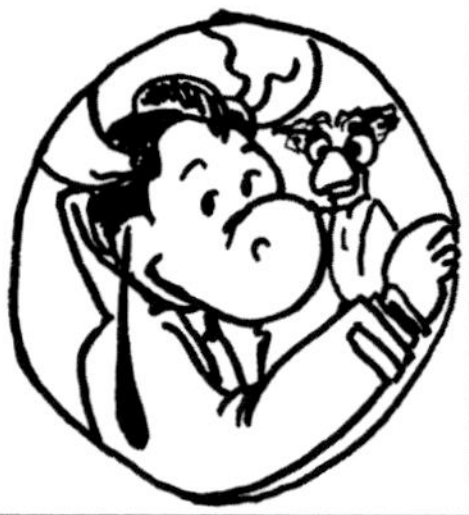

PER SPE CTI VES

WARNING:
GRAPHIC **DEATH AND REBIRTH** AHEAD,
NOT FOR THE FAINT OF HEART!

MELVIN G. MOOSE
TOODE DICK
CHAPTER (4) FOUR
"**FOUR BULLETS**"
©2012
JEFFREY
EDWARD
PETERS

"UP AND OUT
OF THE
INKWELL"

THIS ONE IS FOR:
THE **SUPPORTERS** OF
COMMUTER COMICS
AND
COMICOLOGY.TV
ALL OF WHOM
HELPED ME
REALIZE
AND **ACHIEVE**
MY **DREAM(S)**.
YOU KNOW WHO
YOU ARE...
MY FRIENDS.

"TAKE SOMETHING YOU LOVE, TELL PEOPLE ABOUT IT, BRING TOGETHER PEOPLE WHO SHARE YOUR LOVE, AND HELP MAKE IT BETTER. ULTIMATELY, YOU'LL HAVE MORE OF WHATEVER YOU LOVE FOR YOURSELF AND THE WORLD."
- JULIUS SCHWARTZ

DEAREST THREEDER,

WHAT A **WILD** RIDE, SO FAR! **FLOPPING** AND FLIPPING AROUND LIKE FOUR **FROGS** PLAYING POKER IN A SKILLET! WE'RE **HALFWAY** THROUGH AND THE INSANITY WON'T LET UP FOR ANOTHER THREE ISSUES. SOME DAYS, EVEN **I'M** NOT SURE WHAT WILL HAPPEN NEXT! I'M ONLY THE **SCRIBE**, FAITHFULLY **RECORDING** THE STORY AS IT HAPPENS, WITH NO CONTROL OVER THE FINAL **OUTCOME**. PERHAPS THAT'S JUST MY OVER-ACTIVE **IMAGINATION**... HOW MUCH **TROUBLE** CAN WE REALLY GET INTO ANYWAY, IT'S ONLY **INK** ON **PAPER**, ISN'T IT? OR **IS** IT? WE'LL **SEE**.

AT THIS POINT IN OUR SAGA, WE'VE **MET** ALL THE MAJOR PLAYERS, SO OUR TALE CAN **ROCKET** ALONG WITHOUT TOO MUCH MORE INTERRUPTION. BUT NOT TO WORRY, MORE NEW **IDEAS**, **CONCEPTS**, AND **CHARACTERS** WILL APPEAR IN THE FOLLOWING **PAGES**. IF YOU'RE READING THIS, YOU'RE ALREADY **ALONG** FOR THE RIDE, BUT MORE ON THAT **LATER**.

FOR THOSE OF YOU WHO MAY BE **LOST**, CONFUSED, OR NOT QUITE FOLLOWING THE **ANTIC** PROCEEDINGS, WE HAVE THE **LUXURY** AND CONVENIENCE OF THIS DELIGHTFUL LITERARY **DEVICE**;

OUR **STORY** THUS FAR:

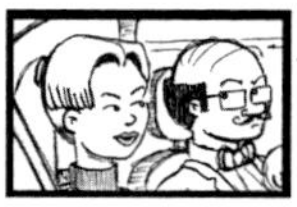

THREE UNSOLVED **MURDERS** CONFOUND OUR DETECTIVES:
ALISE ADAMS & HERBERT MIGGS

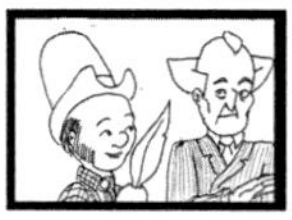

A SECRET **SOCIETY** HAS CHARGED A CARTOONIST TO **RESHAPE** PRINT TO CONFORM WITH AN INCREASINGLY DIGITAL WORLD:
TEX TAYLOR & THE ILLUSTRATI

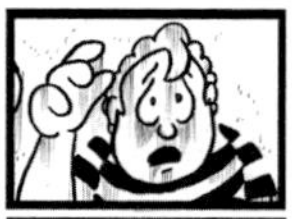

A MAN-CHILD IS **LOST** AND ABANDONED IN A STRANGE UNIVERSE:
MATTY THE BRATTY

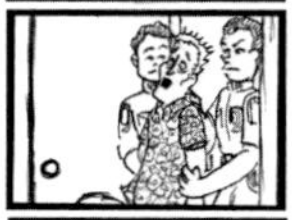

HIS CREATOR SEEKS A METHOD OF **ESCAPE**:
RUDY HARMONY

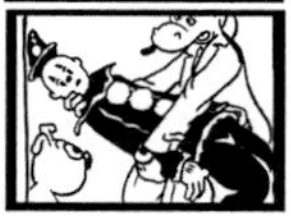

A **CLOWN** ABUSED BY THE POWER-MAD MUSES, GOES BACK TO THE **INK**:
KO-KO

MISSING PANEL **BORDERS** CREATE CHAOS IN TOODEOPOLIS AND NYC:
OUR SUPPORTING CAST OF THOUSANDS

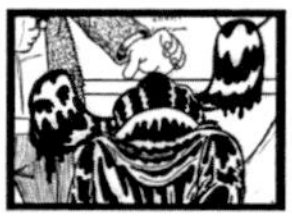

OUR **HERO** HAS ESCAPED TOODEOPOLIS THROUGH THE FOUNT OF INSPIRATION. **TRAPPED** IN THE INKWORLD, HE FINDS A WAY OUT:
MELVIN G. MOOSE, TOODE DICK

IF THAT DOESN'T **HELP** YOU UNDERSTAND THE TWISTS, TURNS, FLOPS, AND FLIPS OF OUR MYTHICAL TALE, THEN GO **BUY** THE FIRST THREE ISSUES, CHEAPSKATE!

YOURS UNTIL THE FINAL ISSUE -

JEFF PETERS 4/8/2012

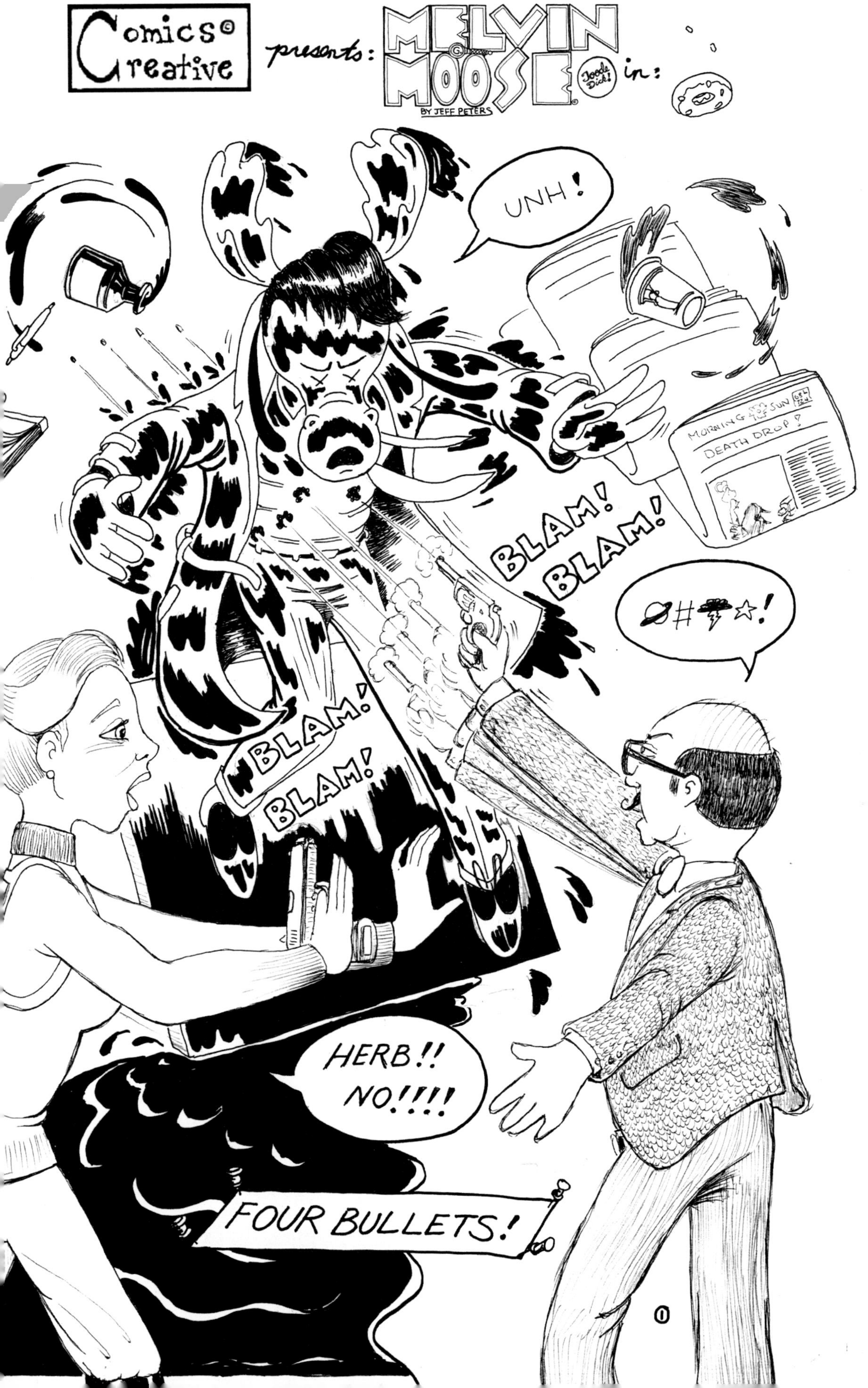
Comics© Creative
presents:
MELVIN G. MOOSE©
Joode Dick!
in:
BY JEFF PETERS
UNH!
MORNING SUN
DEATH DROP?
BLAM! BLAM!
BLAM! BLAM!
HERB!! NO!!!!
FOUR BULLETS!

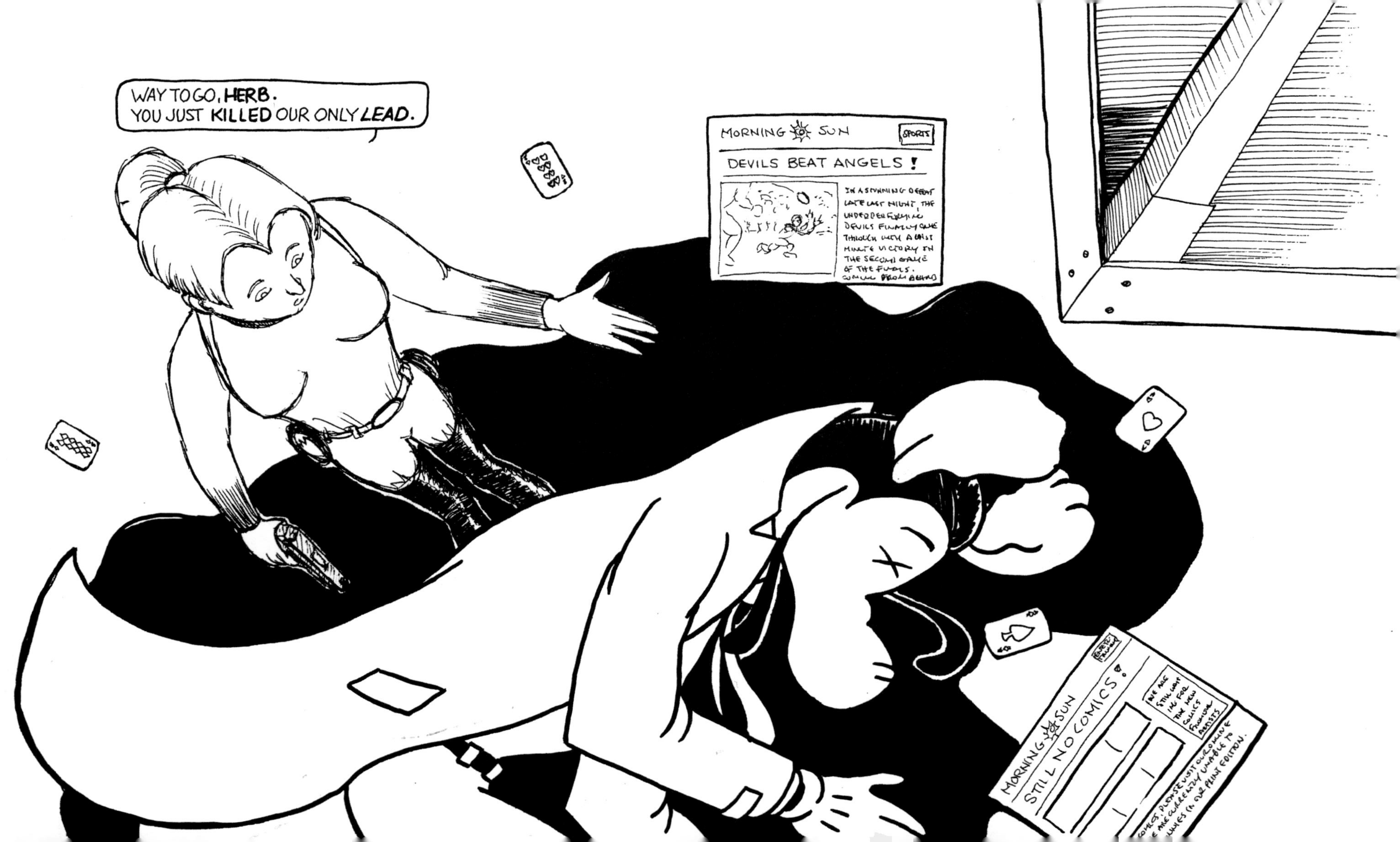
WAY TO GO, HERB.
YOU JUST KILLED OUR ONLY LEAD.
MORNING SUN
SPORTS
DEVILS BEAT ANGELS!
MORNING SUN
STILL NO COMICS?

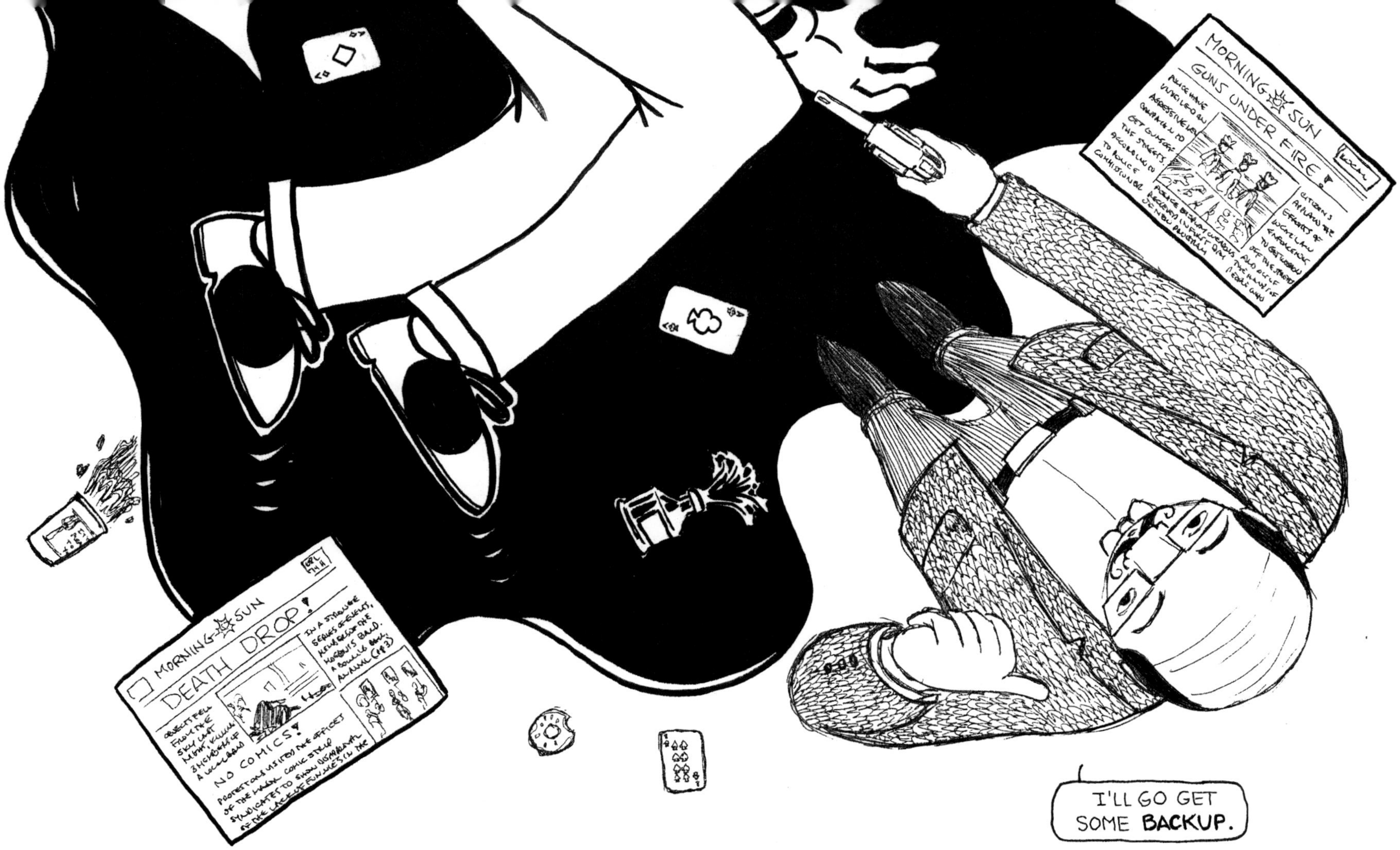
MORNING SUN
GUNS UNDER FIRE!
MORNING SUN
DEATH DROP!
NO COMICS!
I'LL GO GET SOME BACKUP.

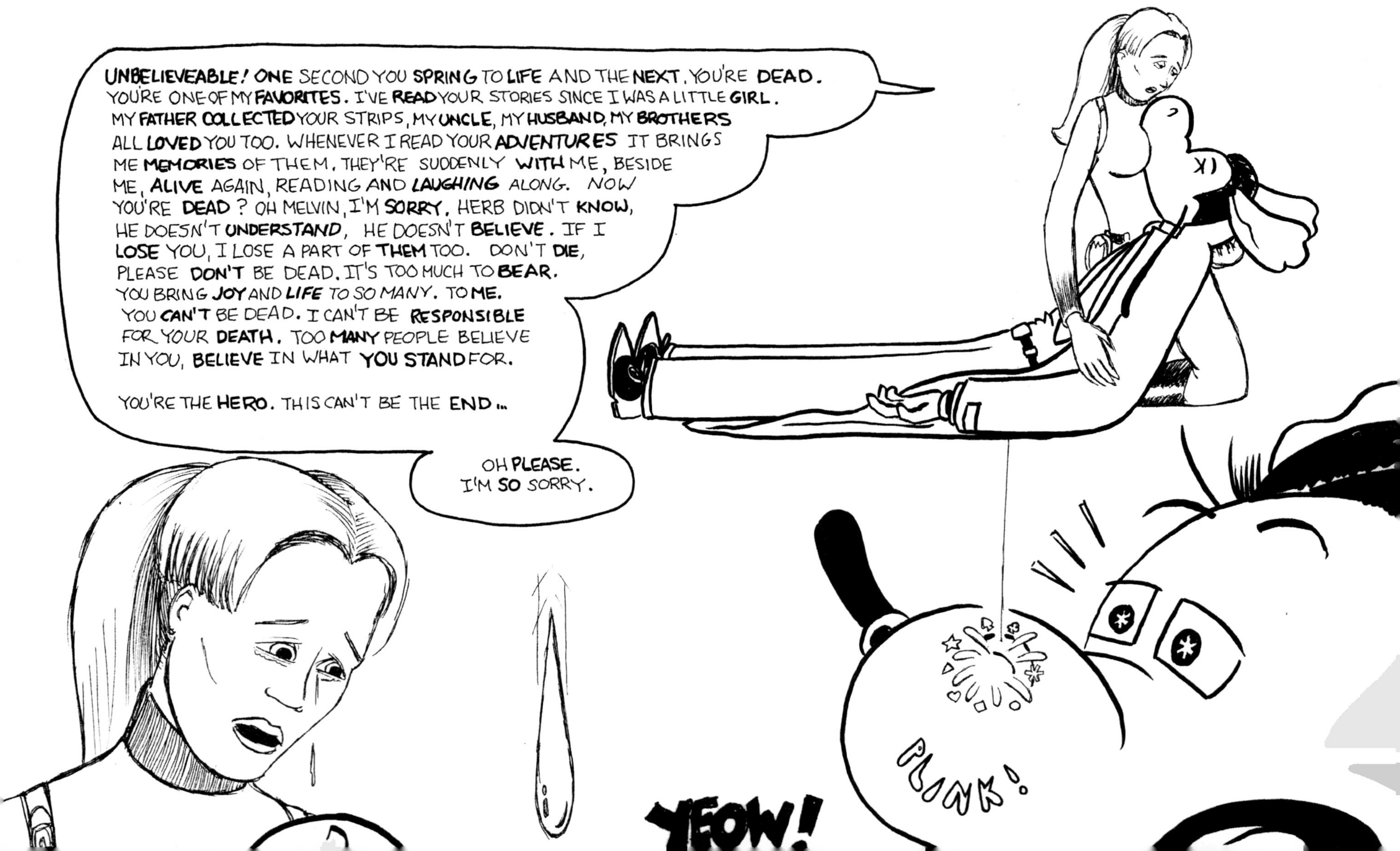
UNBELIEVEABLE! ONE SECOND YOU SPRING TO LIFE AND THE NEXT, YOU'RE DEAD. YOU'RE ONE OF MY FAVORITES. I'VE READ YOUR STORIES SINCE I WAS A LITTLE GIRL. MY FATHER COLLECTED YOUR STRIPS, MY UNCLE, MY HUSBAND, MY BROTHERS ALL LOVED YOU TOO. WHENEVER I READ YOUR ADVENTURES IT BRINGS ME MEMORIES OF THEM. THEY'RE SUDDENLY WITH ME, BESIDE ME, ALIVE AGAIN, READING AND LAUGHING ALONG. NOW YOU'RE DEAD? OH MELVIN, I'M SORRY. HERB DIDN'T KNOW, HE DOESN'T UNDERSTAND, HE DOESN'T BELIEVE. IF I LOSE YOU, I LOSE A PART OF THEM TOO. DON'T DIE, PLEASE DON'T BE DEAD. IT'S TOO MUCH TO BEAR. YOU BRING JOY AND LIFE TO SO MANY. TO ME. YOU CAN'T BE DEAD. I CAN'T BE RESPONSIBLE FOR YOUR DEATH. TOO MANY PEOPLE BELIEVE IN YOU, BELIEVE IN WHAT YOU STAND FOR.
YOU'RE THE HERO. THIS CAN'T BE THE END...
OH PLEASE. I'M SO SORRY.
PLINK!
YEOW!

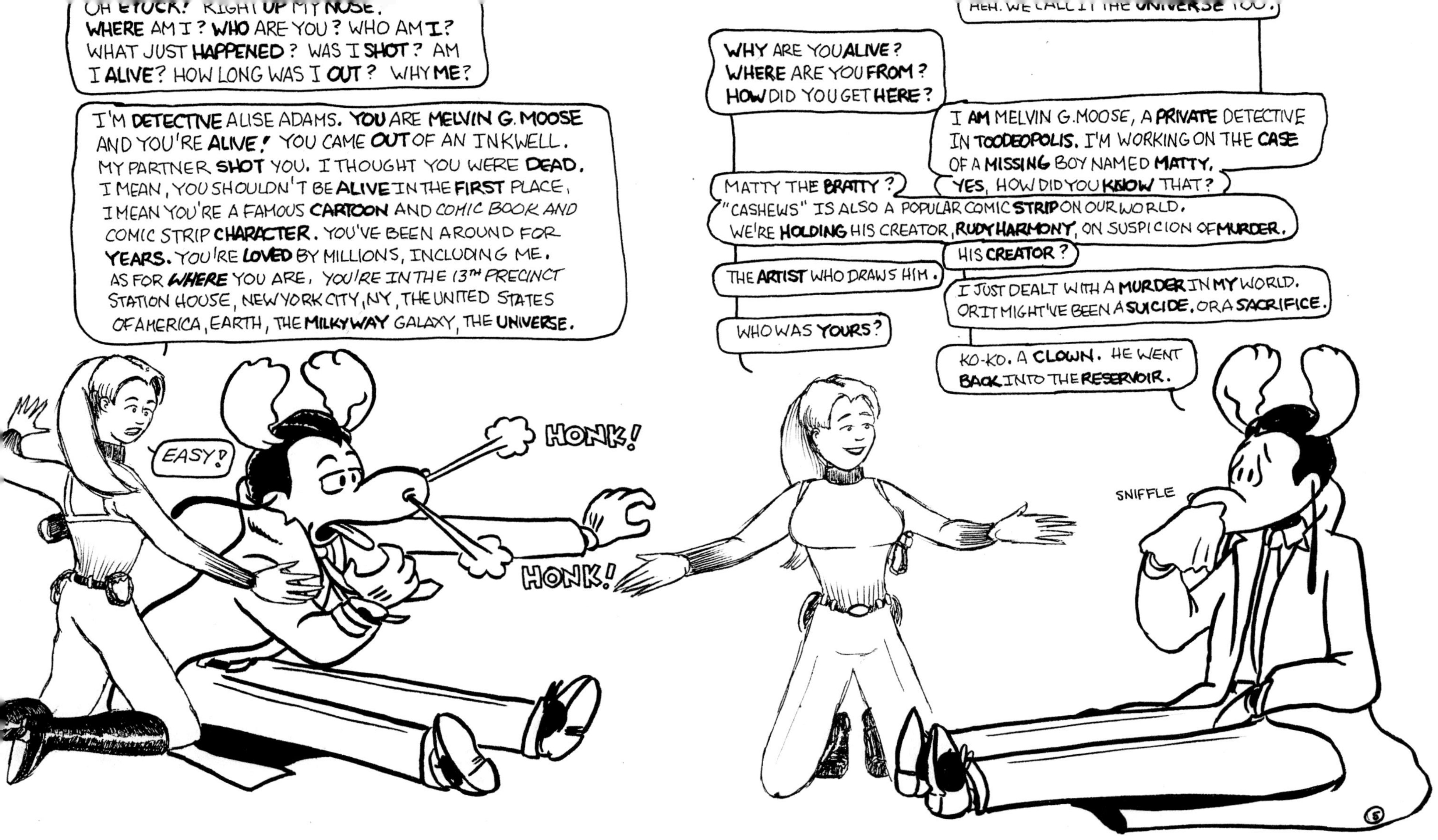
OH BUCK! RIGHT UP MY NOSE.
WHERE AM I? WHO ARE YOU? WHO AM I? WHAT JUST HAPPENED? WAS I SHOT? AM I ALIVE? HOW LONG WAS I OUT? WHY ME?
I'M DETECTIVE ALISE ADAMS. YOU ARE MELVIN G. MOOSE AND YOU'RE ALIVE! YOU CAME OUT OF AN INKWELL. MY PARTNER SHOT YOU. I THOUGHT YOU WERE DEAD. I MEAN, YOU SHOULDN'T BE ALIVE IN THE FIRST PLACE. I MEAN YOU'RE A FAMOUS CARTOON AND COMIC BOOK AND COMIC STRIP CHARACTER. YOU'VE BEEN AROUND FOR YEARS. YOU'RE LOVED BY MILLIONS, INCLUDING ME. AS FOR WHERE YOU ARE, YOU'RE IN THE 13TH PRECINCT STATION HOUSE, NEW YORK CITY, NY, THE UNITED STATES OF AMERICA, EARTH, THE MILKY WAY GALAXY, THE UNIVERSE.
EASY!
HONK!
HONK!
HEH. WE CALL IT THE UNIVERSE TOO.
WHY ARE YOU ALIVE? WHERE ARE YOU FROM? HOW DID YOU GET HERE?
I AM MELVIN G. MOOSE, A PRIVATE DETECTIVE IN TOODEOPOLIS. I'M WORKING ON THE CASE OF A MISSING BOY NAMED MATTY.
MATTY THE BRATTY?
YES, HOW DID YOU KNOW THAT?
"CASHEWS" IS ALSO A POPULAR COMIC STRIP ON OUR WORLD. WE'RE HOLDING HIS CREATOR, RUDY HARMONY, ON SUSPICION OF MURDER.
HIS CREATOR?
THE ARTIST WHO DRAWS HIM.
I JUST DEALT WITH A MURDER IN MY WORLD. OR IT MIGHT'VE BEEN A SUICIDE, OR A SACRIFICE.
WHO WAS YOURS?
KO-KO. A CLOWN. HE WENT BACK INTO THE RESERVOIR.
SNIFFLE

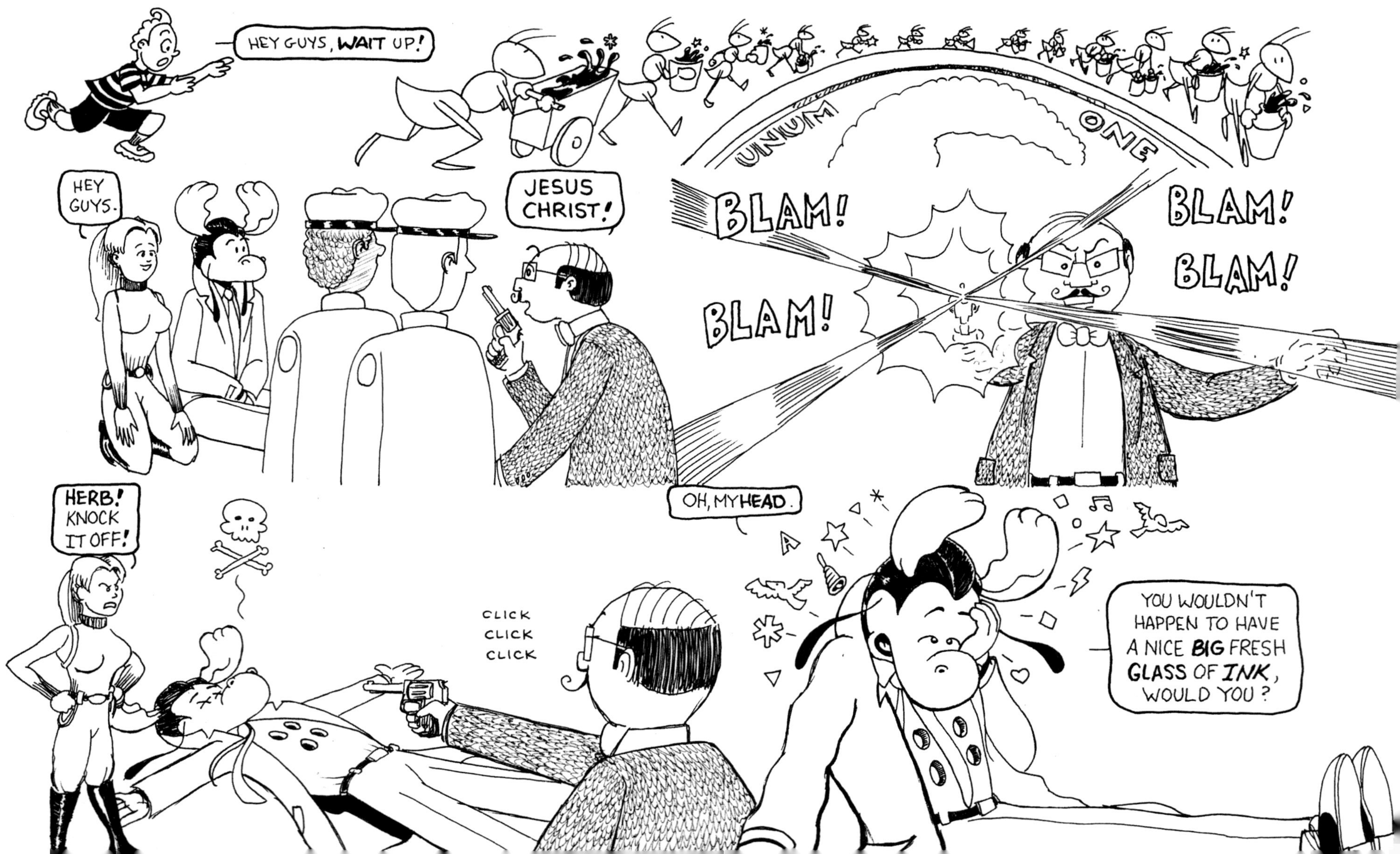
HEY GUYS, WAIT UP!
UNUM
ONE
HEY GUYS.
JESUS CHRIST!
BLAM!
BLAM!
BLAM!
BLAM!
OH, MY HEAD.
HERB! KNOCK IT OFF!
CLICK CLICK CLICK
YOU WOULDN'T HAPPEN TO HAVE A NICE BIG FRESH GLASS OF INK, WOULD YOU?

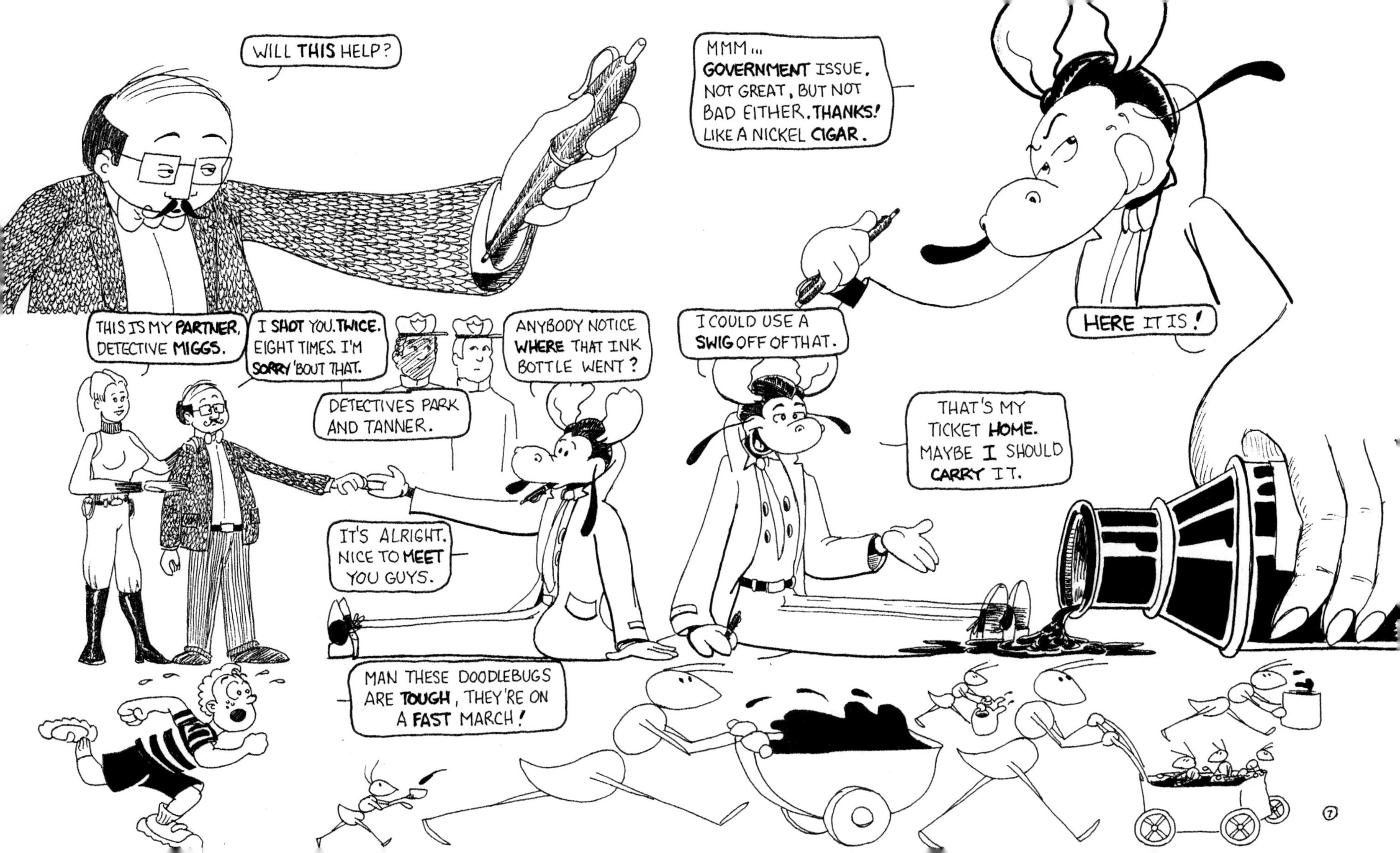
WILL THIS HELP?
MMM... GOVERNMENT ISSUE. NOT GREAT, BUT NOT BAD EITHER. THANKS! LIKE A NICKEL CIGAR.
HERE IT IS!
THIS IS MY PARTNER, DETECTIVE MIGGS.
I SHOT YOU. TWICE. EIGHT TIMES. I'M SORRY 'BOUT THAT.
DETECTIVES PARK AND TANNER.
ANYBODY NOTICE WHERE THAT INK BOTTLE WENT?
I COULD USE A SWIG OFF OF THAT.
THAT'S MY TICKET HOME. MAYBE I SHOULD CARRY IT.
IT'S ALRIGHT. NICE TO MEET YOU GUYS.
MAN THESE DOODLEBUGS ARE TOUGH, THEY'RE ON A FAST MARCH!

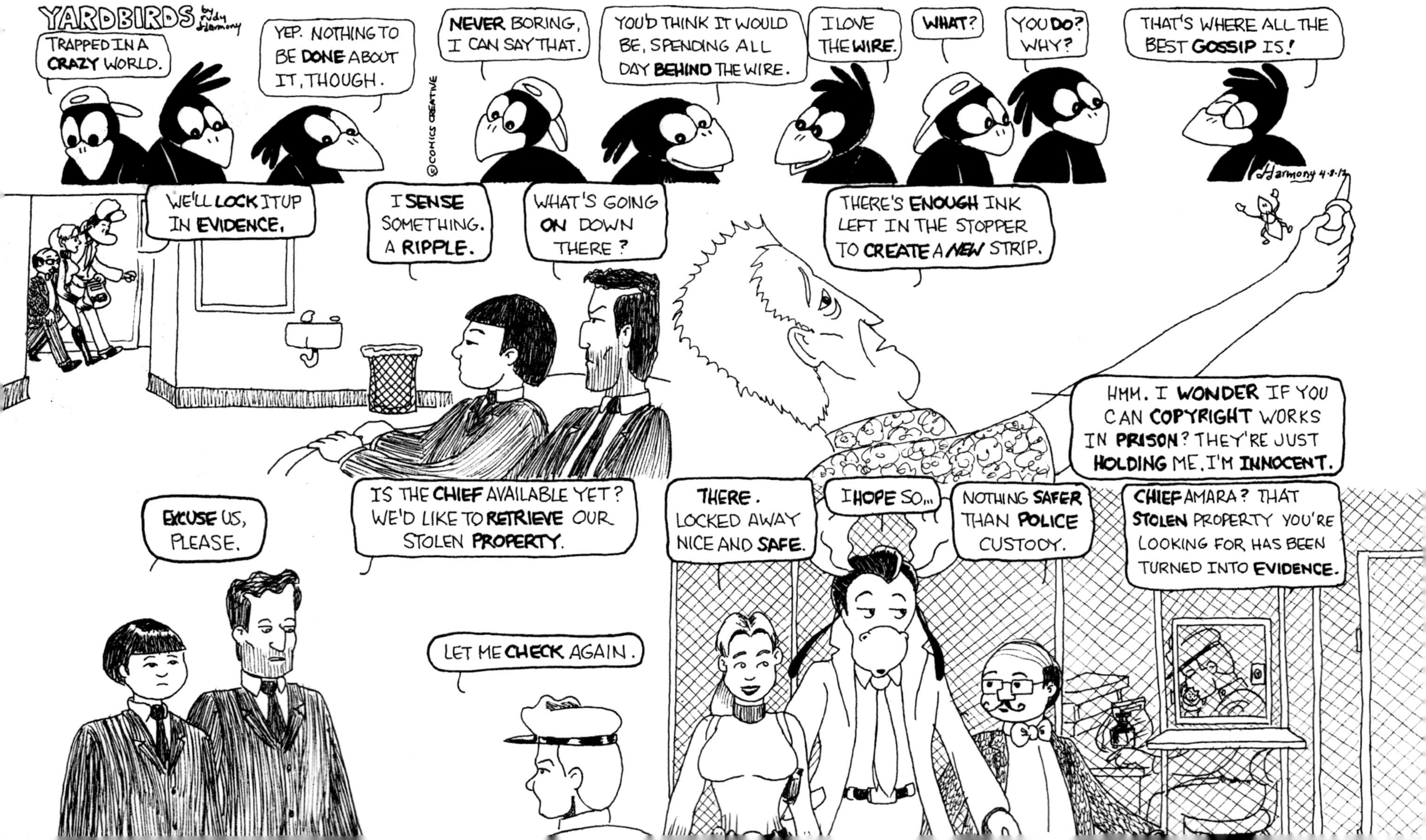

YARDBIRDS by rudy deHarmony
TRAPPED IN A CRAZY WORLD.
YEP. NOTHING TO BE DONE ABOUT IT, THOUGH.
©COMICS CREATIVE
NEVER BORING, I CAN SAY THAT.
YOU'D THINK IT WOULD BE, SPENDING ALL DAY BEHIND THE WIRE.
I LOVE THE WIRE.
WHAT?
YOU DO? WHY?
THAT'S WHERE ALL THE BEST GOSSIP IS!
deHarmony 4·8·12
WE'LL LOCK IT UP IN EVIDENCE.
I SENSE SOMETHING. A RIPPLE.
WHAT'S GOING ON DOWN THERE?
THERE'S ENOUGH INK LEFT IN THE STOPPER TO CREATE A NEW STRIP.
HMM. I WONDER IF YOU CAN COPYRIGHT WORKS IN PRISON? THEY'RE JUST HOLDING ME. I'M INNOCENT.
EXCUSE US, PLEASE.
IS THE CHIEF AVAILABLE YET? WE'D LIKE TO RETRIEVE OUR STOLEN PROPERTY.
LET ME CHECK AGAIN.
THERE. LOCKED AWAY NICE AND SAFE.
I HOPE SO...
NOTHING SAFER THAN POLICE CUSTODY.
CHIEF AMARA? THAT STOLEN PROPERTY YOU'RE LOOKING FOR HAS BEEN TURNED INTO EVIDENCE.

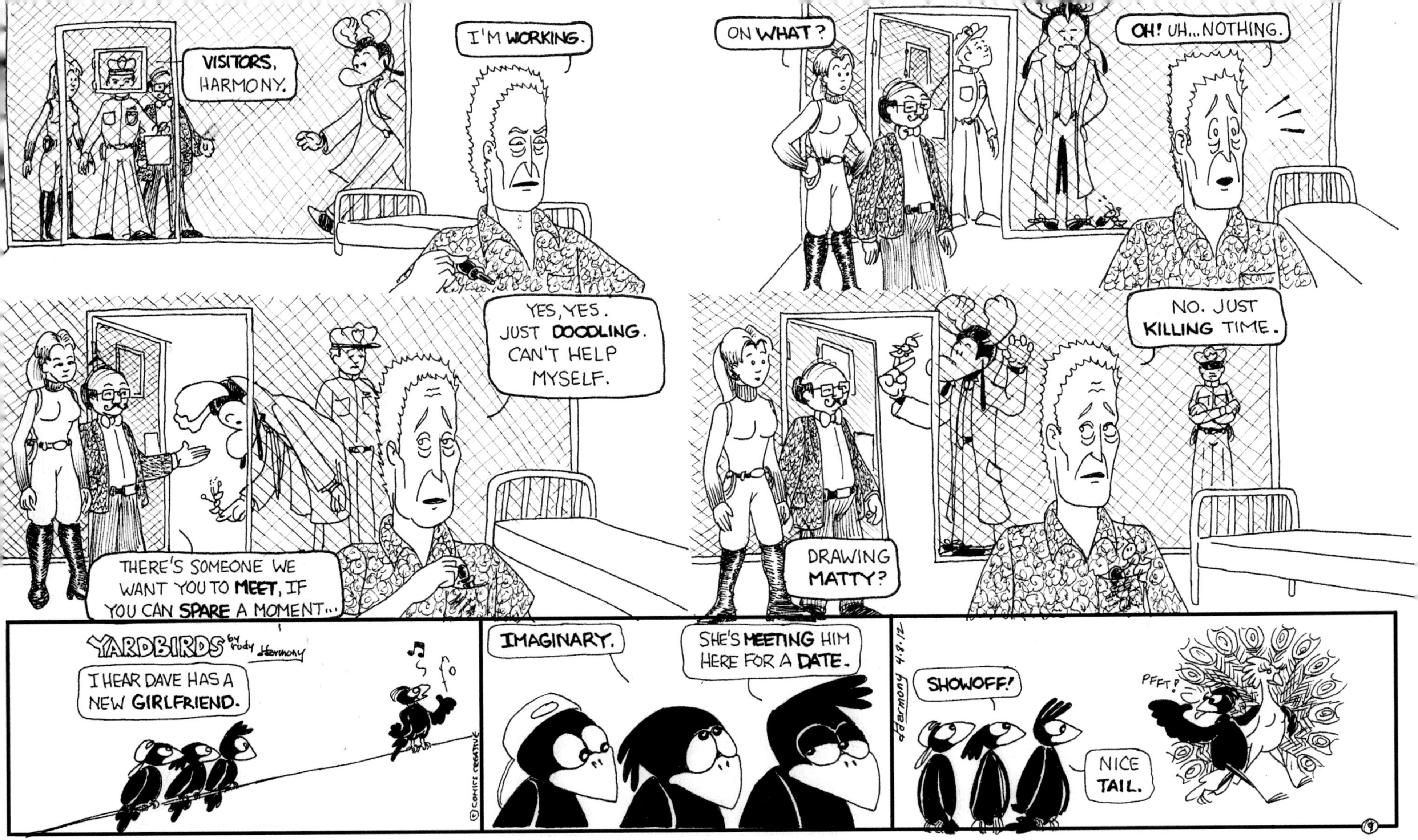
VISITORS, HARMONY.
I'M WORKING.
ON WHAT?
OH! UH...NOTHING.
YES, YES. JUST DOODLING. CAN'T HELP MYSELF.
THERE'S SOMEONE WE WANT YOU TO MEET, IF YOU CAN SPARE A MOMENT...
DRAWING MATTY?
NO. JUST KILLING TIME.
YARDBIRDS by rudy Harmony
I HEAR DAVE HAS A NEW GIRLFRIEND.
© COMICS CREATIVE
IMAGINARY.
SHE'S MEETING HIM HERE FOR A DATE.
dHarmony 4.8.12
SHOWOFF!
NICE TAIL.
PFFT!

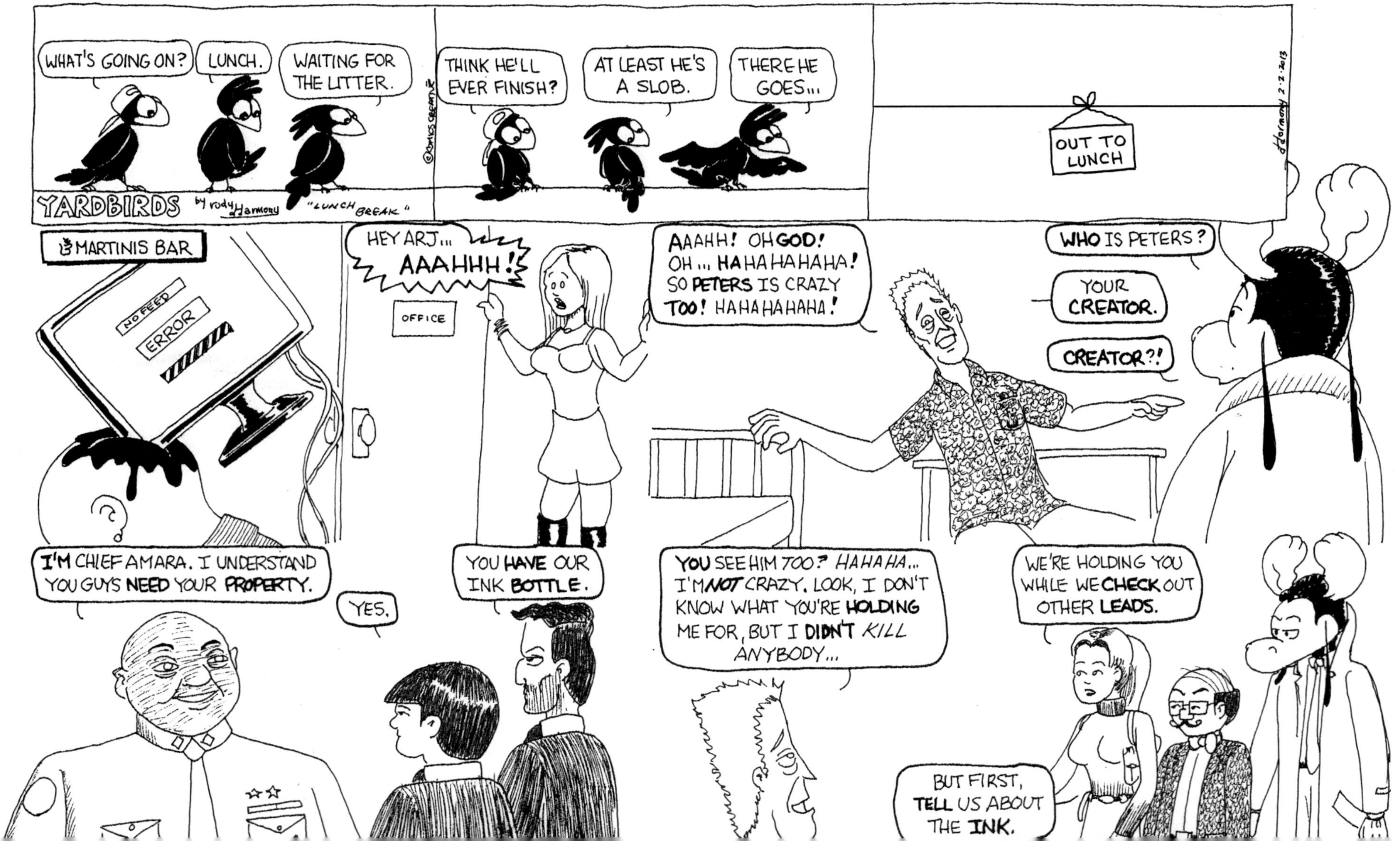

WHAT'S GOING ON?
LUNCH.
WAITING FOR THE LITTER.
YARDBIRDS by rody Harmony "LUNCH BREAK"
©COMICS CREATIVE
THINK HE'LL EVER FINISH?
AT LEAST HE'S A SLOB.
THERE HE GOES...
OUT TO LUNCH
Harmony 2·2·2013
MARTINIS BAR
NO FEED
ERROR
HEY ARJ... AAAHHH!!
OFFICE
AAAHH! OH GOD! OH... HAHAHAHAHA! SO PETERS IS CRAZY TOO! HAHAHAHAHA!
WHO IS PETERS?
YOUR CREATOR.
CREATOR?!
I'M CHIEF AMARA. I UNDERSTAND YOU GUYS NEED YOUR PROPERTY.
YES.
YOU HAVE OUR INK BOTTLE.
YOU SEE HIM TOO? HAHAHA... I'M NOT CRAZY. LOOK, I DON'T KNOW WHAT YOU'RE HOLDING ME FOR, BUT I DIDN'T KILL ANYBODY...
WE'RE HOLDING YOU WHILE WE CHECK OUT OTHER LEADS.
BUT FIRST, TELL US ABOUT THE INK.

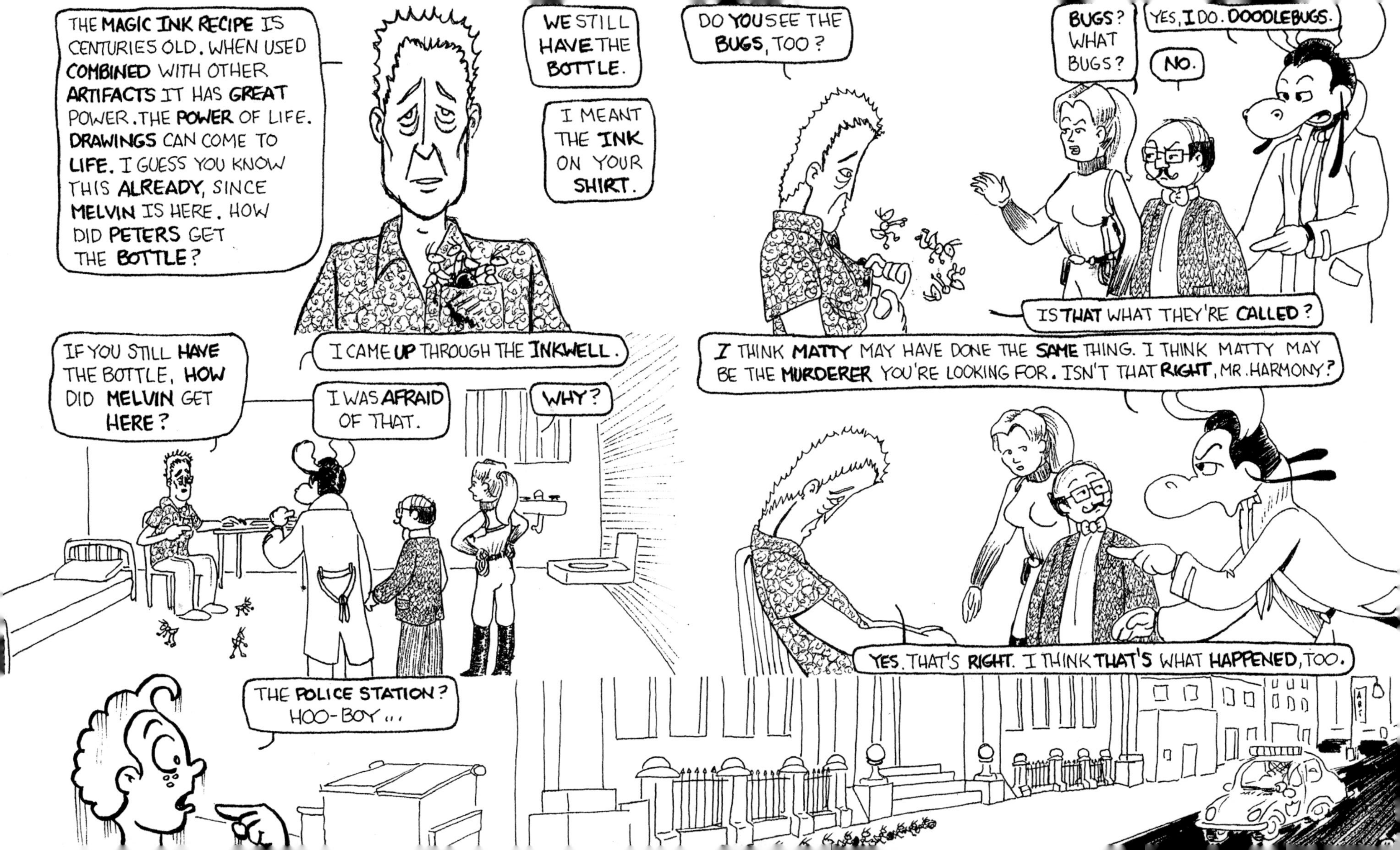
THE MAGIC INK RECIPE IS CENTURIES OLD. WHEN USED COMBINED WITH OTHER ARTIFACTS IT HAS GREAT POWER. THE POWER OF LIFE. DRAWINGS CAN COME TO LIFE. I GUESS YOU KNOW THIS ALREADY, SINCE MELVIN IS HERE. HOW DID PETERS GET THE BOTTLE?
WE STILL HAVE THE BOTTLE.
I MEANT THE INK ON YOUR SHIRT.
DO YOU SEE THE BUGS, TOO?
BUGS? WHAT BUGS?
YES, I DO. DOODLEBUGS.
NO.
IS THAT WHAT THEY'RE CALLED?
IF YOU STILL HAVE THE BOTTLE, HOW DID MELVIN GET HERE?
I CAME UP THROUGH THE INKWELL.
I WAS AFRAID OF THAT.
WHY?
I THINK MATTY MAY HAVE DONE THE SAME THING. I THINK MATTY MAY BE THE MURDERER YOU'RE LOOKING FOR. ISN'T THAT RIGHT, MR. HARMONY?
YES. THAT'S RIGHT. I THINK THAT'S WHAT HAPPENED, TOO.
THE POLICE STATION? HOO-BOY...

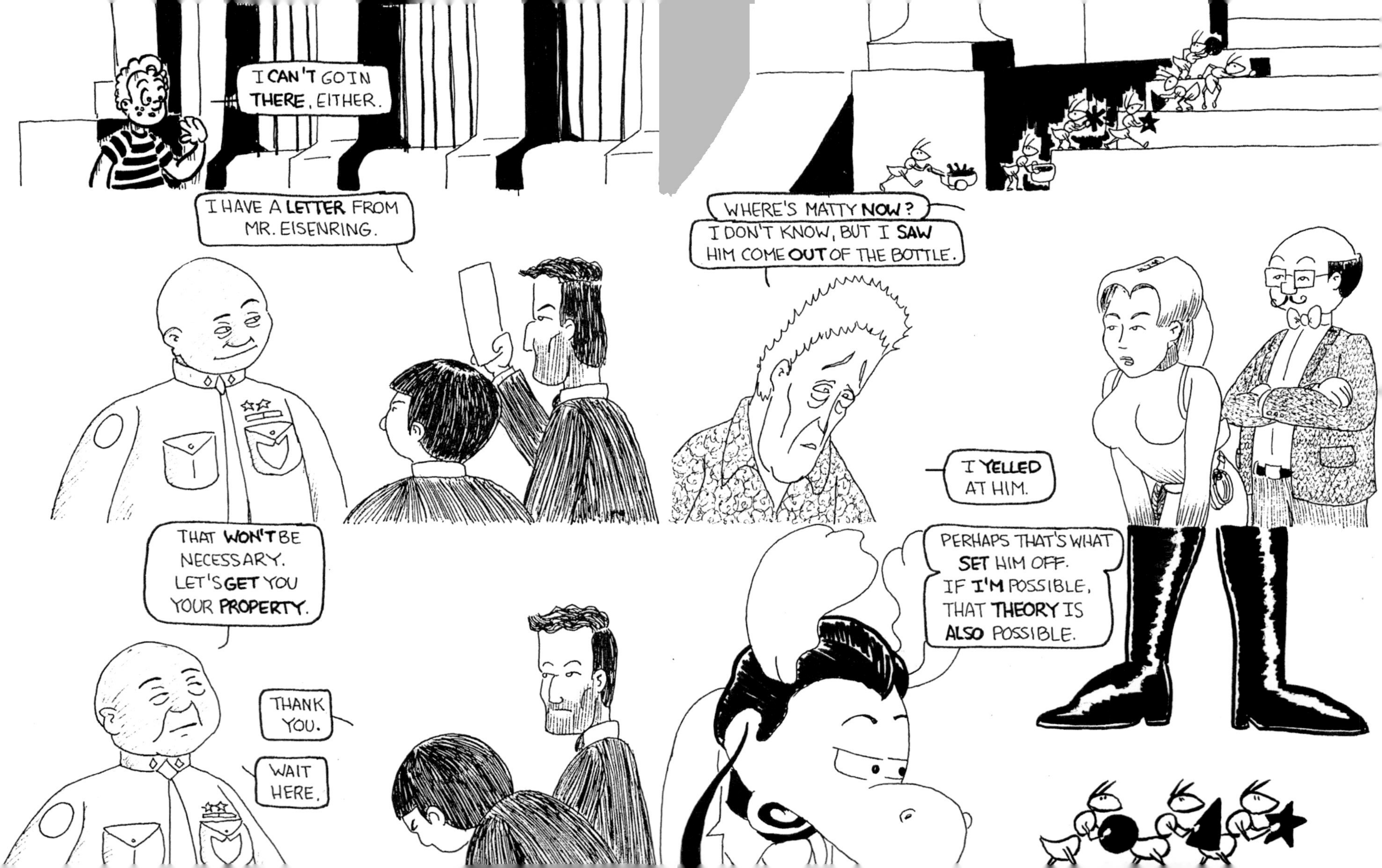
I CAN'T GO IN THERE, EITHER.
I HAVE A LETTER FROM MR. EISENRING.
THAT WON'T BE NECESSARY. LET'S GET YOU YOUR PROPERTY.
THANK YOU.
WAIT HERE.
WHERE'S MATTY NOW?
I DON'T KNOW, BUT I SAW HIM COME OUT OF THE BOTTLE.
I YELLED AT HIM.
PERHAPS THAT'S WHAT SET HIM OFF. IF I'M POSSIBLE, THAT THEORY IS ALSO POSSIBLE.

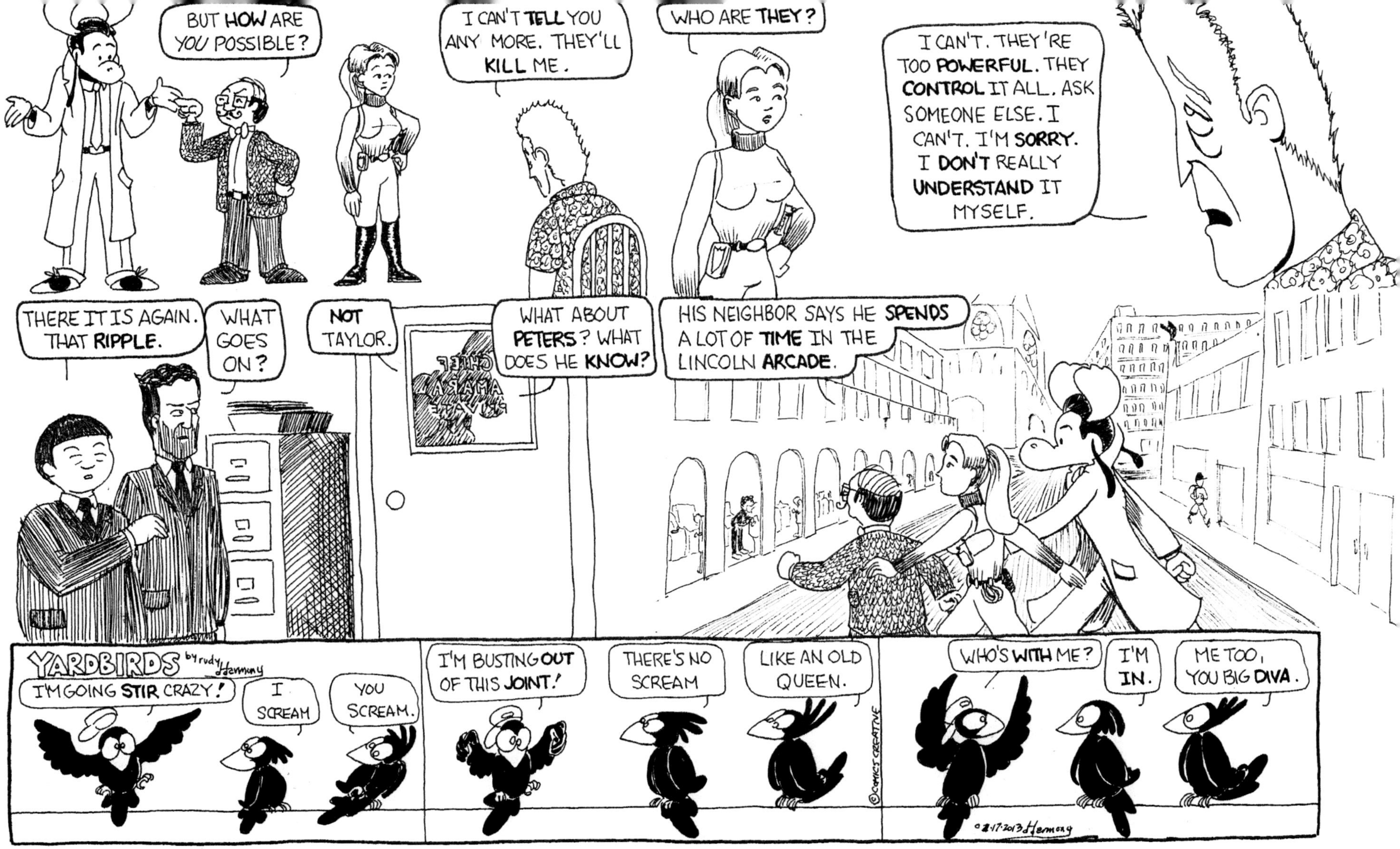
BUT **HOW** ARE *YOU* POSSIBLE?
I CAN'T **TELL** YOU ANY MORE. THEY'LL **KILL** ME.
WHO ARE **THEY**?
I CAN'T. THEY'RE TOO **POWERFUL**. THEY **CONTROL** IT ALL. ASK SOMEONE ELSE. I CAN'T. I'M **SORRY**. I **DON'T** REALLY **UNDERSTAND** IT MYSELF.
THERE IT IS AGAIN. THAT **RIPPLE**.
WHAT GOES ON?
NOT TAYLOR.
WHAT ABOUT **PETERS**? WHAT DOES HE **KNOW**?
HIS NEIGHBOR SAYS HE **SPENDS** A LOT OF **TIME** IN THE LINCOLN **ARCADE**.
YARDBIRDS by rudy Harmony
I'M GOING **STIR** CRAZY!
I SCREAM
YOU SCREAM.
I'M BUSTING **OUT** OF THIS **JOINT**!
THERE'S NO SCREAM
LIKE AN OLD QUEEN.
©COMICS CREATIVE
WHO'S **WITH** ME?
I'M **IN**.
ME TOO, YOU BIG **DIVA**.
©2·17·2013 Harmony

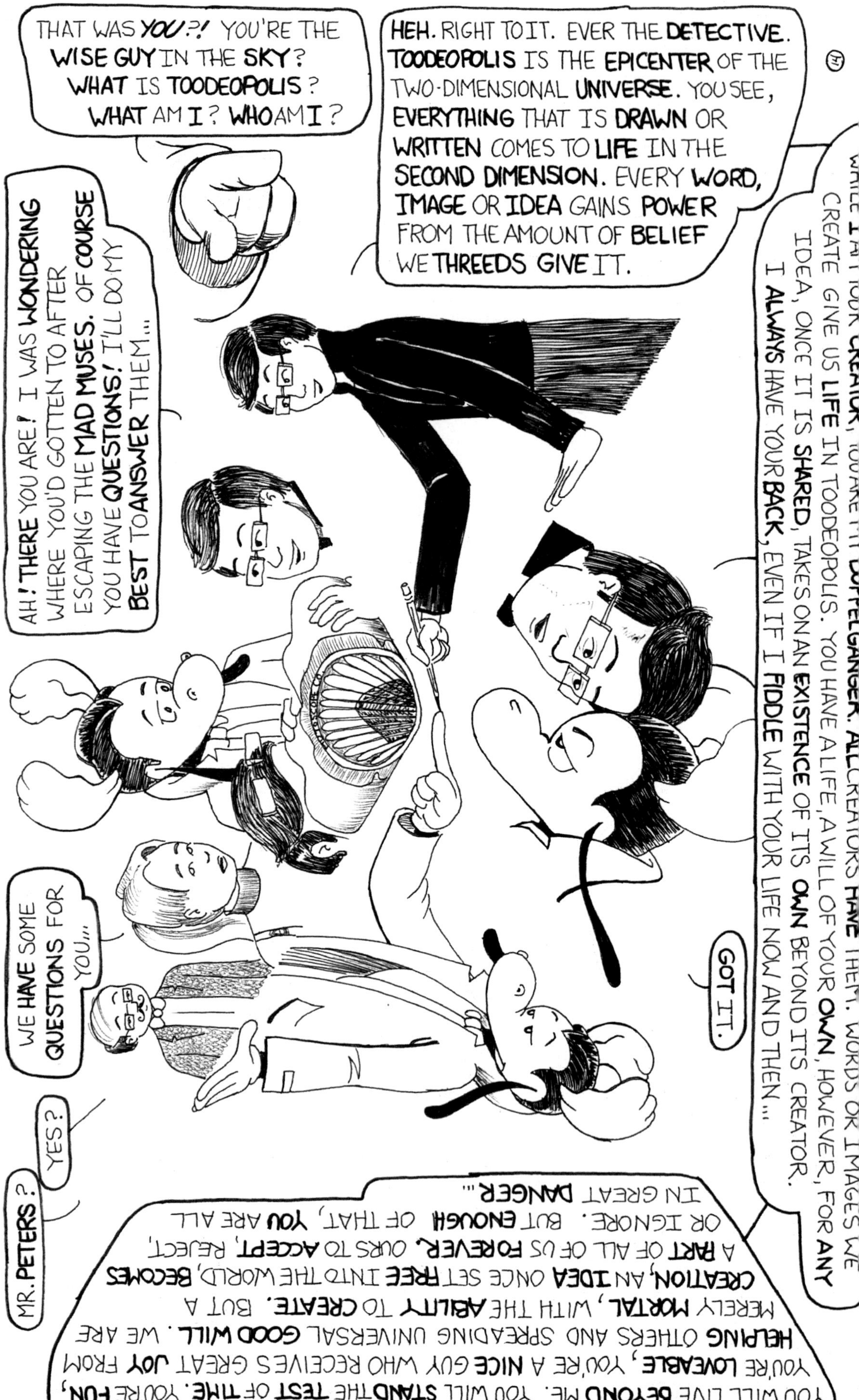
MR. PETERS?
YES?
WE HAVE SOME QUESTIONS FOR YOU...
AH! THERE YOU ARE! I WAS WONDERING WHERE YOU'D GOTTEN TO AFTER ESCAPING THE MAD MUSES. OF COURSE YOU HAVE QUESTIONS! I'LL DO MY BEST TO ANSWER THEM...
THAT WAS YOU?! YOU'RE THE WISE GUY IN THE SKY? WHAT IS TOODEOPOLIS? WHAT AM I? WHO AM I?
HEH. RIGHT TO IT. EVER THE DETECTIVE. TOODEOPOLIS IS THE EPICENTER OF THE TWO-DIMENSIONAL UNIVERSE. YOU SEE, EVERYTHING THAT IS DRAWN OR WRITTEN COMES TO LIFE IN THE SECOND DIMENSION. EVERY WORD, IMAGE OR IDEA GAINS POWER FROM THE AMOUNT OF BELIEF WE THREEDS GIVE IT.
WHILE I AM YOUR CREATOR, YOU ARE MY DOPPELGANGER. ALL CREATORS HAVE THEM. WORDS OR IMAGES WE CREATE GIVE US LIFE IN TOODEOPOLIS. YOU HAVE A LIFE, A WILL OF YOUR OWN, HOWEVER, FOR ANY IDEA, ONCE IT IS SHARED, TAKES ON AN EXISTENCE OF ITS OWN BEYOND ITS CREATOR. I ALWAYS HAVE YOUR BACK, EVEN IF I FIDDLE WITH YOUR LIFE NOW AND THEN...
GOT IT.
YOU WILL LIVE BEYOND ME. YOU WILL STAND THE TEST OF TIME. YOU'RE FUN, YOU'RE LOVEABLE, YOU'RE A NICE GUY WHO RECEIVES GREAT JOY FROM HELPING OTHERS AND SPREADING UNIVERSAL GOOD WILL. WE ARE MERELY MORTAL, WITH THE ABILITY TO CREATE. BUT A CREATION, AN IDEA ONCE SET FREE INTO THE WORLD, BECOMES A PART OF ALL OF US FOREVER, OURS TO ACCEPT, REJECT, OR IGNORE. BUT ENOUGH OF THAT, YOU ARE ALL IN GREAT DANGER...

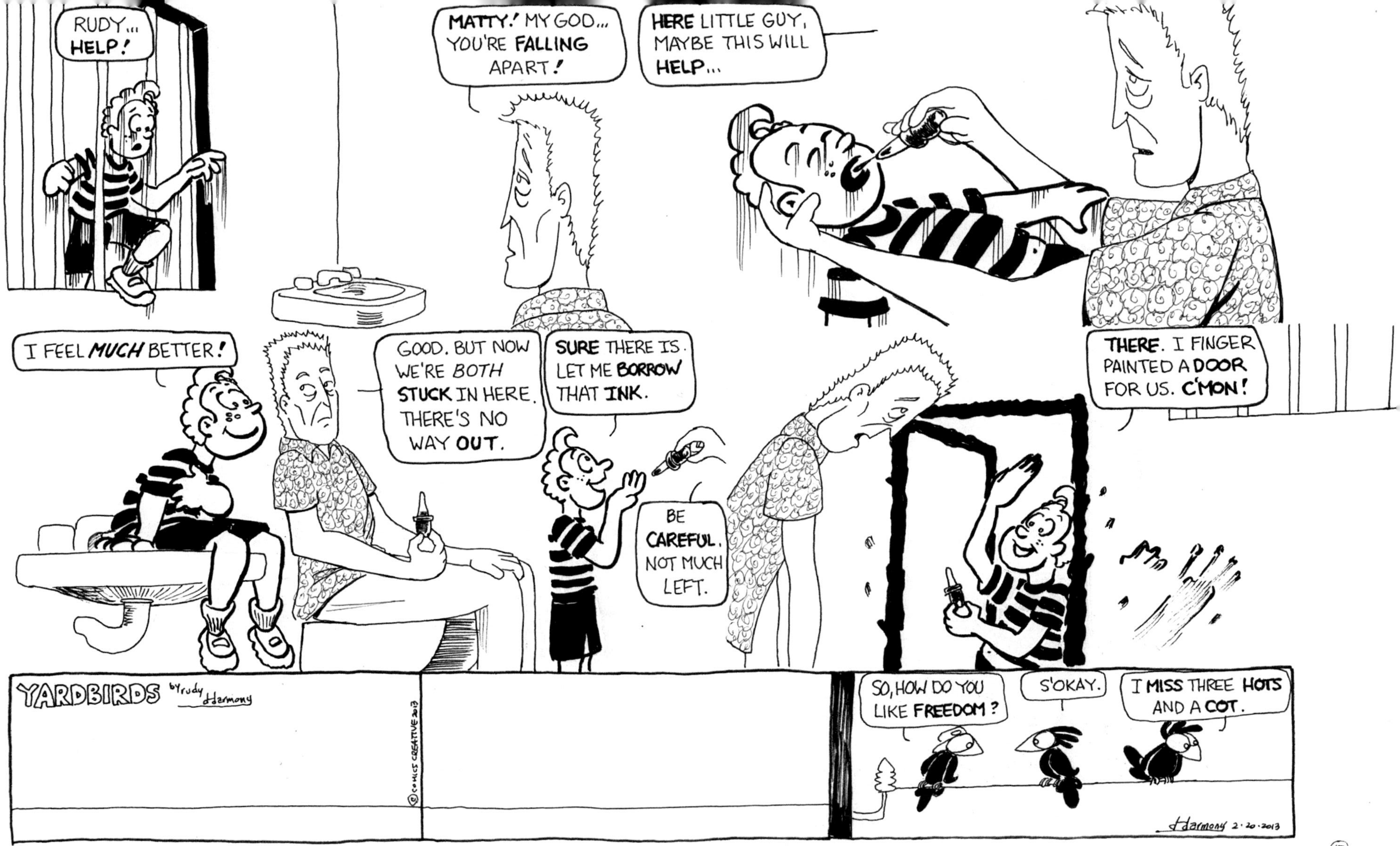

RUDY... HELP!
MATTY! MY GOD... YOU'RE FALLING APART!
HERE LITTLE GUY, MAYBE THIS WILL HELP...
I FEEL MUCH BETTER!
GOOD. BUT NOW WE'RE BOTH STUCK IN HERE. THERE'S NO WAY OUT.
SURE THERE IS. LET ME BORROW THAT INK.
BE CAREFUL. NOT MUCH LEFT.
THERE. I FINGER PAINTED A DOOR FOR US. C'MON!
YARDBIRDS by rudy harmony
© COMICS CREATIVE 2013
SO, HOW DO YOU LIKE FREEDOM?
S'OKAY.
I MISS THREE HOTS AND A COT.
harmony 2·20·2013

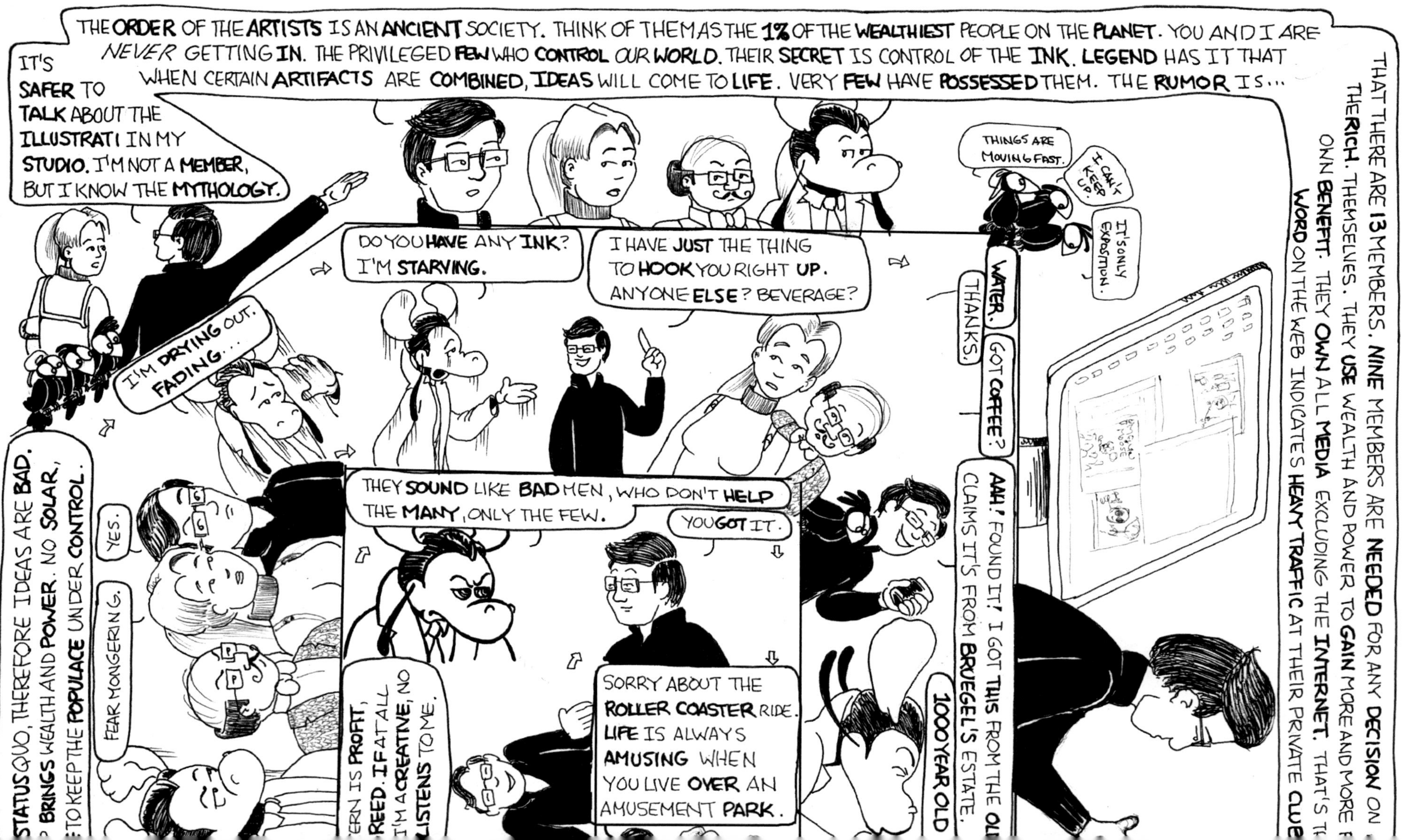
THE ORDER OF THE ARTISTS IS AN ANCIENT SOCIETY. THINK OF THEM AS THE 1% OF THE WEALTHIEST PEOPLE ON THE PLANET. YOU AND I ARE NEVER GETTING IN. THE PRIVILEGED FEW WHO CONTROL OUR WORLD. THEIR SECRET IS CONTROL OF THE INK. LEGEND HAS IT THAT WHEN CERTAIN ARTIFACTS ARE COMBINED, IDEAS WILL COME TO LIFE. VERY FEW HAVE POSSESSED THEM. THE RUMOR IS...
IT'S SAFER TO TALK ABOUT THE ILLUSTRATI IN MY STUDIO. I'M NOT A MEMBER, BUT I KNOW THE MYTHOLOGY.
THINGS ARE MOVING FAST.
I CAN'T KEEP UP.
IT'S ONLY EXPOSITION.
THAT THERE ARE 13 MEMBERS. NINE MEMBERS ARE NEEDED FOR ANY DECISION ON
THE RICH. THEMSELVES. THEY USE WEALTH AND POWER TO GAIN MORE AND MORE
OWN BENEFIT. THEY OWN ALL MEDIA EXCLUDING THE INTERNET. THAT'S T
WORD ON THE WEB INDICATES HEAVY TRAFFIC AT THEIR PRIVATE CLUB
I'M DRYING OUT. FADING...
DO YOU HAVE ANY INK? I'M STARVING.
I HAVE JUST THE THING TO HOOK YOU RIGHT UP. ANYONE ELSE? BEVERAGE?
WATER.
THANKS.
GOT COFFEE?
AAH! FOUND IT! I GOT THIS FROM THE OL
CLAIMS IT'S FROM BRUEGEL'S ESTATE.
1000 YEAR OLD
STATUS QUO, THEREFORE IDEAS ARE BAD.
BRINGS WEALTH AND POWER. NO SOLAR,
TO KEEP THE POPULACE UNDER CONTROL.
YES.
FEAR MONGERING.
THEY SOUND LIKE BAD MEN, WHO DON'T HELP THE MANY, ONLY THE FEW.
YOU GOT IT.
ERN IS PROFIT,
REED. IF AT ALL
I'M A CREATIVE, NO
LISTENS TO ME.
SORRY ABOUT THE ROLLER COASTER RIDE. LIFE IS ALWAYS AMUSING WHEN YOU LIVE OVER AN AMUSEMENT PARK.

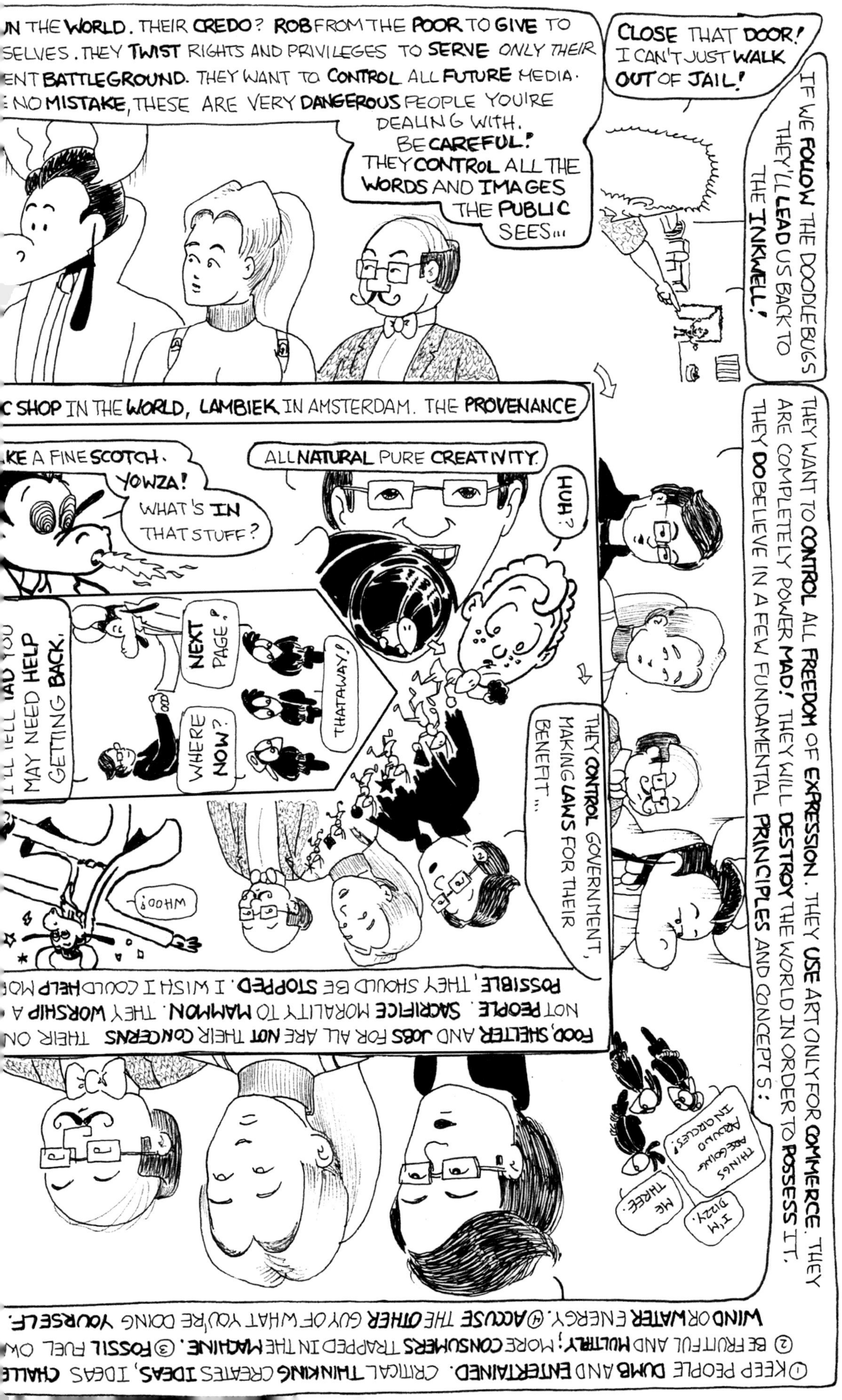

N THE WORLD. THEIR CREDO? ROB FROM THE POOR TO GIVE TO
SELVES. THEY TWIST RIGHTS AND PRIVILEGES TO SERVE ONLY THEIR
ENT BATTLEGROUND. THEY WANT TO CONTROL ALL FUTURE MEDIA.
NO MISTAKE, THESE ARE VERY DANGEROUS PEOPLE YOU'RE DEALING WITH.
BE CAREFUL! THEY CONTROL ALL THE WORDS AND IMAGES THE PUBLIC SEES...
CLOSE THAT DOOR! I CAN'T JUST WALK OUT OF JAIL!
IF WE FOLLOW THE DOODLEBUGS THEY'LL LEAD US BACK TO THE INKWELL!
C SHOP IN THE WORLD, LAMBIEK IN AMSTERDAM. THE PROVENANCE
KE A FINE SCOTCH.
ALL NATURAL PURE CREATIVITY.
YOWZA! WHAT'S IN THAT STUFF?
HUH?
THEY WANT TO CONTROL ALL FREEDOM OF EXPRESSION. THEY USE ART ONLY FOR COMMERCE. THEY ARE COMPLETELY POWER MAD! THEY WILL DESTROY THE WORLD IN ORDER TO POSSESS IT. THEY DO BELIEVE IN A FEW FUNDAMENTAL PRINCIPLES AND CONCEPTS:
MAY NEED HELP GETTING BACK.
NEXT PAGE!
WHERE NOW?
THATAWAY!
THEY CONTROL GOVERNMENT, MAKING LAWS FOR THEIR BENEFIT...
WHOOP!
FOOD, SHELTER AND JOBS FOR ALL ARE NOT THEIR CONCERNS. THEIR ON
NOT PEOPLE. SACRIFICE MORALITY TO MAMMON. THEY WORSHIP A
POSSIBLE. THEY SHOULD BE STOPPED. I WISH I COULD HELP MO
THINGS ARE GOING AROUND IN CIRCLES!
I'M DIZZY.
ME THREE.
① KEEP PEOPLE DUMB AND ENTERTAINED. CRITICAL THINKING CREATES IDEAS, IDEAS CHALLE
② BE FRUITFUL AND MULTIPLY; MORE CONSUMERS TRAPPED IN THE MACHINE. ③ FOSSIL FUEL OW
WIND OR WATER ENERGY. ④ ACCUSE THE OTHER GUY OF WHAT YOU'RE DOING YOURSELF.

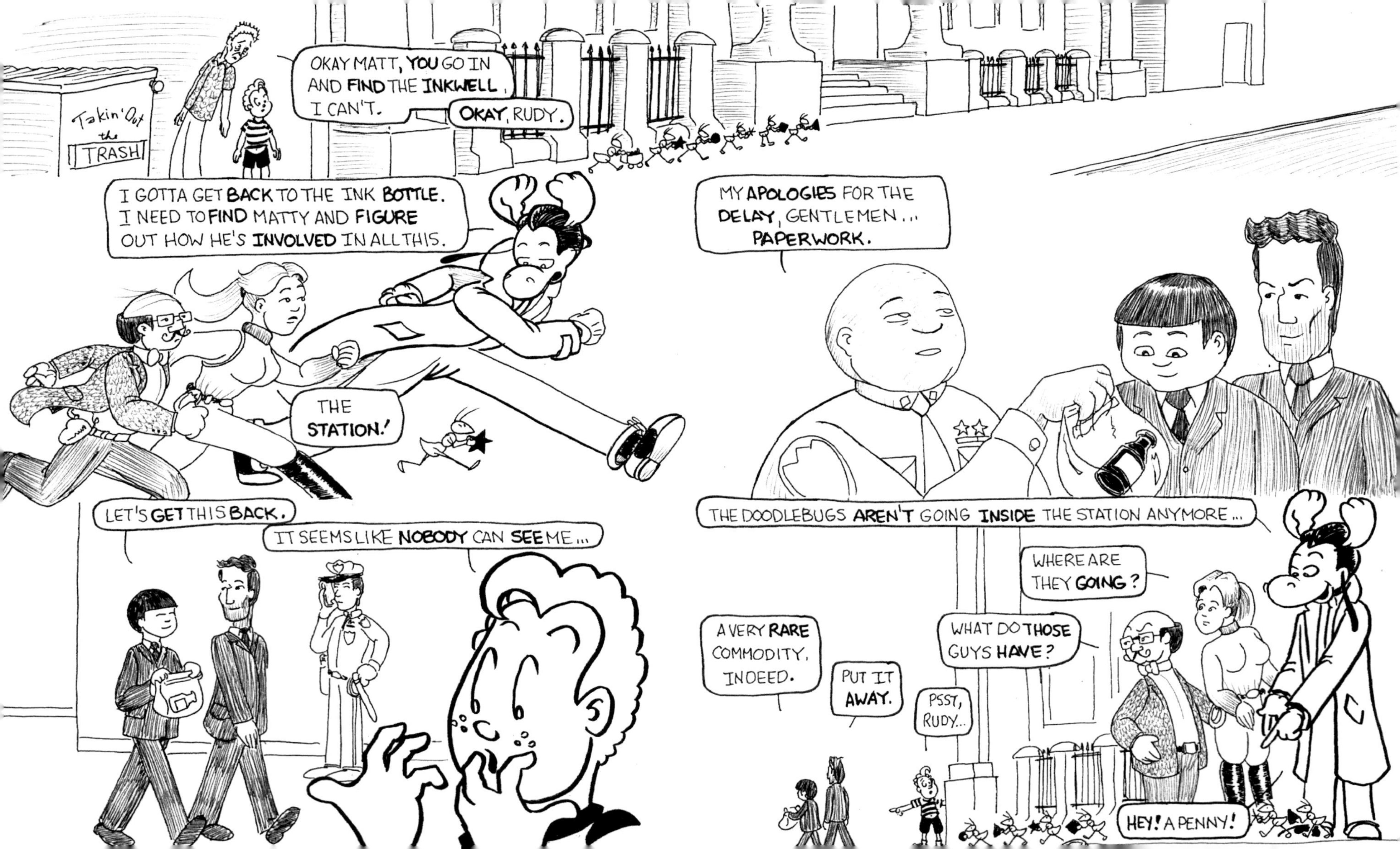
Takin' Out the TRASH
OKAY MATT, YOU GO IN AND FIND THE INKWELL, I CAN'T.
OKAY, RUDY.
I GOTTA GET BACK TO THE INK BOTTLE. I NEED TO FIND MATTY AND FIGURE OUT HOW HE'S INVOLVED IN ALL THIS.
THE STATION!
LET'S GET THIS BACK.
IT SEEMS LIKE NOBODY CAN SEE ME...
MY APOLOGIES FOR THE DELAY, GENTLEMEN... PAPERWORK.
THE DOODLEBUGS AREN'T GOING INSIDE THE STATION ANYMORE...
WHERE ARE THEY GOING?
WHAT DO THOSE GUYS HAVE?
A VERY RARE COMMODITY, INDEED.
PUT IT AWAY.
PSST, RUDY...
HEY! A PENNY!

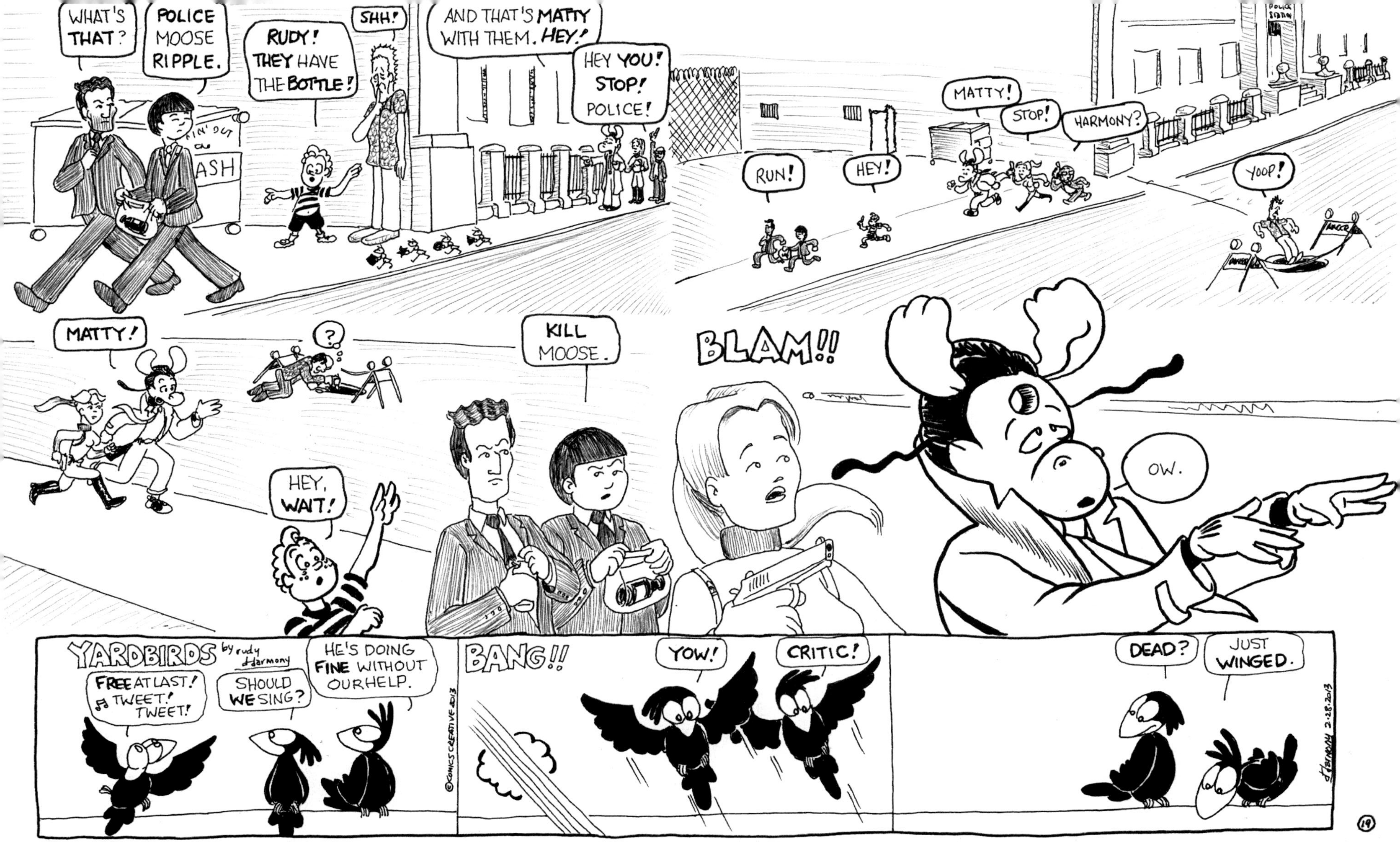
WHAT'S THAT?
POLICE MOOSE RIPPLE.
RUDY! THEY HAVE THE BOTTLE!
SHH!
AND THAT'S MATTY WITH THEM. HEY!
HEY YOU! STOP! POLICE!
RUN!
HEY!
MATTY!
STOP!
HARMONY?
YOOP!
POLICE STATION
MATTY!
?
KILL MOOSE.
HEY, WAIT!
BLAM!!
OW.
YARDBIRDS by rudy harmony
FREE AT LAST! TWEET! TWEET!
SHOULD WE SING?
HE'S DOING FINE WITHOUT OUR HELP.
©COMICS CREATIVE 2013
BANG!!
YOW!
CRITIC!
DEAD?
JUST WINGED.
d harmony 2.28.2013

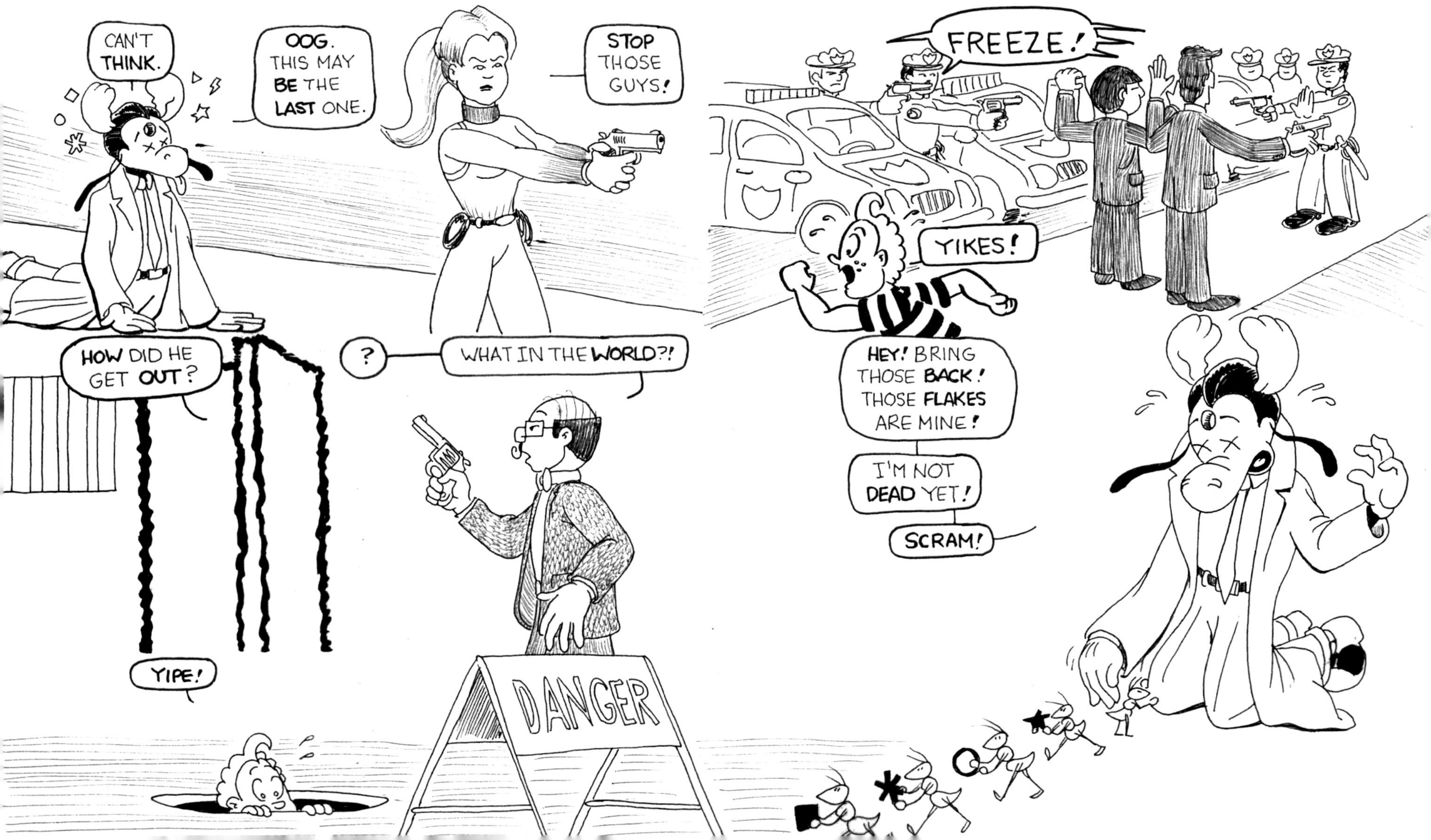
CAN'T THINK.
OOG. THIS MAY BE THE LAST ONE.
STOP THOSE GUYS!
HOW DID HE GET OUT?
?
WHAT IN THE WORLD?!
YIPE!
DANGER
FREEZE!
YIKES!
HEY! BRING THOSE BACK! THOSE FLAKES ARE MINE!
I'M NOT DEAD YET!
SCRAM!

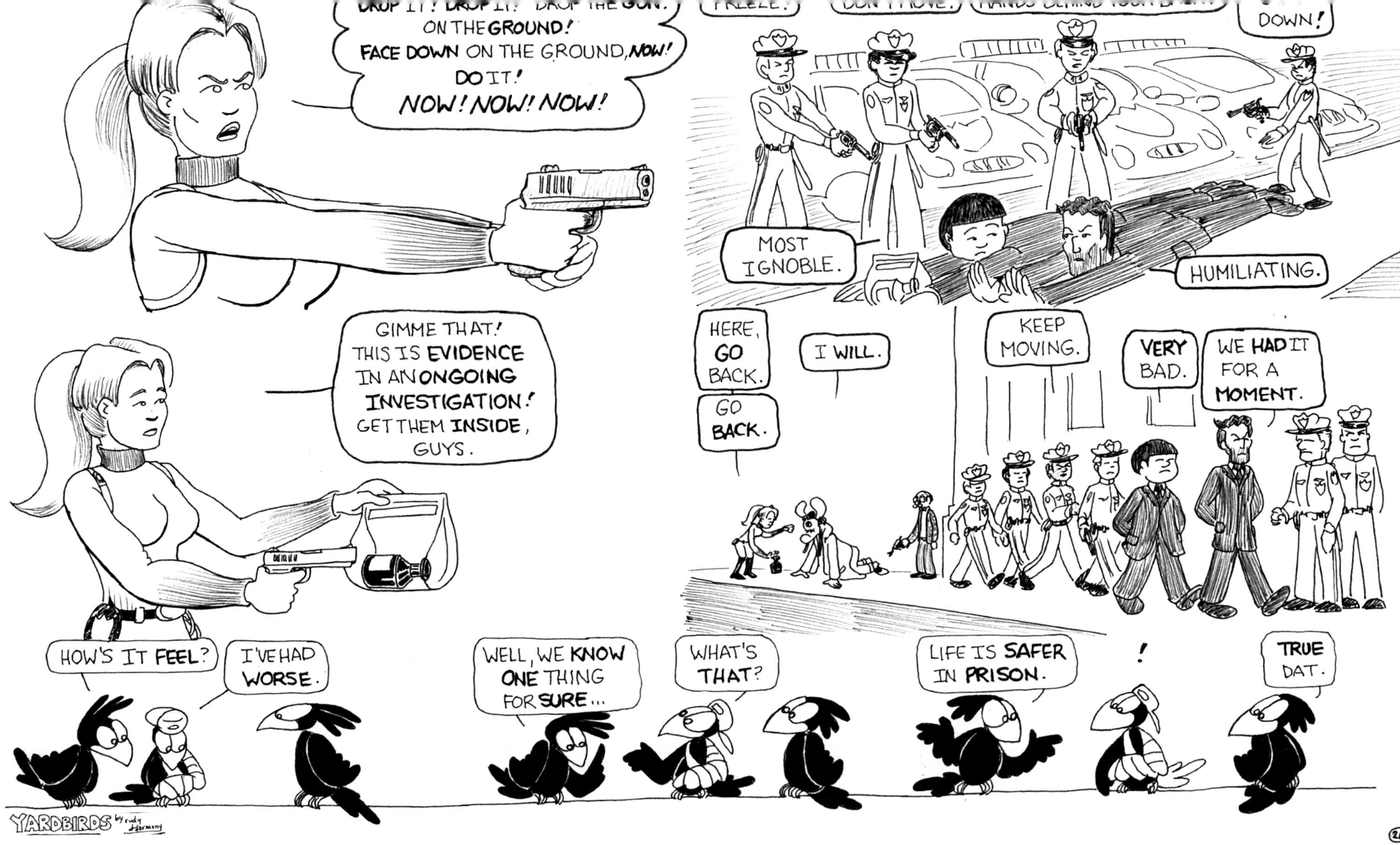
ON THE GROUND!
FACE DOWN ON THE GROUND, NOW!
DO IT!
NOW! NOW! NOW!
DOWN!
MOST IGNOBLE.
HUMILIATING.
GIMME THAT! THIS IS EVIDENCE IN AN ONGOING INVESTIGATION! GET THEM INSIDE, GUYS.
HERE, GO BACK.
GO BACK.
I WILL.
KEEP MOVING.
VERY BAD.
WE HAD IT FOR A MOMENT.
HOW'S IT FEEL?
I'VE HAD WORSE.
WELL, WE KNOW ONE THING FOR SURE...
WHAT'S THAT?
LIFE IS SAFER IN PRISON.
!
TRUE DAT.
YARDBIRDS by rudy harmony

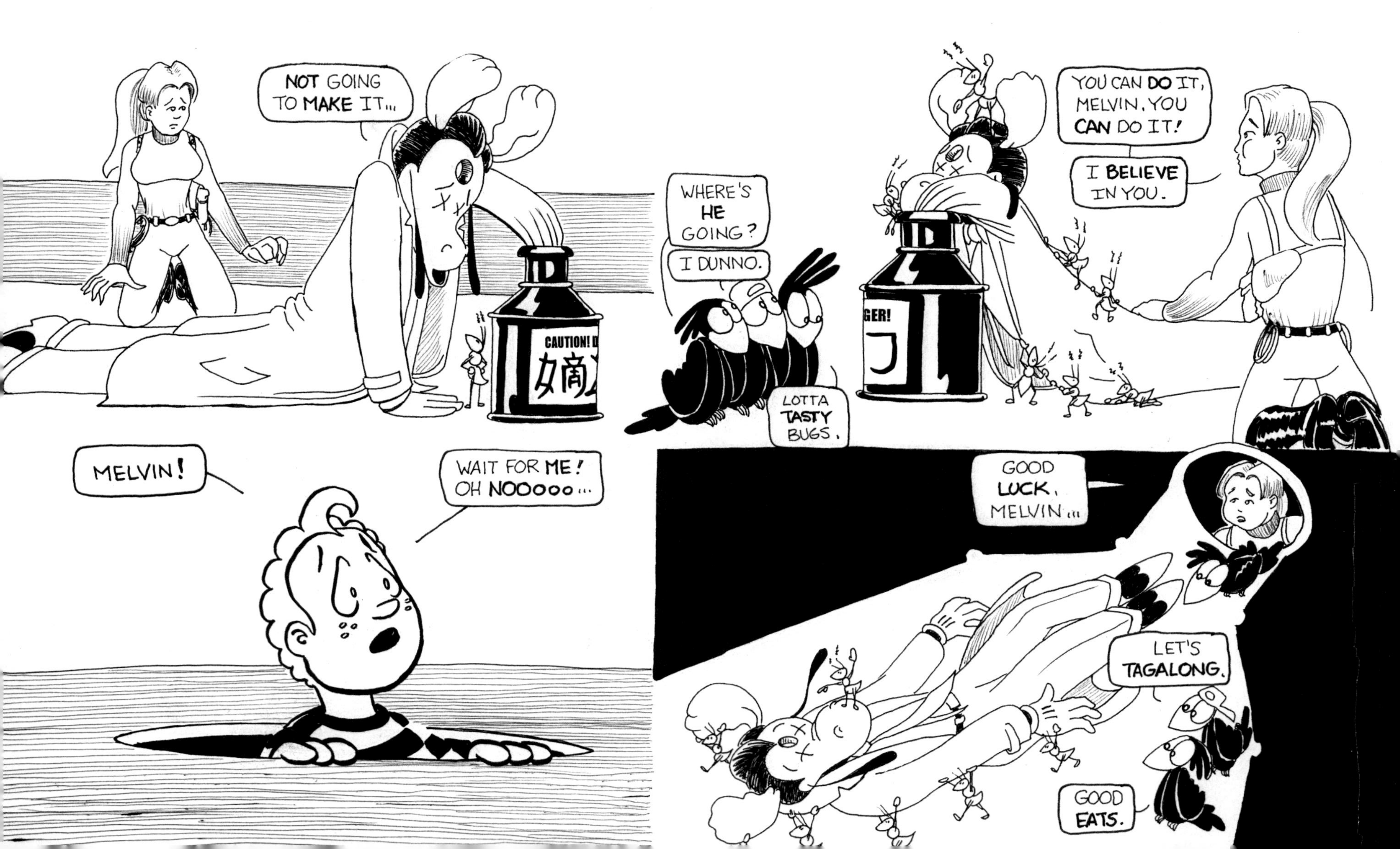
NOT GOING TO MAKE IT...
CAUTION! D
WHERE'S HE GOING?
I DUNNO.
LOTTA TASTY BUGS.
GER!
YOU CAN DO IT, MELVIN. YOU CAN DO IT!
I BELIEVE IN YOU.
MELVIN!
WAIT FOR ME! OH NOOooo...
GOOD LUCK, MELVIN...
LET'S TAGALONG.
GOOD EATS.

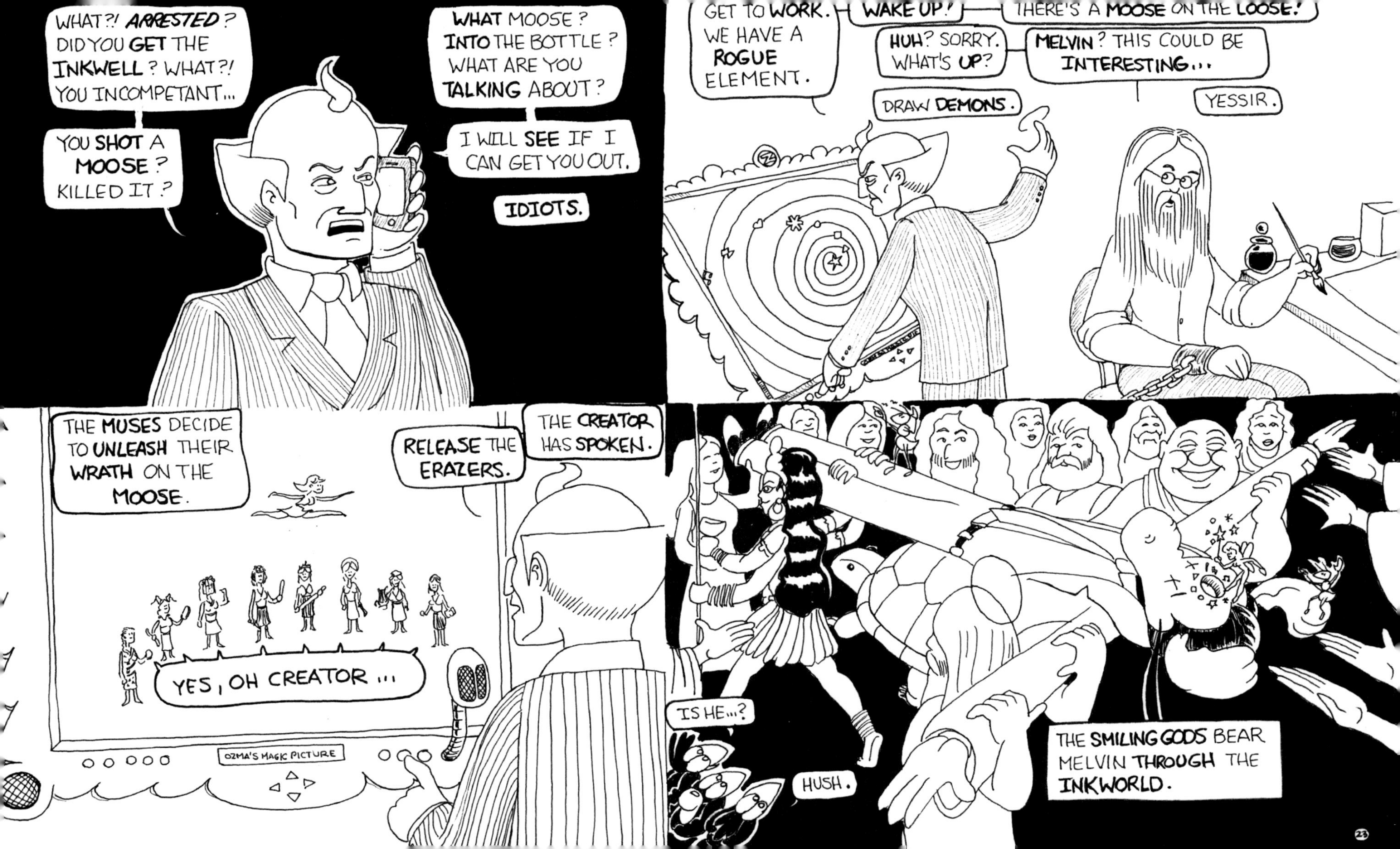
WHAT?! ARRESTED? DID YOU GET THE INKWELL? WHAT?! YOU INCOMPETANT...
YOU SHOT A MOOSE? KILLED IT?
WHAT MOOSE? INTO THE BOTTLE? WHAT ARE YOU TALKING ABOUT?
I WILL SEE IF I CAN GET YOU OUT.
IDIOTS.
GET TO WORK. WE HAVE A ROGUE ELEMENT.
WAKE UP!
THERE'S A MOOSE ON THE LOOSE!
HUH? SORRY. WHAT'S UP?
MELVIN? THIS COULD BE INTERESTING...
DRAW DEMONS.
YESSIR.
THE MUSES DECIDE TO UNLEASH THEIR WRATH ON THE MOOSE.
RELEASE THE ERAZERS.
THE CREATOR HAS SPOKEN.
YES, OH CREATOR ...
OZMA'S MAGIC PICTURE
IS HE...?
HUSH.
THE SMILING GODS BEAR MELVIN THROUGH THE INKWORLD.
23

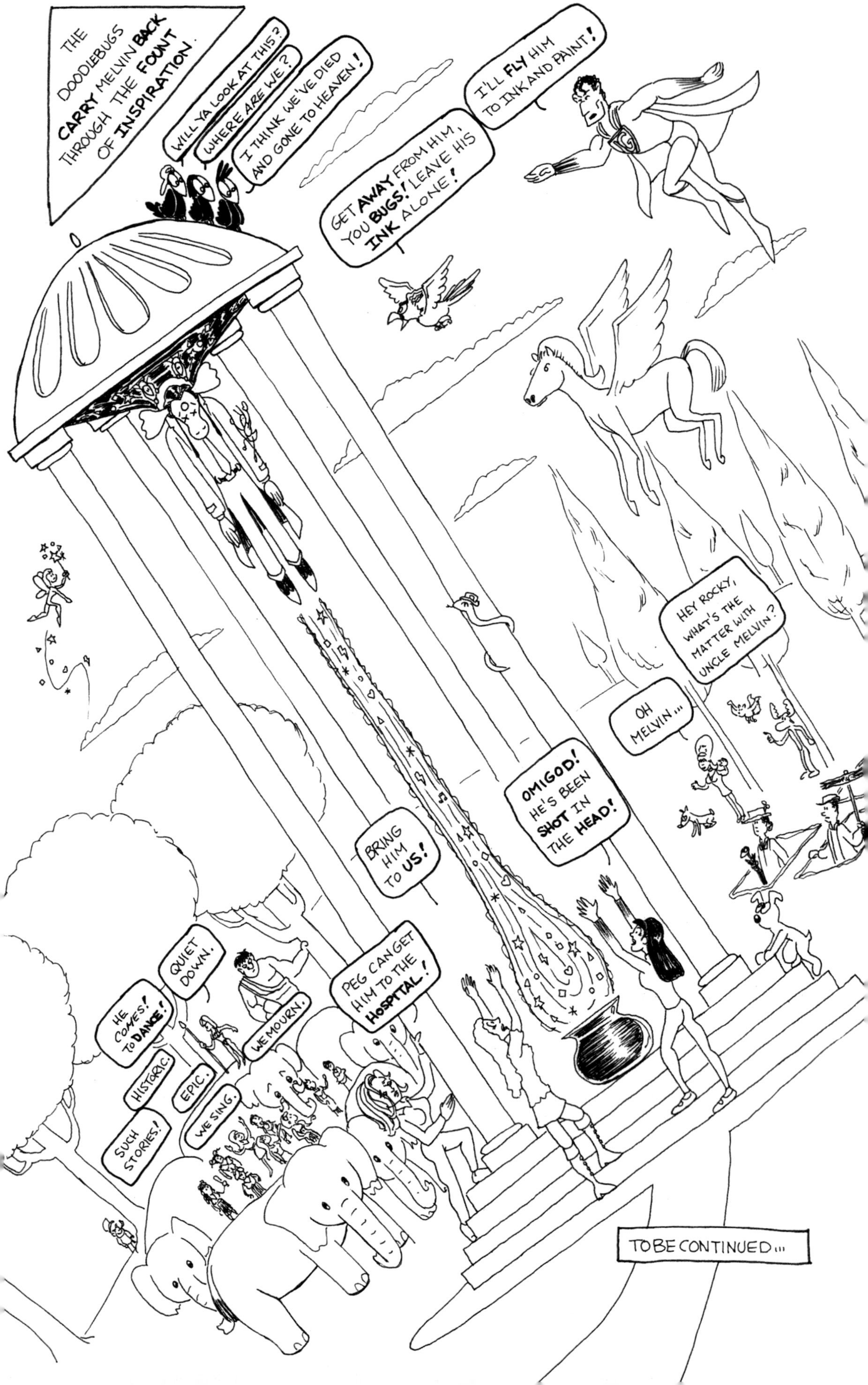

THE DOODLEBUGS CARRY MELVIN BACK THROUGH THE FOUNT OF INSPIRATION.
WILL YA LOOK AT THIS?
WHERE ARE WE?
I THINK WE'VE DIED AND GONE TO HEAVEN!
I'LL FLY HIM TO INK AND PAINT!
GET AWAY FROM HIM, YOU BUGS! LEAVE HIS INK ALONE!
HEY ROCKY, WHAT'S THE MATTER WITH UNCLE MELVIN?
OH MELVIN...
OMIGOD! HE'S BEEN SHOT IN THE HEAD!
BRING HIM TO US!
PEG CAN GET HIM TO THE HOSPITAL!
QUIET DOWN.
HE COMES! TO DANCE!
WE MOURN.
HISTORIC.
EPIC.
WE SING.
SUCH STORIES!
TO BE CONTINUED...

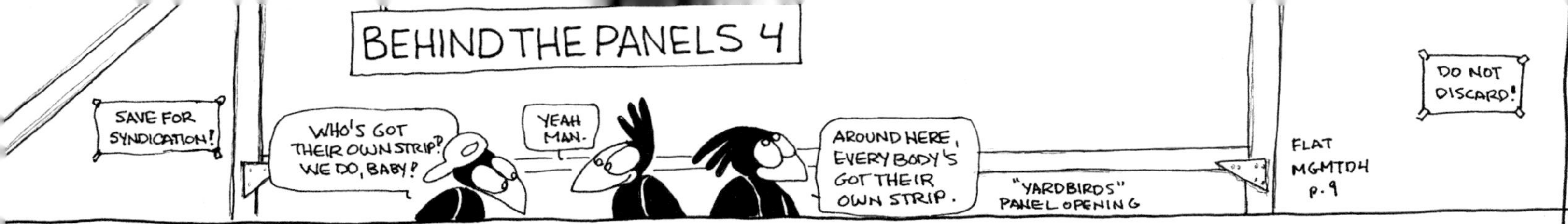
BEHIND THE PANELS 4
SAVE FOR SYNDICATION!
WHO'S GOT THEIR OWN STRIP? WE DO, BABY!
YEAH MAN.
AROUND HERE, EVERYBODY'S GOT THEIR OWN STRIP.
"YARDBIRDS" PANEL OPENING
FLAT MGMTD4 p. 9
DO NOT DISCARD!

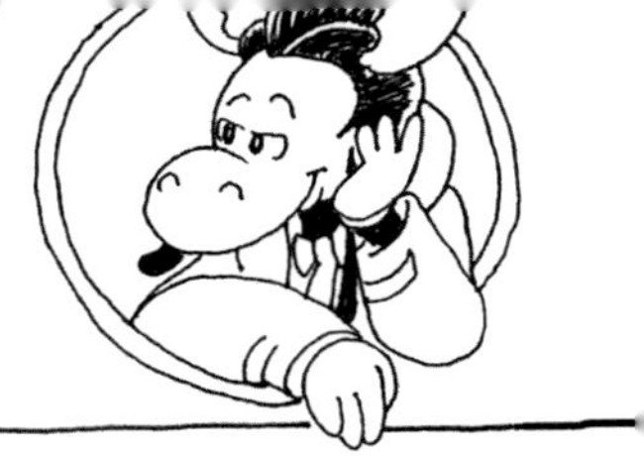

re: incarnations

THE METAPHORICAL MOOSE

WHAT'S A **METAPHOR**? FOR A **MOOSE**, IT'S OFTEN FOR BREAKFAST, LUNCH, AND DINNER.

BUT ALL **PUNS** ASIDE, THE MOOSE SYMBOLIZES **LONGEVITY**, WHICH IS **EVIDENT** FROM THE FACT THAT THE ANCESTORS OF THE **MOOSE** HAVE **INHABITED** THE EARTH FOR OVER **2.6 MILLION** YEARS. THE **MODERN** MOOSE HAS **SURVIVED** AND **EVOLVED** THROUGHOUT THE NORTHERN HEMISPHERE FOR THE LAST **10,000 YEARS.** LONGEVITY INDEED.

AS A SPIRIT AND ANIMAL **TOTEM**, THE MOOSE REPRESENTS MANY CHARACTER **TRAITS**, INCLUDING **COURAGE**, **WISDOM**, AND SHARING **JOY** IN **ACHIEVEMENT**.

MOOSE **CALVES** ARE **BORN** WITH THEIR **EYES OPEN**, WHICH DENOTES AN OPEN **INNER** EYE IN TOUCH WITH UNIVERSAL CONSCIOUSNESS AT BIRTH. MOOSE **ANTLERS** REPRESENT A **CROWN** OF CONSCIOUSNESS WHICH **COLLECTS** UNIVERSAL **ENERGY** THROUGHOUT THEIR LIVES. MOOSE ALSO REPRESENT **FEMININE** ENERGY AND **REBIRTH**. THEIR EASE IN **WATER** (THE GREAT **WOMB** FROM WHICH ALL **LIFE** SPRINGS FORTH) AND ABILITY TO **SUBMERGE** AND **EMERGE** WITH LIFE **SUSTENANCE** DENOTE THE POWER OF **DEATH** AND **REBIRTH**. FINALLY, MOOSE HAVE THE INNATE **POWER** OF **INVISIBILITY.** ALTHOUGH THEY ARE HUGE, **MAJESTIC** CREATURES, THEY CAN **CAMOUFLAGE** THEMSELVES QUICKLY BY BLENDING **MYSTICALLY** INTO THEIR SURROUNDINGS. IN OUR STORY, A **TOODE'S INVISIBILITY** IN THE THREED WORLD **DEPENDS** ON THE AMOUNT OF **BELIEF** AND **AWARENESS** OF THE **THREED** WHO IS **LOOKING.**

HOW MUCH DO **YOU** SEE, **DEAREST THREEDER**?

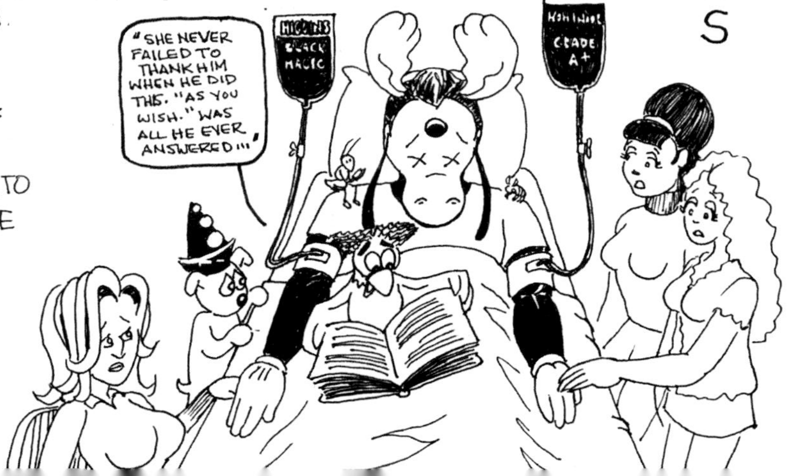
"SHE NEVER FAILED TO THANK HIM WHEN HE DID THIS. "AS YOU WISH." WAS ALL HE EVER ANSWERED!!!"

PETERS 3·5·2013

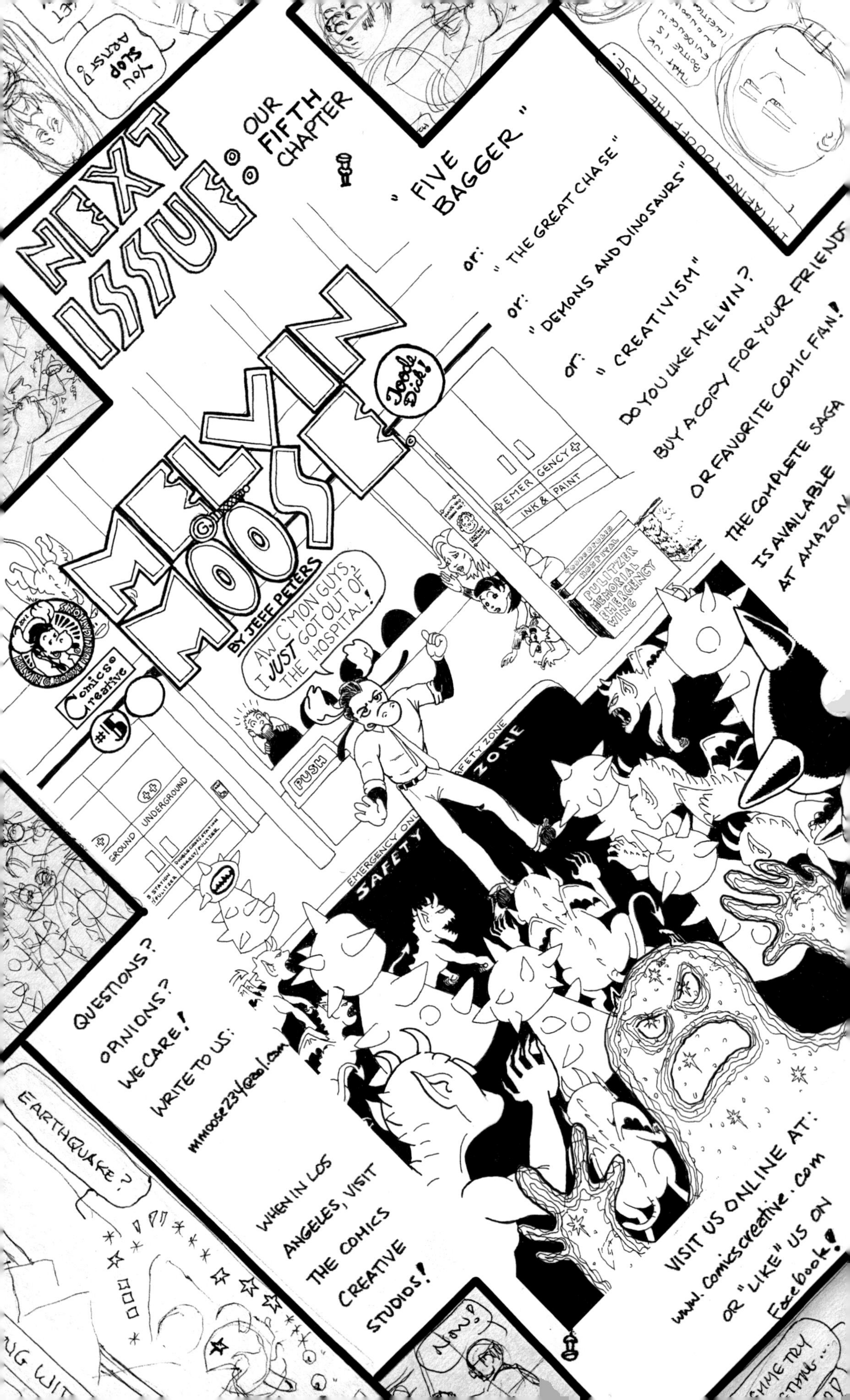
NEXT ISSUE
OUR FIFTH CHAPTER
"FIVE BAGGER"
or: "THE GREAT CHASE"
or: "DEMONS AND DINOSAURS"
or: "CREATIVISM"
DO YOU LIKE MELVIN?
BUY A COPY FOR YOUR FRIENDS OR FAVORITE COMIC FAN!
THE COMPLETE SAGA IS AVAILABLE AT AMAZON
MELVIN MOOSE
Toodle Dick!
BY JEFF PETERS
Comicsc Creative
#5
AW C'MON GUYS, I JUST GOT OUT OF THE HOSPITAL!
PUSH
EMER GENCY
INK & PAINT
TOODEOPOLIS HOSPITAL
PULITZER MEMORIAL EMERGENCY WING
GROUND
UNDERGROUND
SAFETY ZONE
EMERGENCY ONLY
QUESTIONS? OPINIONS? WE CARE! WRITE TO US: mmoose234@aol.com
WHEN IN LOS ANGELES, VISIT THE COMICS CREATIVE STUDIOS!
VISIT US ONLINE AT: www.comicscreative.com OR "LIKE" US ON Facebook!
EARTHQUAKE?

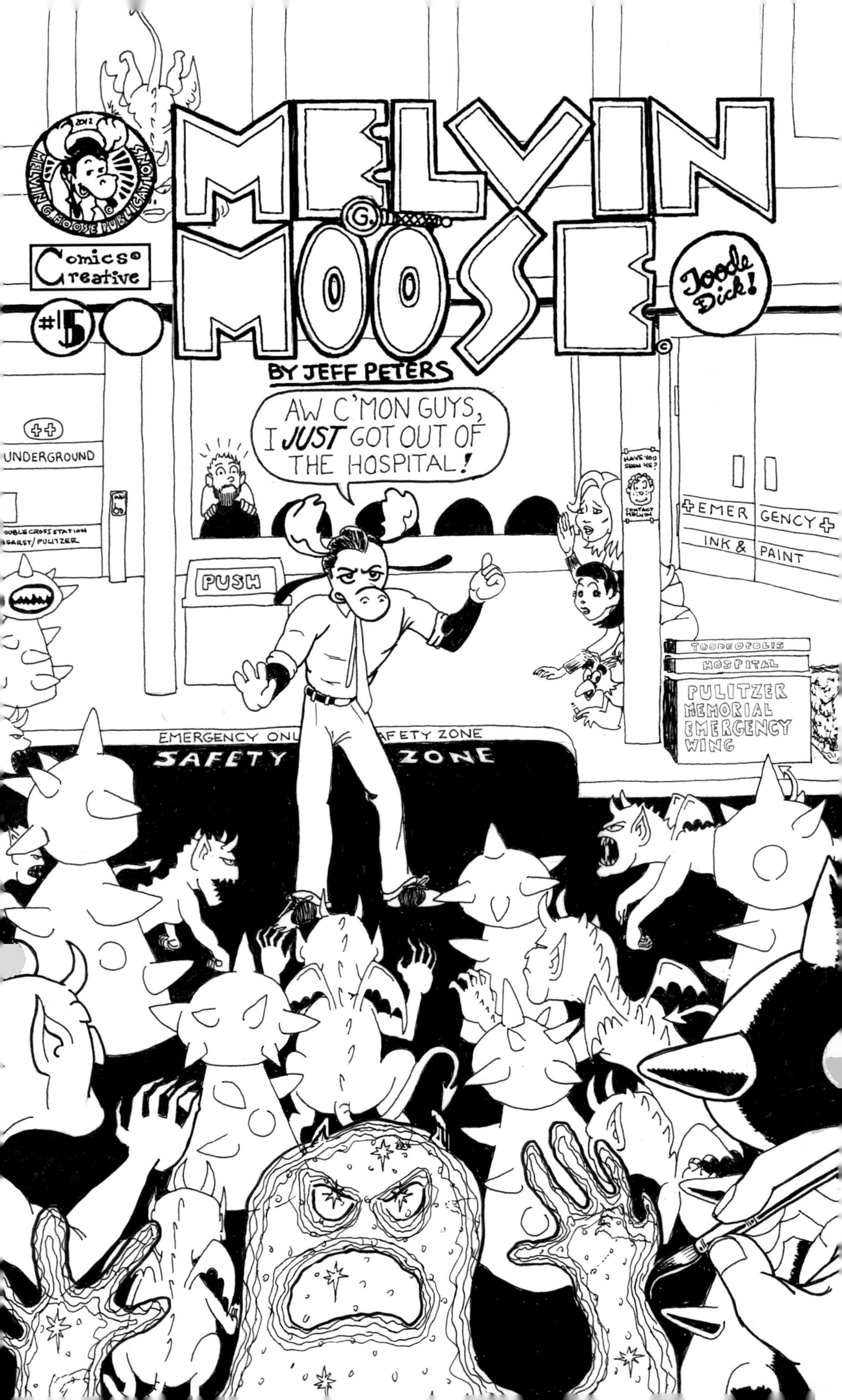
MELVIN G. MOOSE PUBLICATIONS
2012
Comics Creative
#15
MELVIN G. MOOSE
Toode Dick!
BY JEFF PETERS
AW C'MON GUYS, I JUST GOT OUT OF THE HOSPITAL!
UNDERGROUND
PUSH
HAVE YOU SEEN ME?
CONTACT MELVIN
EMERGENCY
INK & PAINT
TOODEOPOLIS
HOSPITAL
PULITZER MEMORIAL EMERGENCY WING
SAFETY ZONE

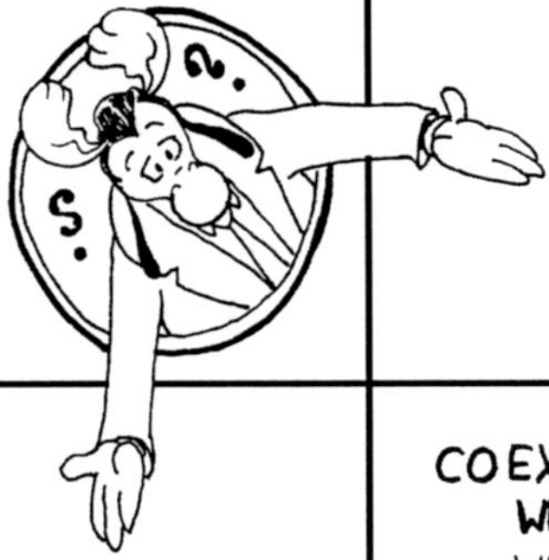

Perceptions...

MELVIN G. MOOSE
TOODE DICK
CHAPTER (5) FIVE
"FIVE BAGGER"

JEFFREY
EDWARD
PETERS

"THROUGH THE LOOKING GLASS DARKLY."

THIS ONE IS FOR THOSE WHO HAVE CHASED ME, AND THOSE WHOM I HAVE CHASED.

COEXISTENCE

WHY CAN'T WE ALL JUST GET **ALONG**?

WHEN TWO **ENTITIES** MEET, THEY HAVE A BRIEF MOMENT TO DETERMINE WHETHER THEY WILL BE **ALLIES** OR **ENEMIES**. IF THEY HAVE A **LIKE-MINDEDNESS** OF SPIRIT, THEY BECOME **FRIENDS** AND MAYBE MORE. IF ONE PERCIEVES THE OTHER TO BE A **THREAT**, OR NO **COMPROMISE** CAN BE MADE BETWEEN THEIR **WORLD VIEWS**, THE TWO FORCES MAY ATTEMPT TO **DESTROY** EACH OTHER. THIS DEMONSTRATION OF **POWER** MAY DRAW OTHER ALLIES AND ENEMIES INTO THEIR **STRUGGLE**. THESE CONFLICTS ARE WHAT MAKE **HIGH DRAMA** AND GREAT **CHASE** SCENES. SUCH IS THE CASE BETWEEN **MELVIN G. MOOSE** AND THE **ILLUSTRATI**.

AND SO, WE'RE **OFF** AND **RUNNING**!

GOT INK?

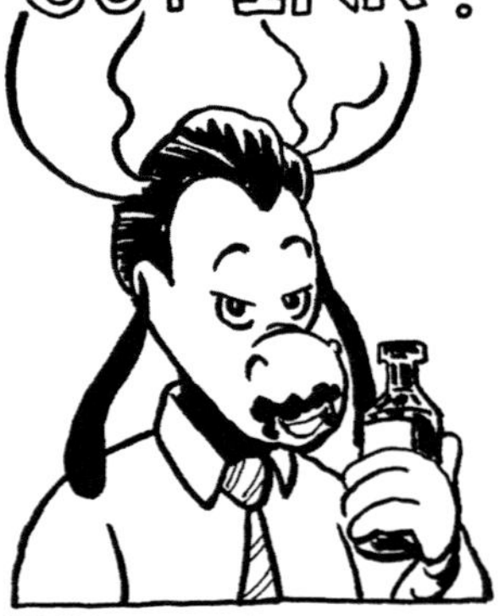

INK DOES A TOODE BODY GOODE!

brought to you by:

THE TOODEOPOLIS INK COUNCIL

SINCE THE BEGINNING OF RECORDED HISTORY.

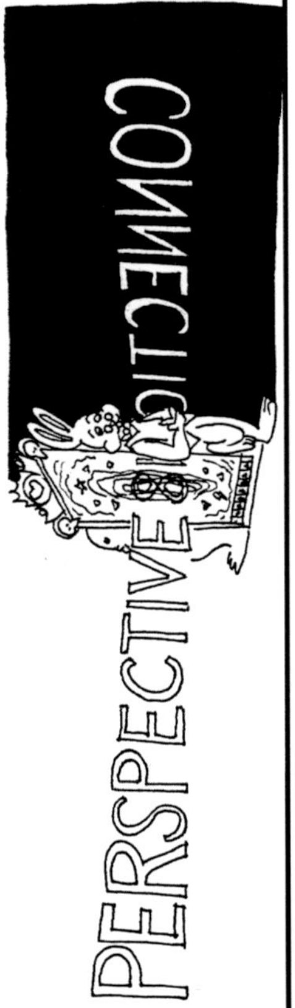
PERSPECTIVE
CONNECTIO

POPPING IN AND OUT OF PAVEMENT PICTURES

"HOW DO **I** GET INTO TOODEOPOLIS?" IS THE NUMBER ONE **QUESTION** I AM **ASKED** BY MY **DEAREST** THREADERS. LET ME **COUNT** A FEW OF THE **WAYS**...

1. IMAGINATION (THROUGHOUT THE CITY)
2. DREAMS (SLUMBERLAND APARTMENTS : OLD STRIP)
3. DAYDREAMS (SEE RALPH : AMINATION)
4. BRAINSTORMS (ie TORNADOES : OZ)
5. MYSTERIOUS ISLANDS (BERMUDA TRIANGLE : INTERNATIONAL WATERS)
6. SPIKE OF POWER (LAS VEGAS : STORYVILLE)
7. TOONTOWN TUNNEL (ACME WAREHOUSE : AMINATION)
8. CHALK PICTURES (HYDE PARK : FOUNT OF INSPIRATION)
9. COSMIC CUBE (FOOMTOWN)
10. COSMIC TREADMILL (NATIONAL CITY)
11. MUNDEN'S BAR (CYNOSURE : INDEPENDENT HEIGHTS)
12. TELEPHONE (DIGITAL STRIP MATRICES)
13. INKWELL (CREATIVE RESERVOIR)
14. OZMA'S MAGIC PICTURE (ILLUSTRATI CLUB)
15. THE TENNIEL MIRROR (ILLUSTRATI CLUB LOBBY : TOODEOPOLIS WHEREABOUTS ARE CURRENTLY UNKNOWN)

OR, YOU CAN SIMPLY **FLOP** THE **PAGE**.
HERE WE **GO**!

JEFF PETERS 3·22·2013

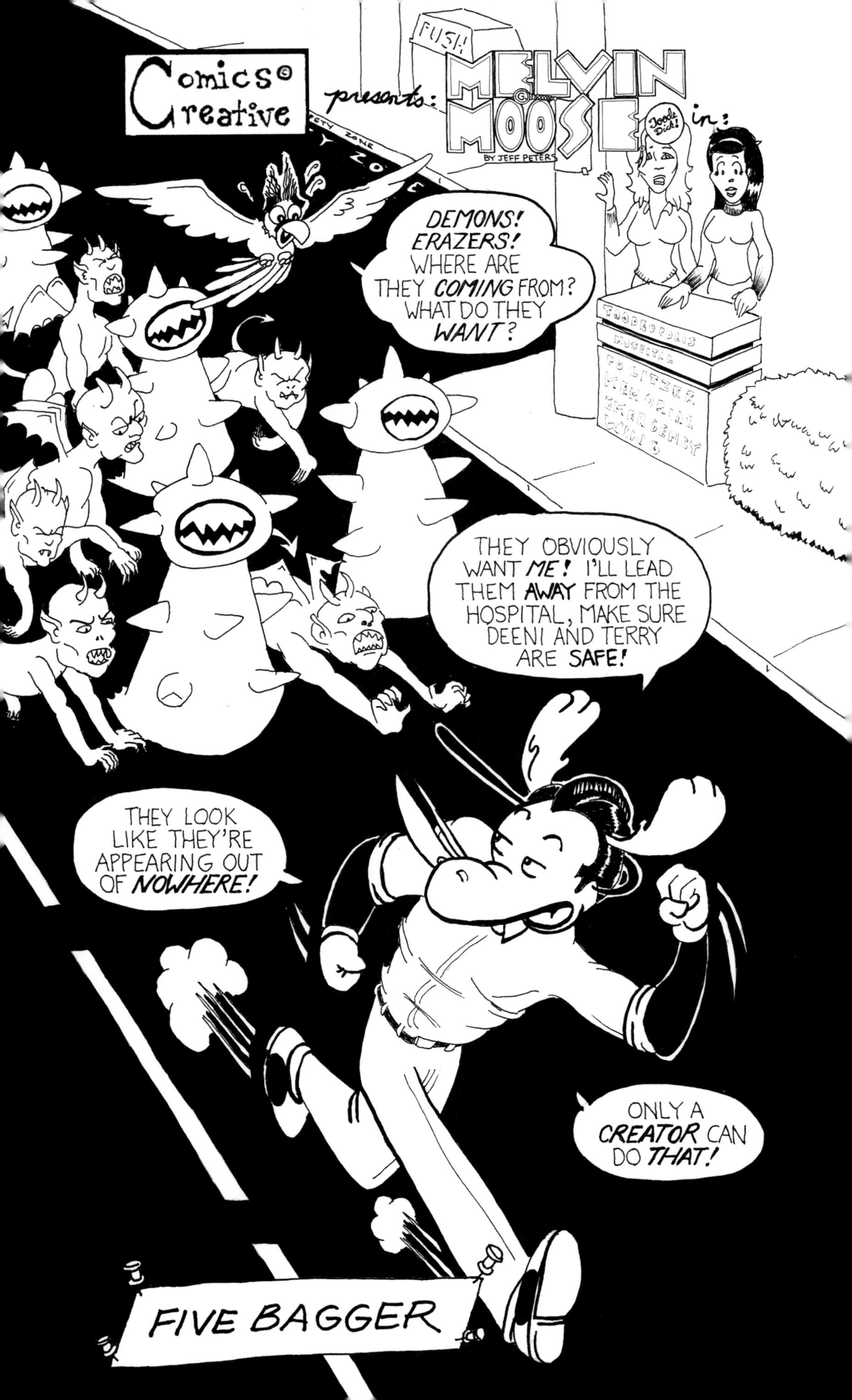Comics© Creative
presents:
MELVIN G. MOOSE
Toodle Dick!
BY JEFF PETERS
in:
PUSH
DEMONS! ERAZERS! WHERE ARE THEY COMING FROM? WHAT DO THEY WANT?
TOODEOPOLIS HOSPITAL
PULITZER MEMORIAL EMERGENCY WING
THEY OBVIOUSLY WANT ME! I'LL LEAD THEM AWAY FROM THE HOSPITAL, MAKE SURE DEENI AND TERRY ARE SAFE!
THEY LOOK LIKE THEY'RE APPEARING OUT OF NOWHERE!
ONLY A CREATOR CAN DO THAT!
FIVE BAGGER

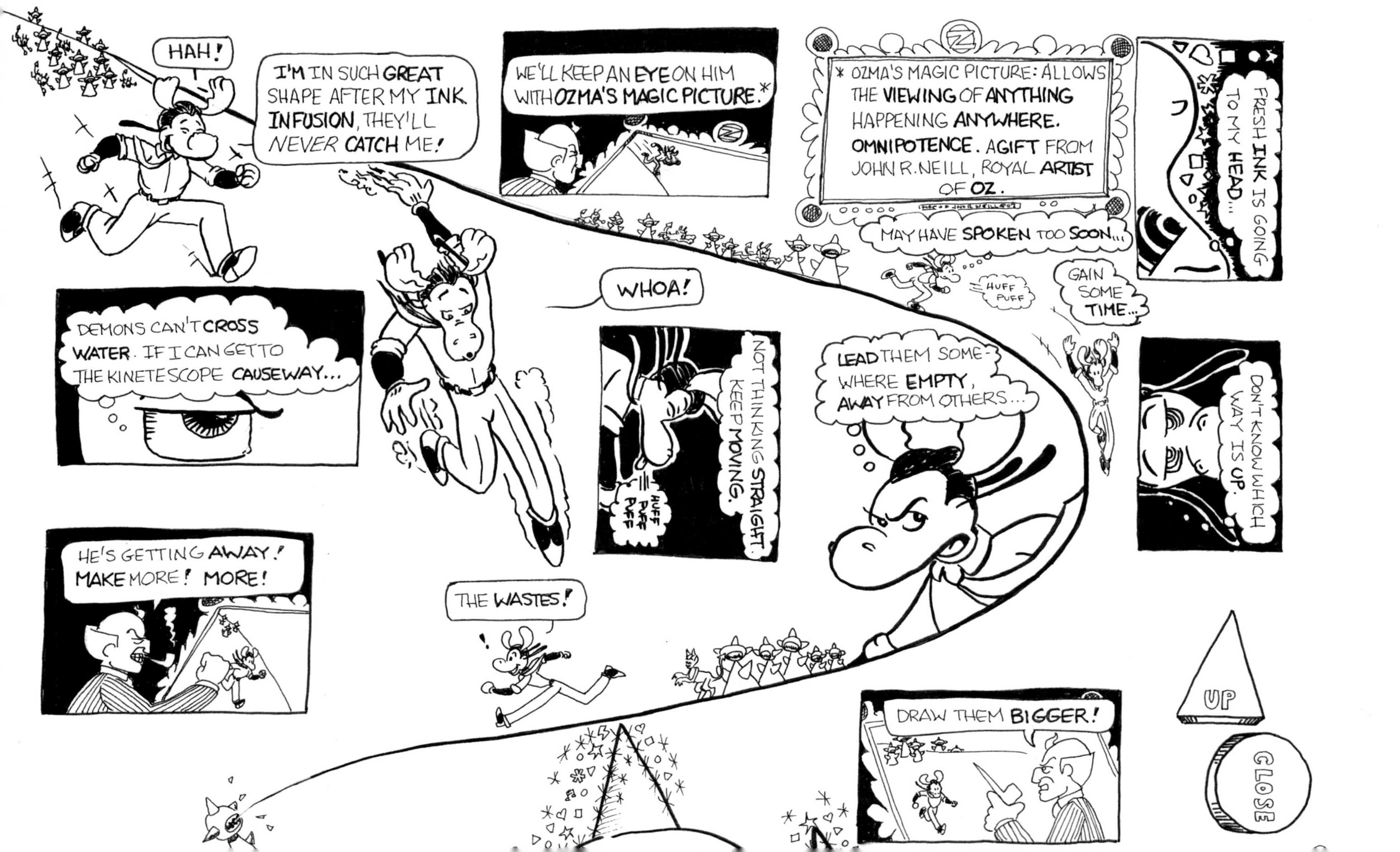
HAH!
I'M IN SUCH GREAT SHAPE AFTER MY INK INFUSION, THEY'LL NEVER CATCH ME!
WE'LL KEEP AN EYE ON HIM WITH OZMA'S MAGIC PICTURE.*
* OZMA'S MAGIC PICTURE: ALLOWS THE VIEWING OF ANYTHING HAPPENING ANYWHERE. OMNIPOTENCE. A GIFT FROM JOHN R. NEILL, ROYAL ARTIST OF OZ.
FRESH INK IS GOING TO MY HEAD...
MAY HAVE SPOKEN TOO SOON...
HUFF PUFF
GAIN SOME TIME...
DEMONS CAN'T CROSS WATER. IF I CAN GET TO THE KINETESCOPE CAUSEWAY...
WHOA!
NOT THINKING STRAIGHT. KEEP MOVING.
HUFF PUFF PUFF
LEAD THEM SOME-WHERE EMPTY, AWAY FROM OTHERS...
DON'T KNOW WHICH WAY IS UP.
HE'S GETTING AWAY! MAKE MORE! MORE!
THE WASTES!
DRAW THEM BIGGER!
UP
CLOSE

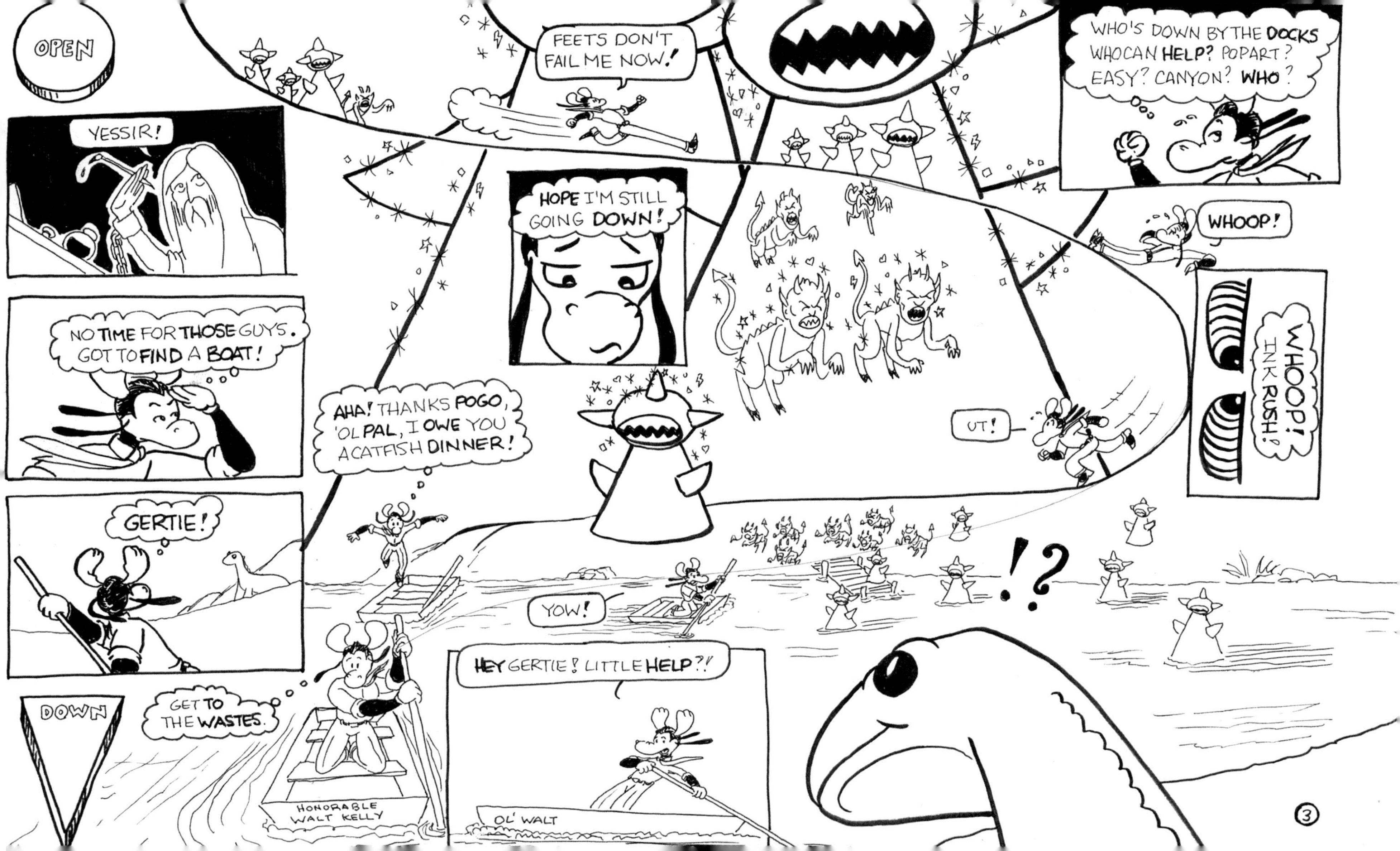
OPEN
YESSIR!
NO TIME FOR THOSE GUYS. GOT TO FIND A BOAT!
GERTIE!
DOWN
GET TO THE WASTES.
HONORABLE WALT KELLY
FEETS DON'T FAIL ME NOW!
HOPE I'M STILL GOING DOWN!
AHA! THANKS POGO, 'OL PAL, I OWE YOU A CATFISH DINNER!
YOW!
HEY GERTIE! LITTLE HELP?!
OL' WALT
WHO'S DOWN BY THE DOCKS WHO CAN HELP? POPART? EASY? CANYON? WHO?
WHOOP!
WHOOP! INK RUSH!
UT!
!?
3

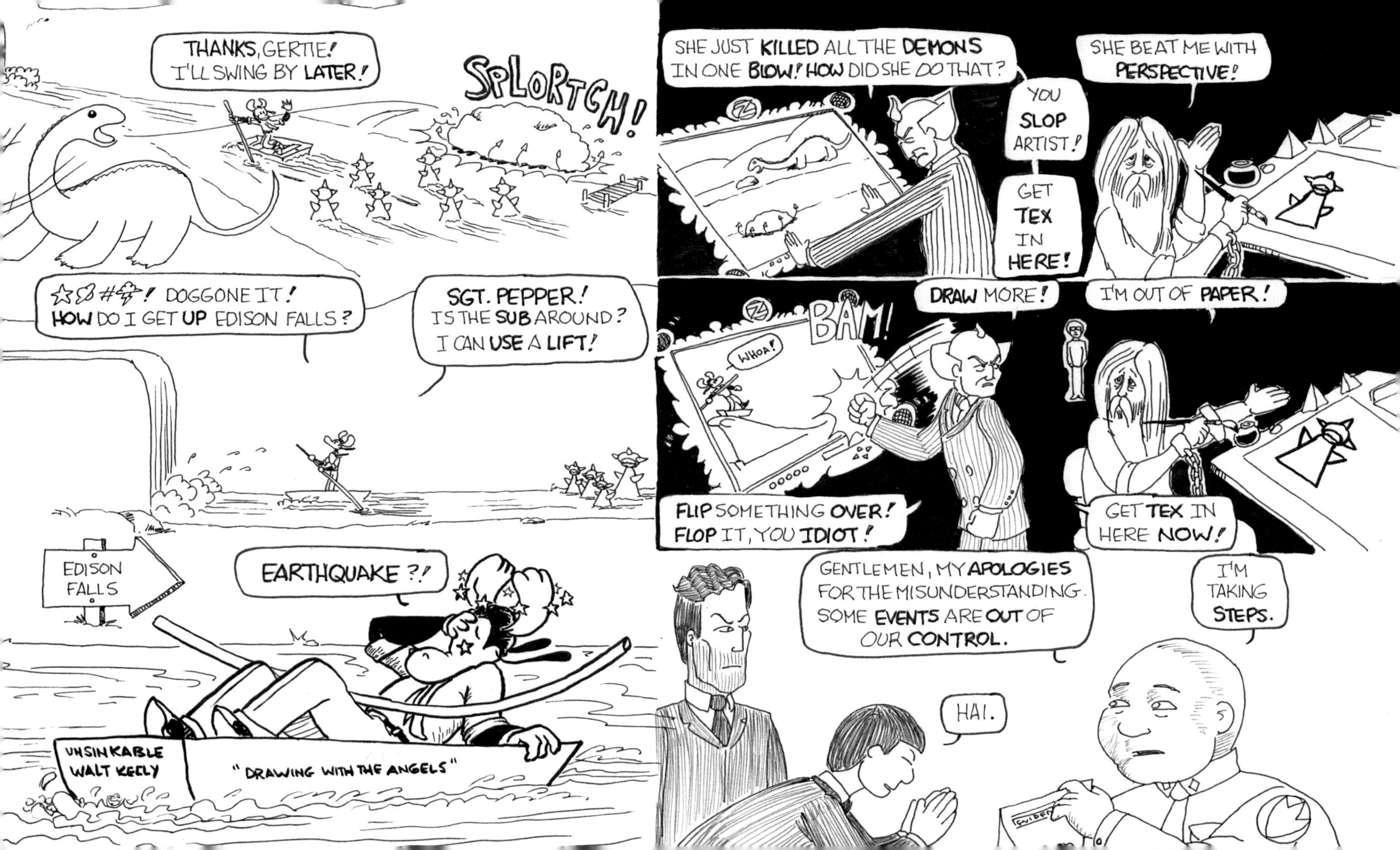
THANKS, GERTIE! I'LL SWING BY LATER!
SPLORTCH!
☆✪#⚡! DOGGONE IT! HOW DO I GET UP EDISON FALLS?
SGT. PEPPER! IS THE SUB AROUND? I CAN USE A LIFT!
EDISON FALLS
EARTHQUAKE?!
UNSINKABLE WALT KEELY
"DRAWING WITH THE ANGELS"
SHE JUST KILLED ALL THE DEMONS IN ONE BLOW! HOW DID SHE DO THAT?
YOU SLOP ARTIST!
GET TEX IN HERE!
SHE BEAT ME WITH PERSPECTIVE!
DRAW MORE!
I'M OUT OF PAPER!
BAM!
WHOA!
FLIP SOMETHING OVER! FLOP IT, YOU IDIOT!
GET TEX IN HERE NOW!
GENTLEMEN, MY APOLOGIES FOR THE MISUNDERSTANDING. SOME EVENTS ARE OUT OF OUR CONTROL.
I'M TAKING STEPS.
HAI.

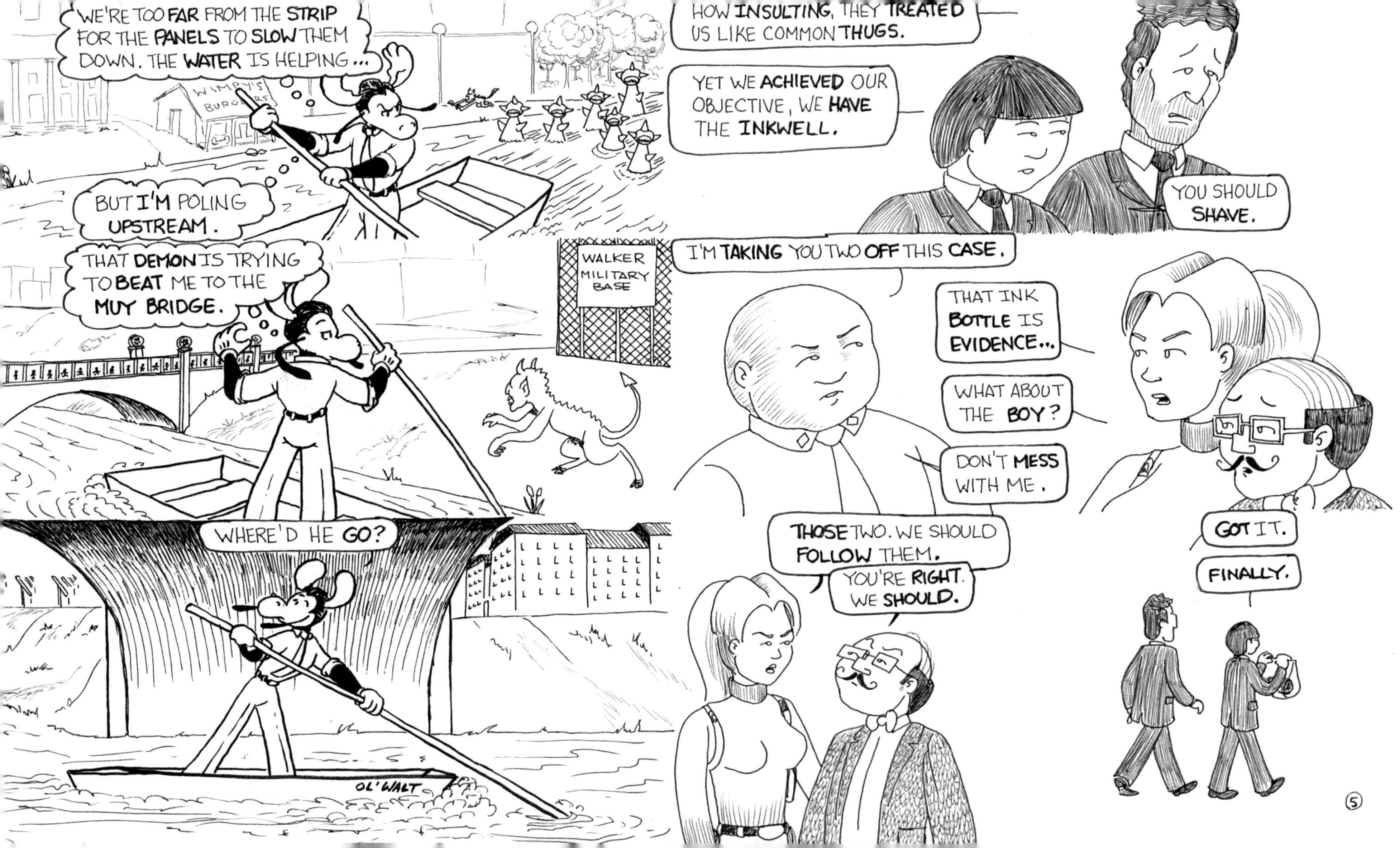
WE'RE TOO FAR FROM THE STRIP FOR THE PANELS TO SLOW THEM DOWN. THE WATER IS HELPING...
WIMPY'S BURGERS
BUT I'M POLING UPSTREAM.
THAT DEMON IS TRYING TO BEAT ME TO THE MUY BRIDGE.
WALKER MILITARY BASE
WHERE'D HE GO?
OL' WALT
HOW INSULTING, THEY TREATED US LIKE COMMON THUGS.
YET WE ACHIEVED OUR OBJECTIVE, WE HAVE THE INKWELL.
YOU SHOULD SHAVE.
I'M TAKING YOU TWO OFF THIS CASE.
THAT INK BOTTLE IS EVIDENCE...
WHAT ABOUT THE BOY?
DON'T MESS WITH ME.
THOSE TWO. WE SHOULD FOLLOW THEM.
YOU'RE RIGHT. WE SHOULD.
GOT IT.
FINALLY.

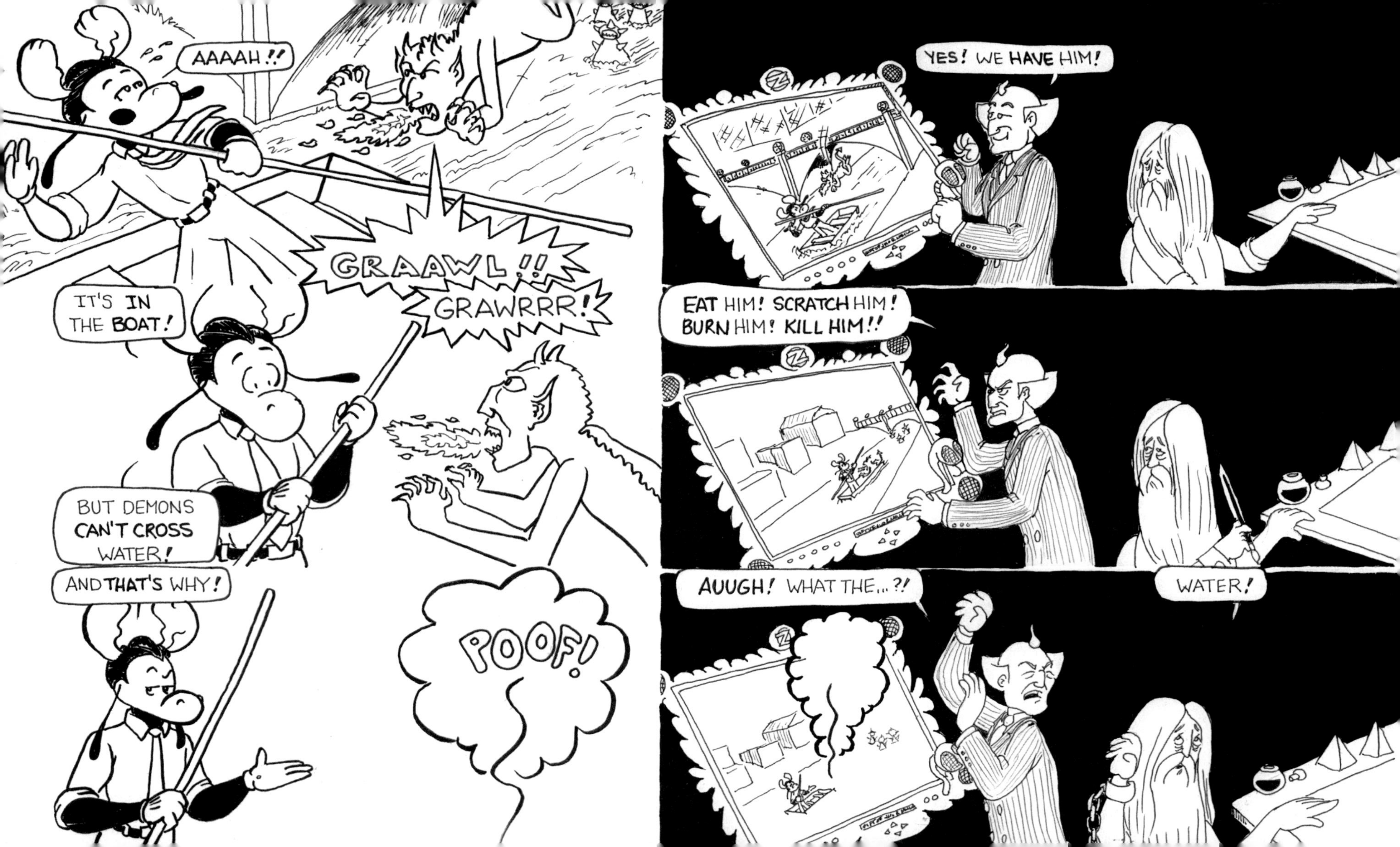
AAAAH!!
GRAAWL!!
GRAWRRR!
IT'S IN THE BOAT!
BUT DEMONS CAN'T CROSS WATER!
AND THAT'S WHY!
POOF!
YES! WE HAVE HIM!
EAT HIM! SCRATCH HIM! BURN HIM! KILL HIM!!
AUUGH! WHAT THE...?!
WATER!

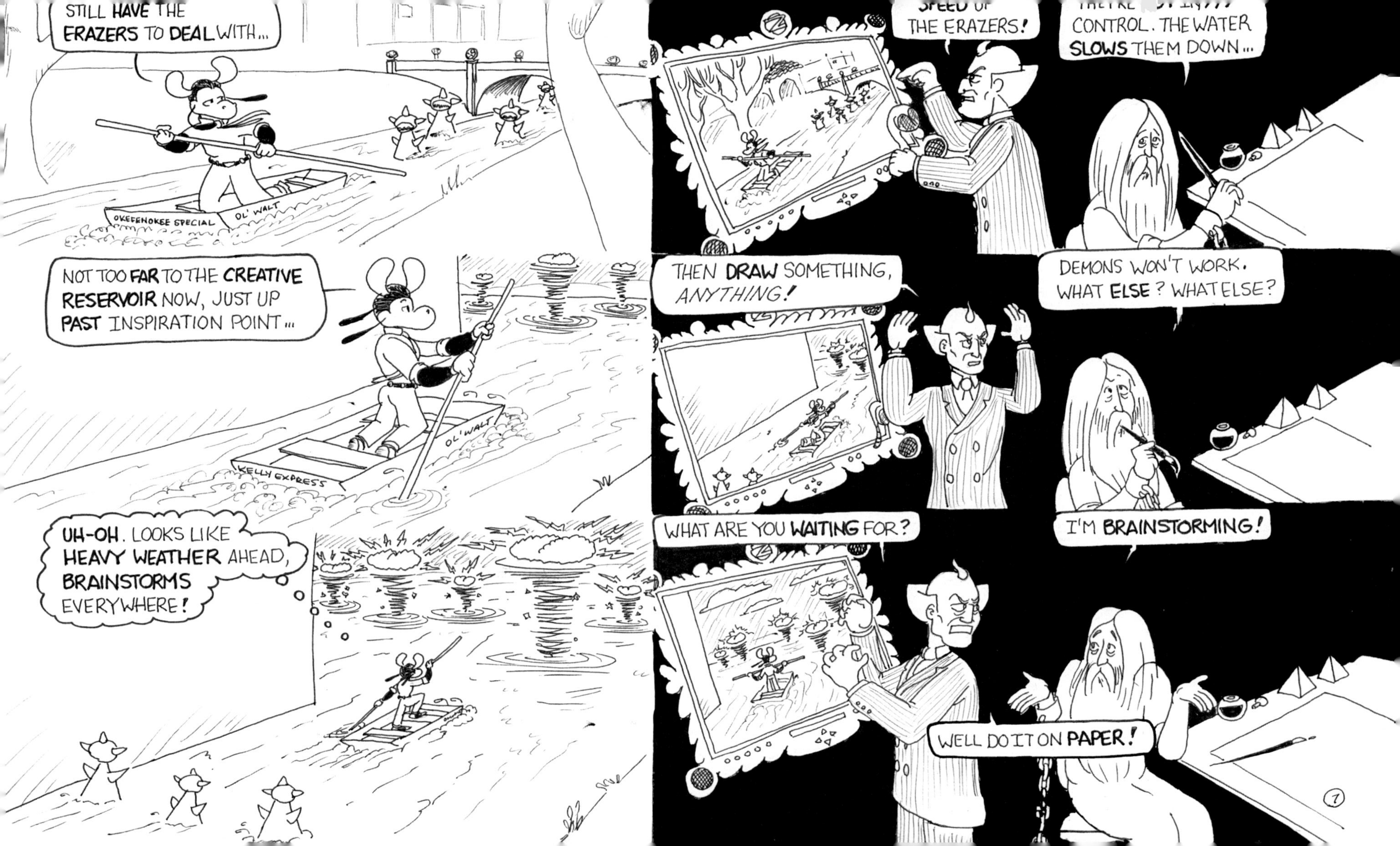
STILL HAVE THE ERAZERS TO DEAL WITH...
OKEFENOKEE SPECIAL
OL' WALT
NOT TOO FAR TO THE CREATIVE RESERVOIR NOW, JUST UP PAST INSPIRATION POINT...
OL' WALT
KELLY EXPRESS
UH-OH. LOOKS LIKE HEAVY WEATHER AHEAD, BRAINSTORMS EVERYWHERE!
THE ERAZERS!
CONTROL. THE WATER SLOWS THEM DOWN...
THEN DRAW SOMETHING, ANYTHING!
DEMONS WON'T WORK. WHAT ELSE? WHAT ELSE?
WHAT ARE YOU WAITING FOR?
I'M BRAINSTORMING!
WELL DO IT ON PAPER!
7

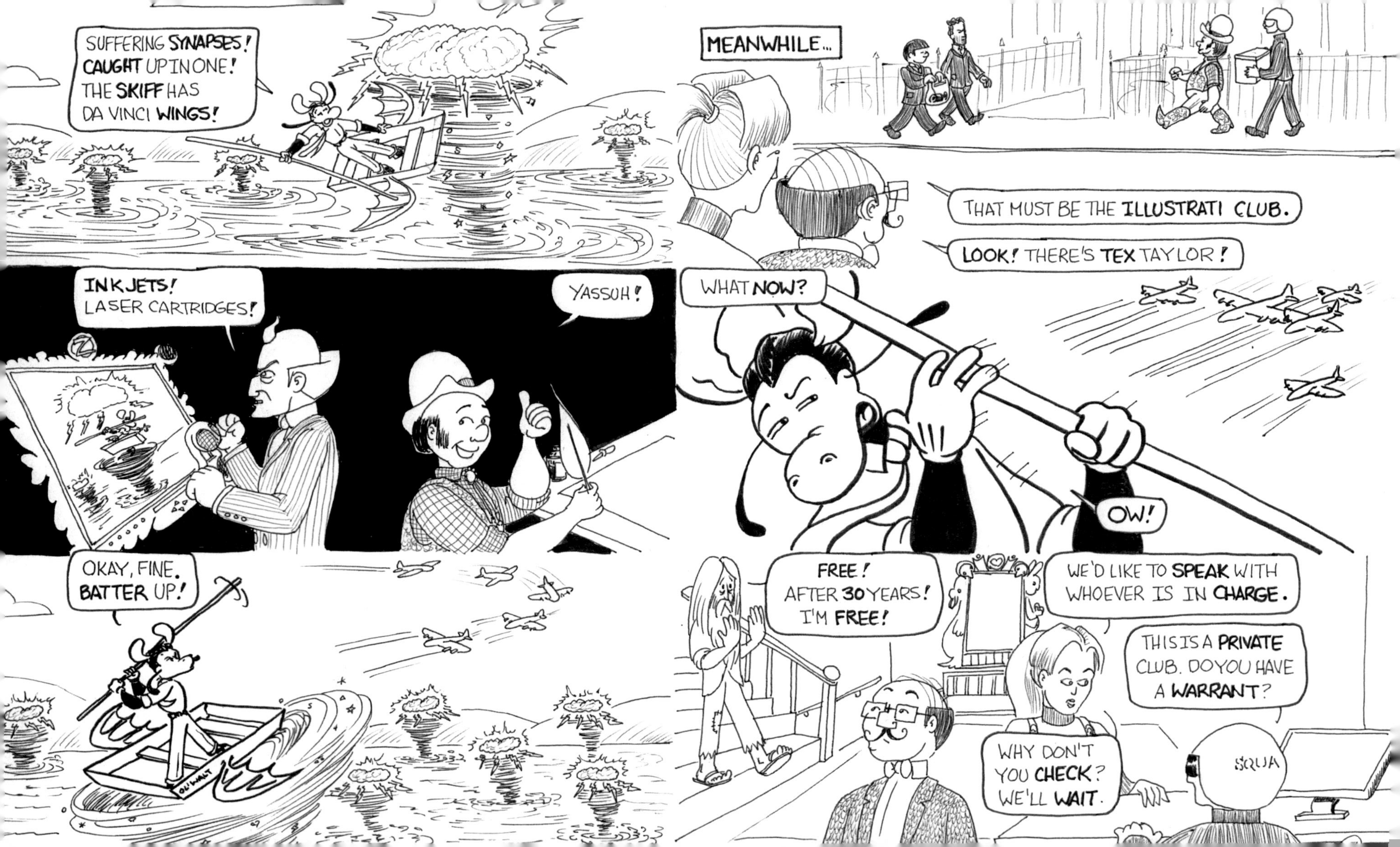
SUFFERING SYNAPSES! CAUGHT UP IN ONE! THE SKIFF HAS DA VINCI WINGS!
INKJETS! LASER CARTRIDGES!
YASSUH!
OKAY, FINE. BATTER UP!
OL' WALT
MEANWHILE...
THAT MUST BE THE ILLUSTRATI CLUB.
LOOK! THERE'S TEX TAYLOR!
WHAT NOW?
OW!
FREE! AFTER 30 YEARS! I'M FREE!
WE'D LIKE TO SPEAK WITH WHOEVER IS IN CHARGE.
THIS IS A PRIVATE CLUB. DO YOU HAVE A WARRANT?
WHY DON'T YOU CHECK? WE'LL WAIT.
SQUA

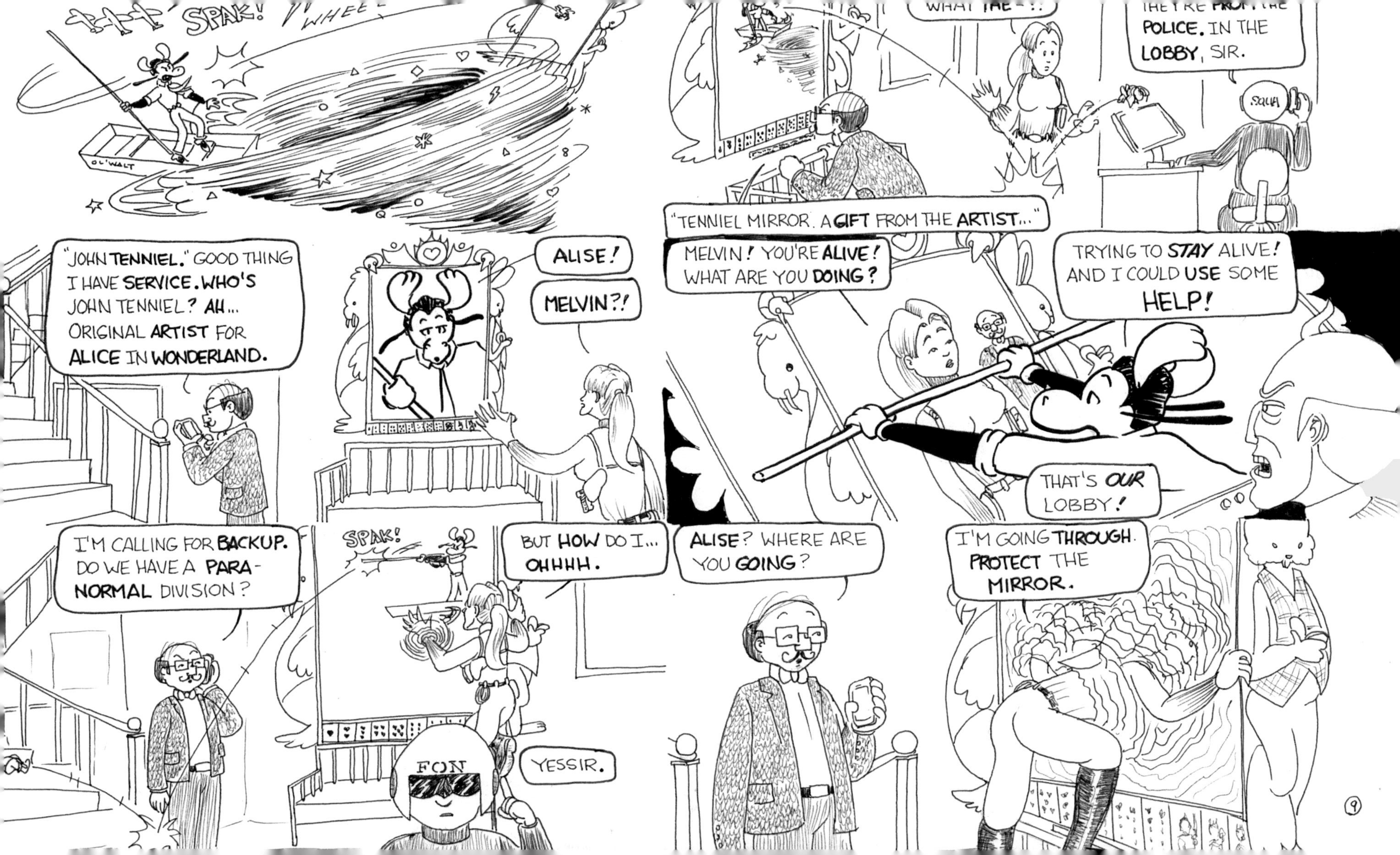
SPAK!
WHEE
OL' WALT
WHAT THE—?!
THEY'RE FROM THE POLICE. IN THE LOBBY, SIR.
SQUA
"TENNIEL MIRROR. A GIFT FROM THE ARTIST..."
"JOHN TENNIEL." GOOD THING I HAVE SERVICE. WHO'S JOHN TENNIEL? AH... ORIGINAL ARTIST FOR ALICE IN WONDERLAND.
ALISE!
MELVIN?!
MELVIN! YOU'RE ALIVE! WHAT ARE YOU DOING?
TRYING TO STAY ALIVE! AND I COULD USE SOME HELP!
THAT'S OUR LOBBY!
I'M CALLING FOR BACKUP. DO WE HAVE A PARA-NORMAL DIVISION?
SPAK!
BUT HOW DO I... OHHHH.
FON
YESSIR.
ALISE? WHERE ARE YOU GOING?
I'M GOING THROUGH. PROTECT THE MIRROR.

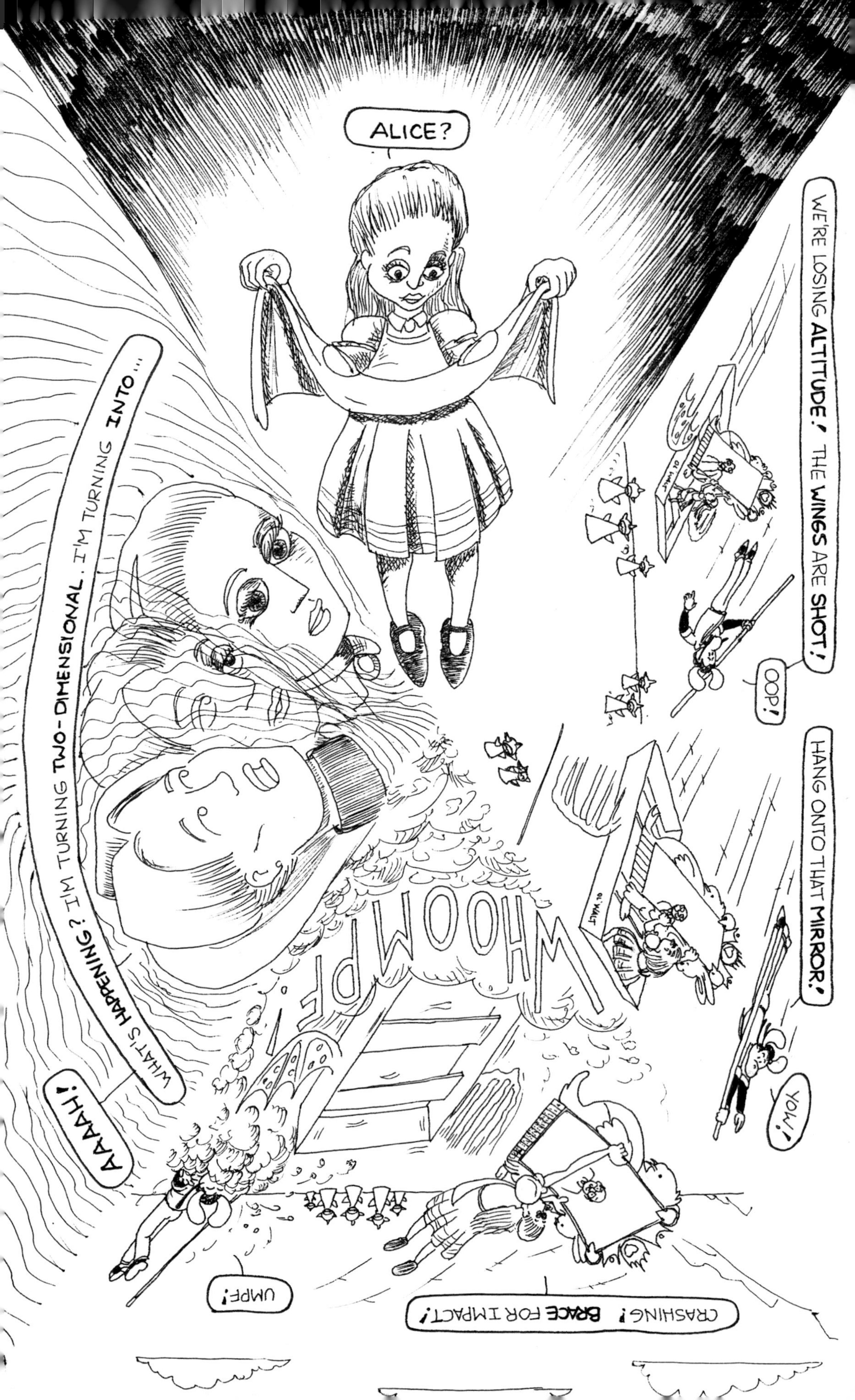
ALICE?
WHAT'S HAPPENING? I'M TURNING TWO-DIMENSIONAL. I'M TURNING INTO...
WE'RE LOSING ALTITUDE! THE WINGS ARE SHOT!
OOP!
HANG ONTO THAT MIRROR!
YOW!
WHOOMPF!
AAAAH!
CRASHING! BRACE FOR IMPACT!
UMPF!

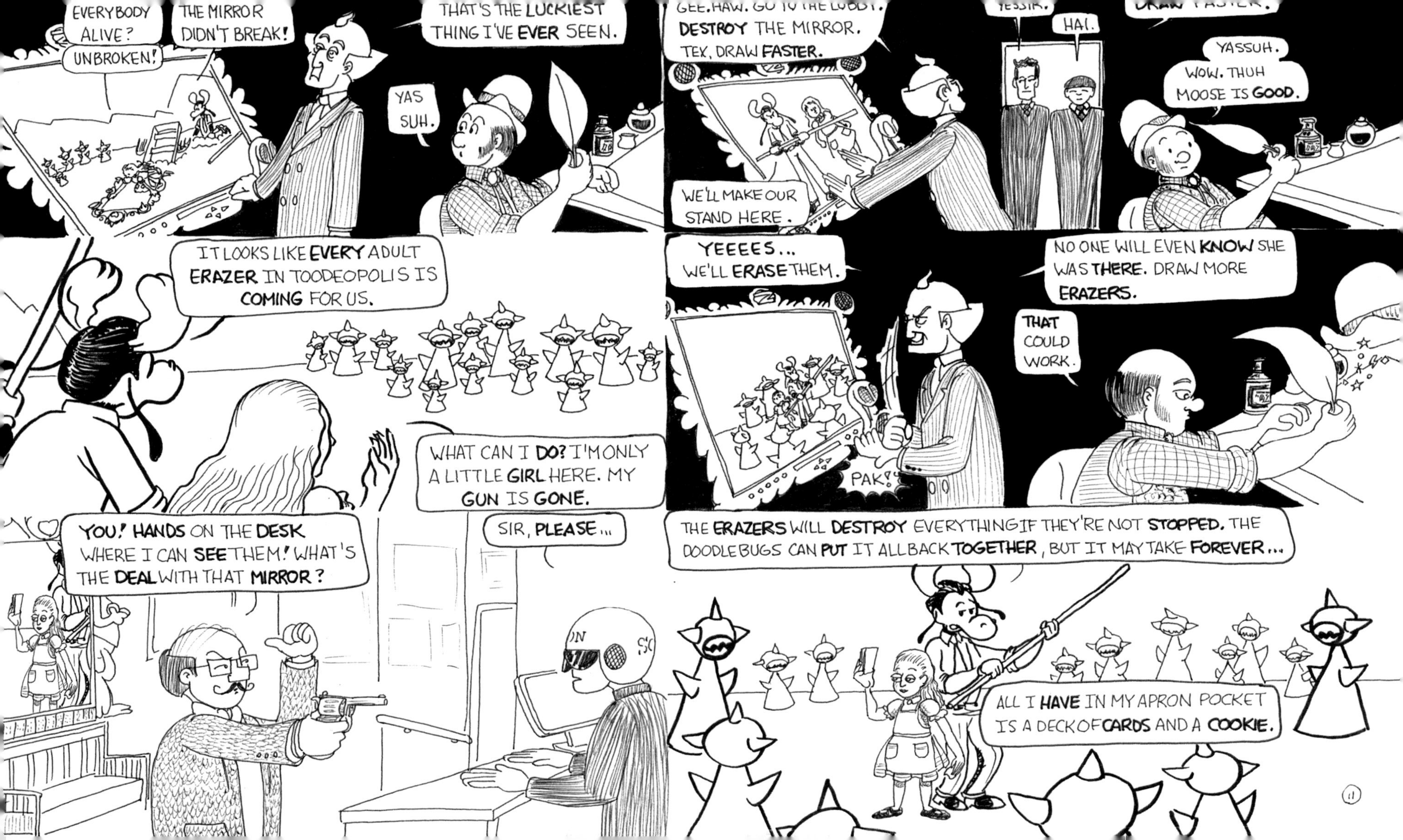
EVERYBODY ALIVE?
THE MIRROR DIDN'T BREAK!
UNBROKEN!
THAT'S THE LUCKIEST THING I'VE EVER SEEN.
YAS SUH.
IT LOOKS LIKE EVERY ADULT ERAZER IN TOODEOPOLIS IS COMING FOR US.
WHAT CAN I DO? I'M ONLY A LITTLE GIRL HERE. MY GUN IS GONE.
SIR, PLEASE...
YOU! HANDS ON THE DESK WHERE I CAN SEE THEM! WHAT'S THE DEAL WITH THAT MIRROR?
DESTROY THE MIRROR. TEX, DRAW FASTER.
HAI.
YASSUH.
WOW. THUH MOOSE IS GOOD.
WE'LL MAKE OUR STAND HERE.
YEEEES... WE'LL ERASE THEM.
NO ONE WILL EVEN KNOW SHE WAS THERE. DRAW MORE ERAZERS.
THAT COULD WORK.
PAK!
THE ERAZERS WILL DESTROY EVERYTHING IF THEY'RE NOT STOPPED. THE DOODLEBUGS CAN PUT IT ALL BACK TOGETHER, BUT IT MAY TAKE FOREVER...
ALL I HAVE IN MY APRON POCKET IS A DECK OF CARDS AND A COOKIE.

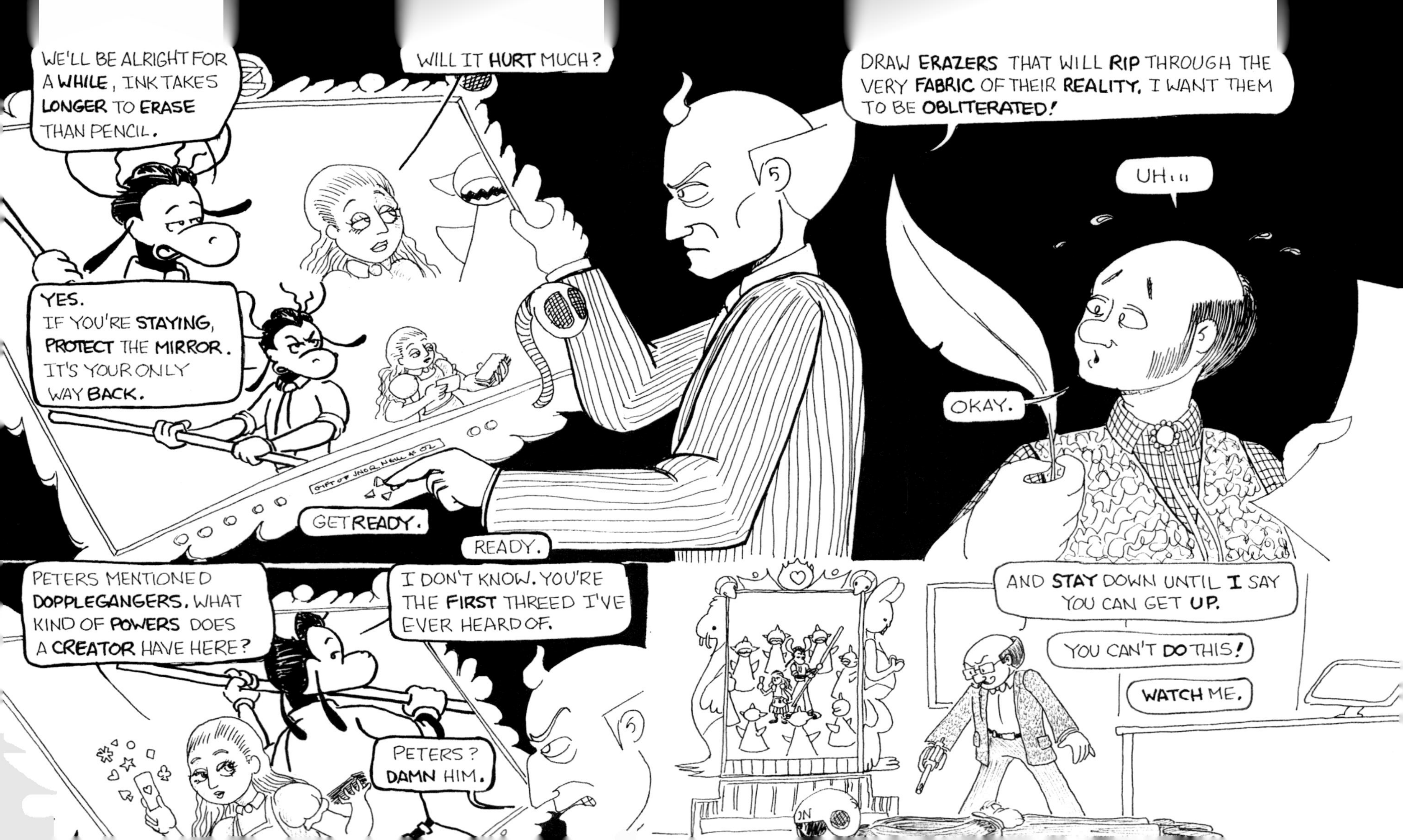

WE'LL BE ALRIGHT FOR A WHILE, INK TAKES LONGER TO ERASE THAN PENCIL.
YES. IF YOU'RE STAYING, PROTECT THE MIRROR. IT'S YOUR ONLY WAY BACK.
WILL IT HURT MUCH?
GET READY.
READY.
DRAW ERAZERS THAT WILL RIP THROUGH THE VERY FABRIC OF THEIR REALITY, I WANT THEM TO BE OBLITERATED!
UH...
OKAY.
PETERS MENTIONED DOPPLEGANGERS. WHAT KIND OF POWERS DOES A CREATOR HAVE HERE?
I DON'T KNOW. YOU'RE THE FIRST THREED I'VE EVER HEARD OF.
PETERS? DAMN HIM.
AND STAY DOWN UNTIL I SAY YOU CAN GET UP.
YOU CAN'T DO THIS!
WATCH ME.

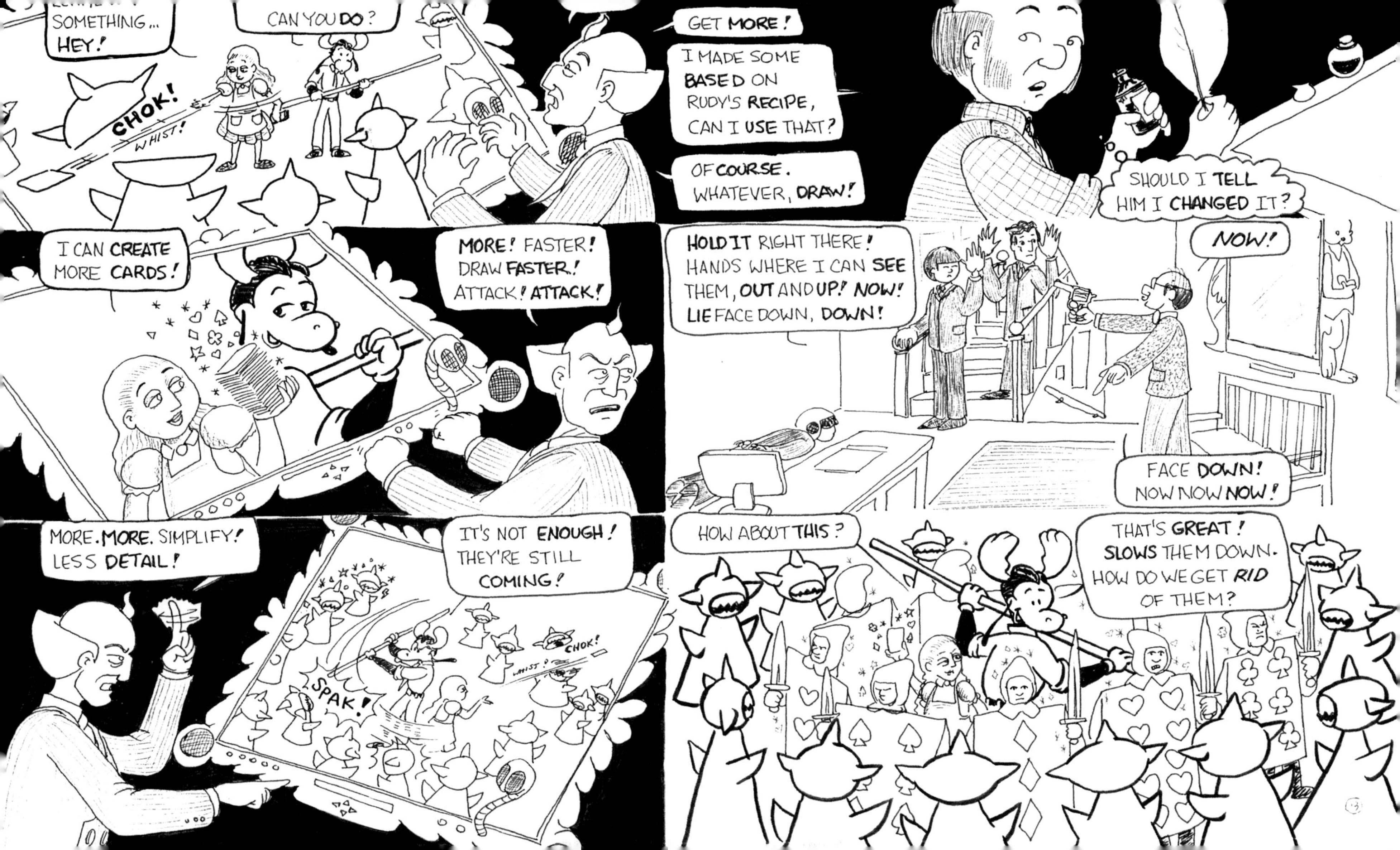
SOMETHING... HEY!
CHOK!
WHIST!
CAN YOU DO?
GET MORE!
I MADE SOME BASED ON RUDY'S RECIPE, CAN I USE THAT?
OF COURSE. WHATEVER, DRAW!
SHOULD I TELL HIM I CHANGED IT?
I CAN CREATE MORE CARDS!
MORE! FASTER! DRAW FASTER! ATTACK! ATTACK!
HOLD IT RIGHT THERE! HANDS WHERE I CAN SEE THEM, OUT AND UP! NOW! LIE FACE DOWN, DOWN!
NOW!
FACE DOWN! NOW NOW NOW!
MORE. MORE. SIMPLIFY! LESS DETAIL!
IT'S NOT ENOUGH! THEY'RE STILL COMING!
CHOK!
SPAK!
HOW ABOUT THIS?
THAT'S GREAT! SLOWS THEM DOWN. HOW DO WE GET RID OF THEM?
13

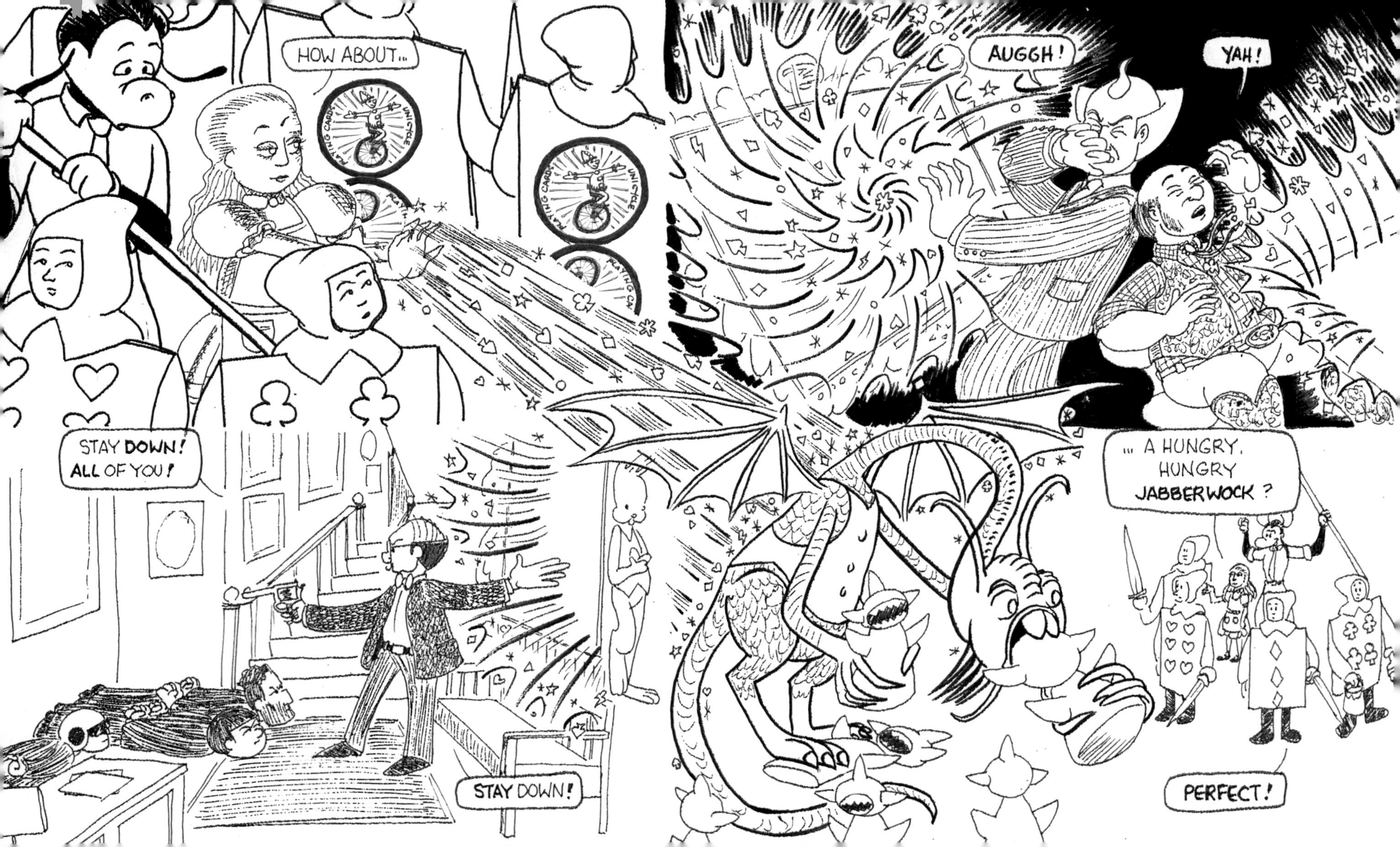
HOW ABOUT...
UNICYCLE
PLAYING CARDS
STAY DOWN! ALL OF YOU!
STAY DOWN!
AUGGH!
YAH!
... A HUNGRY, HUNGRY JABBERWOCK?
PERFECT!

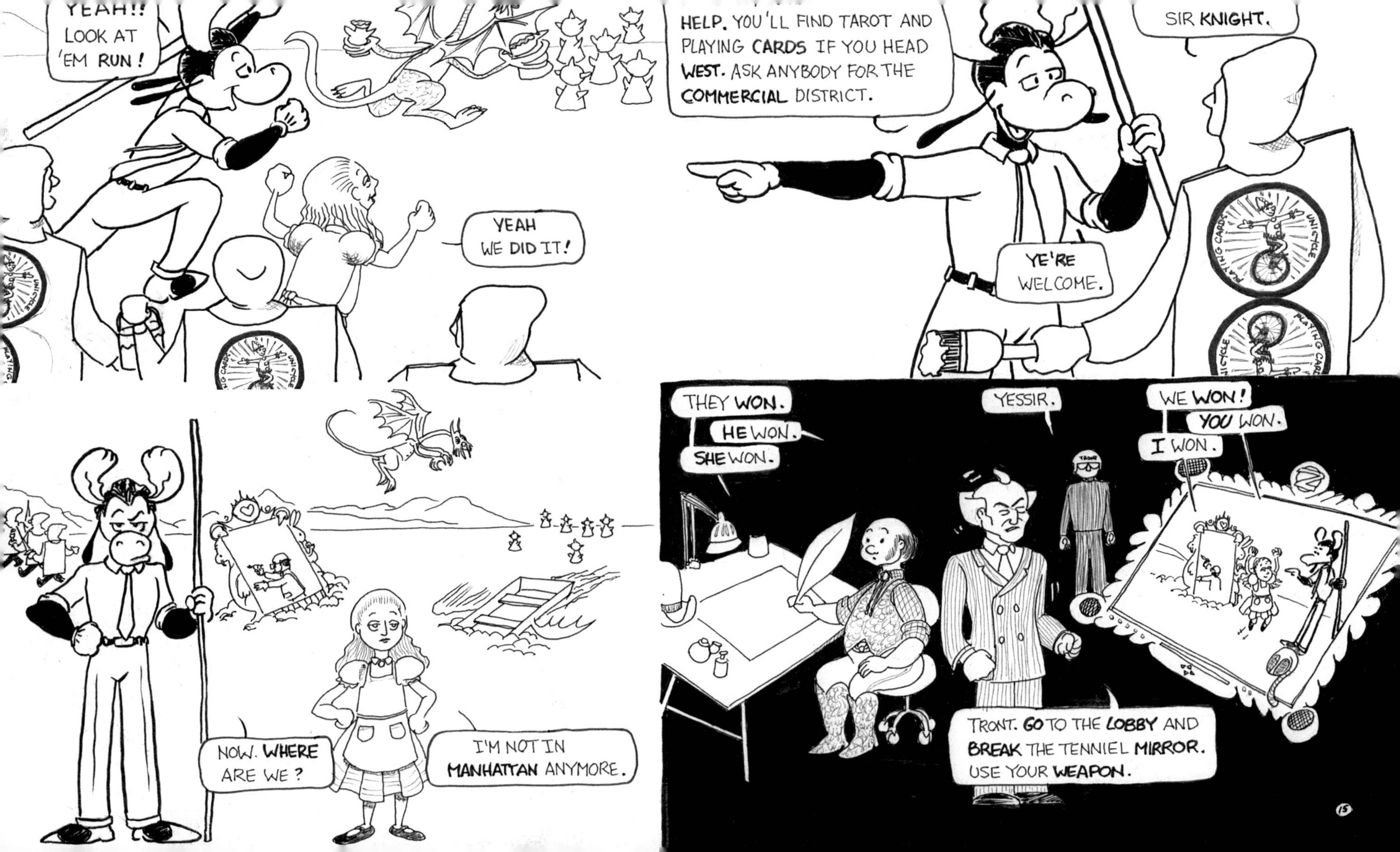
YEAH!! LOOK AT 'EM RUN!
YEAH WE DID IT!
SIR KNIGHT.
YE'RE WELCOME.
HELP. YOU'LL FIND TAROT AND PLAYING CARDS IF YOU HEAD WEST. ASK ANYBODY FOR THE COMMERCIAL DISTRICT.
UNICYCLE
PLAYING CARDS
NOW. WHERE ARE WE?
I'M NOT IN MANHATTAN ANYMORE.
THEY WON.
HE WON.
SHE WON.
YESSIR.
WE WON!
YOU WON.
I WON.
TRONT. GO TO THE LOBBY AND BREAK THE TENNIEL MIRROR. USE YOUR WEAPON.

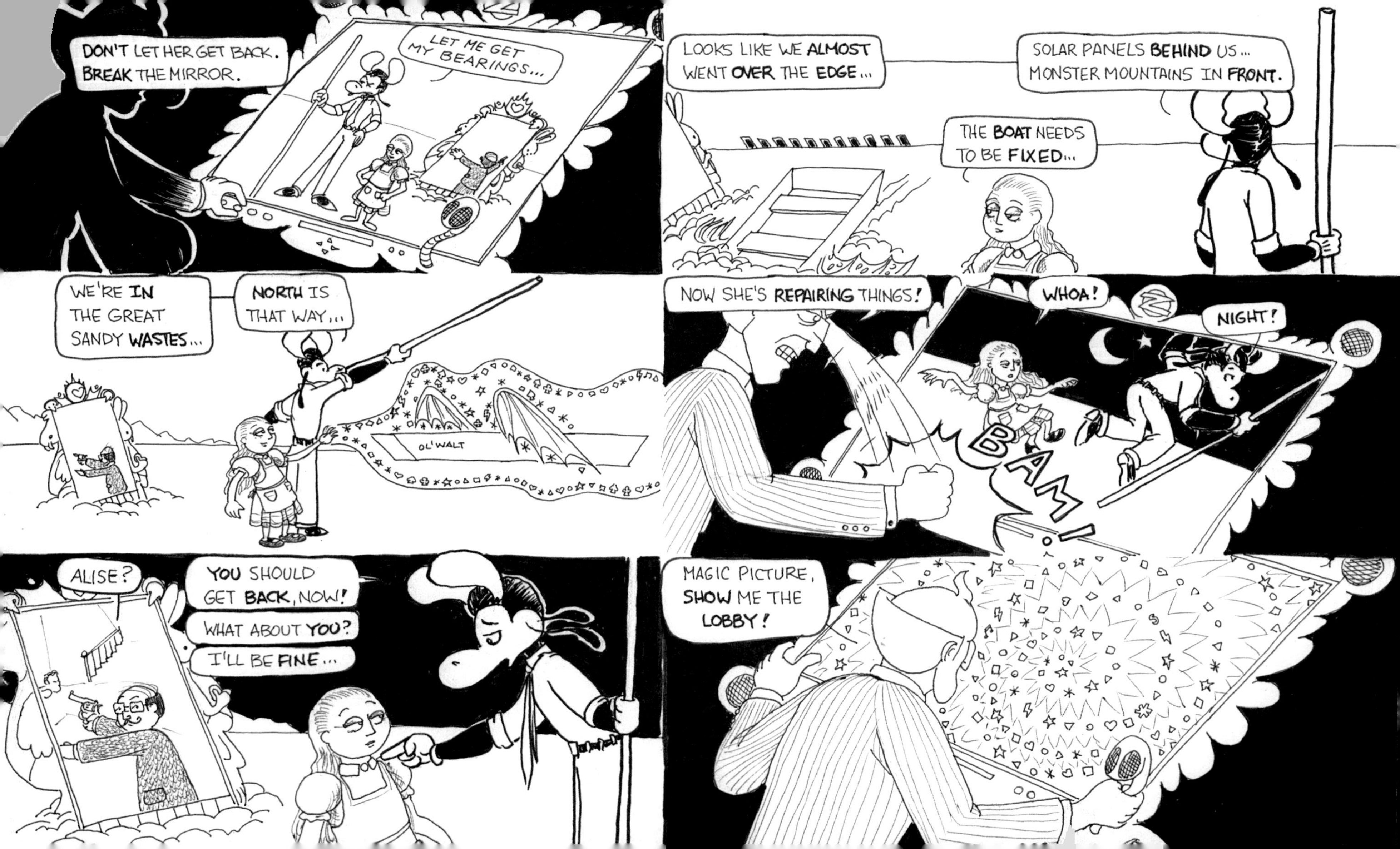
DON'T LET HER GET BACK. BREAK THE MIRROR.
LET ME GET MY BEARINGS...
WE'RE IN THE GREAT SANDY WASTES...
NORTH IS THAT WAY...
OL' WALT
ALISE?
YOU SHOULD GET BACK, NOW!
WHAT ABOUT YOU?
I'LL BE FINE...
LOOKS LIKE WE ALMOST WENT OVER THE EDGE...
SOLAR PANELS BEHIND US... MONSTER MOUNTAINS IN FRONT.
THE BOAT NEEDS TO BE FIXED...
NOW SHE'S REPAIRING THINGS!
WHOA!
NIGHT!
BAM!
MAGIC PICTURE, SHOW ME THE LOBBY!

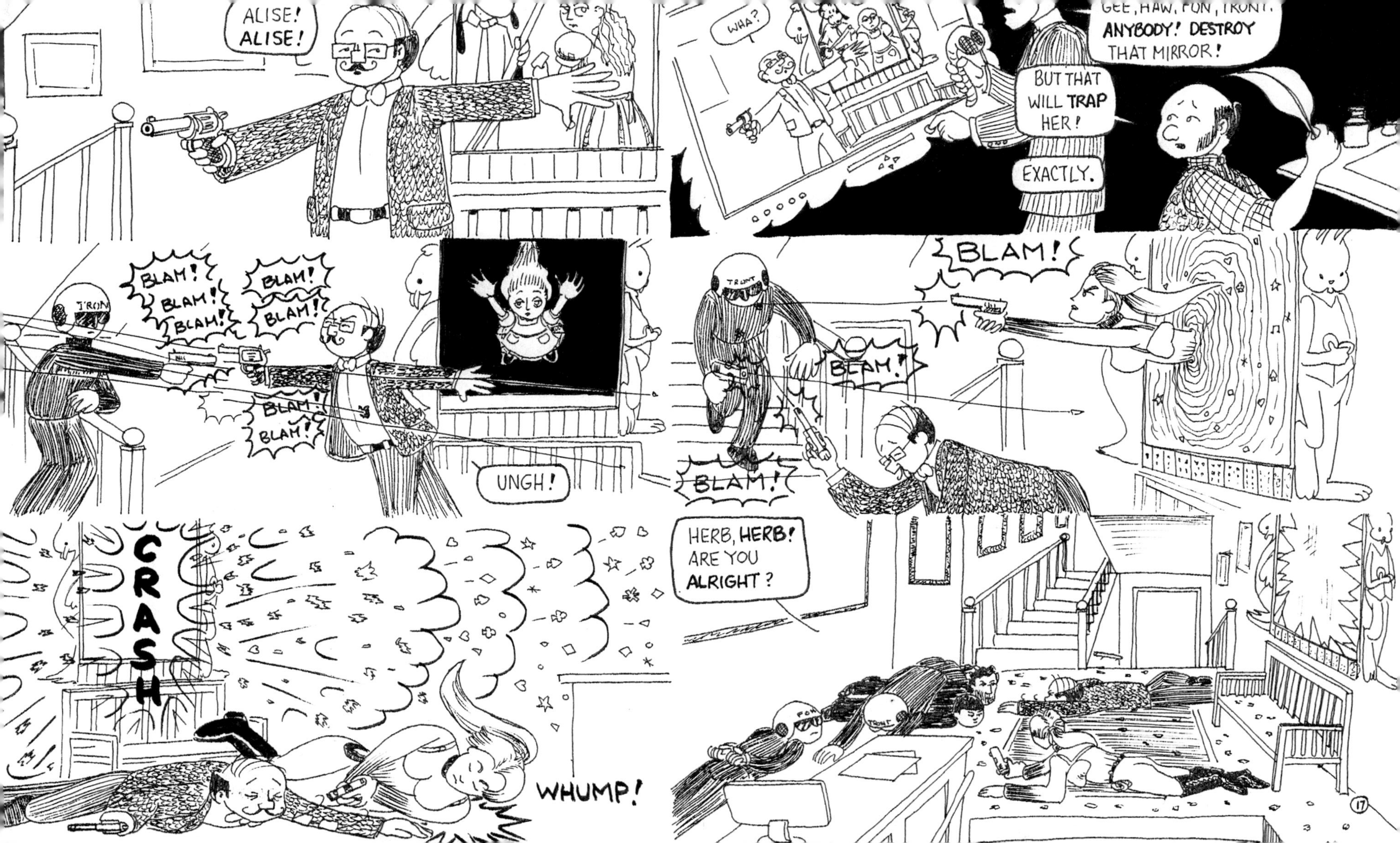
ALISE!
ALISE!
BLAM!
BLAM!
BLAM!
BLAM!
BLAM!
BLAM!
BLAM!
UNGH!
CRASH
WHUMP!
WHA?
GEE, HAW, FON, TRONT!
ANYBODY! DESTROY
THAT MIRROR!
BUT THAT
WILL TRAP
HER!
EXACTLY.
BLAM!
BLAM!
BLAM!
HERB, HERB!
ARE YOU
ALRIGHT?

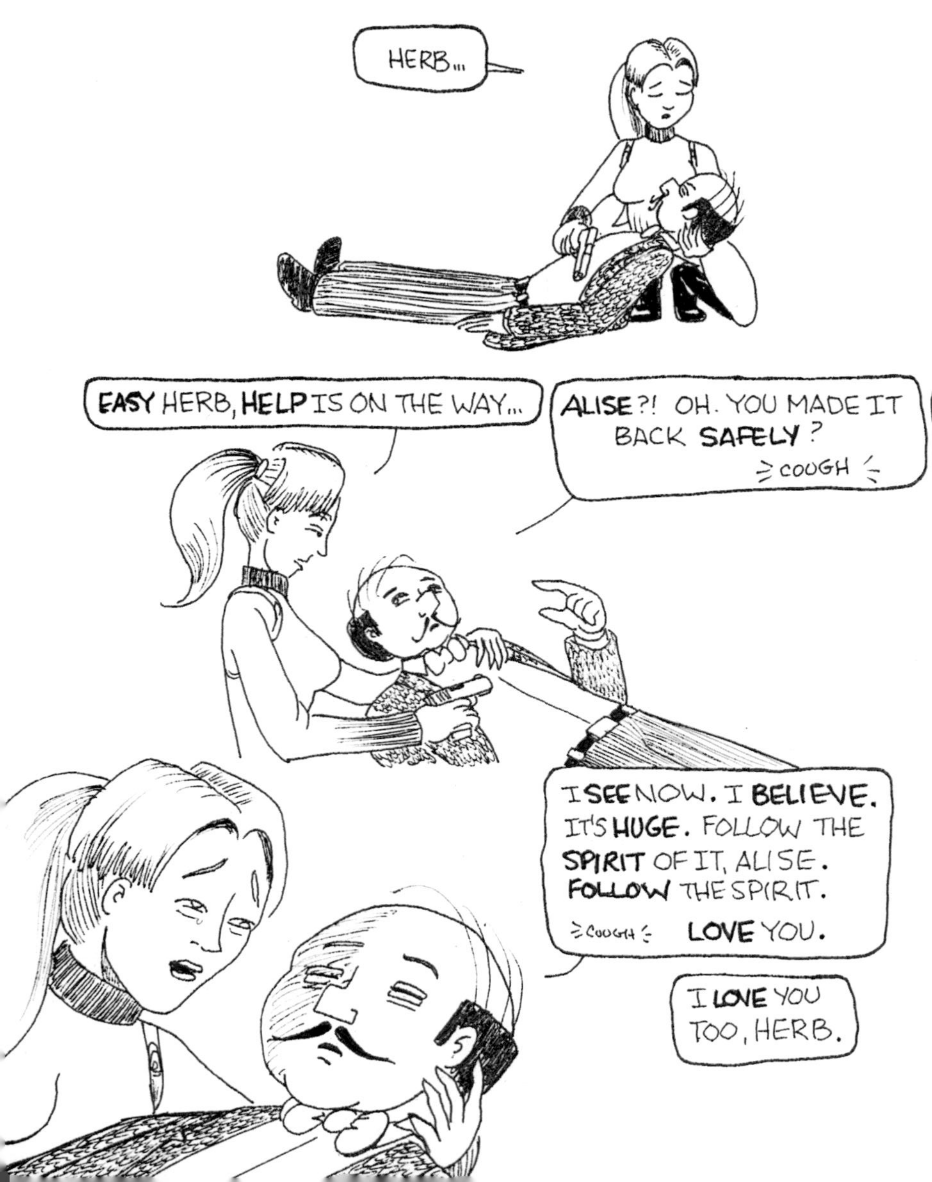
HERB...
EASY HERB, HELP IS ON THE WAY...
ALISE?! OH. YOU MADE IT BACK SAFELY? ≥COUGH≤
I SEE NOW. I BELIEVE. IT'S HUGE. FOLLOW THE SPIRIT OF IT, ALISE. FOLLOW THE SPIRIT. ≥COUGH≤ LOVE YOU.
I LOVE YOU TOO, HERB.

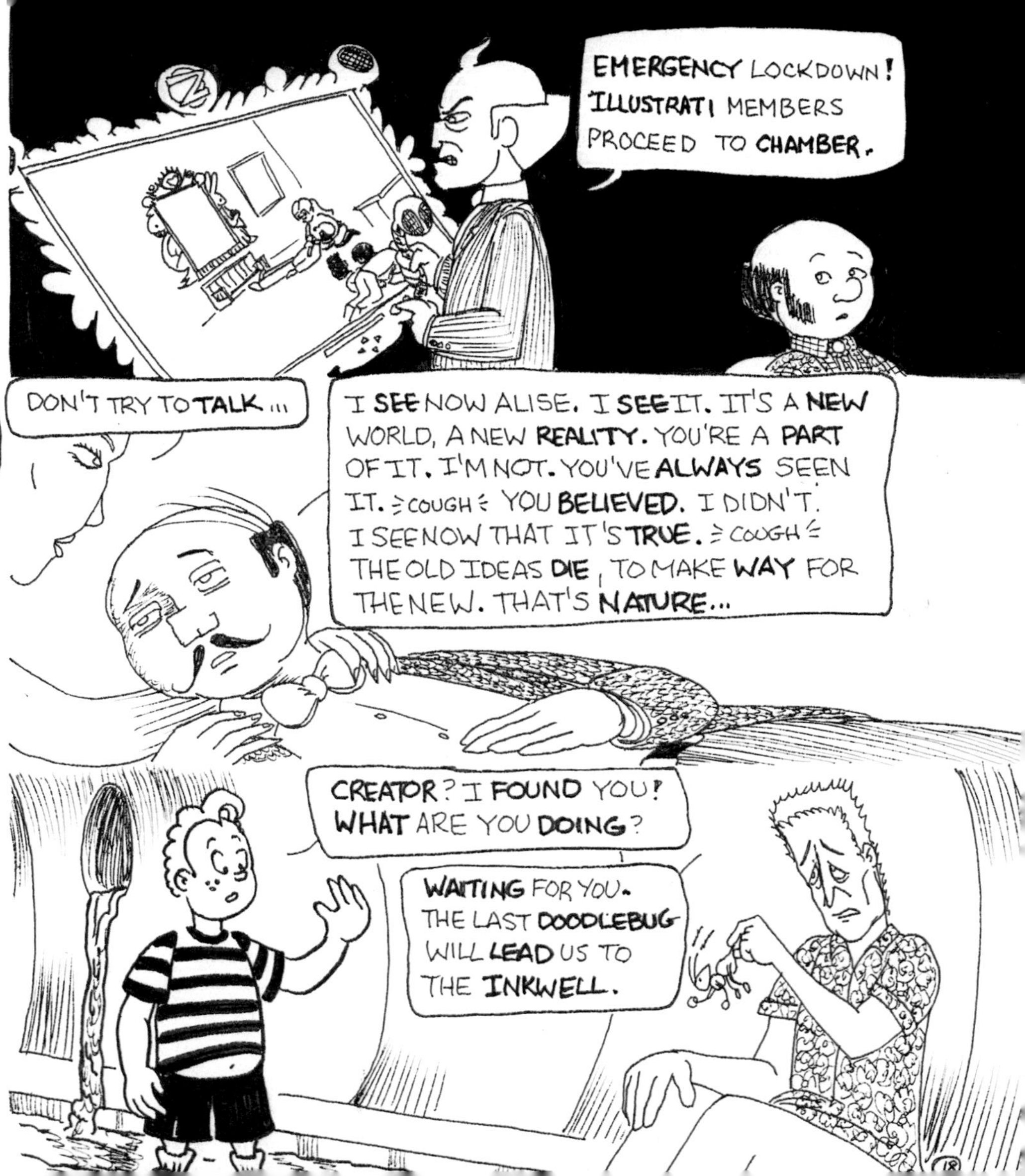
EMERGENCY LOCKDOWN! ILLUSTRATI MEMBERS PROCEED TO CHAMBER.
DON'T TRY TO TALK...
I SEE NOW ALISE. I SEE IT. IT'S A NEW WORLD, A NEW REALITY. YOU'RE A PART OF IT. I'M NOT. YOU'VE ALWAYS SEEN IT. ≥COUGH≤ YOU BELIEVED. I DIDN'T. I SEE NOW THAT IT'S TRUE. ≥COUGH≤ THE OLD IDEAS DIE, TO MAKE WAY FOR THE NEW. THAT'S NATURE...
CREATOR? I FOUND YOU! WHAT ARE YOU DOING?
WAITING FOR YOU. THE LAST DOODLEBUG WILL LEAD US TO THE INKWELL.

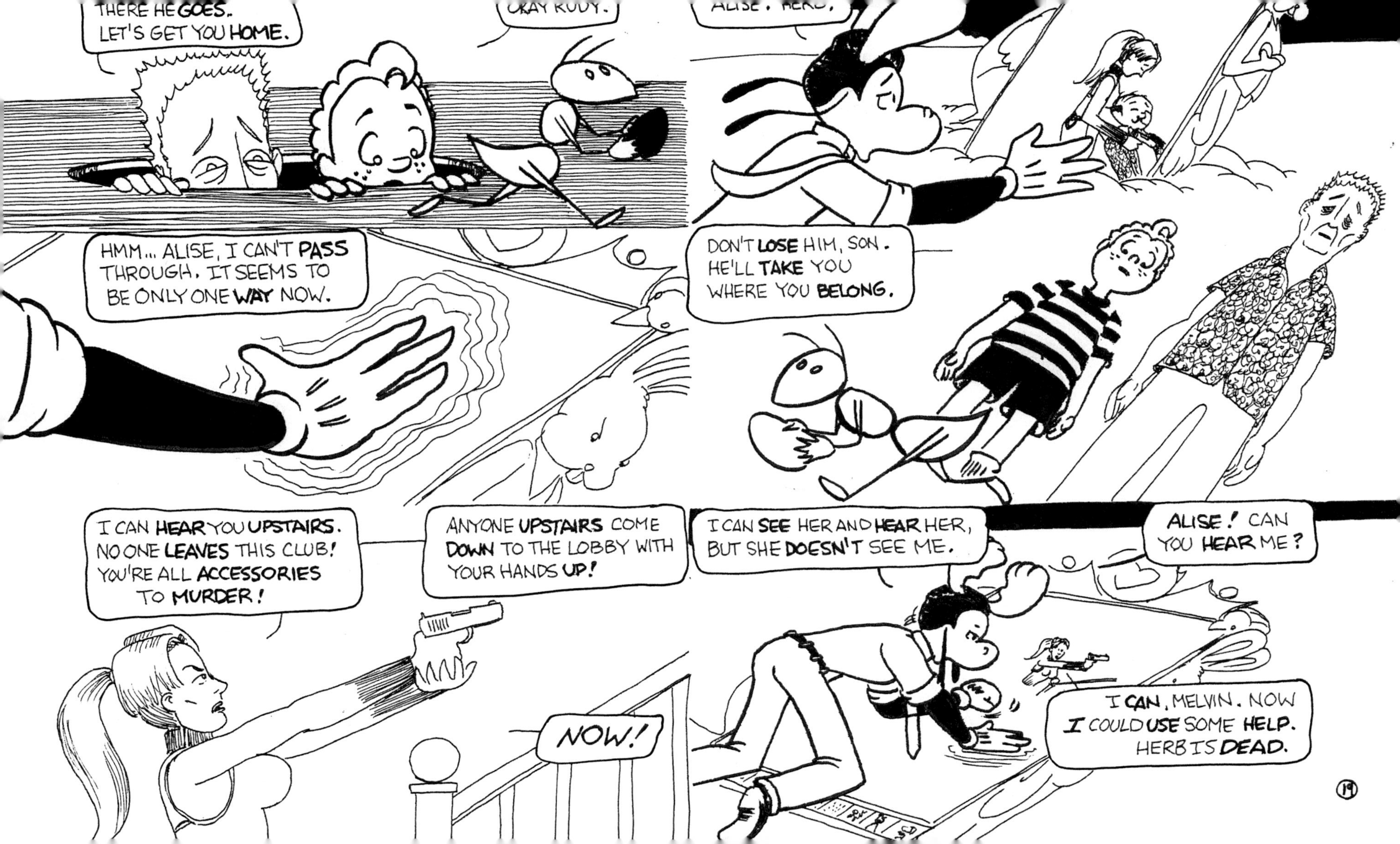
THERE HE GOES. LET'S GET YOU HOME.
HMM... ALISE, I CAN'T PASS THROUGH. IT SEEMS TO BE ONLY ONE WAY NOW.
DON'T LOSE HIM, SON. HE'LL TAKE YOU WHERE YOU BELONG.
I CAN HEAR YOU UPSTAIRS. NO ONE LEAVES THIS CLUB! YOU'RE ALL ACCESSORIES TO MURDER!
ANYONE UPSTAIRS COME DOWN TO THE LOBBY WITH YOUR HANDS UP!
NOW!
I CAN SEE HER AND HEAR HER, BUT SHE DOESN'T SEE ME.
ALISE! CAN YOU HEAR ME?
I CAN, MELVIN. NOW I COULD USE SOME HELP. HERB IS DEAD.

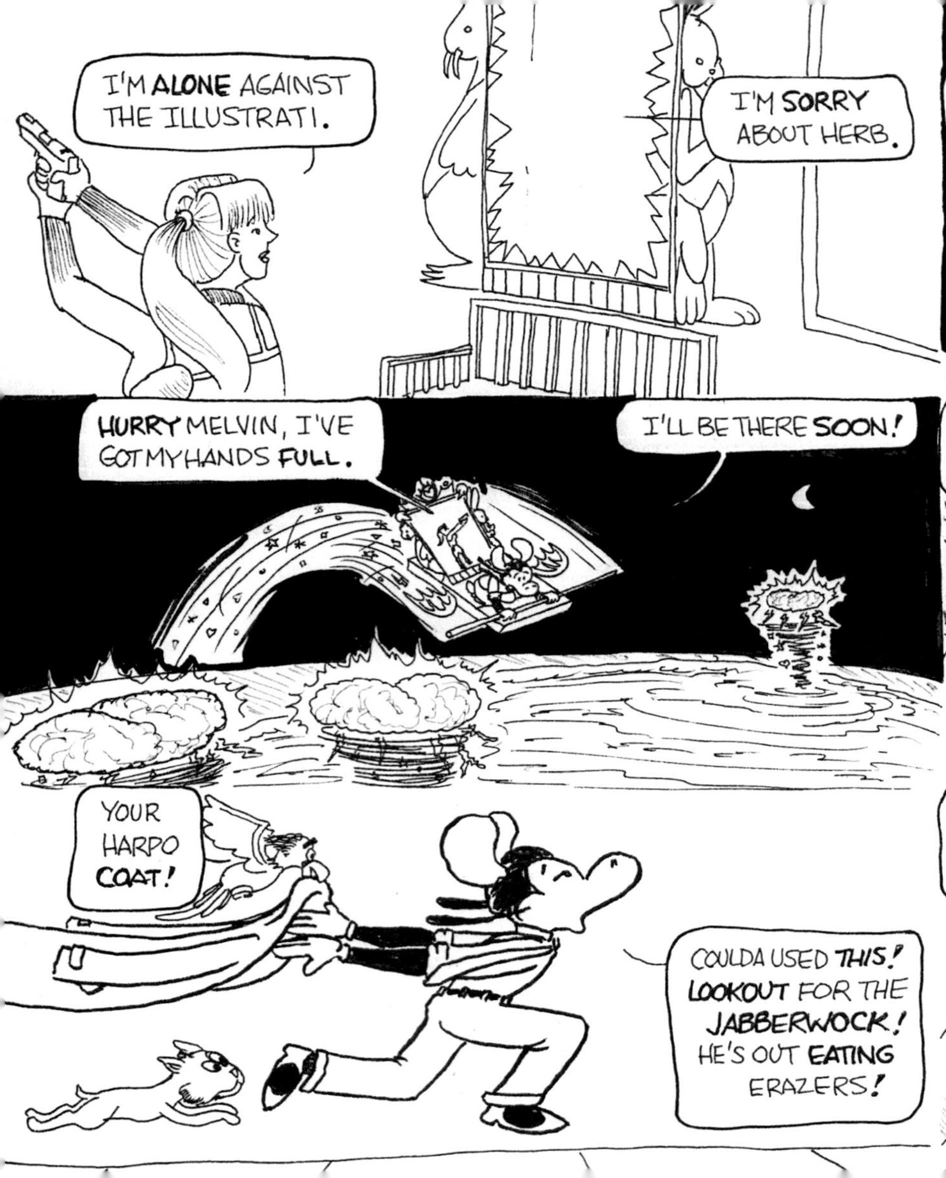
I'M **ALONE** AGAINST THE ILLUSTRATI.
I'M **SORRY** ABOUT HERB.
HURRY MELVIN, I'VE GOT MY HANDS **FULL**.
I'LL BE THERE **SOON**!
YOUR HARPO **COAT**!
COULDA USED **THIS**! **LOOKOUT** FOR THE **JABBERWOCK**! HE'S OUT **EATING** ERAZERS!

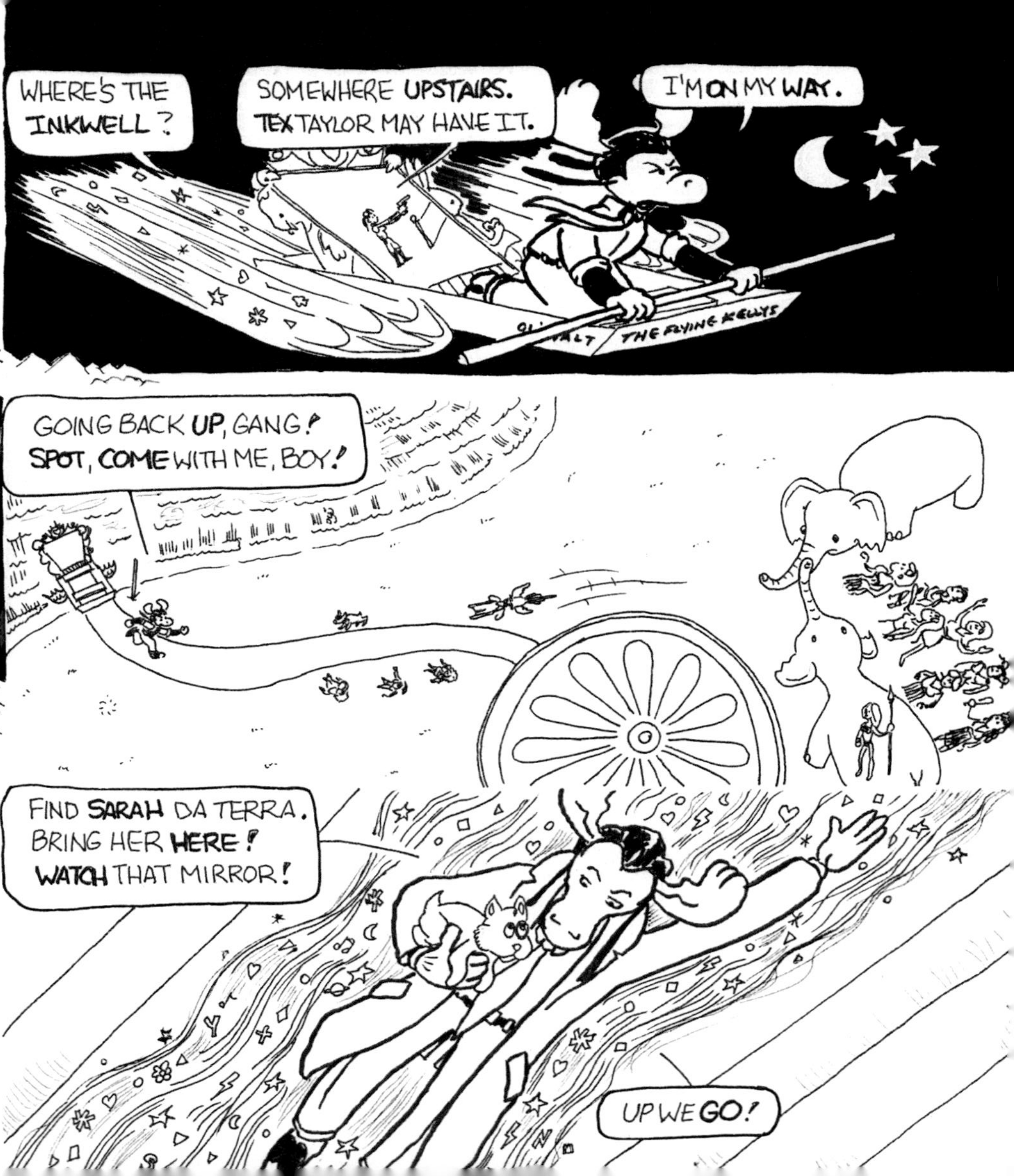
WHERE'S THE **INKWELL**?
SOMEWHERE **UPSTAIRS**. **TEX** TAYLOR MAY HAVE IT.
I'M **ON** MY **WAY**.
THE FLYING KELLYS
GOING BACK **UP**, GANG! **SPOT**, **COME** WITH ME, BOY!
FIND **SARAH** DA TERRA. BRING HER **HERE**! **WATCH** THAT MIRROR!
UP WE **GO**!

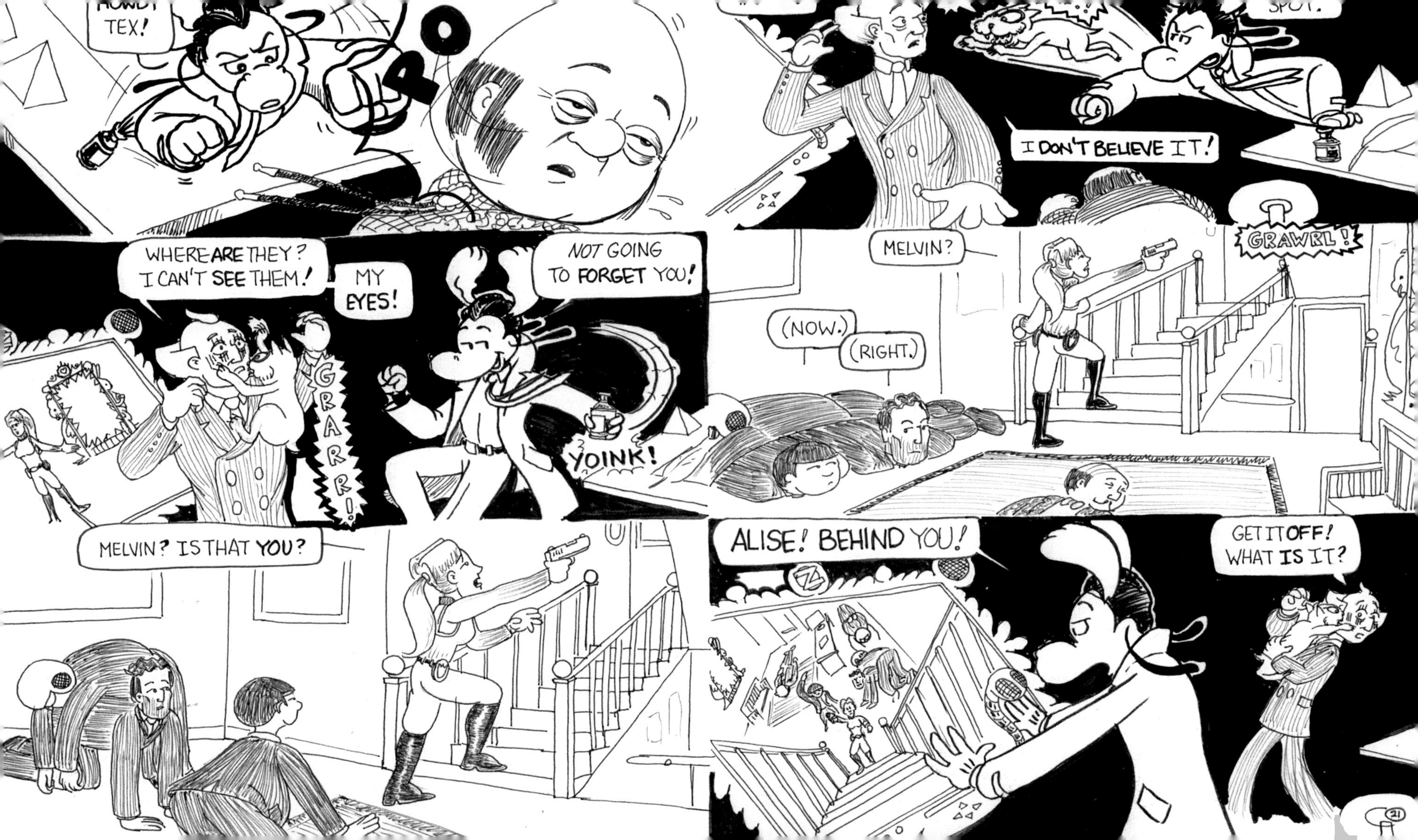
TEX!
WHERE ARE THEY? I CAN'T SEE THEM!
MY EYES!
GRARR!
NOT GOING TO FORGET YOU!
YOINK!
MELVIN? IS THAT YOU?
I DON'T BELIEVE IT!
MELVIN?
GRAWRL!
(NOW.)
(RIGHT.)
ALISE! BEHIND YOU!
GET IT OFF! WHAT IS IT?
21

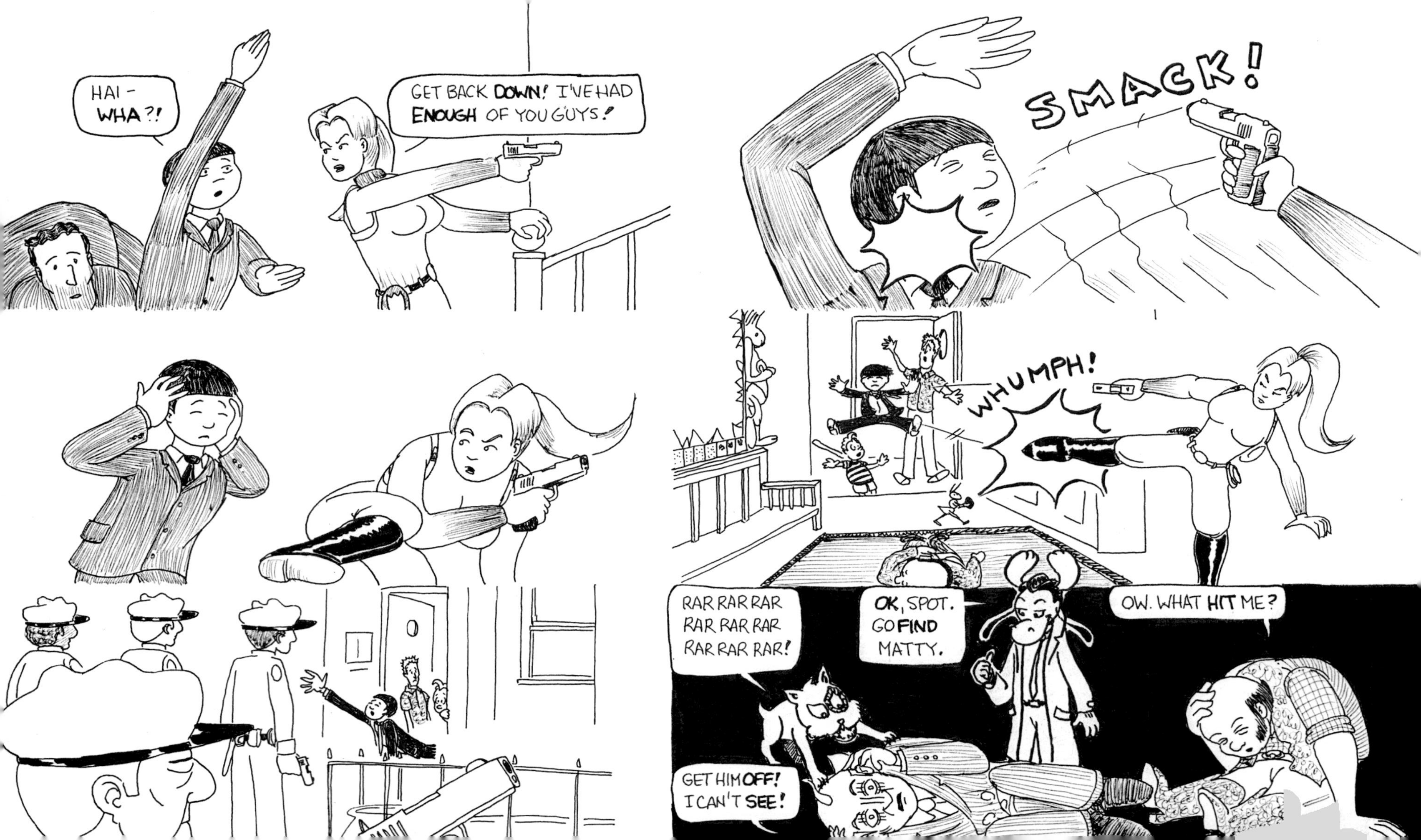
HAI - WHA?!
GET BACK DOWN! I'VE HAD ENOUGH OF YOU GUYS!
SMACK!
WHUMPH!
RAR RAR RAR RAR RAR RAR RAR RAR RAR!
OK, SPOT. GO FIND MATTY.
OW. WHAT HIT ME?
GET HIM OFF! I CAN'T SEE!

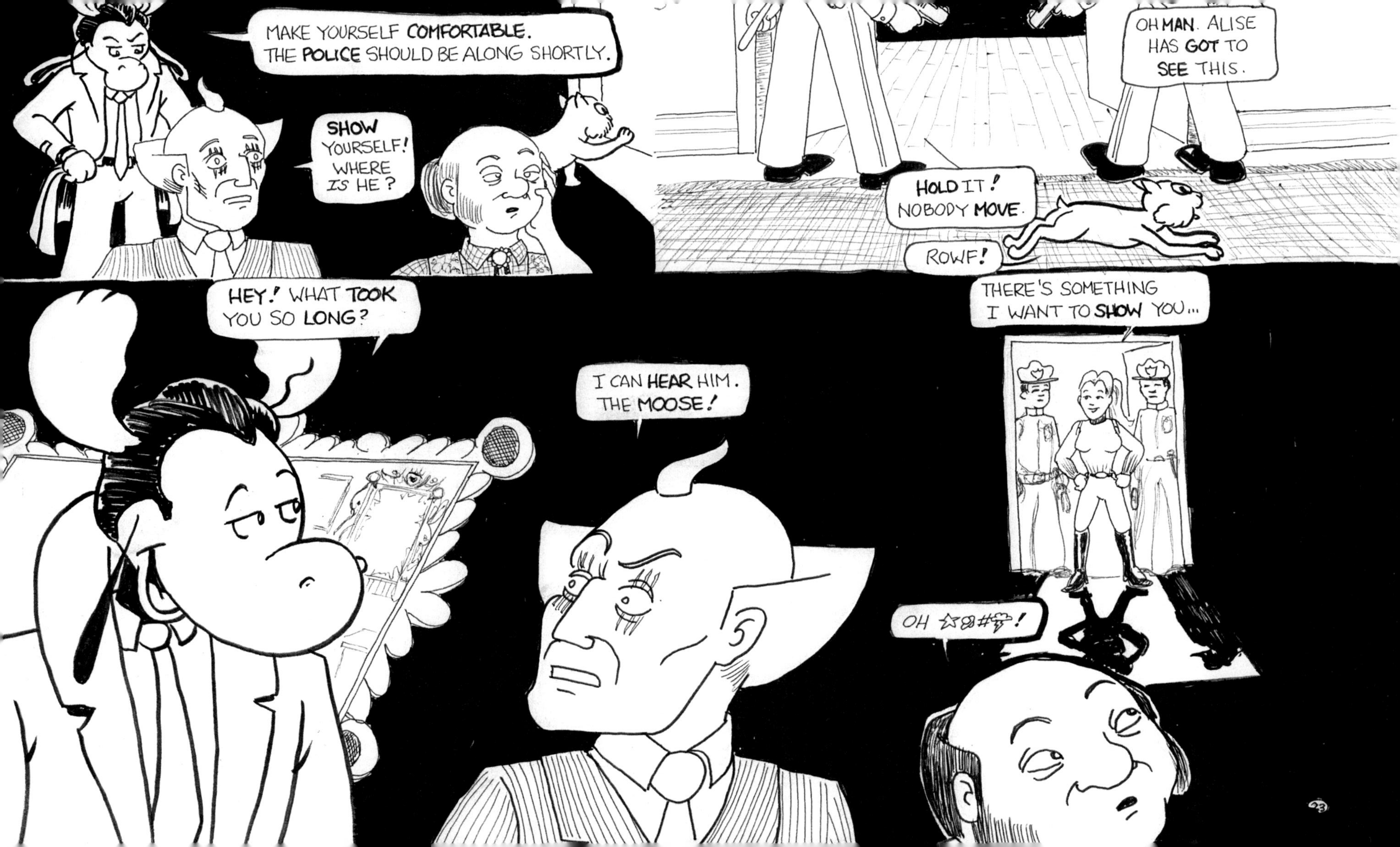
MAKE YOURSELF **COMFORTABLE**. THE **POLICE** SHOULD BE ALONG SHORTLY.
SHOW YOURSELF! WHERE IS HE?
HOLD IT! NOBODY **MOVE**.
OH **MAN**. ALISE HAS **GOT** TO **SEE** THIS.
ROWF!
HEY! WHAT **TOOK** YOU SO **LONG**?
I CAN **HEAR** HIM. THE **MOOSE**!
THERE'S SOMETHING I WANT TO **SHOW** YOU...
OH ☆✿#⚡!
23

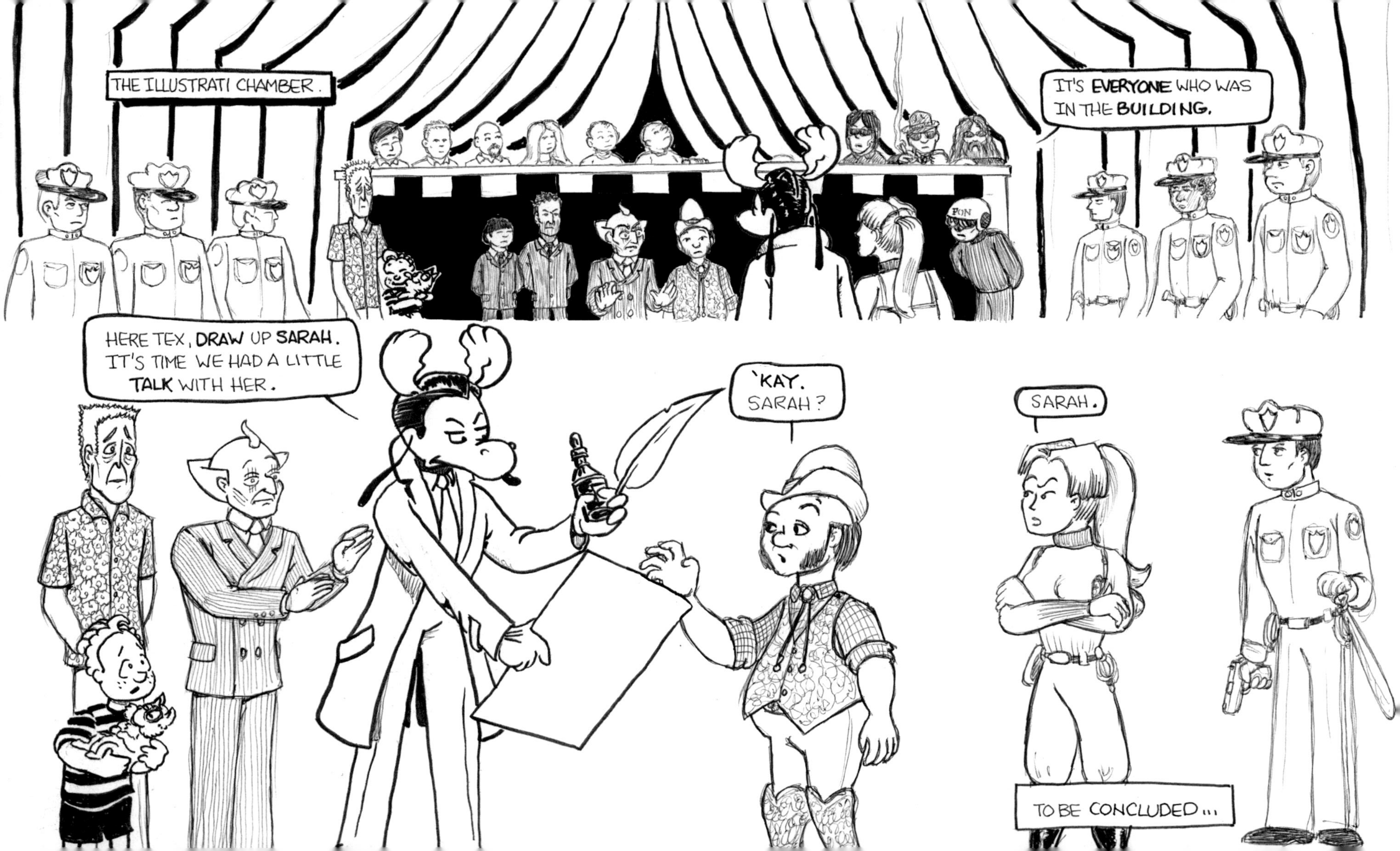
THE ILLUSTRATI CHAMBER.
IT'S EVERYONE WHO WAS IN THE BUILDING.
HERE TEX, DRAW UP SARAH. IT'S TIME WE HAD A LITTLE TALK WITH HER.
`KAY. SARAH?
SARAH.
TO BE CONCLUDED...

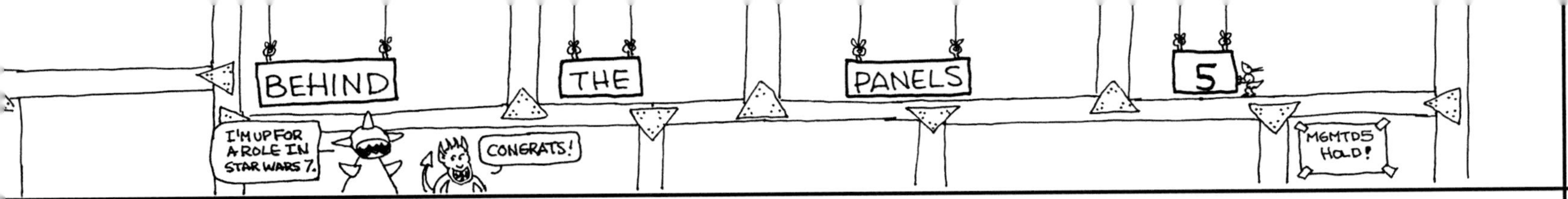
BEHIND
THE
PANELS
5
I'M UP FOR A ROLE IN STAR WARS 7.
CONGRATS!
MGMTDS HOLD!

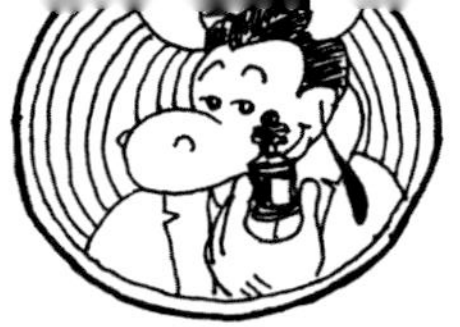

re: READING

A FEW FAVORITE FICTIONS

DEAREST THREADER -

SINCE **YOU'RE** STILL **HERE**, I CERTAINLY DON'T NEED TO CONVEY OR EXPLAIN MY **LOVE** OF **READING** TO YOU. NOR DO I NEED TO CONVINCE YOU OF HOW THE **PLEASURE** THAT COMES FROM **READING** CAN EXPAND THE **RICHNESS** OF YOUR **LIFE**. BUT I CAN **SHARE** SOME OF MY FAVORITE BOOKSHELF **TREASURES** AND **ESCAPES** OF THE MIND WITH YOU. THESE STORIES THAT I **RETURN** TO AGAIN AND AGAIN, BECAUSE OF THE SHEER **JOY** I FIND WITHIN THEIR **PAGES**. YOU WILL FIND MANY OF THEIR **REFLECTIONS** IN THE PAGES OF **MELVIN G. MOOSE**, TOODE DICK.

THE **OZ** BOOKS, WRITTEN BY L. FRANK BAUM, ILLUSTRATED BY JOHN. R. NEILL
SHERLOCK HOLMES, WRITTEN BY ARTHUR CONAN DOYLE, ILLUSTRATED BY SIDNEY PAGET
WALT DISNEY'S COMICS + STORIES / UNCLE SCROOGE, WRITTEN AND ILLUSTRATED BY CARL BARKS
THE FLAMING CARROT, WRITTEN AND ILLUSTRATED BY BOB BURDEN
THE SPIRIT, BY WILL EISNER, et al **POGO**, BY WALT KELLY **LI'L ABNER**, BY AL CAPP
BONE, BY JEFF SMITH **THE ROCKETEER**, BY DAVE STEVENS **PEANUTS**, BY CHARLES SCHULZ
MICKEY MOUSE NEWSPAPER COMIC STRIPS (1930-1955) BY FLOYD GOTTFREDSON

THE **COMPLETE** LIST IS FAR TOO **LONG** TO INCLUDE HERE. HOWEVER, THESE **ILLUSTRATI** MEMBERS HAVE CREATED **MASTERPIECES** THAT WILL **DELIGHT** YOUR IMAGINATION AND **TRANSPORT** YOU FAR **BEYOND** THEIR TWO DIMENSIONAL **REALITIES**. CHECK YOUR LOCAL **LIBRARY**, OR CALL: **1-888-COMIC BOOK** TO FIND YOUR LOCAL COMIC STORE.

WHEN YOU **SEE** THESE CHARACTERS IN THE **MIND'S** EYE OF YOUR **IMAGINATION**, PLEASE SAY **HELLO** AND TELL THEM **MELVIN** SENT YOU. HE'S CLOSE **FRIENDS** WITH THEM **ALL**.

4/30/2013

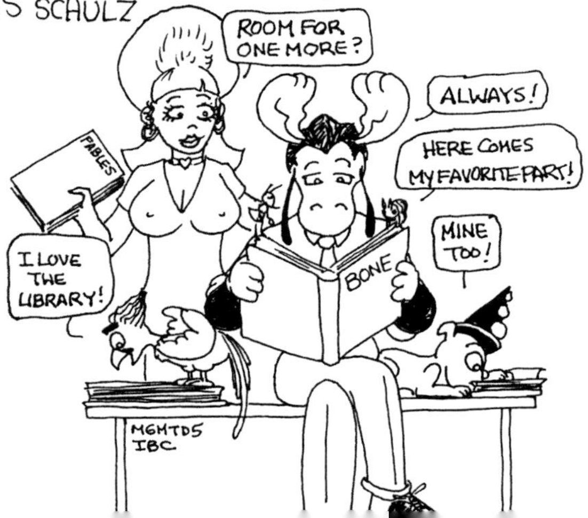
ROOM FOR ONE MORE?
ALWAYS!
HERE COMES MY FAVORITE PART!
MINE TOO!
I LOVE THE LIBRARY!
FABLES
BONE
MGMTDS IBC

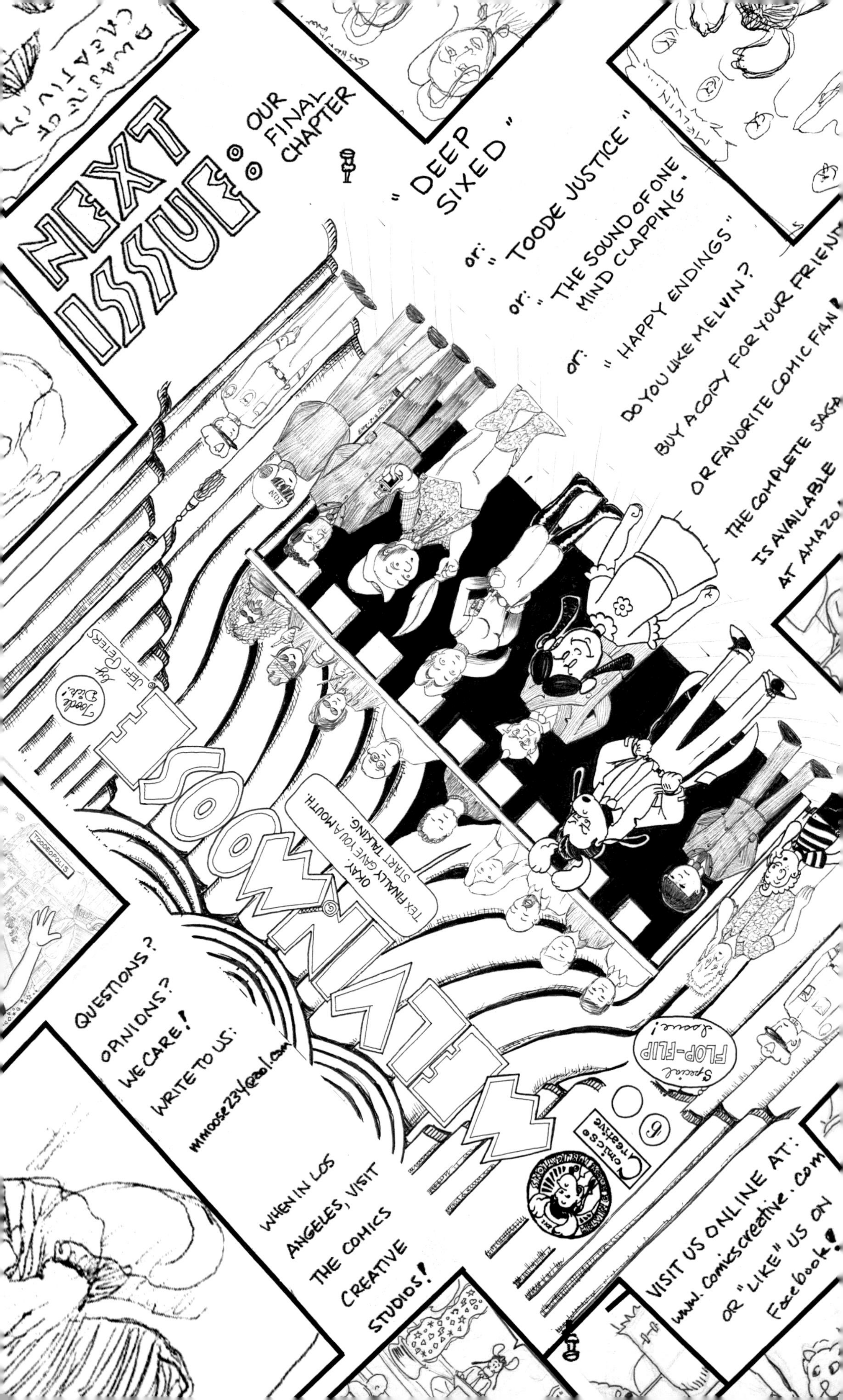

NEXT ISSUE
OUR FINAL CHAPTER
"DEEP SIXED"
or: "TOODE JUSTICE"
or: "THE SOUND OF ONE MIND CLAPPING."
or: "HAPPY ENDINGS"
DO YOU LIKE MELVIN?
BUY A COPY FOR YOUR FRIEND
OR FAVORITE COMIC FAN!
THE COMPLETE SAGA
IS AVAILABLE
AT AMAZON
OKAY. TEX FINALLY GAVE YOU A MOUTH. START TALKING.
Toode Dude!
by JEFF PETERS
Special FLOP-FLIP Issue!
Comics Creative
6
QUESTIONS?
OPINIONS?
WE CARE!
WRITE TO US:
mmoose234@aol.com
WHEN IN LOS ANGELES, VISIT THE COMICS CREATIVE STUDIOS!
VISIT US ONLINE AT:
www.comicscreative.com
OR "LIKE" US ON
Facebook!

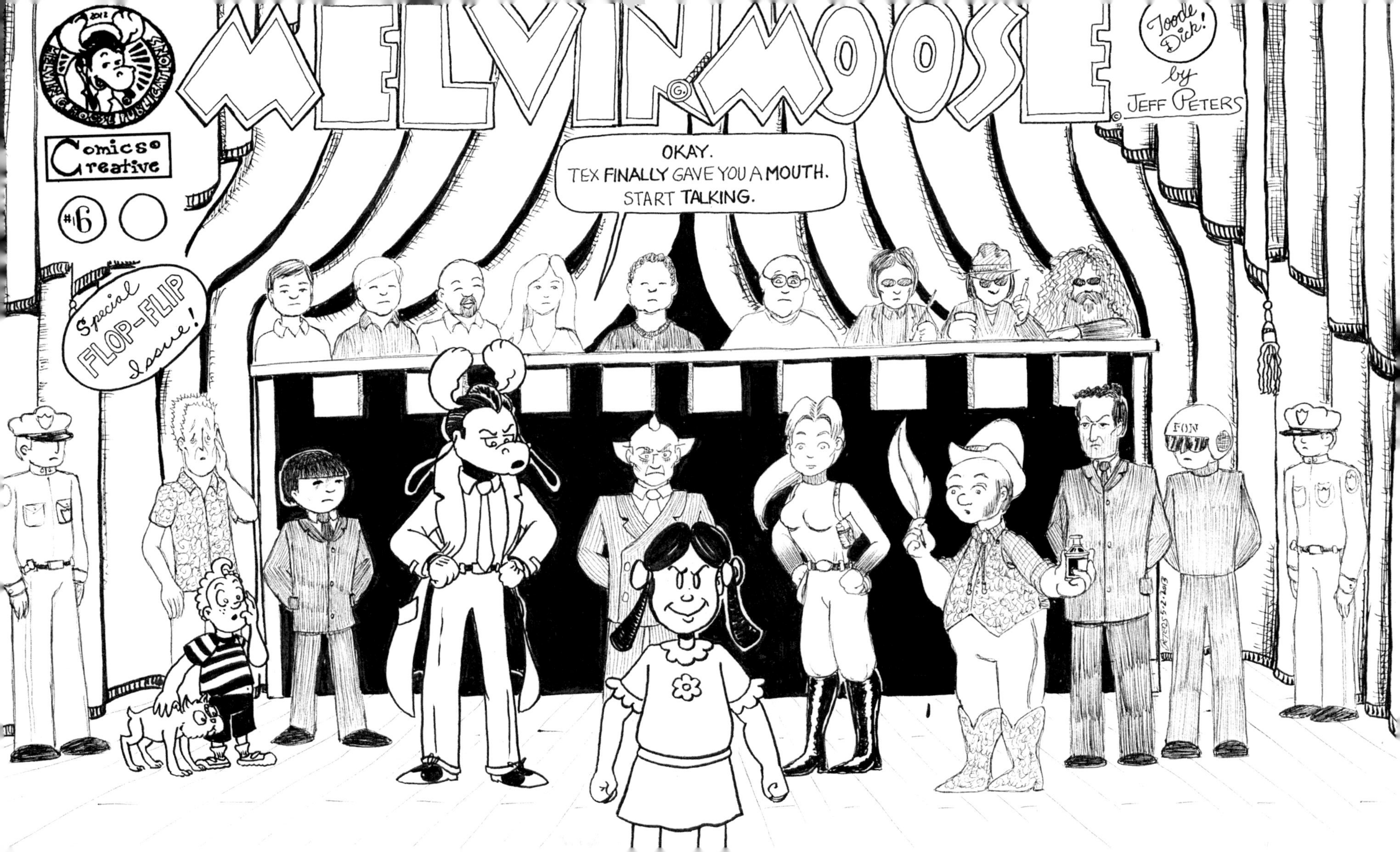
MELVIN G. MOOSE
Toodle Dick!
by JEFF PETERS
Comics Creative
#6
OKAY.
TEX FINALLY GAVE YOU A MOUTH.
START TALKING.
Special FLOP-FLIP Issue!
Melvin G. Moose Publications
2012

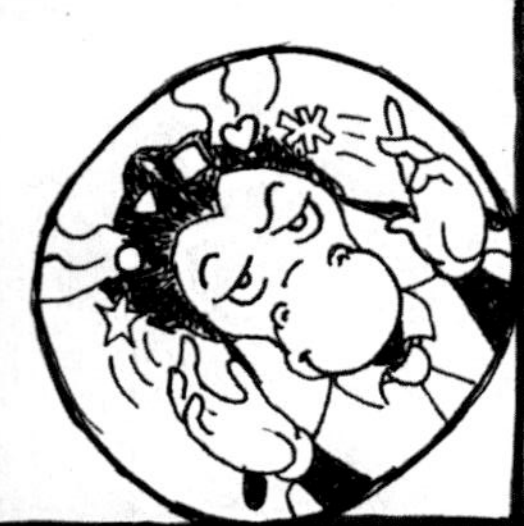

PERSPECTIVES PERCEPTIONS

MELVING MOOSE
TOODE DICK
CHAPTER (6) SIX
"DEEP SIXED"

or
"JUMPING TO CONCLUSIONS"

THIS ONE IS FOR:
YOU
DEAREST THREADER
FOR MAKING IT
TO THE END!

☆♡□❄△○ϟ

TYING THE
MAGIC
TOGETHER.
5 · 8 · 2013

FINAL COURSES

APPETIZER: PUNISHMENT AND CRIME

HOW DOES ONE **PUNISH** AN **IDEA**? HOW CAN WE **DISCIPLINE** OR CHASTIZE THE **EPHEMERAL**? A **CONCEPT** CAN **THRIVE** OR **DIE** ON ITS OWN **MERITS**, BUT CAN IT BE **KILLED**? IS THERE SUCH A THING AS **CORPORAL** PUNISHMENT FOR A **FIGMENT** OF THE IMAGINATION, A WILL O' THE **WISP**? OR "**CORPOREAL** PUNISHMENT" MERELY A CRIMINAL **PUN**?

MAIN COURSE: END OF OUR TALE

CONGRATULATIONS, DEAREST THREADER, YOU'VE MADE IT TO THE **FINALE!** IF I'VE DONE MY JOB **PROPERLY**, ALL THE LOOSE **ENDS** WILL BE **TIED** UP, EXCEPT FOR THE ONES I PURPOSELY LEAVE DANGLING. PERHAPS THE NEXT TIME YOU REGARD **WORDS** AND **PICTURES**, YOU'LL **SEE** THEM A LITTLE **DIFFERENTLY**. REALITY IS WHAT YOU **DECIDE** TO MAKE IT EVERY DAY. WHAT **YOU** BELIEVE IS YOUR **OWN** AND BECOMES YOUR **REALITY**. **ACT** ON YOUR BELIEFS, MAKE THEM **REAL**. I BELIEVE YOU **CAN** DO IT.

DESERT: STORYBOARD COMICS

THIS **SPECIAL** ISSUE HAS PURPOSELY BEEN **FLOPPED** ON IT'S SIDE TO **CHANGE** YOUR PERCEPTIONS OF HOW **PRINTED** INFORMATION CAN BE **SHARED**. I'VE ALSO HAD YOU **SPIN** THE PAGES THROUGHOUT OUR TALE IN ORDER TO **CHALLENGE** YOUR PRECONCIEVED **NOTIONS**. THANK YOU FOR **INDULGING** ME IN MY **ATTEMPTS** TO MAKE PRINT **ALIVE**. AS YOU CAN SEE, ITS NOT **THAT** DIFFICULT TO **READ** IN **LANDSCAPE** RATHER THAN PORTRAIT. IF YOU'RE READING THIS **ELECTRONICALLY**, YOU CAN SEE THAT IT **FITS** YOUR SCREEN **BETTER**. YOU'RE ALSO PART OF THE NEW **COMICS CREATIVE PARADIGM**; STORYBOARD COMICS. MELVIN HAS SET THE STAGE FOR **MORE** FUN TO COME... BUT FOR **NOW**, LET'S GET BACK TO OUR **ADVENTURE**...

IF YOU'RE READING THIS, YOU'RE TURNED THE WRONG WAY! FLOP IT! THIS IS YOUR FINAL WARNING! FLIP IT!

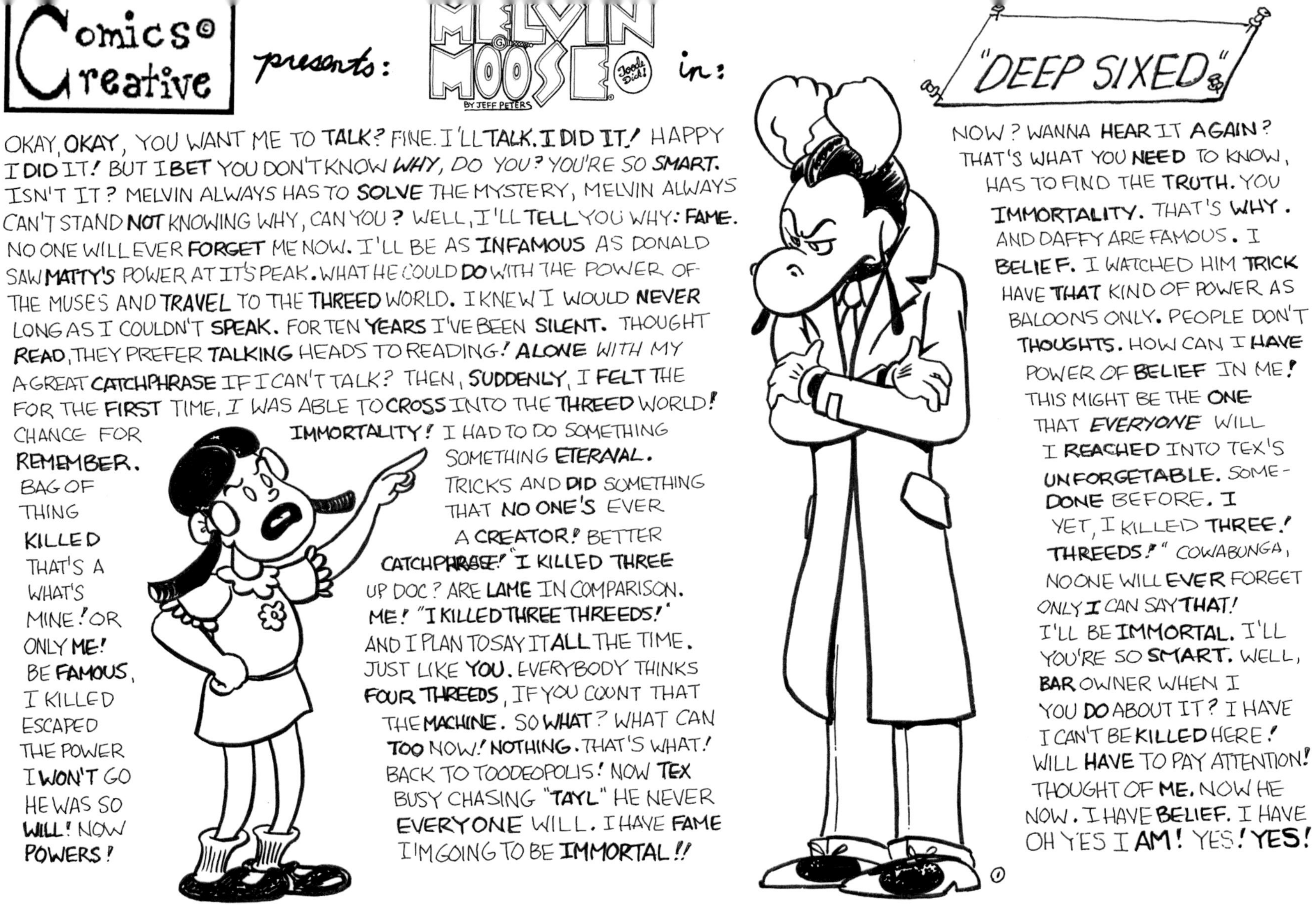

Comics© Creative
presents:
MELVIN G. MOOSE
BY JEFF PETERS
Toodle Dick!
in:
"DEEP SIXED"
OKAY, OKAY, YOU WANT ME TO TALK? FINE. I'LL TALK. I DID IT! HAPPY
I DID IT! BUT I BET YOU DON'T KNOW WHY, DO YOU? YOU'RE SO SMART.
ISN'T IT? MELVIN ALWAYS HAS TO SOLVE THE MYSTERY, MELVIN ALWAYS
CAN'T STAND NOT KNOWING WHY, CAN YOU? WELL, I'LL TELL YOU WHY: FAME.
NO ONE WILL EVER FORGET ME NOW. I'LL BE AS INFAMOUS AS DONALD
SAW MATTY'S POWER AT IT'S PEAK. WHAT HE COULD DO WITH THE POWER OF
THE MUSES AND TRAVEL TO THE THREED WORLD. I KNEW I WOULD NEVER
LONG AS I COULDN'T SPEAK. FOR TEN YEARS I'VE BEEN SILENT. THOUGHT
READ, THEY PREFER TALKING HEADS TO READING! ALONE WITH MY
A GREAT CATCHPHRASE IF I CAN'T TALK? THEN, SUDDENLY, I FELT THE
FOR THE FIRST TIME, I WAS ABLE TO CROSS INTO THE THREED WORLD!
CHANCE FOR
REMEMBER.
BAG OF
THING
KILLED
THAT'S A
WHAT'S
MINE! OR
ONLY ME!
BE FAMOUS,
I KILLED
ESCAPED
THE POWER
I WON'T GO
HE WAS SO
WILL! NOW
POWERS!
IMMORTALITY! I HAD TO DO SOMETHING
SOMETHING ETERNAL.
TRICKS AND DID SOMETHING
THAT NO ONE'S EVER
A CREATOR! BETTER
CATCHPHRASE! "I KILLED THREE
UP DOC? ARE LAME IN COMPARISON.
ME! "I KILLED THREE THREEDS!"
AND I PLAN TO SAY IT ALL THE TIME.
JUST LIKE YOU. EVERYBODY THINKS
FOUR THREEDS, IF YOU COUNT THAT
THE MACHINE. SO WHAT? WHAT CAN
TOO NOW! NOTHING. THAT'S WHAT!
BACK TO TOODEOPOLIS! NOW TEX
BUSY CHASING "TAYL" HE NEVER
EVERYONE WILL. I HAVE FAME
I'M GOING TO BE IMMORTAL!!
NOW? WANNA HEAR IT AGAIN?
THAT'S WHAT YOU NEED TO KNOW,
HAS TO FIND THE TRUTH. YOU
IMMORTALITY. THAT'S WHY.
AND DAFFY ARE FAMOUS. I
BELIEF. I WATCHED HIM TRICK
HAVE THAT KIND OF POWER AS
BALOONS ONLY. PEOPLE DON'T
THOUGHTS. HOW CAN I HAVE
POWER OF BELIEF IN ME!
THIS MIGHT BE THE ONE
THAT EVERYONE WILL
I REACHED INTO TEX'S
UNFORGETABLE. SOME-
DONE BEFORE. I
YET, I KILLED THREE!
THREEDS!" COWABUNGA,
NO ONE WILL EVER FORGET
ONLY I CAN SAY THAT!
I'LL BE IMMORTAL. I'LL
YOU'RE SO SMART. WELL,
BAR OWNER WHEN I
YOU DO ABOUT IT? I HAVE
I CAN'T BE KILLED HERE!
WILL HAVE TO PAY ATTENTION!
THOUGHT OF ME. NOW HE
NOW. I HAVE BELIEF. I HAVE
OH YES I AM! YES! YES!

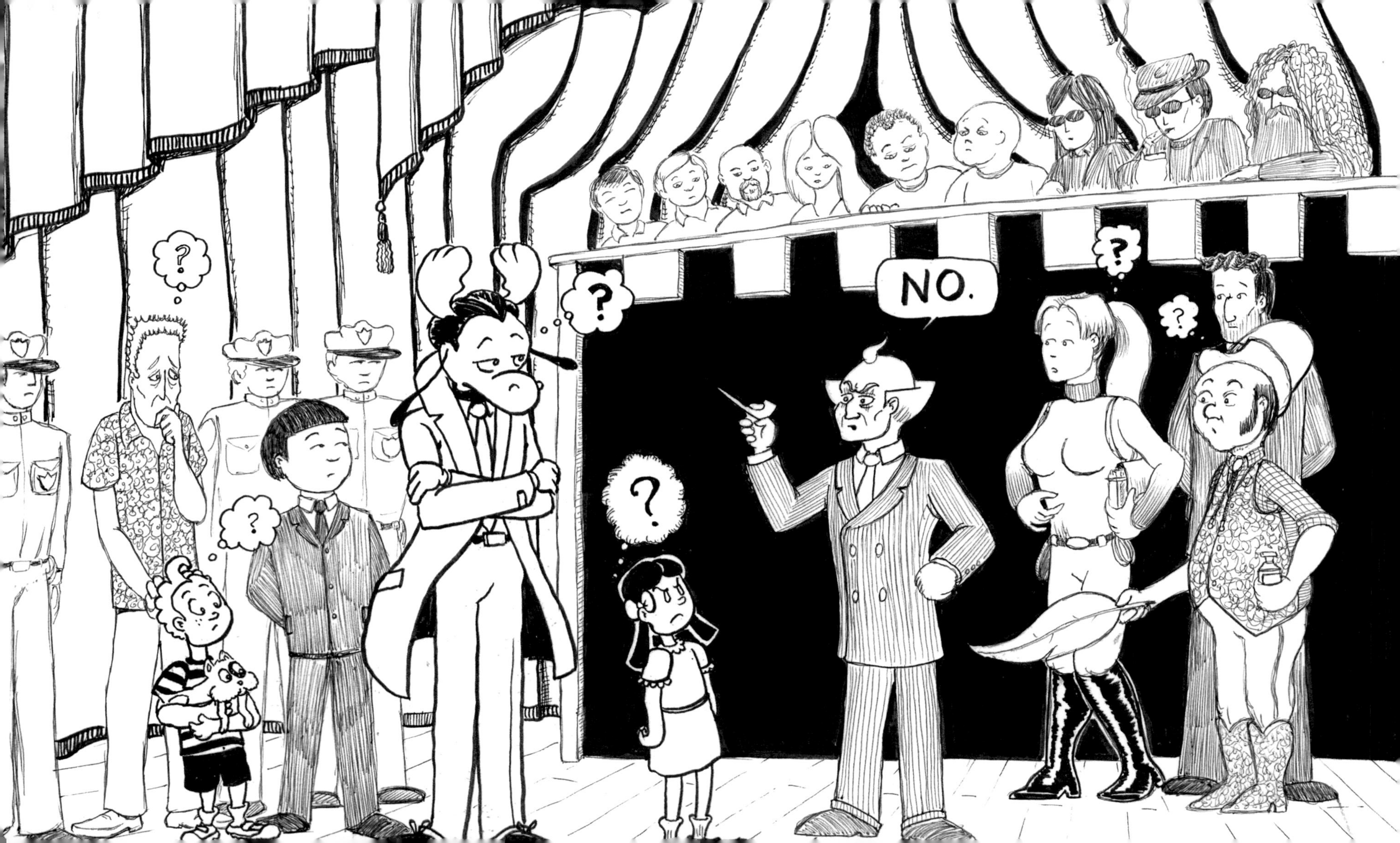
NO.

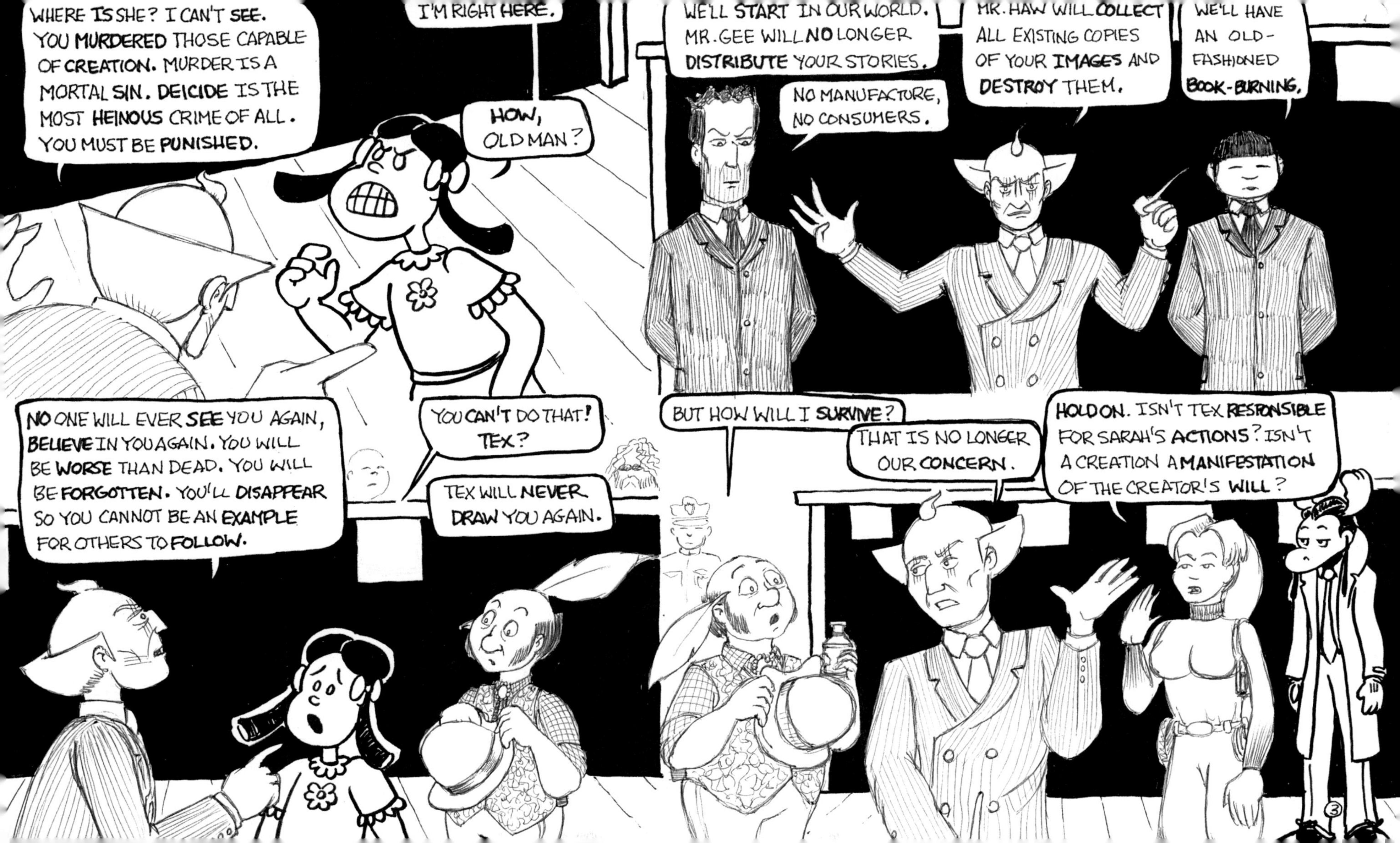
WHERE IS SHE? I CAN'T SEE. YOU MURDERED THOSE CAPABLE OF CREATION. MURDER IS A MORTAL SIN. DEICIDE IS THE MOST HEINOUS CRIME OF ALL. YOU MUST BE PUNISHED.
I'M RIGHT HERE.
HOW, OLD MAN?
WE'LL START IN OUR WORLD. MR. GEE WILL NO LONGER DISTRIBUTE YOUR STORIES.
NO MANUFACTURE, NO CONSUMERS.
MR. HAW WILL COLLECT ALL EXISTING COPIES OF YOUR IMAGES AND DESTROY THEM.
WE'LL HAVE AN OLD-FASHIONED BOOK-BURNING.
NO ONE WILL EVER SEE YOU AGAIN, BELIEVE IN YOU AGAIN. YOU WILL BE WORSE THAN DEAD. YOU WILL BE FORGOTTEN. YOU'LL DISAPPEAR SO YOU CANNOT BE AN EXAMPLE FOR OTHERS TO FOLLOW.
YOU CAN'T DO THAT! TEX?
TEX WILL NEVER DRAW YOU AGAIN.
BUT HOW WILL I SURVIVE?
THAT IS NO LONGER OUR CONCERN.
HOLD ON. ISN'T TEX RESPONSIBLE FOR SARAH'S ACTIONS? ISN'T A CREATION A MANIFESTATION OF THE CREATOR'S WILL?
3

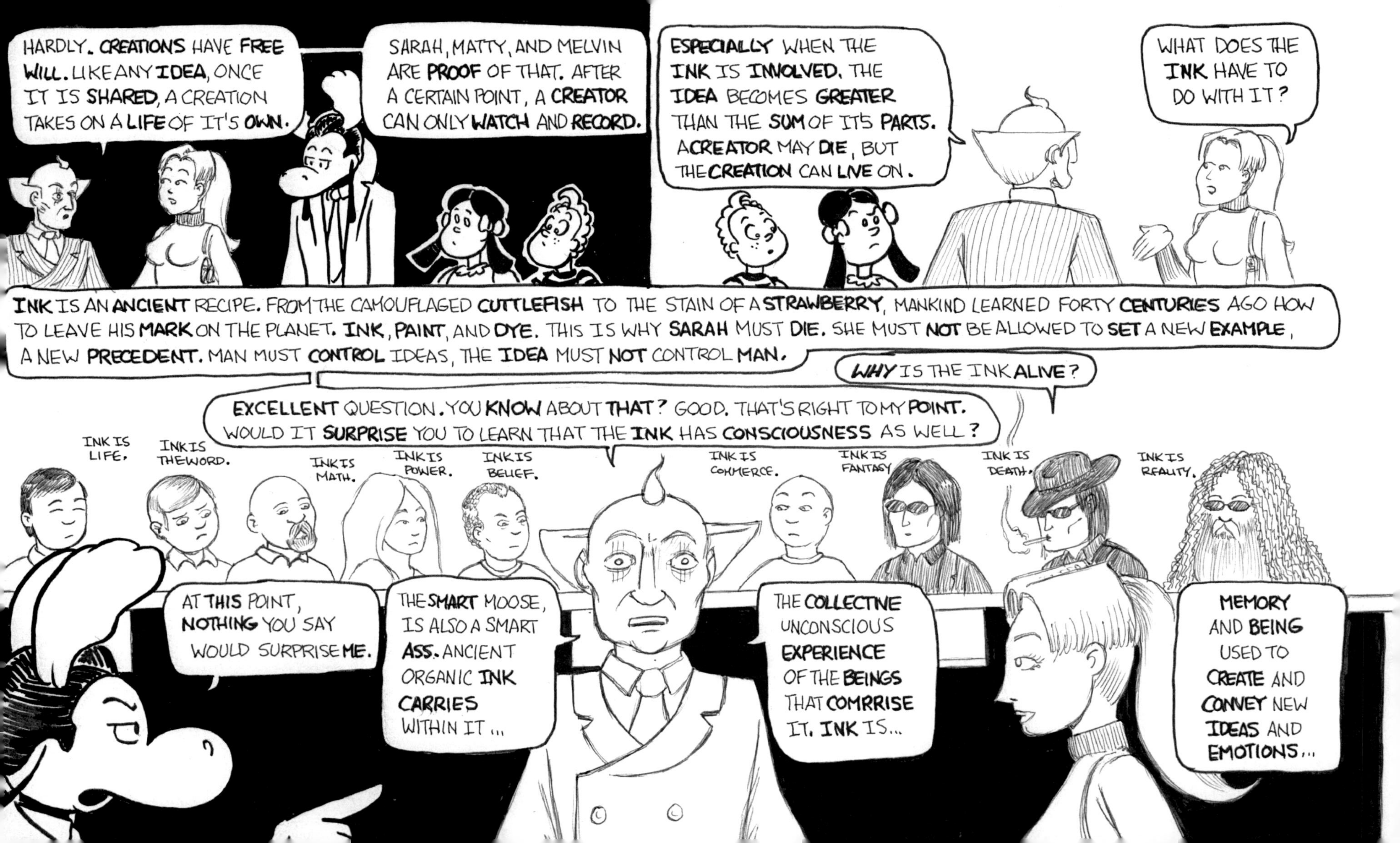
HARDLY. CREATIONS HAVE FREE WILL. LIKE ANY IDEA, ONCE IT IS SHARED, A CREATION TAKES ON A LIFE OF IT'S OWN.
SARAH, MATTY, AND MELVIN ARE PROOF OF THAT. AFTER A CERTAIN POINT, A CREATOR CAN ONLY WATCH AND RECORD.
ESPECIALLY WHEN THE INK IS INVOLVED. THE IDEA BECOMES GREATER THAN THE SUM OF IT'S PARTS. A CREATOR MAY DIE, BUT THE CREATION CAN LIVE ON.
WHAT DOES THE INK HAVE TO DO WITH IT?
INK IS AN ANCIENT RECIPE. FROM THE CAMOUFLAGED CUTTLEFISH TO THE STAIN OF A STRAWBERRY, MANKIND LEARNED FORTY CENTURIES AGO HOW TO LEAVE HIS MARK ON THE PLANET. INK, PAINT, AND DYE. THIS IS WHY SARAH MUST DIE. SHE MUST NOT BE ALLOWED TO SET A NEW EXAMPLE, A NEW PRECEDENT. MAN MUST CONTROL IDEAS, THE IDEA MUST NOT CONTROL MAN.
WHY IS THE INK ALIVE?
EXCELLENT QUESTION. YOU KNOW ABOUT THAT? GOOD. THAT'S RIGHT TO MY POINT. WOULD IT SURPRISE YOU TO LEARN THAT THE INK HAS CONSCIOUSNESS AS WELL?
INK IS LIFE.
INK IS THE WORD.
INK IS MATH.
INK IS POWER.
INK IS BELIEF.
INK IS COMMERCE.
INK IS FANTASY
INK IS DEATH.
INK IS REALITY.
AT THIS POINT, NOTHING YOU SAY WOULD SURPRISE ME.
THE SMART MOOSE, IS ALSO A SMART ASS. ANCIENT ORGANIC INK CARRIES WITHIN IT...
THE COLLECTIVE UNCONSCIOUS EXPERIENCE OF THE BEINGS THAT COMRRISE IT. INK IS...
MEMORY AND BEING USED TO CREATE AND CONVEY NEW IDEAS AND EMOTIONS...

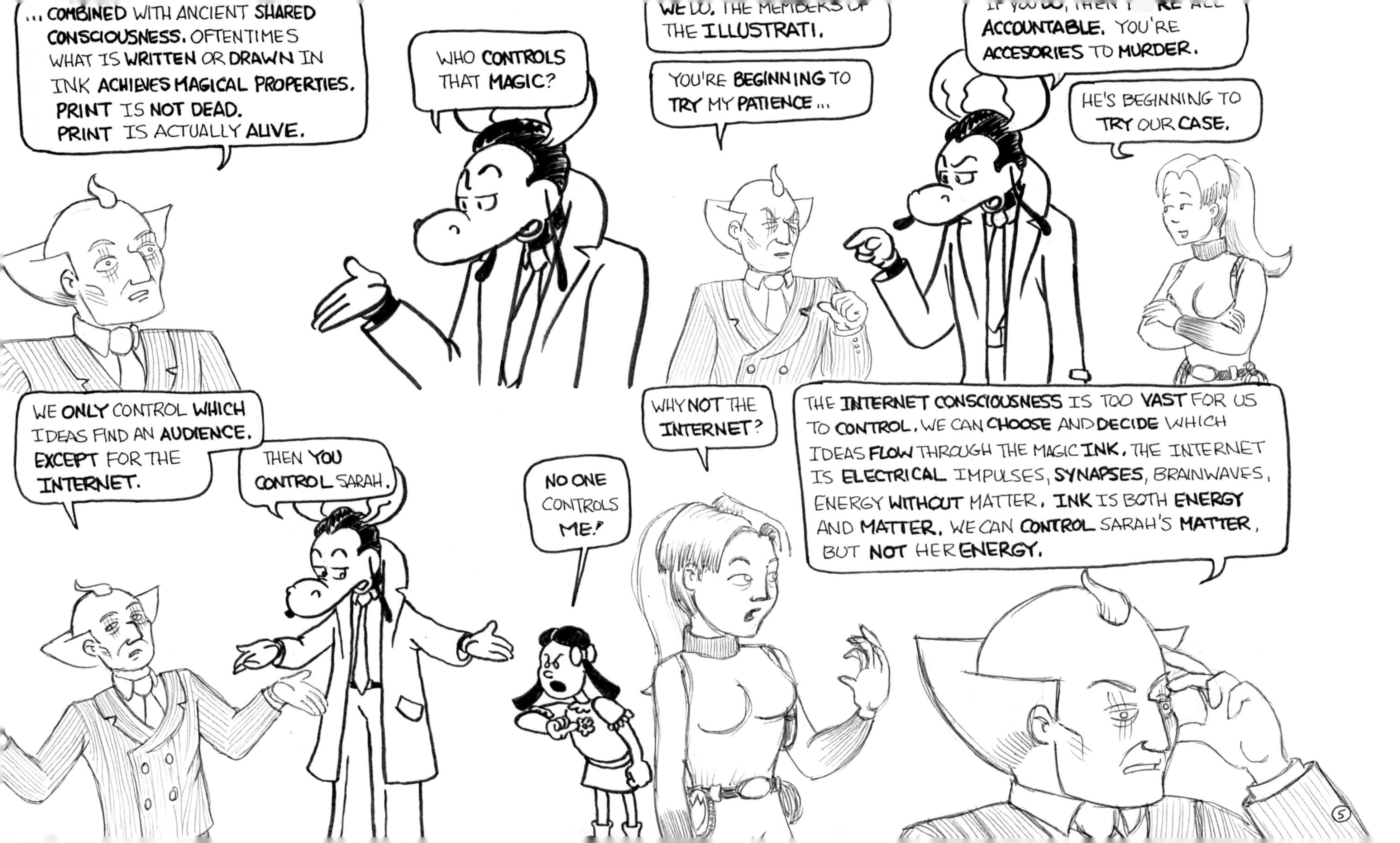
... COMBINED WITH ANCIENT SHARED CONSCIOUSNESS. OFTENTIMES WHAT IS WRITTEN OR DRAWN IN INK ACHIEVES MAGICAL PROPERTIES. PRINT IS NOT DEAD. PRINT IS ACTUALLY ALIVE.
WHO CONTROLS THAT MAGIC?
WE DO. THE MEMBERS OF THE ILLUSTRATI.
YOU'RE BEGINNING TO TRY MY PATIENCE...
ACCOUNTABLE. YOU'RE ACCESORIES TO MURDER.
HE'S BEGINNING TO TRY OUR CASE.
WE ONLY CONTROL WHICH IDEAS FIND AN AUDIENCE. EXCEPT FOR THE INTERNET.
THEN YOU CONTROL SARAH.
NO ONE CONTROLS ME!
WHY NOT THE INTERNET?
THE INTERNET CONSCIOUSNESS IS TOO VAST FOR US TO CONTROL. WE CAN CHOOSE AND DECIDE WHICH IDEAS FLOW THROUGH THE MAGIC INK. THE INTERNET IS ELECTRICAL IMPULSES, SYNAPSES, BRAINWAVES, ENERGY WITHOUT MATTER. INK IS BOTH ENERGY AND MATTER. WE CAN CONTROL SARAH'S MATTER, BUT NOT HER ENERGY.
5

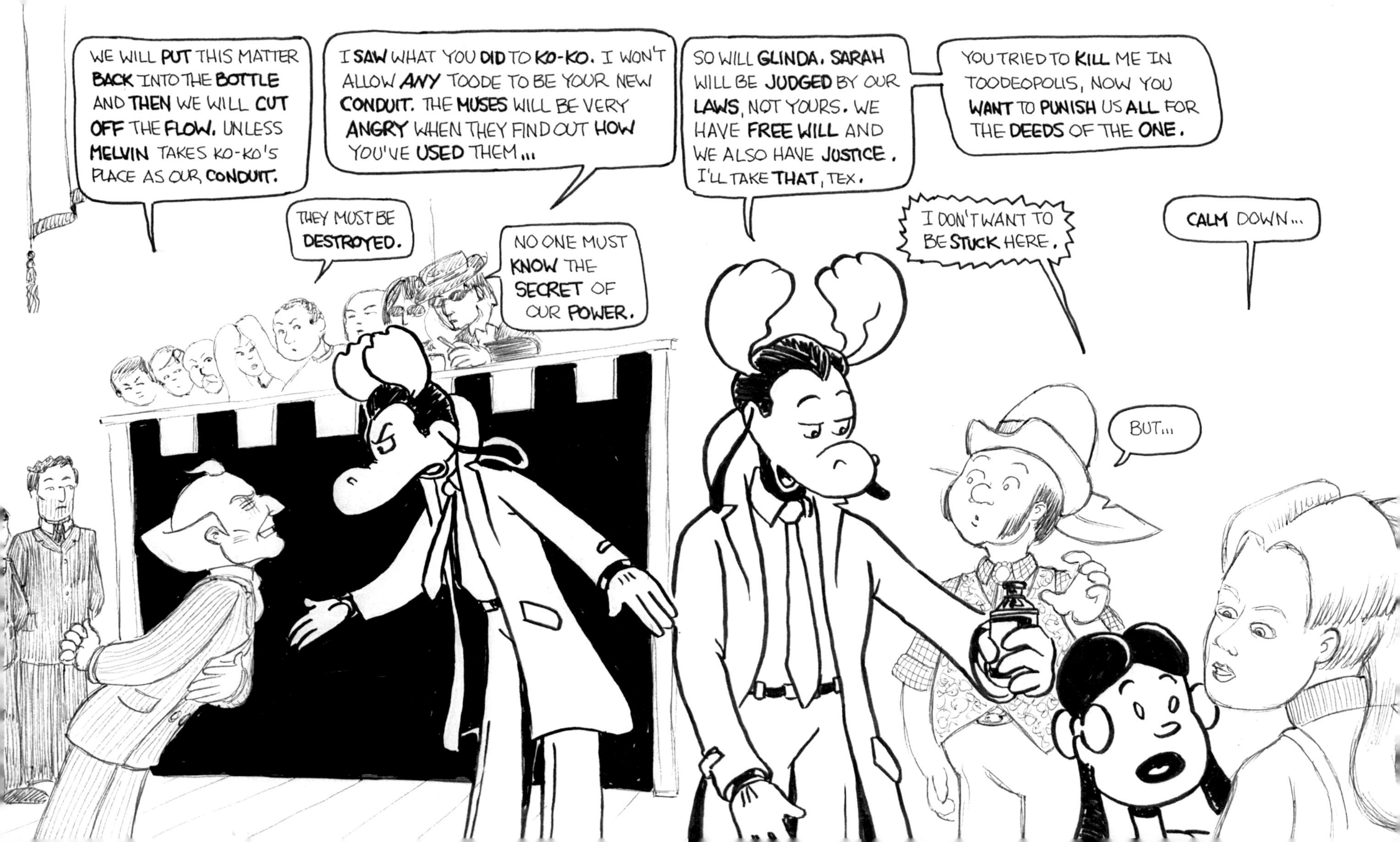
WE WILL PUT THIS MATTER BACK INTO THE BOTTLE AND THEN WE WILL CUT OFF THE FLOW. UNLESS MELVIN TAKES KO-KO'S PLACE AS OUR CONDUIT.
THEY MUST BE DESTROYED.
I SAW WHAT YOU DID TO KO-KO. I WON'T ALLOW ANY TOODE TO BE YOUR NEW CONDUIT. THE MUSES WILL BE VERY ANGRY WHEN THEY FIND OUT HOW YOU'VE USED THEM...
NO ONE MUST KNOW THE SECRET OF OUR POWER.
SO WILL GLINDA. SARAH WILL BE JUDGED BY OUR LAWS, NOT YOURS. WE HAVE FREE WILL AND WE ALSO HAVE JUSTICE. I'LL TAKE THAT, TEX.
YOU TRIED TO KILL ME IN TOODEOPOLIS, NOW YOU WANT TO PUNISH US ALL FOR THE DEEDS OF THE ONE.
I DON'T WANT TO BE STUCK HERE.
CALM DOWN...
BUT...

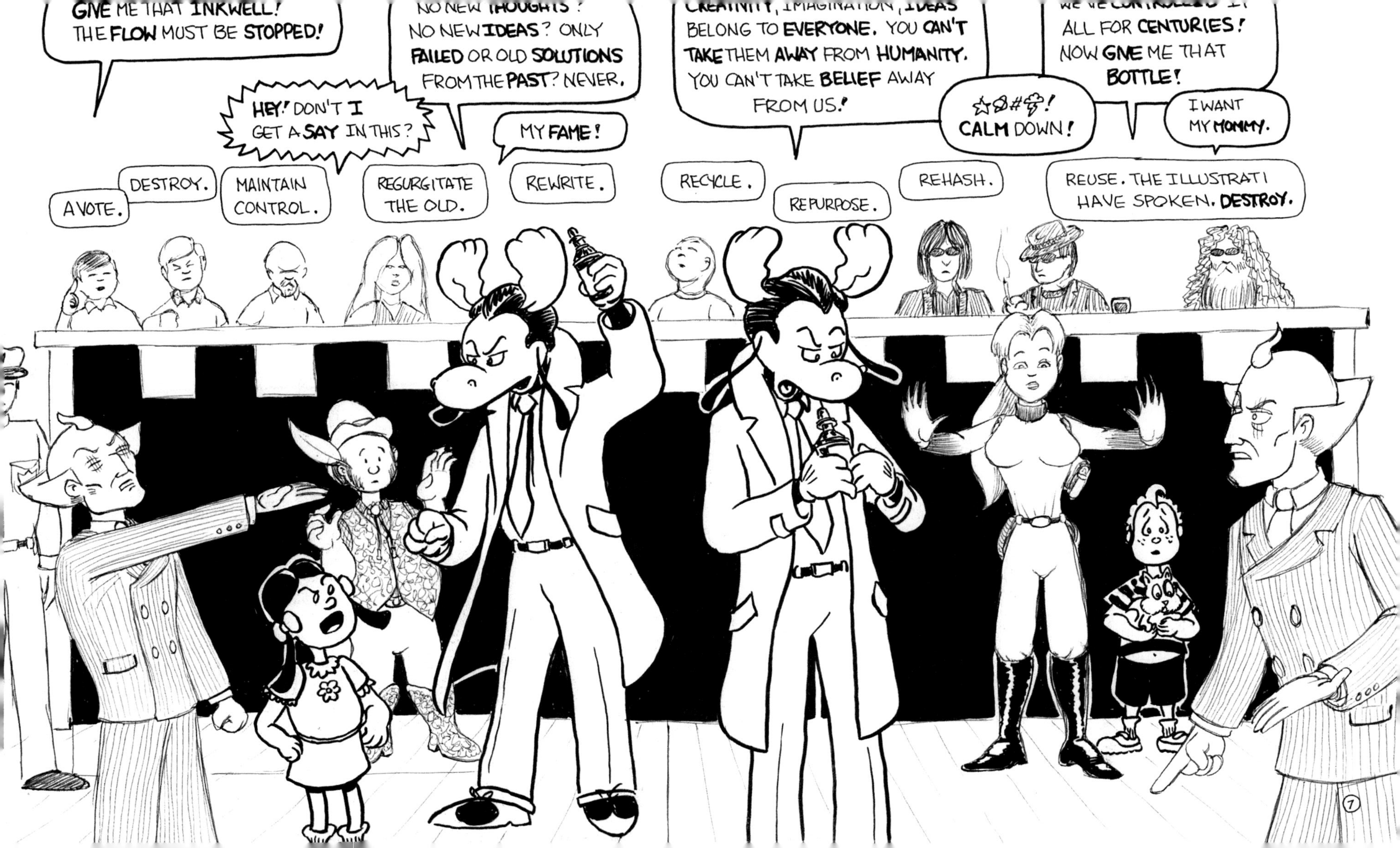
GIVE ME THAT INKWELL! THE FLOW MUST BE STOPPED!
HEY! DON'T I GET A SAY IN THIS?
NO NEW IDEAS? ONLY FAILED OR OLD SOLUTIONS FROM THE PAST? NEVER.
MY FAME!
BELONG TO EVERYONE. YOU CAN'T TAKE THEM AWAY FROM HUMANITY. YOU CAN'T TAKE BELIEF AWAY FROM US!
CALM DOWN!
ALL FOR CENTURIES! NOW GIVE ME THAT BOTTLE!
I WANT MY MOMMY.
A VOTE.
DESTROY.
MAINTAIN CONTROL.
REGURGITATE THE OLD.
REWRITE.
RECYCLE.
REPURPOSE.
REHASH.
REUSE. THE ILLUSTRATI HAVE SPOKEN. DESTROY.

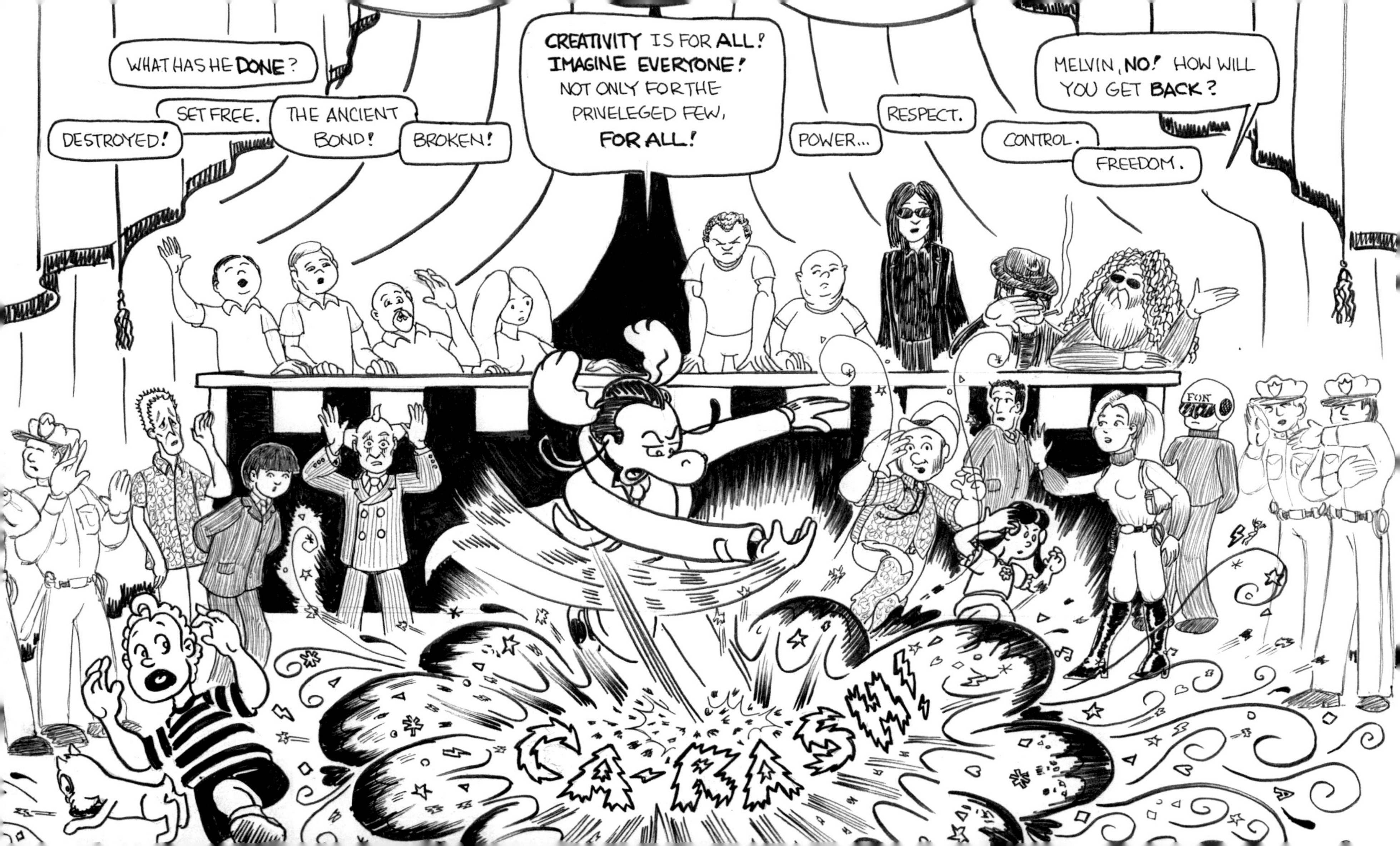
WHAT HAS HE DONE?
SET FREE.
DESTROYED!
THE ANCIENT BOND!
BROKEN!
CREATIVITY IS FOR ALL! IMAGINE EVERYONE! NOT ONLY FOR THE PRIVELEGED FEW, FOR ALL!
POWER...
RESPECT.
CONTROL.
FREEDOM.
MELVIN, NO! HOW WILL YOU GET BACK?

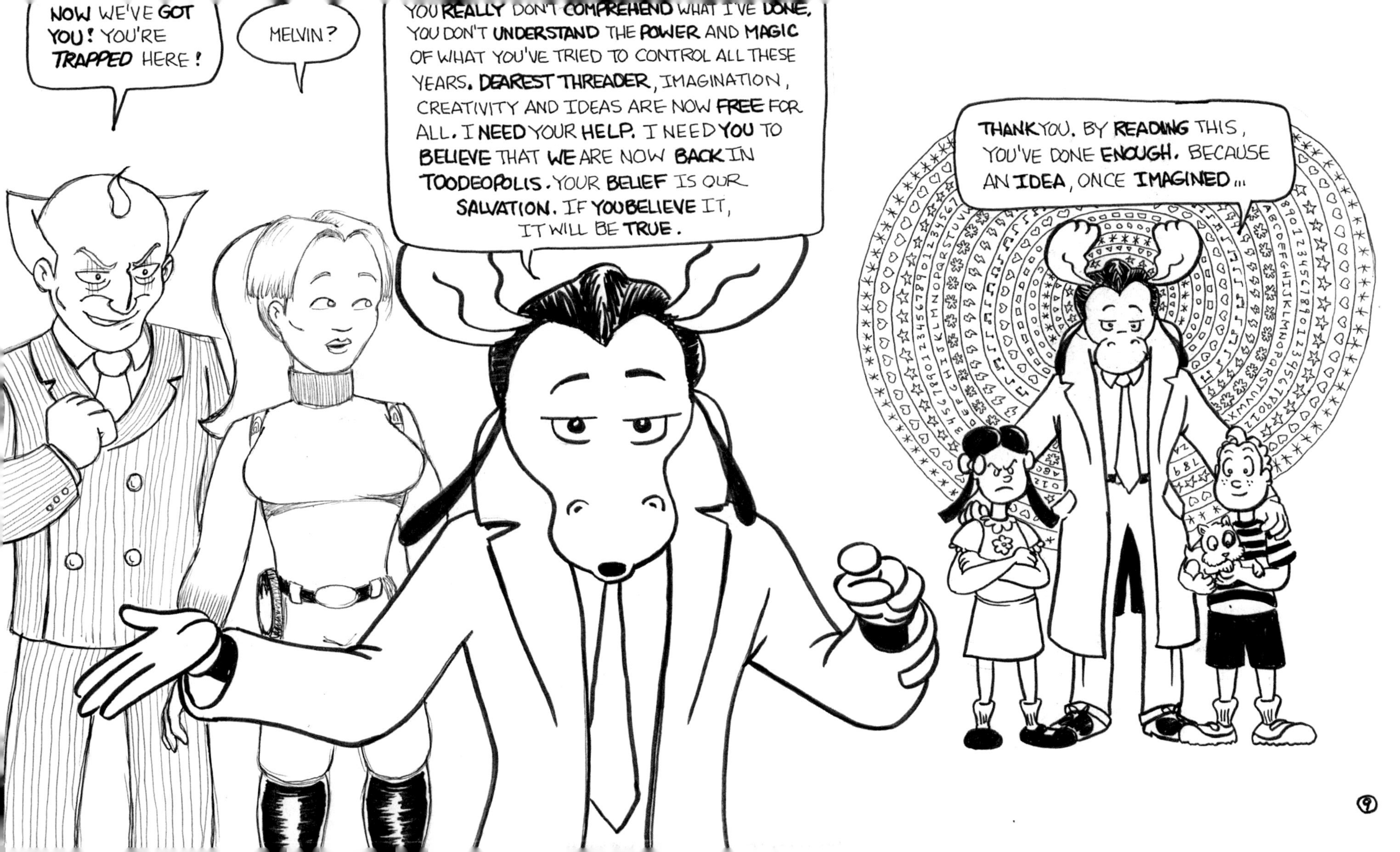
NOW WE'VE GOT YOU! YOU'RE TRAPPED HERE!
MELVIN?
YOU REALLY DON'T COMPREHEND WHAT I'VE DONE. YOU DON'T UNDERSTAND THE POWER AND MAGIC OF WHAT YOU'VE TRIED TO CONTROL ALL THESE YEARS. DEAREST THREADER, IMAGINATION, CREATIVITY AND IDEAS ARE NOW FREE FOR ALL. I NEED YOUR HELP. I NEED YOU TO BELIEVE THAT WE ARE NOW BACK IN TOODEOPOLIS. YOUR BELIEF IS OUR SALVATION. IF YOU BELIEVE IT, IT WILL BE TRUE.
THANK YOU. BY READING THIS, YOU'VE DONE ENOUGH. BECAUSE AN IDEA, ONCE IMAGINED...

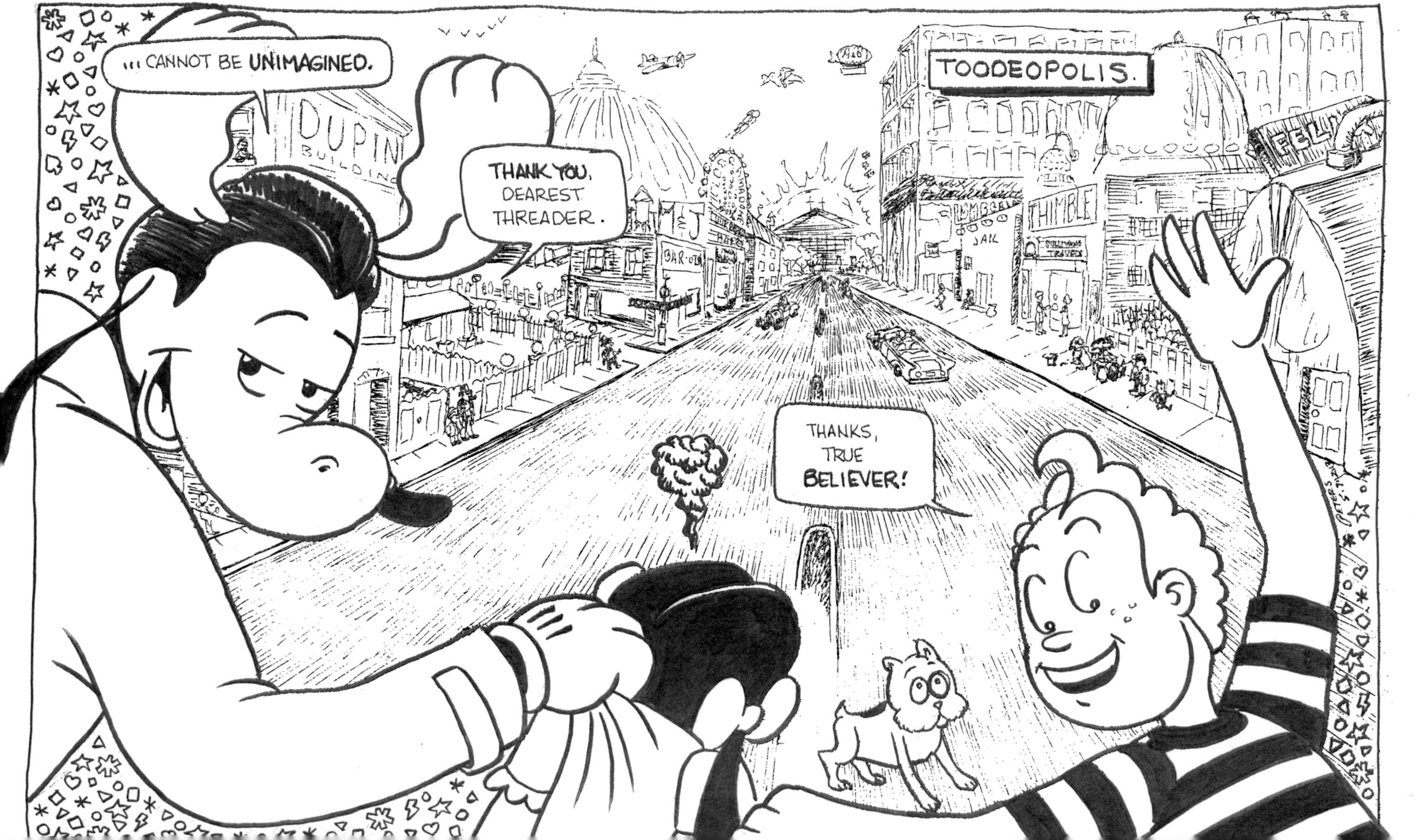

... CANNOT BE UNIMAGINED.
THANK YOU, DEAREST THREADER.
THANKS, TRUE BELIEVER!
TOODEOPOLIS.
DUPIN BUILDING
THIMBLE
JAIL

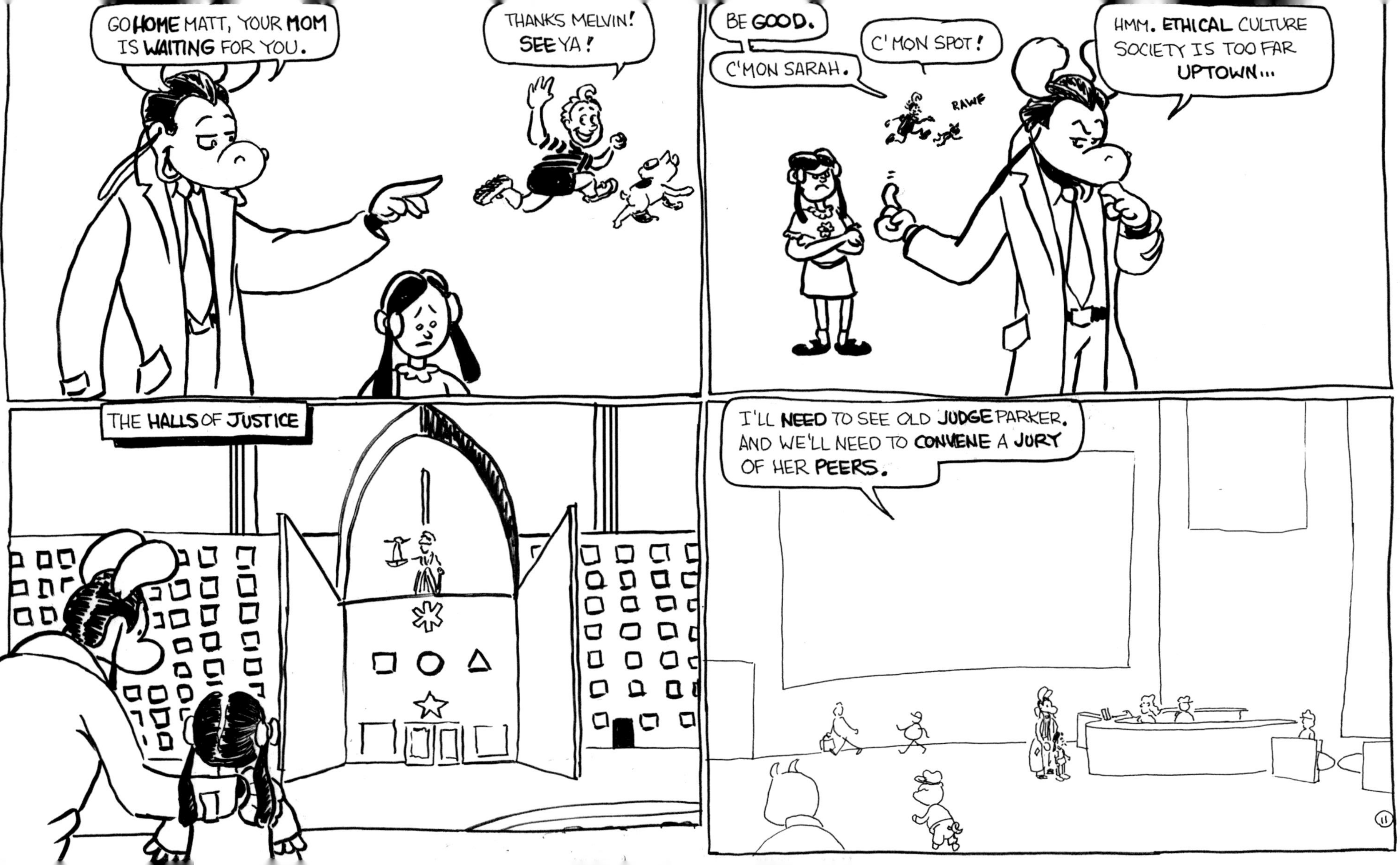
GO HOME MATT, YOUR MOM IS WAITING FOR YOU.
THANKS MELVIN! SEE YA!
BE GOOD.
C'MON SARAH.
C'MON SPOT!
RAWF
HMM. ETHICAL CULTURE SOCIETY IS TOO FAR UPTOWN...
THE HALLS OF JUSTICE
I'LL NEED TO SEE OLD JUDGE PARKER. AND WE'LL NEED TO CONVENE A JURY OF HER PEERS.
11

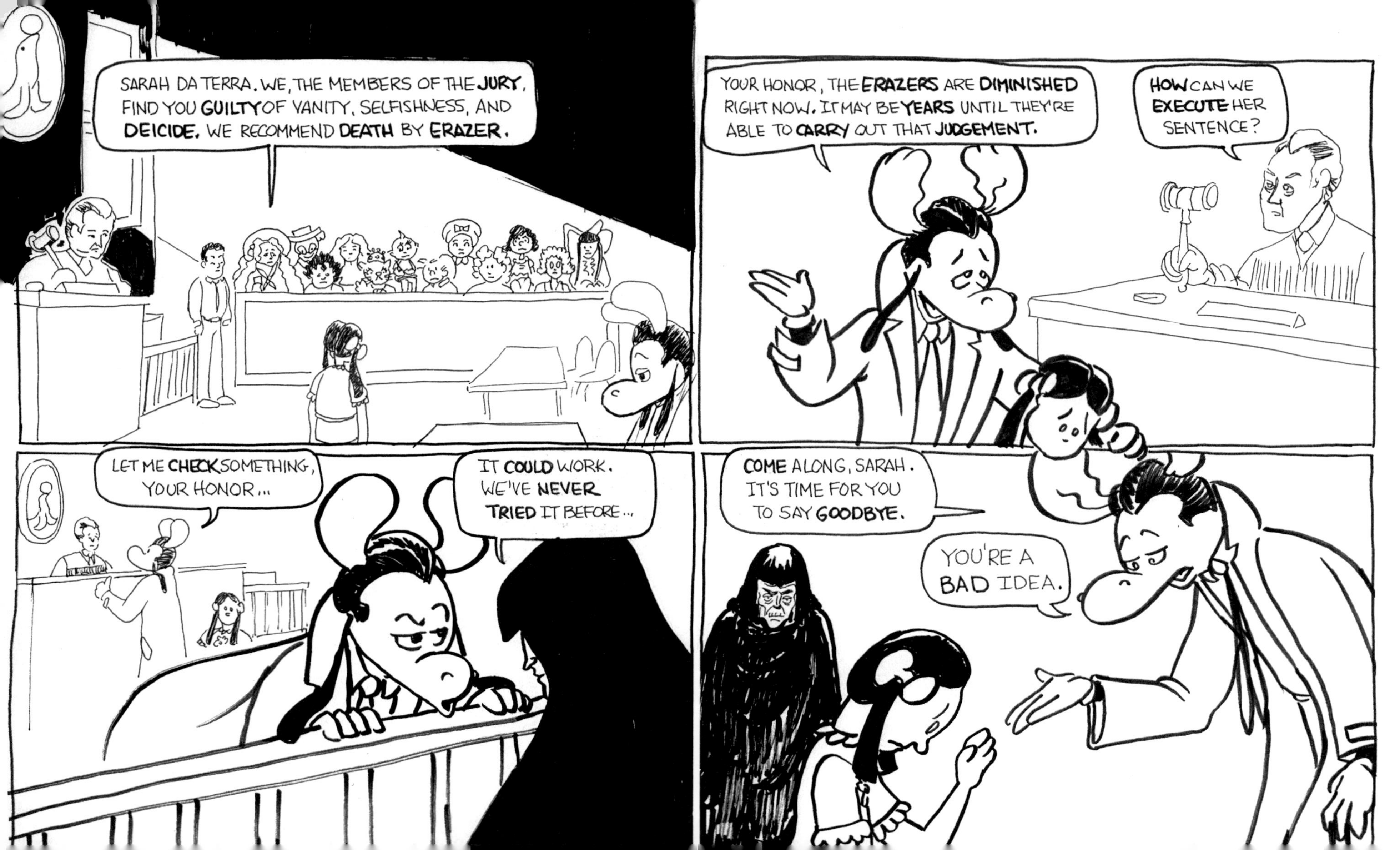
SARAH DA TERRA. WE, THE MEMBERS OF THE JURY, FIND YOU GUILTY OF VANITY, SELFISHNESS, AND DEICIDE. WE RECOMMEND DEATH BY ERAZER.
LET ME CHECK SOMETHING, YOUR HONOR...
IT COULD WORK. WE'VE NEVER TRIED IT BEFORE...
YOUR HONOR, THE ERAZERS ARE DIMINISHED RIGHT NOW. IT MAY BE YEARS UNTIL THEY'RE ABLE TO CARRY OUT THAT JUDGEMENT.
HOW CAN WE EXECUTE HER SENTENCE?
COME ALONG, SARAH. IT'S TIME FOR YOU TO SAY GOODBYE.
YOU'RE A BAD IDEA.

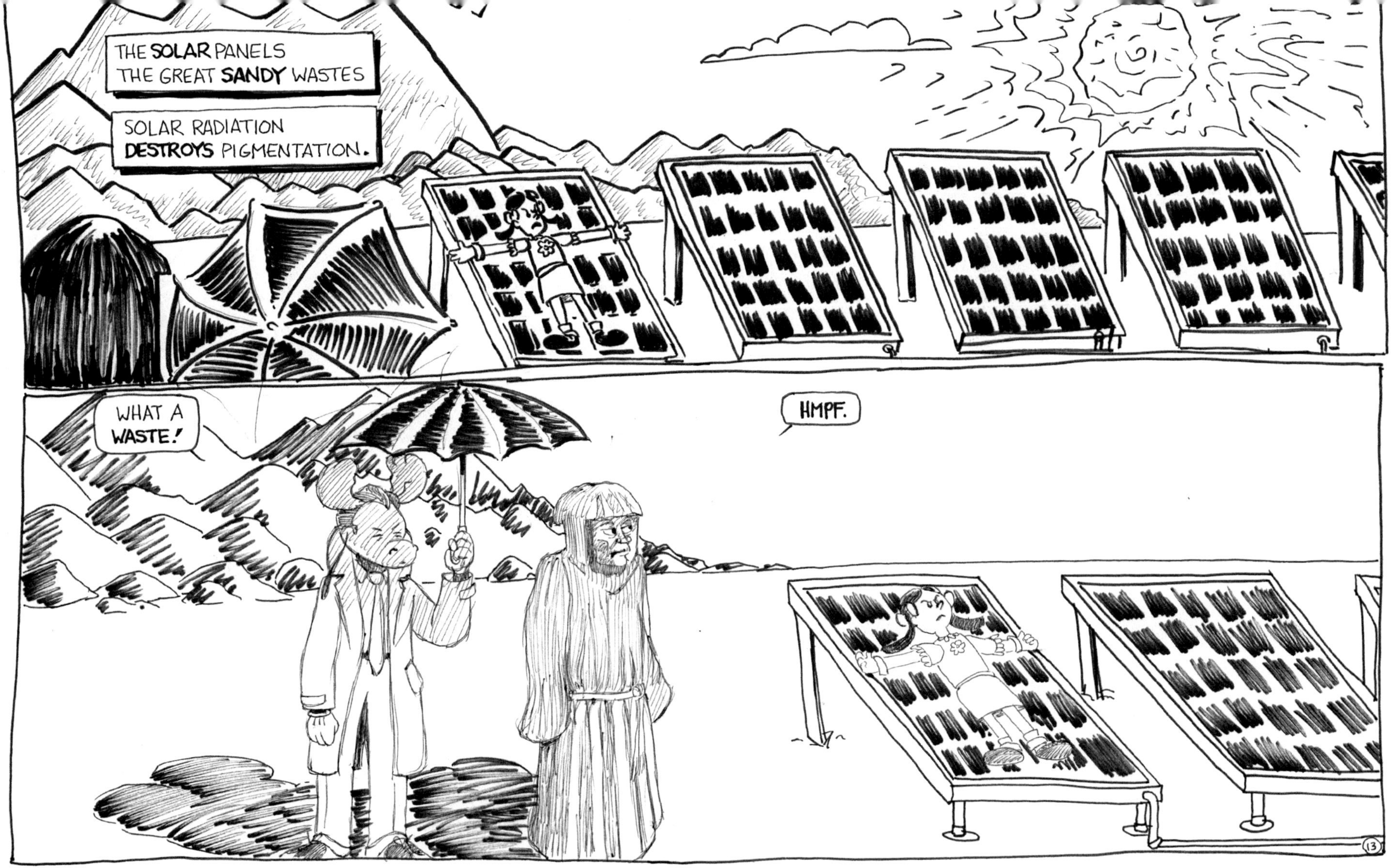
THE SOLAR PANELS
THE GREAT SANDY WASTES
SOLAR RADIATION DESTROYS PIGMENTATION.
WHAT A WASTE!
HMPF.
13

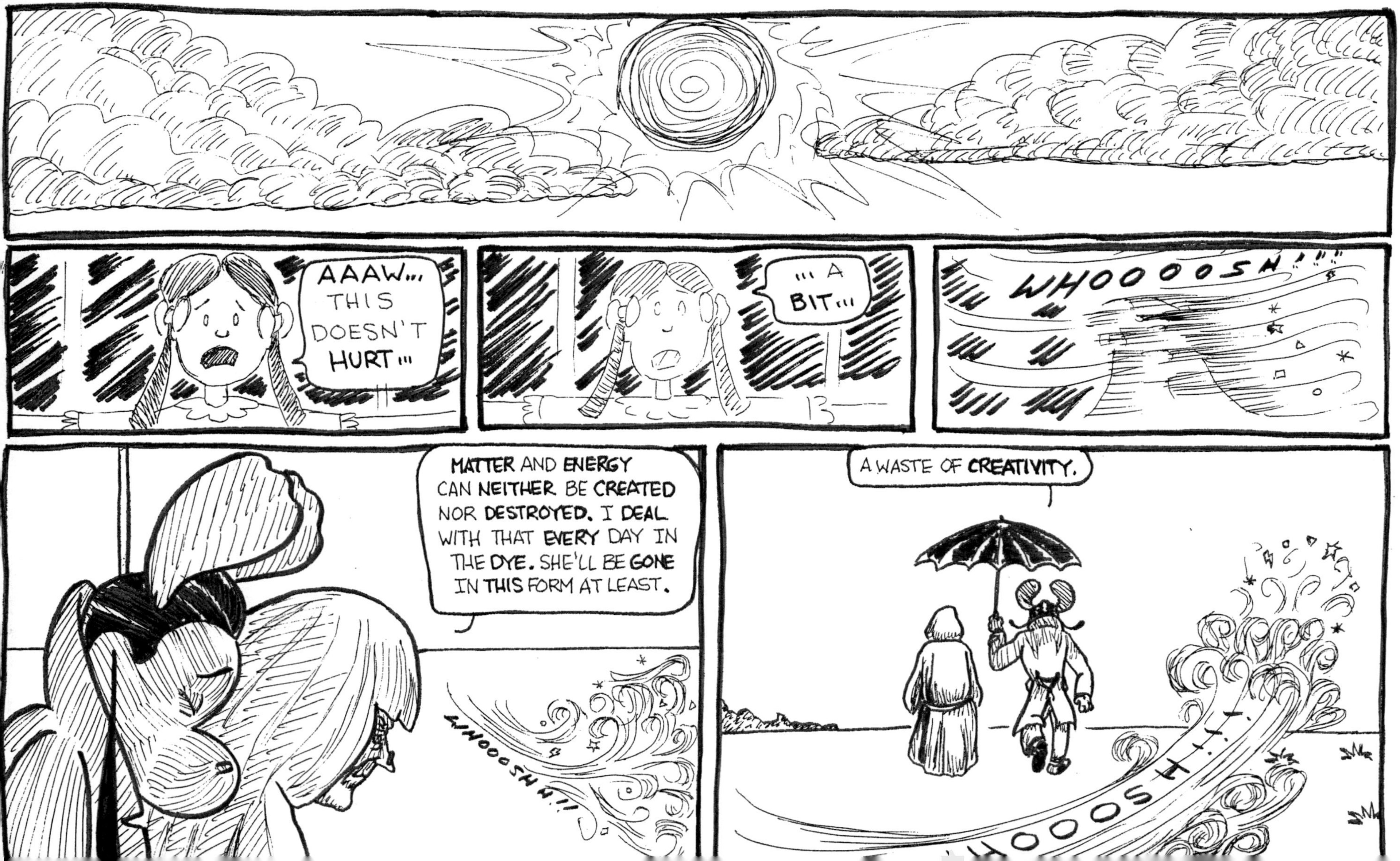
AAAW... THIS DOESN'T HURT...
...A BIT...
WHOOOOOSH!!!!
MATTER AND ENERGY CAN NEITHER BE CREATED NOR DESTROYED. I DEAL WITH THAT EVERY DAY IN THE DYE. SHE'LL BE GONE IN THIS FORM AT LEAST.
WHOOOSH!!
A WASTE OF CREATIVITY.

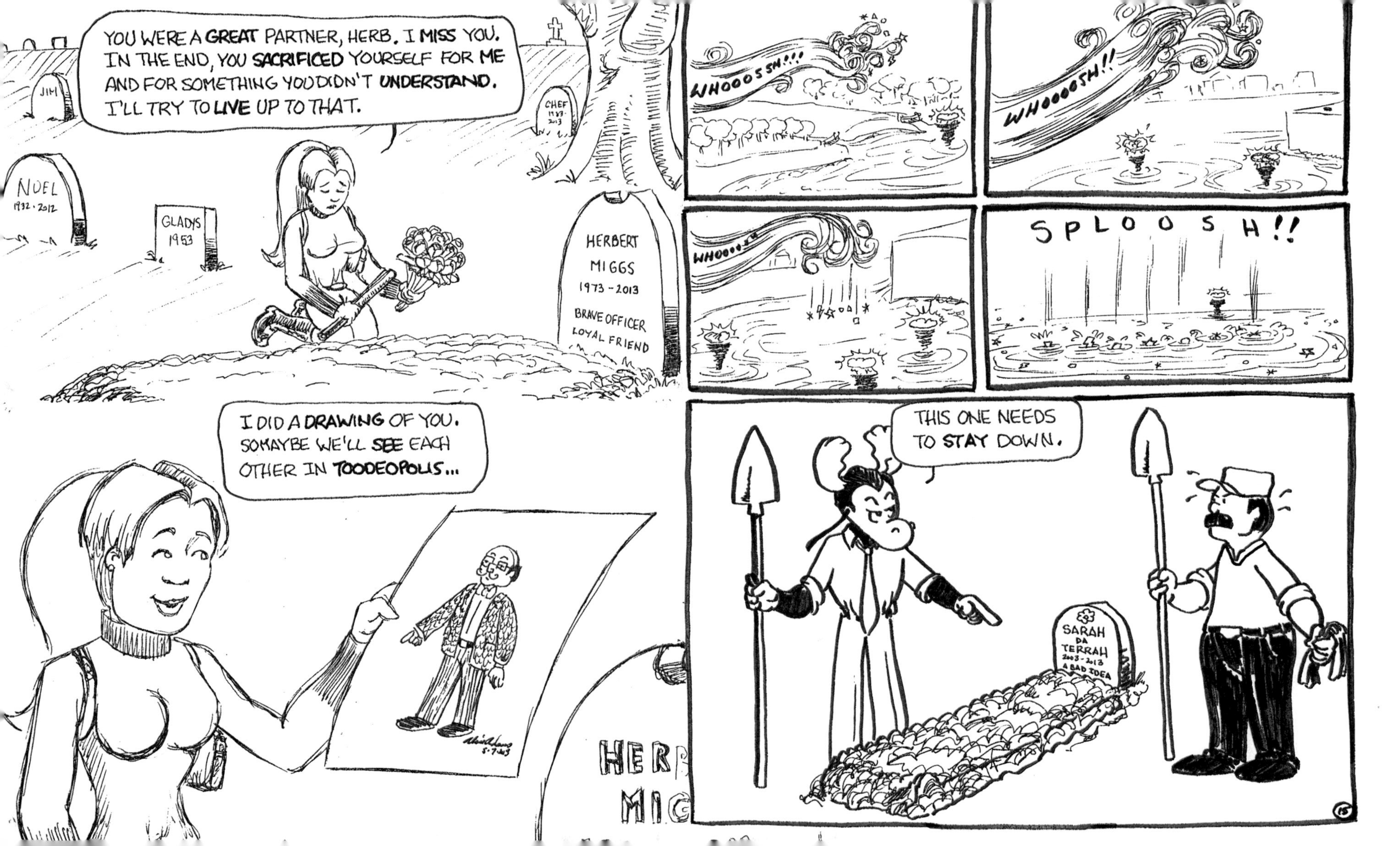
YOU WERE A GREAT PARTNER, HERB. I MISS YOU. IN THE END, YOU SACRIFICED YOURSELF FOR ME AND FOR SOMETHING YOU DIDN'T UNDERSTAND. I'LL TRY TO LIVE UP TO THAT.
JIM
NOEL 1932 - 2012
GLADYS 1953
CHEF
HERBERT MIGGS 1973 - 2013 BRAVE OFFICER LOYAL FRIEND
I DID A DRAWING OF YOU. SO MAYBE WE'LL SEE EACH OTHER IN TOODEOPOLIS...
HER
MIG
WHOOOSSH!!!
WHOOOOSH!!
SPLOOSH!!
THIS ONE NEEDS TO STAY DOWN.
SARAH DA TERRAH 2003 - 2013 A BAD IDEA
15

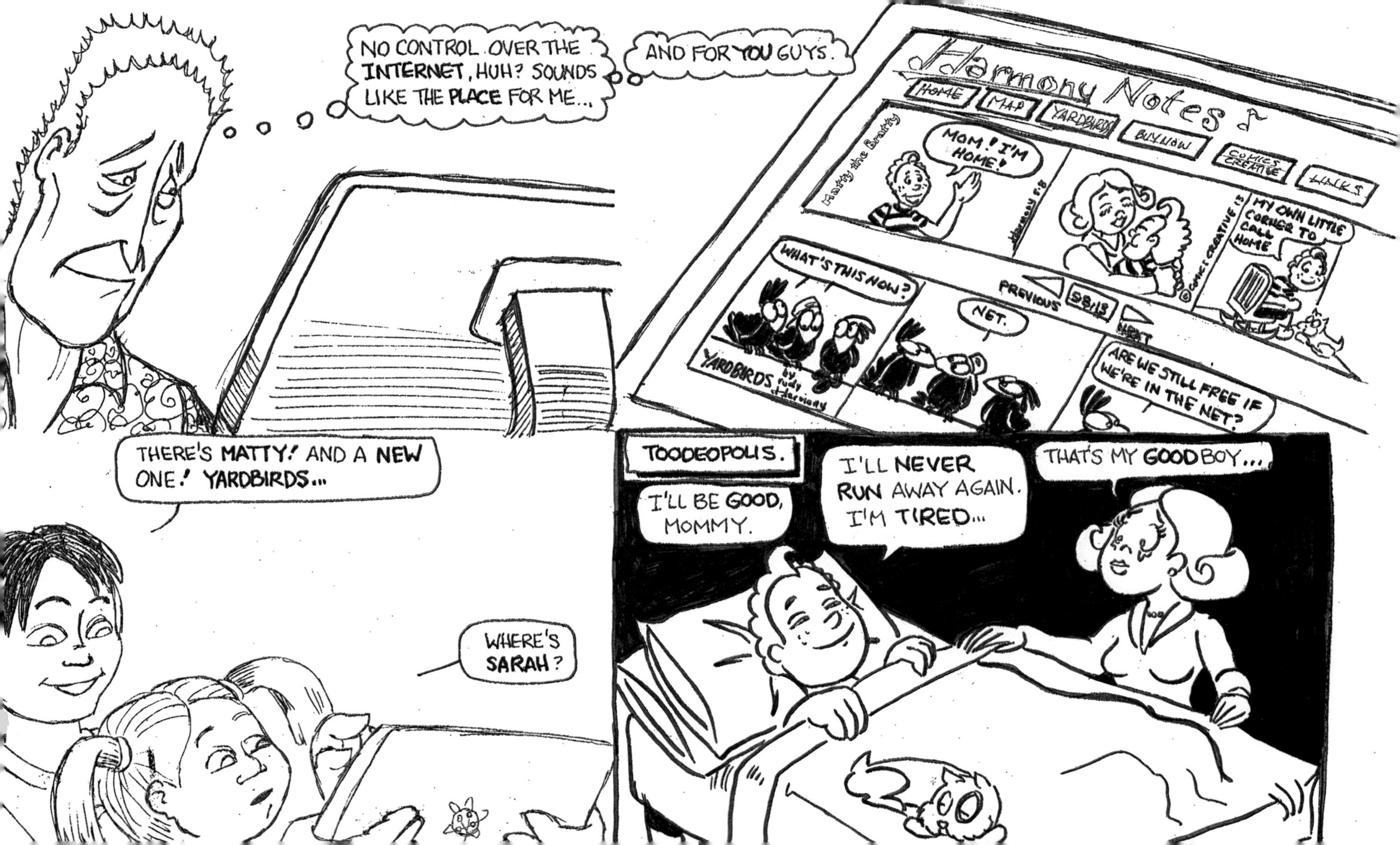
NO CONTROL OVER THE INTERNET, HUH? SOUNDS LIKE THE PLACE FOR ME...
AND FOR YOU GUYS.
Harmony Notes
HOME
MAP
YARDBIRDS
BUY NOW
COMICS CREATIVE
LINKS
Matty the Bratty
MOM! I'M HOME!
MY OWN LITTLE CORNER TO CALL HOME
WHAT'S THIS NOW?
NET.
ARE WE STILL FREE IF WE'RE IN THE NET?
YARDBIRDS by Rudy Harmony
PREVIOUS
98/13
NEXT
THERE'S MATTY! AND A NEW ONE! YARDBIRDS...
WHERE'S SARAH?
TOODEOPOLIS.
I'LL BE GOOD, MOMMY.
I'LL NEVER RUN AWAY AGAIN. I'M TIRED...
THAT'S MY GOOD BOY...

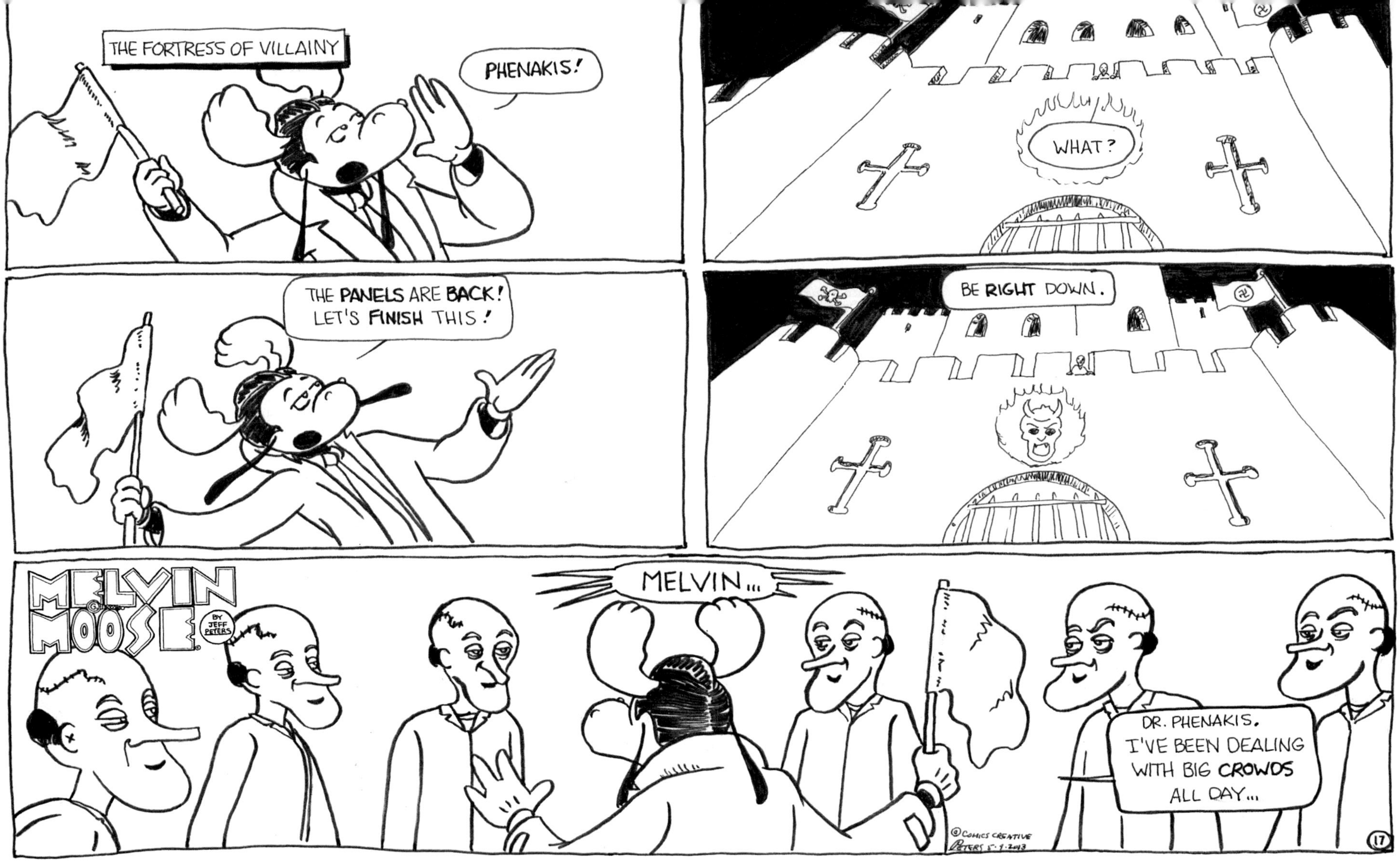
THE FORTRESS OF VILLAINY
PHENAKIS!
WHAT?
THE PANELS ARE BACK! LET'S FINISH THIS!
BE RIGHT DOWN.
MELVIN MOOSE
BY JEFF PETERS
MELVIN...
DR. PHENAKIS. I'VE BEEN DEALING WITH BIG CROWDS ALL DAY...
©COMICS CREATIVE
PETERS 5·9·2013
17

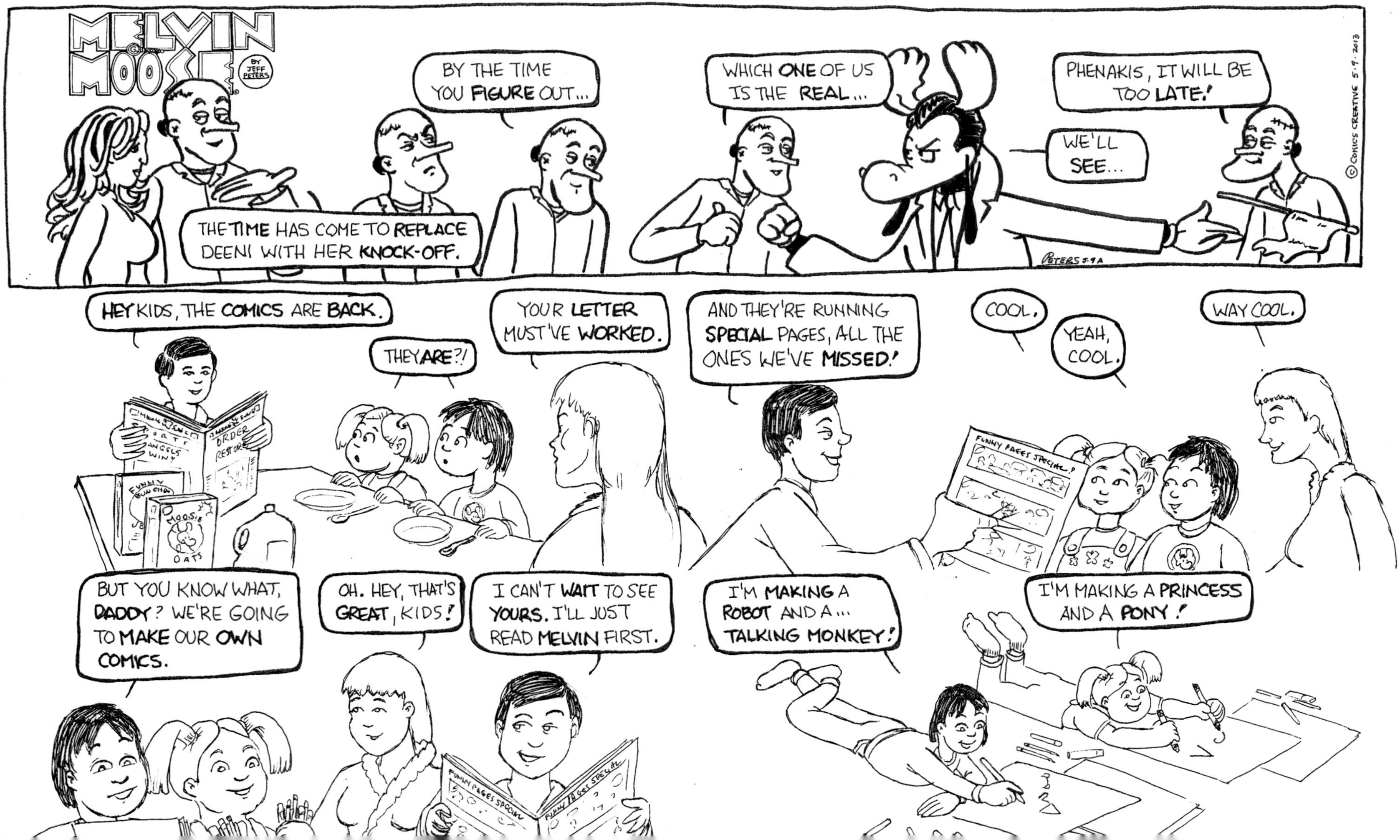
MELVIN MOOSE
BY JEFF PETERS
THE TIME HAS COME TO REPLACE DEENI WITH HER KNOCK-OFF.
BY THE TIME YOU FIGURE OUT...
WHICH ONE OF US IS THE REAL...
PHENAKIS, IT WILL BE TOO LATE!
WE'LL SEE...
PETERS 5-9A
© COMICS CREATIVE 5·9·2013
HEY KIDS, THE COMICS ARE BACK.
THEY ARE?!
YOUR LETTER MUST'VE WORKED.
AND THEY'RE RUNNING SPECIAL PAGES, ALL THE ONES WE'VE MISSED!
COOL.
YEAH, COOL.
WAY COOL.
ORDER RESTORED
MOOSIE OATS
FUNNY PAGES SPECIAL
BUT YOU KNOW WHAT, DADDY? WE'RE GOING TO MAKE OUR OWN COMICS.
OH. HEY, THAT'S GREAT, KIDS!
I CAN'T WAIT TO SEE YOURS. I'LL JUST READ MELVIN FIRST.
I'M MAKING A ROBOT AND A... TALKING MONKEY!
I'M MAKING A PRINCESS AND A PONY!

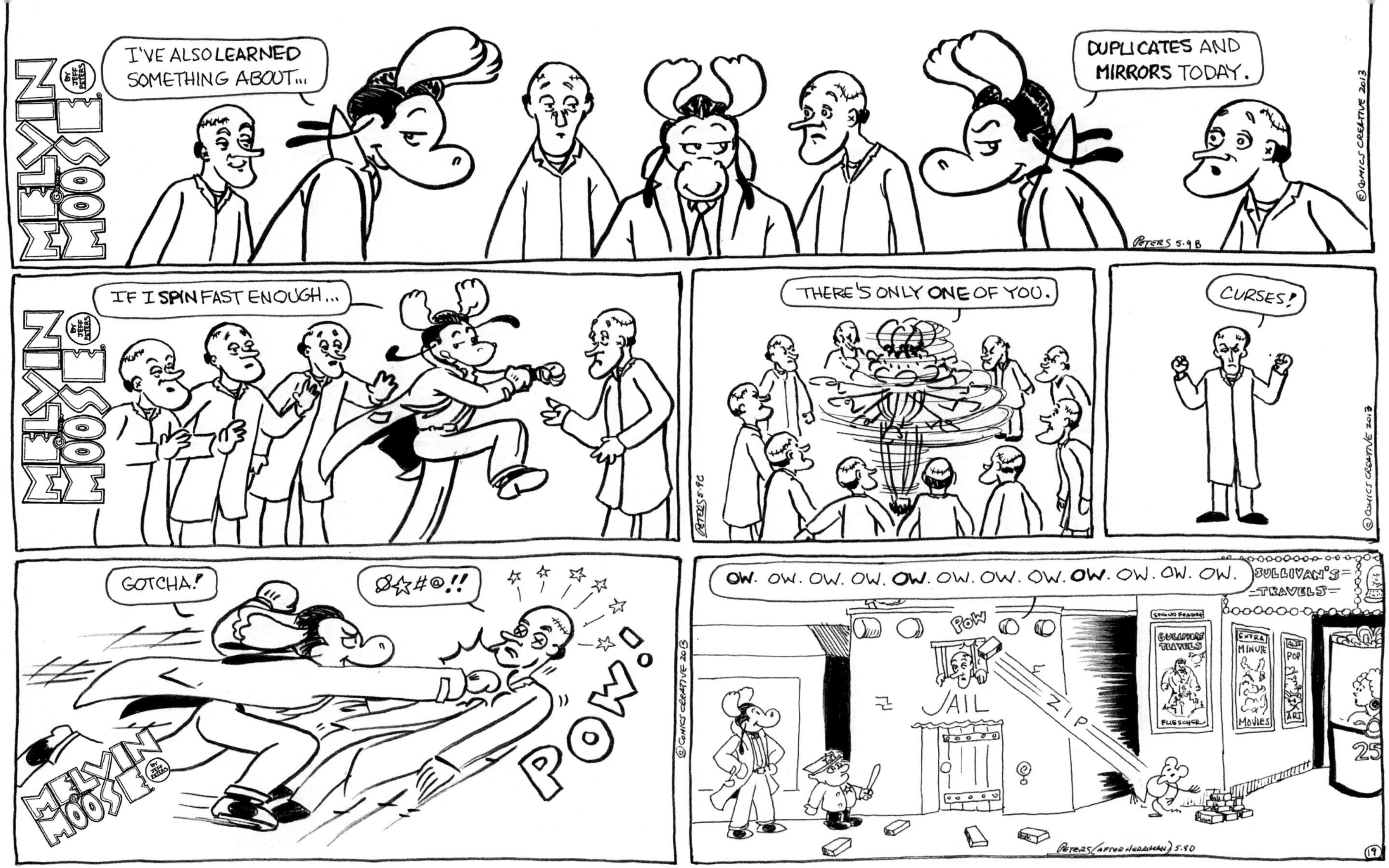
MELVIN MOOSE
BY JEFF PETERS
I'VE ALSO LEARNED SOMETHING ABOUT...
DUPLICATES AND MIRRORS TODAY.
PETERS 5.9B
© COMICS CREATIVE 2013
MELVIN MOOSE
BY JEFF PETERS
IF I SPIN FAST ENOUGH...
THERE'S ONLY ONE OF YOU.
PETERS 5.9C
CURSES!
© COMICS CREATIVE 2013
GOTCHA!
@☆#@!!
POW!
MELVIN MOOSE
BY JEFF PETERS
© COMICS CREATIVE 2013
OW. OW. OW. OW. OW. OW. OW. OW. OW. OW. OW. OW.
SULLIVAN'S TRAVELS
POW
GULLIVER'S TRAVELS
FLEISCHER
EXTRA MINUTE MOVIES
POP ART
JAIL
ZIP
25
PETERS (AFTER HERRIMAN) 5.9D
19

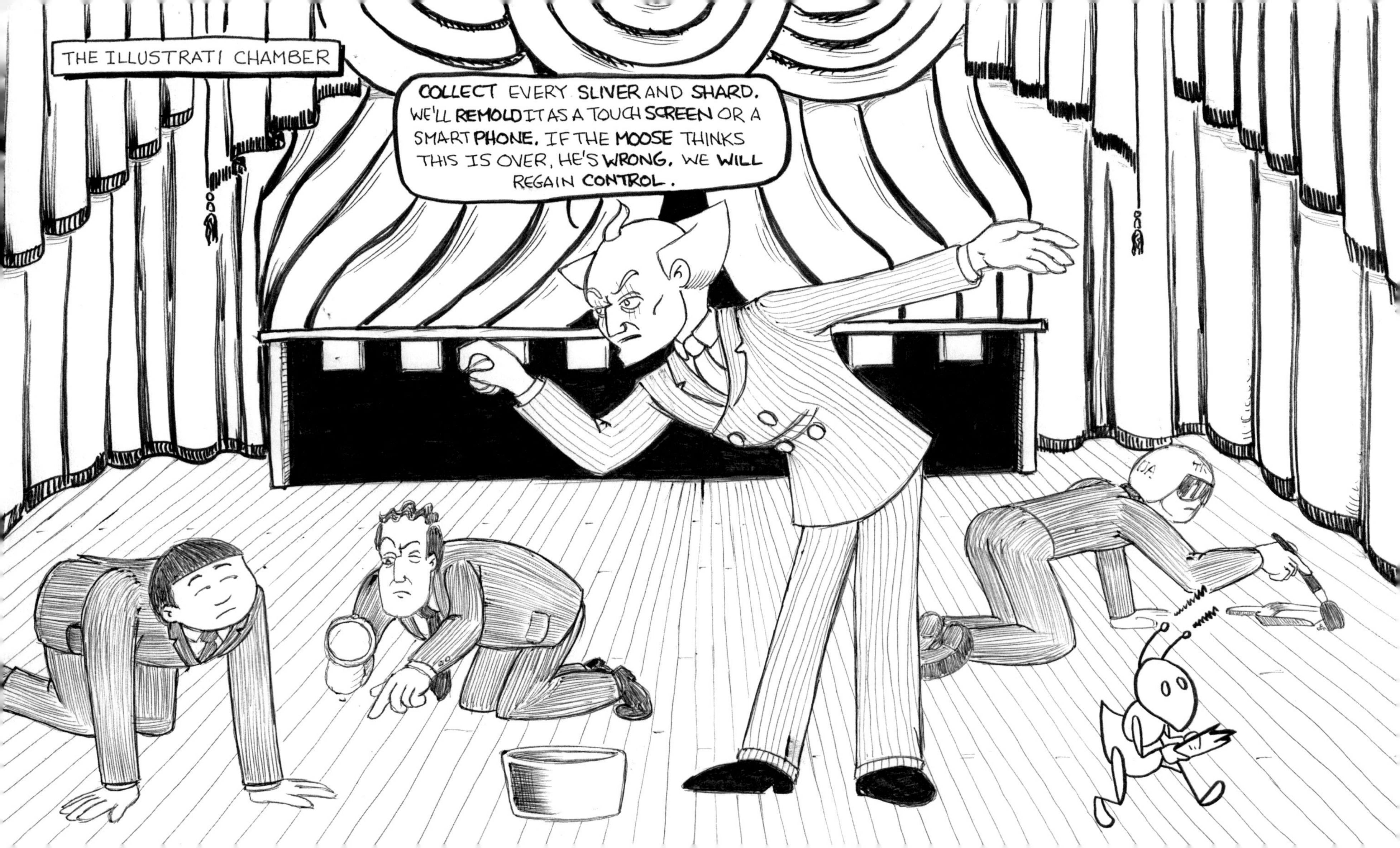
THE ILLUSTRATI CHAMBER
COLLECT EVERY SLIVER AND SHARD. WE'LL REMOLD IT AS A TOUCH SCREEN OR A SMART PHONE. IF THE MOOSE THINKS THIS IS OVER, HE'S WRONG. WE WILL REGAIN CONTROL.

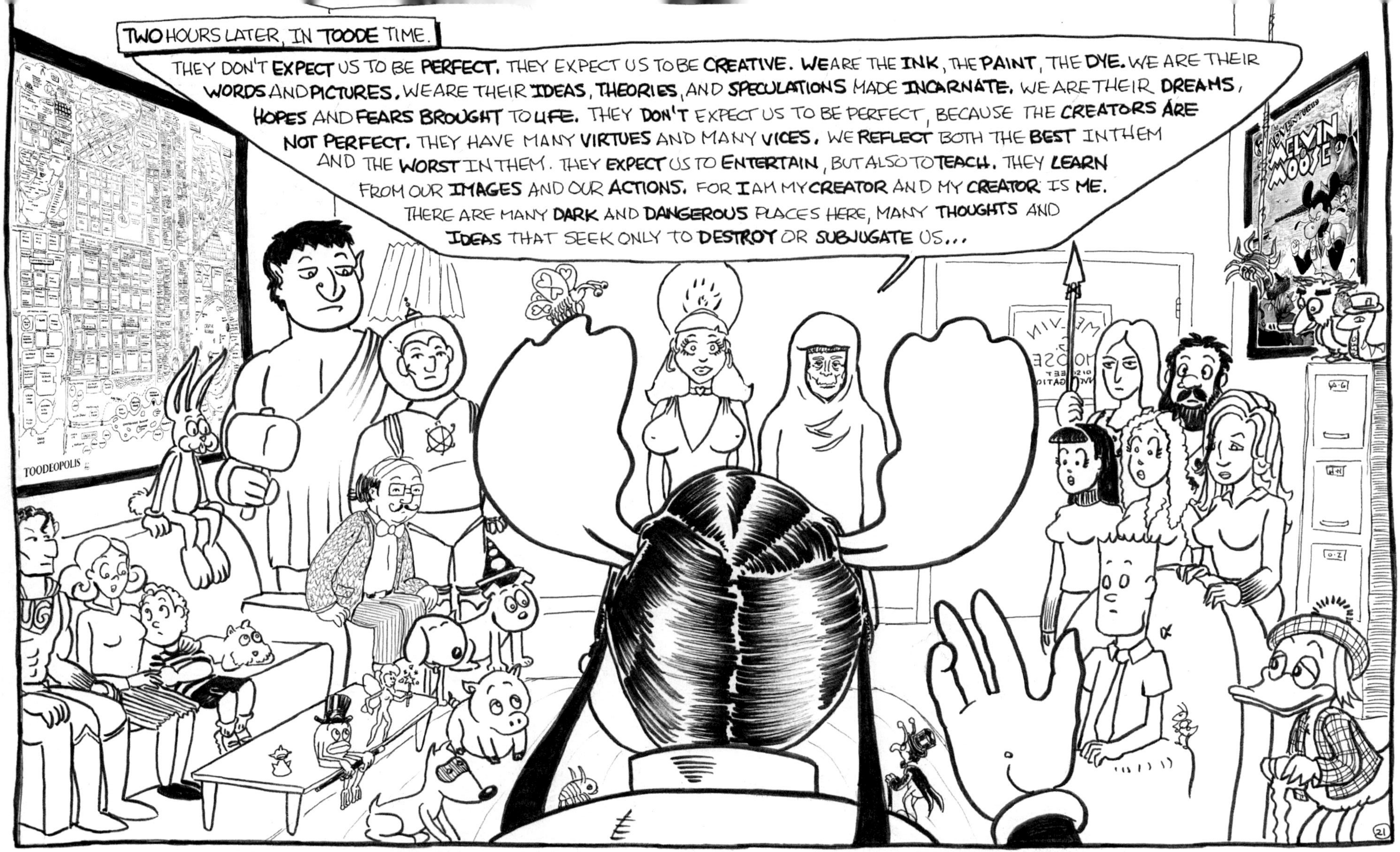
TWO HOURS LATER, IN TOODE TIME.
THEY DON'T EXPECT US TO BE PERFECT. THEY EXPECT US TO BE CREATIVE. WE ARE THE INK, THE PAINT, THE DYE. WE ARE THEIR WORDS AND PICTURES. WE ARE THEIR IDEAS, THEORIES, AND SPECULATIONS MADE INCARNATE. WE ARE THEIR DREAMS, HOPES AND FEARS BROUGHT TO LIFE. THEY DON'T EXPECT US TO BE PERFECT, BECAUSE THE CREATORS ARE NOT PERFECT. THEY HAVE MANY VIRTUES AND MANY VICES. WE REFLECT BOTH THE BEST IN THEM AND THE WORST IN THEM. THEY EXPECT US TO ENTERTAIN, BUT ALSO TO TEACH. THEY LEARN FROM OUR IMAGES AND OUR ACTIONS. FOR I AM MY CREATOR AND MY CREATOR IS ME. THERE ARE MANY DARK AND DANGEROUS PLACES HERE, MANY THOUGHTS AND IDEAS THAT SEEK ONLY TO DESTROY OR SUBJUGATE US...
TOODEOPOLIS
MELVIN MOOSE

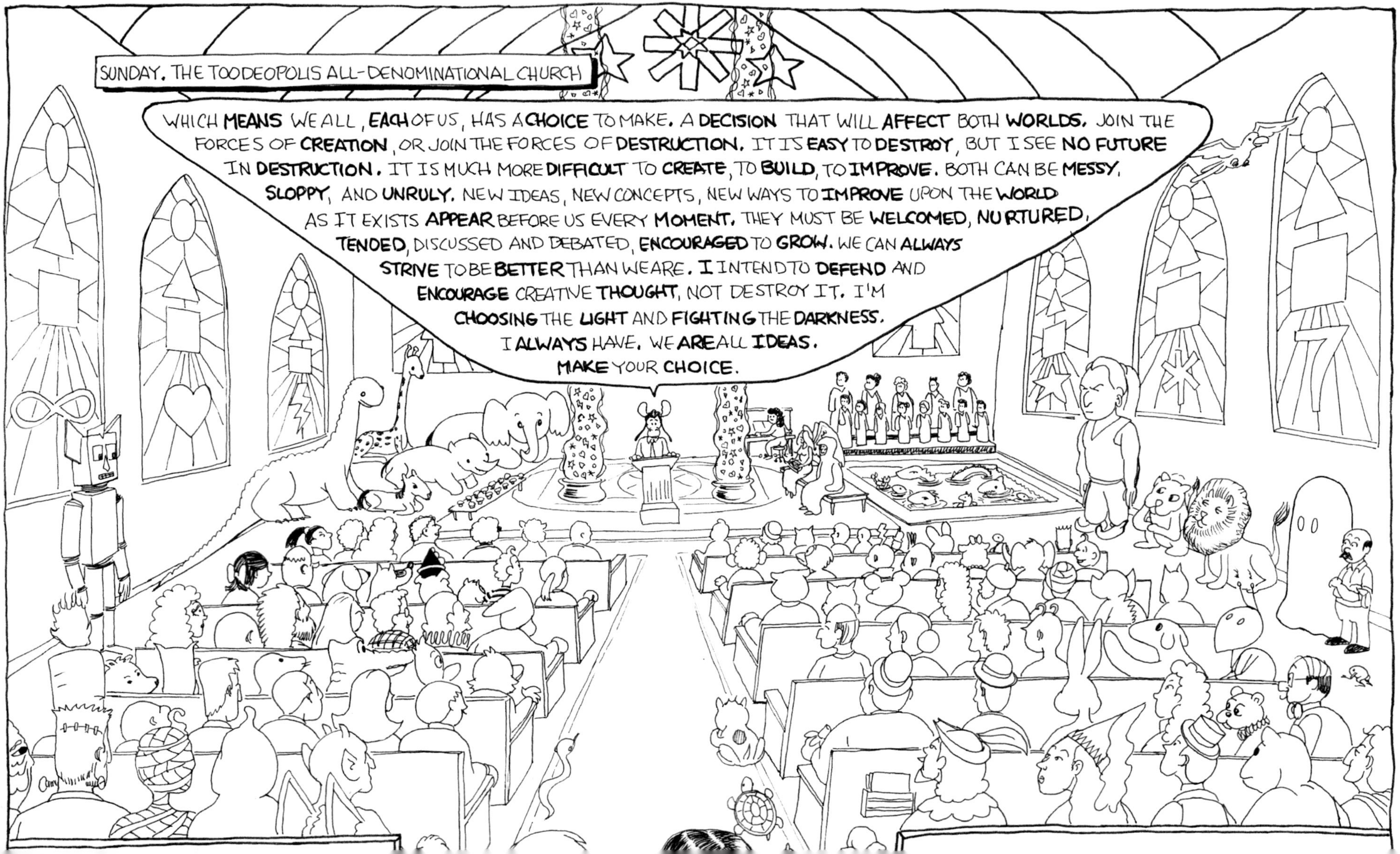
SUNDAY. THE TOODEOPOLIS ALL-DENOMINATIONAL CHURCH
WHICH MEANS WE ALL, EACH OF US, HAS A CHOICE TO MAKE. A DECISION THAT WILL AFFECT BOTH WORLDS. JOIN THE FORCES OF CREATION, OR JOIN THE FORCES OF DESTRUCTION. IT IS EASY TO DESTROY, BUT I SEE NO FUTURE IN DESTRUCTION. IT IS MUCH MORE DIFFICULT TO CREATE, TO BUILD, TO IMPROVE. BOTH CAN BE MESSY, SLOPPY, AND UNRULY. NEW IDEAS, NEW CONCEPTS, NEW WAYS TO IMPROVE UPON THE WORLD AS IT EXISTS APPEAR BEFORE US EVERY MOMENT. THEY MUST BE WELCOMED, NURTURED, TENDED, DISCUSSED AND DEBATED, ENCOURAGED TO GROW. WE CAN ALWAYS STRIVE TO BE BETTER THAN WE ARE. I INTEND TO DEFEND AND ENCOURAGE CREATIVE THOUGHT, NOT DESTROY IT. I'M CHOOSING THE LIGHT AND FIGHTING THE DARKNESS. I ALWAYS HAVE. WE ARE ALL IDEAS. MAKE YOUR CHOICE.

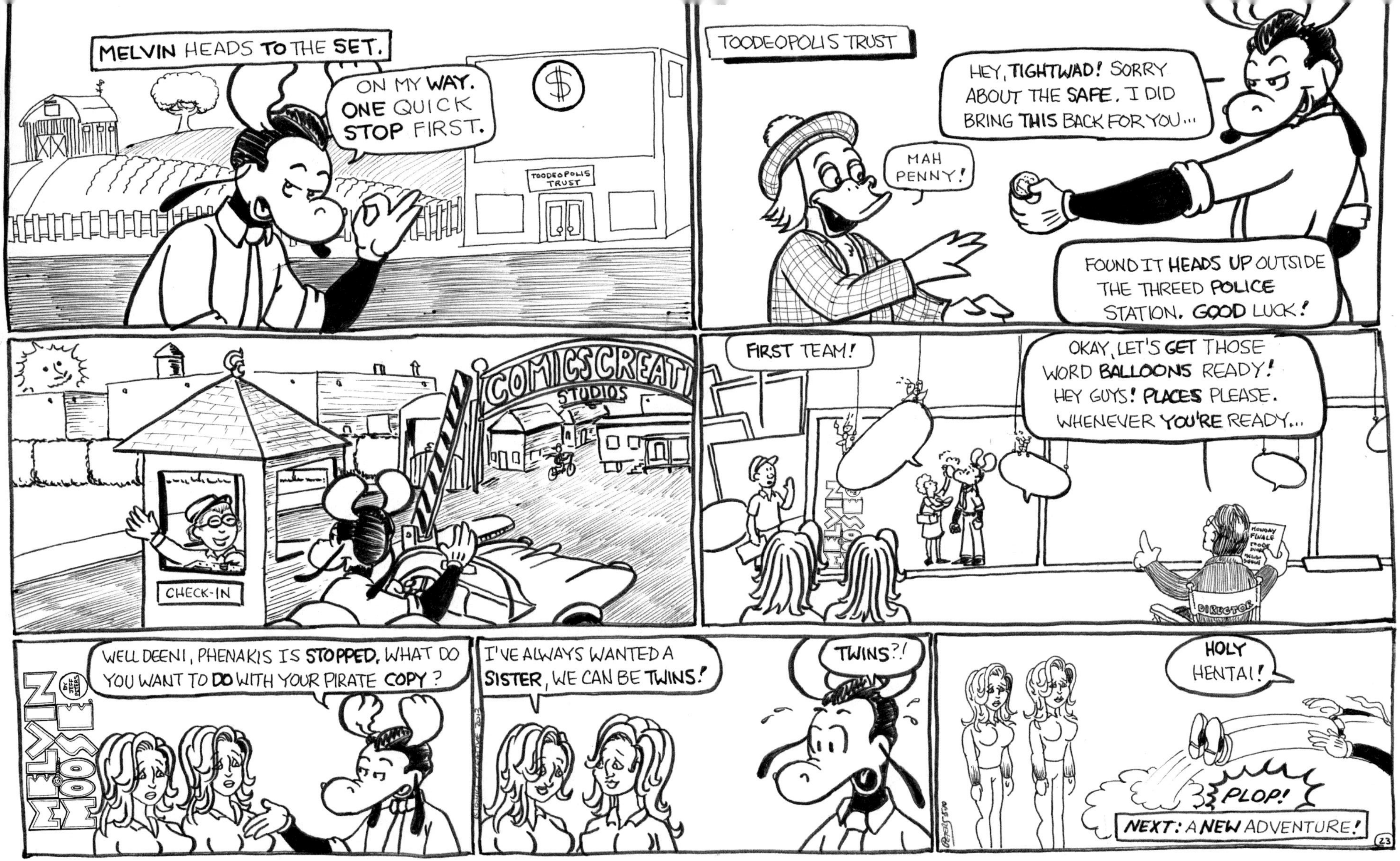
MELVIN HEADS TO THE SET.
ON MY WAY. ONE QUICK STOP FIRST.
TOODEOPOLIS TRUST
TOODEOPOLIS TRUST
HEY, TIGHTWAD! SORRY ABOUT THE SAFE. I DID BRING THIS BACK FOR YOU...
MAH PENNY!
FOUND IT HEADS UP OUTSIDE THE THREED POLICE STATION. GOOD LUCK!
COMICSCREAT
STUDIOS
CHECK-IN
FIRST TEAM!
OKAY, LET'S GET THOSE WORD BALLOONS READY! HEY GUYS! PLACES PLEASE. WHENEVER YOU'RE READY...
DIRECTOR
MELVIN MOOSE BY JEFF PETERS
WELL DEENI, PHENAKIS IS STOPPED. WHAT DO YOU WANT TO DO WITH YOUR PIRATE COPY?
I'VE ALWAYS WANTED A SISTER, WE CAN BE TWINS!
TWINS?!
HOLY HENTAI!
PLOP!
NEXT: A NEW ADVENTURE!
23

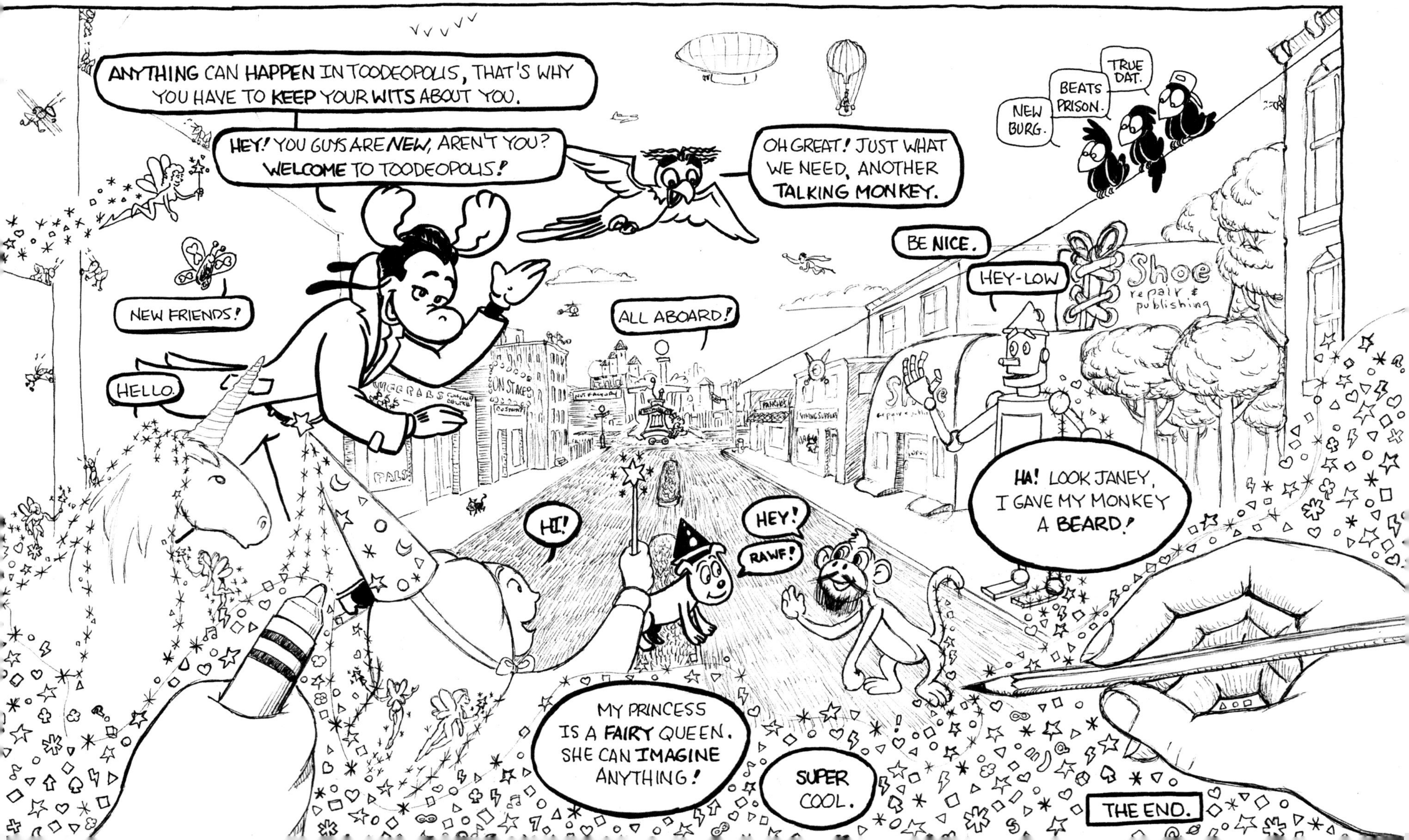
ANYTHING CAN HAPPEN IN TOODEOPOLIS, THAT'S WHY YOU HAVE TO KEEP YOUR WITS ABOUT YOU.
HEY! YOU GUYS ARE NEW, AREN'T YOU? WELCOME TO TOODEOPOLIS!
OH GREAT! JUST WHAT WE NEED, ANOTHER TALKING MONKEY.
NEW BURG.
BEATS PRISON.
TRUE DAT.
BE NICE.
HEY-LOW
Shoe repair & publishing
NEW FRIENDS!
HELLO.
ALL ABOARD!
HA! LOOK JANEY, I GAVE MY MONKEY A BEARD!
HI!
HEY!
RAWF!
MY PRINCESS IS A FAIRY QUEEN. SHE CAN IMAGINE ANYTHING!
SUPER COOL.
THE END.